Sally Neighbour is a reporter with Australia's premier television current affairs program, ABC TV's *4 Corners*, where she has worked since 1996. She has reported extensively on Jemaah Islamiyah and al Qaeda. She was previously Asia correspondent for ABC TV, based in Hong Kong and China and travelling widely throughout Southeast Asia. She is a winner of two Walkley awards, the highest accolades in Australian journalism. Sally lives in Sydney with her husband and son.

IN THE
SHADOW
OF SWORDS

ON THE TRAIL OF TERRORISM
FROM AFGHANISTAN TO AUSTRALIA

SALLY NEIGHBOUR

HarperCollins*Publishers*

HarperCollins*Publishers*

First published in Australia in 2004
by HarperCollins*Publishers* Pty Limited
ABN 36 009 913 517
A member of the HarperCollins*Publishers* (Australia) Pty Limited Group
www.harpercollins.com.au

HarperCollins*Publishers*
25 Ryde Road, Pymble, Sydney NSW 2073, Australia
31 View Road, Glenfield, Auckland 10, New Zealand
77–85 Fulham Palace Road, London W6 8JB, United Kingdom
2 Bloor Street East, 20th Floor, Toronto, Ontario M4W 1A8, Canada
10 East 53rd Street, New York, NY 10022, USA

National Library of Australia Cataloguing-in-publication data:

Neighbour, Sally.
   In the shadow of swords: on the trail of terrorism from
   Afghanistan to Australia.
   Includes index.
   ISBN 0 7322 8010 9.
   1. Jemaah Islamiyah (Organization). 2. Islamic.
   fundamentalism — Asia, Southeastern. 3. Terrorism —
   Religious aspects — Islam. 4. Terrorism — Asia,
   Southeastern. I. Title.
303.6250959

Cover design by Jenny Grigg and Natalie Winter, HarperCollins Design Studio
Internal design by Natalie Winter, HarperCollins Design Studio
Cover photo Village on Basilan, Philippines (litho) by English school (19th century)
Private collection/Bridgeman Art Library
Maps by Laurie Whiddon, Map Illustrations
Typeset in 11.5/14pt Bembo by HarperCollins Design Studio
Printed and bound in Australia by Griffin Press on 79gsm Bulky White

5 4 3 2 1   04 05 06 07

For Michael and Oscar

For the survivors and families of those who died in Bali

And for Des, who would have liked this book

Jihad is your duty under any ruler, be he godly or wicked. A day and a night of fighting on the frontier is better than a month of fasting and prayer. The nip of an ant hurts a martyr more than the thrust of a weapon, for these are more welcome to him than sweet, cold water on a hot summer day . . . Learn to shoot, for the space between the mark and the archer is one of the gardens of Paradise. Paradise is in the shadows of swords

CONTENTS

cᐱ

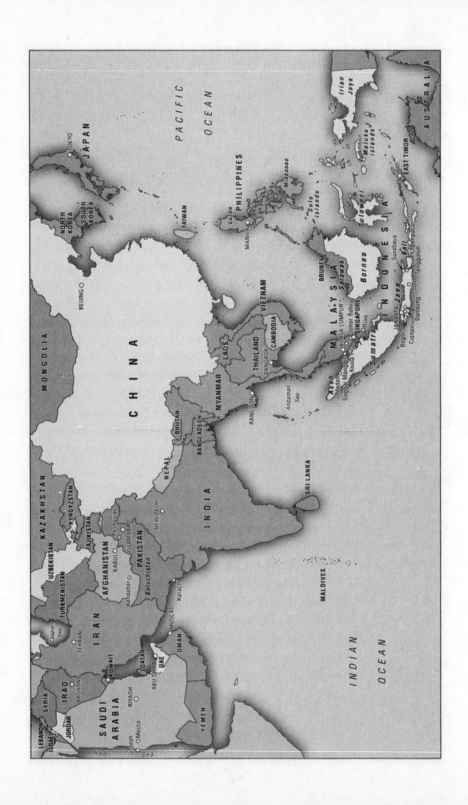

ACKNOWLEDGEMENTS

A great deal of the work for this book was done in conjunction with my friends and colleagues at *4 Corners* in the course of a series of stories we did on JI in 2002 and 2003. I especially want to thank researchers Jo Puccini, Sarah Curnow, Sandra Harvey and Peter Cronau; producers Morag Ramsay, Anne Connolly, Virginia Moncrieff and Lin Buckfield (to whom I owe extra thanks for persuading me to write the book); Neale Maude and Jerry Rickard for their hard work and camaraderie on the road; and executive producer Bruce Belsham for his forbearance and flexibility, without which I couldn't have done it. Thanks also to *4 Corners'* wonderful editors Alec, Jess, Michael, Jonathan and the late, lovely Des; to Adelaide Beavis, Kerryn Kelleway, Cathy Beale, Jenny Crawford and Geraldine Rodwell in the clippings library; and to the army of other dedicated staff including Michelle Baddiley, Ann Connor, Sharnelle, Rosemary and all of my fellow workers.

I am indebted to Sidney Jones of the International Crisis Group for her groundbreaking work on JI and for generously sharing her knowledge and material. Likewise, Rohan Gunaratna, Zachary Abuza, Greg Fealy, Bill Maley, Amin Saikal, Clive Williams, Abdullah Saeed, David Kilcullen and Malcolm McGregor all gave generously of their time and expertise, as did Neil Fergus, Ian Shaw and Bob Costello at Intelligent Risks in Sydney.

Numerous other journalists have reported extensively on JI, enabling me to draw on their fine work. Particular credit goes to Martin Chulov and Colleen Egan of the *Australian*, ABC Jakarta correspondent Tim Palmer, the *7.30 Report*'s Mick O'Donnell in Perth, CNN's Maria Ressa, Sarah McDonald of the BBC, and Margot O'Neill of *Lateline*, who got me onto the story in the first place and inspired me throughout. Thanks also to Alan D'Cruz in Kuala Lumpur, Jackie Chan in Singapore, Sonya Neufeld in Sydney and Debra Mewett in Adelaide for additional research; and to Mary Neighbour for her unpaid editing and Robyn Fallick for her excellent translation.

The Australian Federal Police provided extensive help, for which I am grateful to Mick Keelty, Graham Ashton, Glen Fisher, Anne Lyons and Jane O'Brien. And a big thank you to the numerous other Australian investigators, past and present, who provided such invaluable assistance but who cannot be named.

Many people with direct knowledge of JI or the characters in it went out on a limb to speak to me for the *4 Corners* stories and for this book. Among them were Jack Roche, Ibrahim Fraser, Zainal Arifin, Mohammed Baluel, Gabr el Gafi, John Cooper and numerous others who spoke on condition of anonymity. I am indebted to all of them.

Although I'm assured that it's not obligatory, I do wish to thank Shona Martyn and Helen Littleton at HarperCollins for their enthusiasm, support and endless flexibility with my deadline and, in particular, my marvellous editor Mary Rennie for her patience, encouragement, good nature and painstaking perfectionism. Most importantly, I thank Michael Doyle for his journalist rigour, personal integrity, love and support, for weeding out the worst of my clichés and for putting up with me and this project, which took over our lives.

❧

CHAPTER ONE

RAVINE OF HATE

THE TINNY LOUDSPEAKER WHINED into life and a thin nasal monotone crackled out through the open-air mosque. 'At this time of Friday prayers I would like to explain the nature of Islam's enemies.' With his immaculate white robes and aura of serenity, the elderly man at the lectern looked almost saintly amid the heat and dust and grime of Solo, Central Java. But behind the large gold-rimmed glasses his brown eyes were steely and his voice had a harsh, barking tone as it echoed off the ceramic-tiled walls.

'God has divided humanity into two parts,' he intoned, 'namely the followers of God and those who follow Satan. The party of God and the party of Satan. God's group and Satan's group.' His thin brown face was bland but his tone grew hectoring as he warmed to his theme, one finger poking the air.

'God's group are those who follow Islam, those who are prepared to follow his laws and struggle for the implementation of sharia [Islamic] law ... Meanwhile what is meant by Satan's group are those people who oppose God's law, who wish to bring pressure to bear upon God's law [and] throw obstacles in the path of the implementation of God's law.'

His followers listened entranced. They filled the old mosque and overflowed into the baking, dusty street outside, huddling in the small patch of shade cast by the silver onion dome gleaming under the tropical sun. The crowd murmured its assent as the grim sermon went on. 'For God's warriors, sharia law is more important than life itself. Life without sharia is nothing . . . Everything in the world, if it does not have sharia, means nothing. For God's warriors, one must be prepared to forfeit one's life for sharia.'

Behind the iron fence and the sea of flip-flops left by the congregation at the entrance, a cluster of foreign journalists and TV crews was also hanging on every word. The speaker was Abu Bakar Bashir, spiritual leader of the fanatical Islamist group Jemaah Islamiyah. It was October 2002, just six days after Indonesia's worst terrorist attack, the bombings in Bali. While a massive investigation was just beginning, Bashir's group was already being blamed and demands for his arrest were mounting. The world was watching to see what Bashir had to say and we, the assembled media, were there to record it.

But if we expected some sign of sorrow, there would be none from Bashir — no words of comfort for the grieving families or shocked governments, not even lip service paid to condemning the atrocity. Though his tirade was in Indonesian and Arabic, Bashir's contempt for what the world thought was clear from his tone and from the few words he spat out that we could understand — such as 'jihad', 'terrorist' and 'kafir' (infidel) — and the odd phrase in English like 'God bless Osama bin Laden'.

Bashir's homily was aimed, not at the devotees gathered before him, but at an audience thousands of kilometres away — in Australia, Europe and the United States, in the countries mourning dozens of their nationals slaughtered in Bali. The message to these enemies of Islam, as Bashir sees them, was chillingly plain. No matter the cost or the condemnation, Bashir and his followers would never, *ever* veer from their course.

'We would rather die than follow that which you worship,' he vowed. 'We reject all of your beliefs, we reject all of your ideologies, we reject all of your teachings on social issues, economics or beliefs. Between you and us there will forever be a ravine of hate and we will be enemies until you follow God's law.'

Bashir's words reverberated through the mosque and later around living rooms across Australia and the world. *'Between you and us there will forever be a ravine of hate.'*

Five nights earlier I had stood with a *4 Corners* TV crew amid the smashed glass and rubble of Legian Street in Kuta Beach, where the charred remains of the Sari Club and Paddy's Bar were still smouldering. It was eerily quiet and the stench was terrible. There was no sign of life. We later tramped the chaotic corridors of Denpasar's Sanglah hospital, past the rows of blackened corpses shrouded in white, dumbfounded at what could have motivated such carnage.

Now Abu Bakar Bashir had put it into words, distilled it in a single line. *'Between you and us there will forever be a ravine of hate.'* Bashir's words only compounded the fear and confusion of Australians struggling to comprehend the nation's worst mass loss of life since World War II. To me his sentence was more frightening than the bombing itself. We had found ourselves at war again, only this time it was a war that had never been declared, against an enemy we didn't even know, an enemy driven by a hatred we were at a loss to understand. And Bali was clearly just one battle. Amid the shock and outrage and urge for revenge, there was a desperate need to understand — what was this 'ravine of hate'? And how on earth had we found ourselves on the other side?

✺

CHAPTER TWO

JIHAD IS OUR WAY

A dusty dead-end laneway on the outskirts of Solo leads to a spiked iron gate and a sign announcing the entrance to the Al Mukmin Islamic Boarding School at Ngruki. Beyond the barrier, a gaggle of boys emerges from a greying, white-washed classroom, neat as pins in their pressed white shirts and sarongs. A woman on a bicycle, shrouded head to toe in a burkah, glides into view. The call to prayer drones from a distant loudspeaker. On a wall, a sign in Arabic and English announces 'Jihad is our way. Death in the way of Allah is our highest aspiration.'

Back in the 1970s when it was founded, Abu Bakar Bashir's religious school in the village of Ngruki was a backwater. On the day I was there it was front-page news. A scrum of sweaty journalists and TV crews was pressed up against the wrought-iron gate. On the other side was a phalanx of pint-sized disciples in matching green jackets who confiscated our passports one by one then allowed the cursing press pack to squeeze by turn through the gap in the gate. The green-uniformed minions reminded me of Chairman Mao's Red Guards.

It was October 2002, the same day as Bashir's sermon on the 'ravine of hate'. After a mad car dash from the silver-domed mosque through the back streets of Solo following the navy Mercedes Benz in which the emir was being chauffered, we had ended up back at his famous boarding school to await an audience with Abu Bakar Bashir.

The JI leader swept in, flanked by an entourage of aides and supporters in black vests with the word 'Mujahideen' — holy warrior — emblazoned in yellow on the back. The press pack closed in around Bashir, beatific as always in white robes and cap, matching white scarf elegantly draped. In my grubby checked headscarf, a relic of an earlier assignment to Cambodia, I recalled the facile decree of the Gucci fashion house supremo, Tom Ford, who had declared Hamid Karzai, the leader of desperate, war-torn Afghanistan, to be 'the chicest man on the planet today'. I was sure Tom Ford would approve of Bashir.

Bashir took his seat at a trestle table covered in batik and launched into his speech. 'Ladies and gentlemen and journalists,' he began, 'the situation that I find myself in is associated with politics and in particular with the agendas of the foreign governments that dominate our country . . . The root of all confrontation in the world at this time, which is frequently described as terrorism, is actually the clash between believers in Islam and non-believers. That is the sum of the confrontation.'

With his large ears, bucked teeth and oversized glasses, Bashir at close quarters is not a charismatic man, though the white robes add a certain style. His voice is harsh and clipped, his delivery stridently didactic rather than impassioned. But in contrast to his alarming fulminations at the mosque, his delivery now was measured and his words made sense, whether or not you agreed with them.

'Non-believers endeavour in a variety of ways to extinguish the light of Islam under the guise of opposing terrorism,' Bashir continued. 'I have been victimised due to the fact that I wish to implement Islamic law in its fullest sense. And this is what the enemies of Islam are most afraid of. I ask that you understand this.'

His attendants nodded vigorously in agreement. Bashir's words struck a powerful chord, not only with his followers, but with many Indonesians and countless Muslims around the world, who shared his conviction that the 'war on terror' being waged by the United States and its allies was in fact a war against Islam.

'The terrorists in the world are America and Israel,' Bashir railed. 'America has killed many innocent people. George W. Bush has murdered the people of Afghanistan and has cruelly destroyed their homes. There were even those among them who were enjoying their wedding party and their celebration was bombed, destroyed. Israel has cruelly murdered Palestinians. That is terrorism. There isn't a single Muslim person who has done things like that. It is said that Osama bin

Laden blew up the World Trade Center — where's the evidence? America can't prove it.'

The evidence against Bashir himself was still unclear and the proof of Jemaah Islamiyah's role in Bali had yet to be uncovered. The accusations were all part of a conspiracy against Islam, according to Bashir. When questions were allowed, I yelled above the clamour: 'Mr Bashir, the Australian Government says it has evidence that your organisation was behind the Bali bombings. What is your response to that?' Bashir's gaze was unflinching as he snapped back: 'That is a blatant lie and if the evidence is there, go ahead and present it. It's a lie and I am not involved at all.'

Bashir's contempt for what the West thought was clearly a key part of his appeal. It was echoed in the graffiti scrawled around his school. 'Bush is fucked' read one sample in English daubed in white paint on a wall. 'Bush and Sharon, if you like dead, come to here' said another. In a classroom, childish drawings of bombs and sticks of dynamite scrawled in chalk on a blackboard were later filmed by an ABC TV crew. The principal had a portrait of Osama bin Laden on his door, alongside a poster for the Ngruki school with the slogan 'There is no God but Allah' and a picture of a rifle brandished aloft by a raised arm.[1]

Like bin Laden, Bashir's status had only been enhanced by the growing pressure from the United States and other Western countries for his arrest. 'The preacher wanted by America' was how the fliers for his public appearances described him. It was the same indomitable defiance that had first marked him out as a hero decades before when he had stood up to the dictator Suharto.

⚭

Not far from the silver-domed mosque in Solo lies the Surakarta Palace, the now fading former home of the Mataram kingdom of Central Java. Within the whitewashed palace walls lie ornate pavilions and meditation halls and a treasure trove of heirlooms from Indonesia's rich and turbulent past. The city of Solo was founded here in 1745. The story goes that when the sultan, Pakubuwono II, found himself under siege from Dutch invaders and rivals in his royal family, mysterious voices told him to up and move his kingdom from its old seat to the village of Solo, 10 kilometres to the west, which Allah had decreed would become a great and prosperous city.

In a day-long procession the entire citadel was moved, the king in his royal wagon leading his retinue of troops, horses, courtiers, elephants and even the royal banyan trees, to be transplanted on the site where a sumptuous new palace was built. For all Pakubowono's trouble, his kingdom was soon split up into separate sultanates by the conquering Dutch, one of many realms to have risen and fallen through Indonesia's centuries of civilisation.

Abu Bakar Bashir was born 200 kilometres to the east of Solo, in Mojoagung, a muddy hamlet of thatch-roofed homes, nestled in the emerald volcanic foothills of Eastern Java.[2] The year was 1938. The boy's devout Muslim parents named him after the Prophet Muhammad's most trusted disciple and caliph (deputy), Abu Bakar.

The young Bashir was one of five children in a family descended from Yemeni traders, who were among the seafarers who first brought Islam from the Middle East to Indonesia in the thirteenth century and had plied the trade routes across the Arabian Sea and Indian Ocean ever since. Scattered across the plains around Bashir's home town lay the red clay relics of Indonesia's last great Hindu dynasty, the Majapahit, which fell in the fourteenth century as Islam advanced across the archipelago.

Bashir's family were merchants like their ancestors; his grandfather and father sold textiles, one sibling ran a hardware store and another wove cloth for sarongs. Bashir was ten years old and still attending the village primary school when his father died. It was a time of hardship for his family and for Indonesia itself.

The colonial era was drawing to a violent close. The Dutch had surrendered to the invading Japanese army in 1942, only to return at war's end to reclaim their colony, dismissing Indonesia's declaration of independence. It took four years of bloody struggle before the Dutch relinquished sovereignty in 1949 to the new Republic of Indonesia. Its president, the nationalist Sukarno, faced a formidable task: building a nation out of 13,000 islands flung across more than 5000 kilometres and governing it democratically.

These were heady years in the provincial town of Jombang where young Bashir was just entering high school. A town of timber bungalows fringed by fields of sugar cane, Jombang was at the heart of the surge of nationalism that swept Indonesia to independence. Known as 'the city of 1000 pesantrens' for its scores of Islamic boarding schools, it was a cradle of the Muslim mass movement Nahdlatul Ulama (NU), meaning 'Revival of Islamic Scholars', one of the groups that played a vital role in the independence struggle. NU championed the laid-back style of Islam that has traditionally flourished in Indonesia — a kind of Javanese hybrid influenced by Buddhism, Hinduism and traditional mystical beliefs.

During his school days in Jombang, a rival brand of Islam was competing for the allegiance of young Muslims like Bashir. A powerful Islamic resurgence was sweeping all the way from the Middle East, driven by a backlash against the colonisation of Muslim countries by the West. It was a radical new philosophy known as 'modernism' that aimed to revolutionise the Islamic world. The idea was to modernise Muslim economies and societies, while at the same time reviving the Islamic faith by returning to the 'fundamental truths' of the Koran.

The push was embodied by the Muslim Brotherhood, formed in Egypt in the 1920s, which set up hospitals, schools and factories while promoting a return to the 'pure' Islam of the Prophet Muhammad. Its proponents embraced modernisation but rejected Westernisation emphatically, blaming Western culture for the ills of the modern world. It was a political revolution with religion at its core and it marked a crucial change — the emergence of Islam as no longer simply a matter of personal belief, but an ideology of resistance.

In his early years at high school, Bashir was swept up in the modernists' fervour to transform the Islamic world. He joined the village branch of the Indonesian Islamic Youth Movement, a student group with close ties to the Muslim political party Masyumi, which was dominated by modernists, as was NU's rival grassroots movement Muhammadiyah, or Followers of Muhammad. The modernists in Indonesia believed that Islam had to be be cleansed of its Javanese influences and restored to its pure, original form, just as it was in the time of the Prophet.

Sent off in his mid-teens to senior high school in the industrial city of Surabaya, Bashir quickly found that secular studies held little appeal. And boarding school was a heavy drain on his family's limited funds. So Bashir dropped out before graduating and returned to his village to help out in the family business weaving cloth for sarongs.[3]

But for a zealous young Muslim and student activist, this was no time to be making batik. Politics beckoned. The task of governing the young republic had proved more of a challenge than Sukarno and his colleagues had anticipated. In Indonesia's first elections, Sukarno's Nationalists had secured only 22 per cent of the vote, with the Muslim parties Masyumi and NU winning 21 per cent and 18 per cent respectively, and the Indonesian Communist Party netting 16 per cent. Sukarno was obliged to govern in a fractious coalition, with relations between the Muslim groups and the communists growing steadily more tense.

The Islamic lobby was increasingly disillusioned with the secular nature of the new republic. Having fought for independence and emerged as the single most popular political force, the Muslim parties believed they had won the right to an Islamic state. But a clause enshrining Islamic law in the Constitution had been dumped at the last moment from the official state ideology known as Pancasila, or 'five principles' — belief in one God, justice and civility, the unity of Indonesia, democracy through consensus and social justice.

Radicals like Abu Bakar Bashir never forgave this betrayal. Bashir wrote much later: 'Under the colonisation of the Dutch and the Japanese, the Islamic community of Indonesia saw their rights oppressed and misappropriated in a most brutal fashion . . . With the help of Allah, the Muslims successfully drove the kafir Dutch and Japanese from their soil. At that time Muslims had the perfect opportunity to implement their rights — namely to apply the laws of Islam. However that golden opportunity soon elapsed and instead a new disaster replaced that of before.'[4]

Bashir's hero and the man who spearheaded the rising Muslim resistance to Sukarno was S.M. Kartosuwiryo, a charismatic veteran of Indonesia's struggle for independence. Kartosuwiryo had been a commander in a volunteer muslim militia called Hizbullah — God's Warriors — formed by the occupying Japanese army to help it fight the Allies during World War II. Some of the warriors had revolted against their Japanese masters and then helped drive out the Dutch, renaming themselves the Indonesian Islamic Army. At the birth of the Republic, their leader, Kartosuwiryo, had led the push for an Islamic state. When it failed, he had spurned the job of Defence Minister under Sukarno[5] and announced that, by turning its back on Islam, the new government had made itself 'as evil an enemy as the Dutch'.

In 1949, the same year that Sukarno proclaimed the Republic, Kartosuwiryo declared his own Islamic State of Indonesia — Negara Islam Indonesia, or NII. It extended over most of rural West Java, enforced by an army of 12,000 men and with its own police, tax collectors and civilian administration.[6] Kartosuwiryo called his movement Darul Islam, meaning the Abode of Islam. The phrase invoked an old Islamic tradition which divided the world into 'the abode of Islam' and 'the abode of war', meaning the lands still reigned over by heathens who must be fought until they surrender to Islamic rule.

'It seems that not enough filth of the world was eliminated and chased away in the First and Second World wars,' wrote Kartosuwiryo. 'We are obliged to foment the Third World War and World Revolution [because] God's justice in the form of God's kingdom does not yet exist on earth.' Kartosuwiryo gave Muslims this choice: 'Eliminate all infidels and atheism until they are annihilated and the God-granted state is established in Indonesia, or die as martyrs in a Holy War.'[7]

Unlike Bashir and his cohorts, Kartosuwiryo was no modernist. He hailed from Java's feudal elite, which resented the erosion of its power under Sukarno. He was also a proponent of the mystical Sufi stream of Islam, regarded as heresy by puritanical modernists like Bashir. Kartosuwiryo's followers were mostly poor peasants who yearned for what one scholar called 'a Paradise Lost . . . as opposed to the present Republic, which is held to be governed by a class of urban unbelievers'.[8]

The Darul Islam rebellion spread throughout the 1950s to Aceh, South Sulawesi and parts of Central Java. The rebels bombed cinemas and markets, poisoned water supplies and resorted to banditry, extortion and other 'terror' tactics, as they were described in newspaper accounts of the time. The rebels warned that their enemies would 'in no small number become senseless corpses who are scattered in the middle of roads or swept away in rivers . . . which will always run with corpses smeared with blood'.[9] Sukarno's troops met brutality with force; by the time the civil war ended, some 20,000 people would be dead and half a million homes destroyed.

By the end of the 1950s, Indonesia's fractions fling with parliamentary democracy was coming to an end. In the face of regional rebellions, a declining economy and ongoing discord over how the country should be governed, the military was agitating to take control. In 1957 the army persuaded Sukarno to impose martial law and the following year a band of frustrated army rebels proclaimed their own revolutionary government in Sumatra, openly supported by some Masyumi leaders and covertly propped up by the CIA, which was angling to counter Sukarno's alliance with the communists.[10] The rebellion was quickly put down but Sukarno was finally persuaded of the need to rule the country with a firmer hand.

In 1959, with the army's backing, Sukarno finally dumped the Constitution in favour of a new more authoritarian style of government which he called 'Guided Democracy'. It was basically a return to a system of personal rule, not unlike the Javanese feudalism of old. As Sukarno explained it, with customary Javanese diplomacy: 'OK now, my dear brothers, it is like this and I hope you agree.'[11] As Sukarno reasserted his authority, the Muslim party Masyumi was banned for having supported the regional rebellions and its leaders jailed or forced into exile, leaving the ranks of the Islamists in disarray.

This watershed year in the life of the ten-year-old Republic was a turning point for young Abu Bakar Bashir. At twenty-one, Bashir gave up weaving sarongs and enrolled himself in the Gontor Islamic Boarding School, a famous modernist pesantren in East Java, which combines a modern curriculum and the study of English with intensive studies of Islam and Arabic. Funded by his brothers, Bashir spent four years in this hothouse of Muslim politics, which has produced some of Indonesia's leading Islamic intellectuals, including liberals such as Bashir's classmate, the theologian Nurcholish Madjid, who made a bid to run for president in 2004. Bashir certainly wasn't among the liberals, as Nurcholish recalled: 'We still remember how he was so puritanical, so uncompromising ... And then we parted and I didn't know anything more about him.'[12]

While Bashir was still at Gontor, the Darul Islam rebellion was finally crushed when its leader Kartosuwiryo was captured and executed in 1962. His Islamic state, which had survived for thirteen years, collapsed. For Abu Bakar Bashir and his generation of Muslim activists, the execution of Kartosuwiryo was a profoundly galvanising event. Despite their doctrinal differences, Bashir and his colleagues seized upon the martyred rebel leader as an icon for their cause. His movement, Darul Islam, would live on and inspire Muslim radicals for decades to come.

The following year, after four years at Gontor, Bashir moved to Solo. To the alarm of Muslim activists, the city had become a stronghold of Indonesia's communists, whose determination to enforce land reform was seen as a direct challenge to Islamic groups and whose influence on Sukarno infuriated Islamists like Bashir.

Solo became Bashir's political base. He enrolled in the Al Ikhlas University, a leading hub for Indonesian modernists of Arab descent. Bashir's major was in *dakwah*, or religious proselytising, but he was so caught up in student politics that he never completed his course. He spent most of his time with the Association of Islamic University Students and the Islamic Students Proselytising Foundation, which he headed.

It was in Solo that Bashir met another ardent young activist with whom he formed a crucial partnership. His new soul mate was a chain-smoking scholar by the name of Abdullah Sungkar, who would fulminate against the enemies of Islam through wafts of sweetly-scented smoke from his clove cigarettes.

The two men had much in common. Sungkar had been born in Solo a year before Bashir and was also of Yemeni descent. But his family had been too poor to send him to university so Sungkar had taught himself and then gone to work as a preacher,[13] joining the Islamic party Masyumi and the Indonesian Muslim Islamic Movement, of which Bashir was also a member. An inspiring and passionate ideologue, Sungkar would become a powerful influence on the young Bashir as together they took on the mantle of the Darul Islam struggle.

While Bashir was at university, the latest chapter in Indonesia's history was convulsing to a bloody end. The experiment known as Guided Democracy had failed, destabilised by political infighting, a collapsing economy, a restive army and Sukarno's inability to resolve the hostilities between the Muslim groups, communists and armed forces whom he had tried to unite.

The rising unrest came to a head in September 1965, with an abortive coup attempt by a group of leftist army officers linked to the Communist Party, who kidnapped and killed six generals and a lieutenant, dumping their bodies in a well. A major general named Suharto stepped into the breach, moving swiftly to quell the uprising and enforce order. The Communist Party was blamed for the upheaval, though the evidence of its role remains sketchy to this day.

In the aftermath of the bungled coup, the tensions that had been steadily building were unleashed in an orgy of savagery. Military gangs and civilian vigilantes embarked on an anti-communist rampage in which hundreds of thousands of people were killed, a blood bath the CIA described as 'one of the worst mass murders of the twentieth century.'[14] As the crisis continued, Major General Suharto moved steadily to exert control. With student protestors, urged on by the army, parading around the palace demanding the president's resignation, the besieged Sukarno eventually conceded defeat, handing power to Suharto on 11 March 1966.

After the anarchy of the Sukarno years, Suharto's 'New Order' was greeted by many with relief. The West saw Suharto as a staunch ally in its Cold War against communism, while Muslim activists like Bashir and Abdullah Sunkgar were glad to see the back of Sukarno and his atheist friends. Muslim groups had joined in the anti-communist purges and again expected to reap the political rewards they felt they had long been denied. 'In a repeat of history, the Muslims — by the leave and help of Allah — successfully brought down the Old Order,' Bashir and Sungkar wrote later. 'The Islamic community supposed that this New Order was a realization of the blessings of Allah which would carry the strength of Islam forward.'[15]

But the hopes of Bashir and the Islamic lobby were once again quashed. Like his predecessor the new president, Suharto, would have no truck with calls for an Islamic state and was intent on denying the Muslim parties a meaningful role in his government. Having wiped out the communists, Suharto's armed forces now saw militant Muslims as the next threat to their power. Suharto himself, as a young army commander, had helped cut down the Darul Islam rebellion in Central Java and he was determined to keep it from rising up again. Muslim activists, like anyone else who dared raise their voice in protest, would be ruthlessly suppressed. In the words of Bashir and Sungkar, 'the New Order turned into a disaster worse than and more terrifying than what had been before.'

Abu Bakar Bashir and his friend Abdullah Sungkar were soon on a direct collision course with Suharto's regime. In 1967, after Bashir left university, the pair joined forces to set up their own radio station, the Islamic Proselytisation Radio of Surakarta (Solo), described later in a regional intelligence report as 'a pirate radio station that broadcast the call to jihad across the rice paddies of Central Java.'[16]

Sungkar and Bahsir's credo was that Muslims must live by Islamic law alone. They believed that laws made by men — President Suharto among them — were nothing less than an affront to God. 'Worship of Allah means observing all of Allah's laws, therefore observing laws other than Allah's laws is worship towards others than Allah,' Bashir preached later. 'The making and establishing of laws by others besides Allah and without his permission amounts to the robbery of Allah's rightful authority . . . If there are men who claim the right to make and decide legislation for other men, then in reality they have claimed to possess divinity. This is the same as proclaiming that they are gods or lords alongside Allah!'[17]

Sungkar and Bashir advocated the formation of small *jemaah islamiyah*, meaning Islamic communities, in which their followers would live strictly by Islamic law, as the first step towards establishing an Islamic state. Their dogma was seen as an unacceptable challenge to the regime and their radio station was shut down. But the two extremists soon found a far more potent way of spreading their message.

In 1971, Sungkar and Bashir set up their own religious boarding school, or pesantren, to preach their uncompromising brand of Islam. The school in the dusty cul-de-sac in the village of Ngruki became a symbol of Muslim resistance to Suharto's increasingly authoritarian rule. Sungkar and Bashir refused to fly the Indonesian flag, spurned the official state ideology, Pancasila, and urged their supporters to ignore the laws made by the parliament in Jakarta.[18] As Suharto tightened his grip on the country, the two preachers through their Ngruki school gained a name as courageous dissidents and a solid following among the ranks of their youthful students and the older loyalists of the Darul Islam movement.

Bashir outlined his approach to Islamic education much later, in a speech he made in 2000. 'Religious boarding schools are the bulwarks of Islam . . . The formation of students must be directed towards nurturing their spirit and zeal to magnify the confession of faith, and in an atmosphere of purity of intent, with Allah as the only consideration. In order for a pesantren to truly be a crucible for the formation of cadres of mujahideen, the school must be kept free of all influence of secular thinking and worldly sciences . . . Instruction in the laws of jihad and war must also be included in the curriculum, so that graduates of pesantren truly become preachers and mujahideen.'[19]

Bashir bemoaned the fact, as he saw it, that the enemies of Islam had eradicated 'the spirit of jihad' from the soul of the Muslim community. 'The enemies of Islam know that as long as the *umma* [community] no longer understands jihad and the zeal for martyrdom, they will be easily subjugated . . . For this reason, we must nurture both comprehension of and zeal for jihad so that love for it and for martrydom grow in the soul of the mujahideen.'

Those fighting for an Islamic state had to be like 'the learned men in the early days of Islam,' according to Bashir. 'Besides acting as scholars, missionaries and moral teachers, they were also mujahideen who were always prepared to go to war and didn't just sit back in their mosques or schools giving lessons.'

While Sungkar and Bashir were building up their Ngruki school, the old forces of Darul Islam were regrouping. Secret meetings were held where commanders still loyal to the executed DI leader Kartosuwiryo invited new initiates to swear an oath of allegiance known as the *bai'at* and join the struggle for an Islamic state. Evidence would later emerge that the revival of Darul Islam was secretly encouraged by Indonesian military intelligence, to flush out Muslim militants opposed to the Suharto regime.[20]

According to the Indonesian Government, Sungkar and Bashir were inducted into Darul Islam in 1976 during a meeting at Abdullah Sungkar's home in Solo, where they swore the oath used by Kartosuwiryo and vowed to carry on his fight. Despite their extreme philosophy and strident rhetoric, the two Ngruki preachers were not promoting violent resistance at this time. But Suharto was bent on eradicating any political challenge. As the pair later put it, with their usual overblown rhetoric: 'Suharto, using the armed forces as his instrument, put into force a strategy of deceit and torment which proved to be a hammer blow, and its poison was at its most venomous towards the Creed of the Muslims, as it tried to extinguish the hopes of Islam in Indonesia.'[21]

Sungkar and Bashir were arrested in November 1978 and accused of plotting to overthrow the government by campaigning for an Islamic state. Their indictment said that after swearing allegiance to Darul Islam, Sungkar had been given the title of military governor of the Islamic State of Indonesia (Negara Islam Indonesia — NII) and that the pair had then begun recruiting people to join them. Their group was referred to in court documents for the first time as 'Jemaah Islamiyah', employed the term Bashir used for his individual communities of followers who were implenting Islamic law. The prosecutors also called their group 'Komando Jihad', a phrase apparently coined by the government. Sungkar and Bashir were further accused of circulating a book by one of their teachers, urging Muslims to wage war against the enemies who resisted Islamic law.

'The charges were standard fare for the time,' wrote Sidney Jones, Indonesia specialist with the International Crisis Group, 'broadly worded accusations against two men who dared to criticise the Suharto Government, with nothing to suggest that they advocated violence or were engaged in criminal activity'.[22]

Sungkar and Bashir were found guilty and sentenced to nine years in jail for subversion, later reduced on appeal to three years and ten months. Amnesty International called them 'prisoners of conscience' and said the evidence against them was insubstantial: 'Many commentators have doubted whether a Komando Jihad exists or ever existed and have suggested that these accusations were used to stifle radical Muslim activity.'[23]

With the arrest of the two preachers from Ngruki along with some 200 Darul Islam followers, it seemed that the forces of militant Islam in Indonesia had once again been strangled. But Sungkar and Bashir's incarceration would only burnish their image as heroes persecuted for their faith. During their years in prison, their Ngruki school would become a beacon of defiance against Suharto's rule and a magnet for Muslims across the archipelago drawn by their call to jihad.

CHAPTER THREE

BROTHERS

ONE OF THE ARDENT YOUNG men who flocked to the Ngruki school in Solo was a lanky teenager with a mop of black hair and a big toothy smile by the name of Ali Gufron. He came from Tenggulun in East Java, a dusty village of 2000 people, three mosques and a dirt strip of a main street where fat pigs and scrawny chickens forage in the open drains. The village lies at the end of a bumpy stone road that runs through fields pierced by shards of volcanic rock, the ground so hard in places that the farmers have to plough it by hand to scratch a living from meagre crops of corn and green nuts.

In this barren backwater, young Ali Gufron was better off than most. He was one of thirteen children of the former village secretary Nur Hasyim, a respected leader and strict disciplinarian who ruled over the village for thirty years and had high hopes for his sons. The toothy middle boy and two of his younger brothers were certainly destined for big things, though surely not what their father had hoped for. Ali Gufron would later take the nom de guerre Muklas — and the assignment as controller of the Bali bombings, assisted by his brothers, Amrozi and Ali Imron.

The house that the brothers were raised in is a squat tile-floored bungalow set back from Tenggulun's main street. Except for a pair of mangy kittens wrestling in the dirt, there was little sign of life when I went there with a *4 Corners* film crew in January 2003. Inside, the proud family patriarch, Nur Hasyim, lay wide-eyed and motionless on a threadbare mat on the hard floor, paralysed by motor neurone disease and a stroke. He was tended by the first of his two wives, Tariyem, her small, wizened face wrapped tightly in an orange hijab. Tariyem is the mother of Muklas, Amrozi and Ali Imron, who were by then under arrest and facing the death penalty over the Bali bombings. The elderly couple were in a state of shock and confusion over the arrest of their three sons and the procession of foreign journalists to their remote village.

'It was about this time, after the midday prayer, about one o'clock,' Tariyem told us. 'These people rushed in. I asked, "What's going on?" He said "It's a raid. I'm looking for photos of Amrozi and his passport." He just kept saying that. I said, "He hasn't got a passport." He said, "Yes, he has!" He just kept shouting at me. Then lots of people came in. They put a picture of me on the TV.'

As she recalled the traumatic events of the previous October, her paralysed husband, eyes wide and hands trembling, wept silently at the mention of his sons. Clutching the old man's hand tightly, Tariyem went on. 'Even after the house had been raided I just thought he'd gone for a drive. I asked someone, "Where's Amrozi? Why hasn't he come home?"'

The eldest of the trio, Muklas, was the scholar of the family, but it was Amrozi who was Tariyem's pet son. 'Everybody says Amrozi was the cutest boy in the family,' his mother recalled fondly.[1] Two years younger than the studious Muklas, Amrozi was the black sheep, a mischievous boy with a good nature and a goofy grin, who only made it to year two of high school. '[I am] a naughty person, sir, that's what my family always says about me,' Amrozi would later tell Indonesia's national police chief in a televised interview.

While big brother Muklas was memorising the Koran, Amrozi would be hooning around on his motorbike or flirting with the local girls. 'Amrozi was, indeed, a challenge for the family,' the youngest brother, Ali Imron, said later. Eight years younger than Amrozi, Ali Imron was the baby of the family, a gap-toothed runt of a kid trailing around the village after the bigger boys. Like his older brother Muklas, little Ali was a serious boy who complained bitterly about Amrozi's antics: 'He is the one of my father's children who is extremely difficult to control.'[2]

Just down the road from the home the brothers grew up in is the Islamic boarding school established by their family in 1992. A chipped green sign on a stake beside a low-slung dormitory announces the

'Pesantren Al Islam, Tenggulun'. When we were there, a battered ping-pong ball was being slammed back and forth across an old wooden table out the front by a couple of pubescent combatants urged on by their skinny mates. 'Only for Muslim People' read another sign in English nearby.

The arrival of our foreign TV crew brought the game to a halt and the rowdy barracking turned to sullen stares, an unusual reaction in Indonesia where normally youngsters this age are boisterously friendly. The school's female students were nowhere to be seen. They're kept veiled and segregated somewhere out of public view.

The Al Islam school was modelled on Abu Bakar Bashir's famous pesantren at Ngruki, where the patriarch, Nur Hasyim, had sent four of his eight sons. But compared with the expansive compound housing Bashir's school, the huddle of low wooden buildings with a clapped-out ping-pong table is a modest affair. 'We practically built it from scratch,' boasted Jafar Shodiq, yet another of Muklas's brothers and the Al Islam school's founder. 'We built it with our own hands.'[3]

The school has always been a sore point in the village. 'The people at that school weren't like people at other Islamic schools,' the current village leader, Maskun, told me. 'Their activities were not like other educational institutions, which is why I became suspicious and wondered what was going on there.'[4]

Bashir was regarded as the school's patron and was received as an honoured guest when he travelled from Solo to Tenggulun to officiate at graduation ceremonies. But many of the villagers, who prefer the more laid-back Javanese style of Islam, shunned the visiting preacher from Solo and the rigid doctrine being taught at the school. Maskun said the village leaders refused three times to approve Bashir's visits to Tenggulun: 'He didn't have the respect of the elders.'

The Al Islam school's principal, Zakaria, a round-faced man with a knitted skullcap and a wiry beard, is another graduate of Bashir's Ngruki school. Zakaria emerged to greet us and agreed to an interview but wouldn't meet my eye, let alone shake my hand. We sat on the low wall under his dusty porch, as he outlined his school's program. 'What we teach to the students here is faith. We also teach languages, Arabic, English and Indonesian, as well as Islamic law and ritual obligations. They're the basic things.' No mention of basics like science, literature or maths. And the suspicious stares of Zakaria's pupils made me wonder what they were being taught about foreigners like me. Another journalist reported seeing a classrooms where the words 'mole', 'spy' and 'avenger' were spelt out in English on the blackboard.[5]

The goings-on at the Al Islam school had been the talk of the village for years. 'Their education included military training, rifle drills and war games,' village chief Maskun told me. 'They usually came out to do their military training at night. It was like army training. They did it around eleven, twelve, one o'clock. It might have gone on all night . . . They practised crawling along the ground, push-ups, marching and so on. And there was shooting practice.' According to Maskun, the students were all from trouble spots like Ambon, Aceh and East Timor, where rival Muslim and Christian militia groups were locked in brutal conflict. When the police raided Tenggulun after the Bali bombings, they found a military training manual in Zakaria's home and a cache of weapons and ammunition in the forest near the village.

The actions of Tenggulun's newly infamous brothers had polarised the tiny community. Some people, like Maskun, believed that Muklas, Amrozi and Ali Imron had brought disgrace on village. Others regarded them as home-town heroes, a view echoed in the graffiti seen scrawled on dusty windows, some words in Bahasa Indonesia, some in English: 'Bali for the *jahanam* [evil]' and 'Amrozi group for Paradise'.

Zakaria looked blank when I asked him what he thought of the three brothers and their arrest. 'I think it was a risk that they faced,' he answered. 'They were carrying out jihad and that is the risk of carrying out jihad. It was a choice they made.' And did he agree with their idea of how jihad should be waged? 'I know Amrozi and Muklas — their views on jihad are the ones that Allah and his prophet wanted them to have. If their intent was really to carry out jihad, as I've been told, then that's what they've been taught to do as Muslims when under attack by enemies.'

The glares of the apprentice jihadists clustered in Zakaria's schoolyard became more hostile the longer we stayed. Our driver was edgy and ready to go. But I had another question for Zakaria: Did he believe the killing of those 202 people in Bali was wrong? 'Depends on how you look at it,' he said. 'If Amrozi and the others saw it from the point of view that Indonesian culture was being defiled by the infidels' denial of God, then it's permitted by religion, as long as a warning has been given . . . What I mean by their denial of God is that Indonesian culture protects women's honour. But with the arrival of the infidels, women become more open, freer.' Zakaria threw in a few words in

English to emphasise his view of foreign 'infidels': 'Free life! Free sex! Free free!'

Zakaria's view was all too clear. But I pressed him anyway. The patron of his school, Abu Bakar Bashir, had said that he believed the victims of the Bali bombings would go to hell.[6] I asked Zakaria if he too thought that the people killed in Bali had deserved to die. 'According to the Islamic point of view they were infidels who hadn't seen the light,' Zakaria responded. 'If they had understood that such things were forbidden, and they're forbidden in every religion, then they shouldn't have done them.'

Muklas and his brothers were raised with a stern hand by their father, Nur Hasyim, a follower of the severe Wahhabi school of Islam imported from Saudi Arabia. 'My father, he wanted his children to be warriors, not just to defend Islam — we needed to champion Islam, to glorify Islam,' Amrozi later told an interviewer from the BBC. There was a long tradition of glorifying Islam in the brothers' family tree, their father and mother both the children of Muslim preachers. 'Religious activities were very much reflected in their daily lives,' said Muklas. 'We have been taught since a very early age not to ever skip prayers. Praise be to Allah, all of my siblings have been brought up never to skip prayers — except Amrozi.'

Back in colonial times, the brothers' maternal grandfather had set up Tenggulun's very first pesantren. Kyai Haji Sulaiman was a legendary figure around the village, by Muklas's account. He wore robes down to his ankles — 'proper attire' like the Prophet Muhammad's — with a headdress that Muklas described as just like Ali Baba's, and galloped around the village on his horse, brandishing a stick and a sword. Haji Sulaiman made the hajj pilgrimage to Mecca seven times, a herculean effort for any Muslim nowadays let alone in the 1930s. He stayed away for a year each time, bringing back the latest teachings from Saudi Arabia on his return. To the grandfather's disappointment, his pesantren eventually folded, according to Muklas, 'because there wasn't enough interest'.

Muklas's father, Nur Hasyim, was raised in religious schools and taught strictly by the Koran, paying his own way through secondary school after his father died. Nur Hasyim made the hajj pilgrimage to Mecca once, as did his wife Tariyem; he also adhered to the rigid Wahhabi view that Islam must be practised strictly as it was in the time of the Prophet. 'He was very fanatical with his beliefs,' said Muklas. Nur Hasyim taught his sons that traditional Javanese customs such as grave worship were heresy under Islam and must be eradicated.

Like many of his generation, Nur Hasyim was a veteran of Indonesia's independence struggle against the Dutch. In one battle not far from Tenggulun, he witnessed the death of his own brother, shot by Dutch soldiers. 'It was about 500 metres from where my father was standing,' Muklas recounted. 'He had a premonition that there were Dutch soldiers ahead. So my father asked my uncle to take a different route . . . but my uncle walked on alone. Fifteen minutes later there were gunshots. Apparently my uncle was shot.' To avoid being shot himself or captured, Nur Hasyim had to wait a month to recover his brother's body. 'It was these kinds of stories that inspired me and my younger brothers to be mujahideen,' Muklas explained.

While Amrozi was his mother's pet, Muklas was the star pupil of the family, never more happy than when studying the Koran. After classes at the local state primary school he would head off for religious study at an Islamic school in a neighbouring village. Despite the strict upbringing he was a sunny child. Asked much later why he was always smiling, he replied that that was what he had been taught. 'Never underestimate a tiny kindness, even if it's only to show people your happy face.'[7]

When he wasn't poring over the Koran, Muklas was tending his beloved goats. 'None of my siblings took good care of the pets, so my grandmother gave me a present . . . a mother female goat and a little one, her child. I took care of them. I was the sole person responsible for the goats,' he recalled with pride. Muklas cared for his goats so well that he eventually had a herd of forty which were his constant companions.

'As it turns out, goats are very similar to humans,' he reflected. 'Sometimes they get hiccups. Some are cute, some are nasty, some are scoundrels — you know, exactly like goats.' Muklas was chuffed to learn that as a goatherd he was in good company. 'When I read later on about the history of the Prophet and Islam, the scriptures also said that almost every prophet and disciple had goats. All the way from Noah, Jesus, Muhammad — they all herded goats.'

After graduating from junior high school, Muklas was sent off to Islamic boarding school in a nearby town. His parents had no idea what to do with Amrozi. The mischief-maker of the family had no interest in schoolwork or studying the Koran. At home he would pinch things belonging to his family and sell them for cash, and at school he was a menace. 'He was naughty,' complained Ali Imron. 'He often played pranks on his teachers and friends. All sorts of pranks. The family persisted to try to change Amrozi for the better. Put him through school.' But even at Islamic school Amrozi got into strife: 'He was banned by his teachers — he was expelled before he ever got to senior high.'

If nothing else Amrozi was good with his hands, always mucking about with tools. He eventually made himself useful by becoming the local repairman, fixing everything from cars to mobile phones. He became a fixture around the village with his long hair and oil-stained jeans and and his big goofy grin.

Amrozi would later be described as 'simple' and 'rather shallow' with an intellectual ability lower than normal and a 'disordered' attitude to work and planning, in a police psychiatric report after the Bali bombings. On the positive side, it said he had an 'adventurous spirit' and 'lofty spiritual beliefs', concluding: 'Personality immature, tends to be impulsive and easily influenced by others he respects or is in awe of, and very obsessive.'[8]

The person Amrozi was most in awe of was his big brother Muklas, who disappeared off to boarding school when Amrozi was twelve. 'He never came home,' Amrozi lamented. 'We hadn't seen each other in such a long time.' Amrozi would later credit Muklas's influence with turning him from a delinquent into an Islamic warrior. 'It was Mas [brother] Muklas who raised my awareness to fight the injustice toward Islam.'[9] The effort that went into Amrozi's transformation would prompt Muklas to boast with a chuckle: 'Thank God, with endless patience, bit by bit, to this day, he's also in the league of praiseworthy terrorists.'

After eighteen months at boarding school, Muklas did come home but not for long. He enrolled in a local college to study to be a teacher but soon found, just as Abu Bakar Bashir had, that secular studies were not for him. At fifteen, Muklas was a serious young Muslim with no time for the undergraduate antics of some of his classmates. 'It was during that time that I was extremely challenged by Allah almighty. If it weren't for Allah's grace and direction ... I'm sure I would have slipped. Because my classmates were a wicked lot . . . I had to make acquaintance with adulterers, drinkers, and so on. But Allah almighty gave me the strength to face this . . . I never neglected any prayer and never touched those women.'

His fellow students mocked Muklas's piety and calculated ways to torment him. 'I was once locked in by my friends, locked in a room to be with a prostitute. I just waited. I waited for almost two hours. I just kept quiet. Praise be to Allah — Allah kept me safe at this time.' His devious schoolmates eventually realised that Muklas would not be tempted and let him and the prostitute go.

Just as Muklas resolved that secular studies were not his calling, a chance meeting with an old friend from primary school illuminated the path ahead. His friend told him about a famous boarding school in Solo, run by a celebrated cleric named Abu Bakar Bashir. Muklas immediately began pestering his father to let him go. 'My father seemed indifferent, as if he was half-hearted. But apparently he was trying to collect the money to send me there.' Nur Hasyim eventually scraped together enough money to send four of his sons to Bashir's school.

And so, at the age of nineteen, Muklas waved farewell to his parents, brothers and goats and set off on the 200-kilometre journey to Ngruki, where he would spend the next six years. 'It was at this place,' said Muklas, 'that finally I felt I got the religious, spiritual nourishment that I had been desperately seeking.'

Muklas arrived at the Ngruki school in 1979. Sungkar and Bashir were still in jail, revered from afar as dissidents persecuted for their beliefs. 'When I heard the story from the students here that there are clerics who have been imprisoned I got curious, then I got upset,' recalled Muklas. 'How could this be? How is it that a cleric is imprisoned?'

Despite the absence of its founders, the Ngruki school was caught up in a new wave of Islamic fervour sweeping the Muslim world. In Iran, Ayatollah Khomeini's 1979 revolution toppled the corrupt US-backed Shah from power and ushered in an Islamic state. In the same year the Soviet army invaded Afghanistan and Muslims all over the world rallied to support the Afghan mujahideen. 'The jihad atmosphere dominated our campus,' recalled one student who was there at the time.[10] Students marched around the schoolyard to protest against the Russian invasion and circulated leaflets on behalf of the Afghan resistance urging all Muslims to support their struggle. Some who had finished their studies prepared to rush off to the battlefields of Afghanistan to join the jihad.

For a devoted young Muslim like Muklas, Ngruki was the place to be. 'There were members of Muhammadiyah there, also those from NU. There were children of religious clerics, of all levels,' Muklas related. 'There were children from the government civil service and children of those who were against the government; there were children of terrorists — all were equally accommodated. This boarding school really taught me about the real sense of brotherhood, so we could truly love Islam.'

The new Islamic resurgence was not confined to young zealots like Muklas. Muslims everywhere were flocking back to their faith. Many were disillusioned with what they saw as the corrupt materialism and moral bankruptcy of the West. Like the Muslim modernists earlier in the century, they saw Islam — with its emphasis on charity, morality and social justice — as not just a religion but a total solution to the ills of the modern world.

As one contemporary commentator has written: 'For new Muslim intellectuals and their followers, Islam must entail more than personal piety and public devotion. It must offer an alternative model of politics. It should provide moral discipline in the face of the anarchy and hedonism of the market. It can run schools, operate banks and organise farmers' cooperatives. It may even provide an alternative, some say, to secular nationalism as the moral basis of the national community.'[11] The extreme version of this view, propounded by the likes of Bashir and Sungkar, was that the West — and Islamic countries that replicate its systems — was floundering in corruption and moral decay because the laws made by men had failed; the solution was to replace the rule of men with the rule of God, in the form of Islamic law.

While Sungkar and Bashir were in prison, some of their followers had abandoned peaceful opposition and resorted to violence. A rival cleric in Solo, accused of informing on the two preachers and causing their arrest, was murdered in January 1979. A teacher at the Ngruki school was charged with the murder and later executed by firing squad. Another follower involved in the murder was also accused of planning to kill the judge and prosecutor who had sent one of Bashir's associates to prison for life.[12] The same gang also carried out robberies which they justifying by calling them *fa'i*, an Arabic term that describes raising money by attacking the enemies of Islam. These isolated crimes of violence by a handful of Bashir's followers were used to justify dozens more arrests.

Sungkar and Bashir were released from prison in late 1982. They were hailed as home-coming heroes on their return to Ngruki. Muklas, by then in his early twenties, had graduated the year before and was an apprentice teacher at the school.

Bashir began regrouping supporters and fellow dissidents who had been jailed in the earlier crackdown, forming a religious study group which met monthly at Ngruki. According to a 1988 report by Amnesty International, 'He told them that his aim was to collect together the members of the Jemaah Islamiyah (Islamic community) who had been scattered by the arrests of the previous years.'[13]

People who wished to join his group were asked to swear the *bai'at*, which by one account went like this: 'In the name of Allah, I promise that I will always believe in Allah and will not commit adultery, steal or kill anything forbidden by Allah and will obey the leadership, as long as its orders do not conflict with the will of Allah and his Prophet.' Another account said the oath, in Arabic, was simply: 'I swear to you that I will hear and obey all your commands.'[14]

Bashir's followers were then sent home to their towns and villages to set up individual groups known as *usroh*, meaning family, a concept based on the teachings of the founder of the Muslim Brotherhood, the Egyptian schoolteacher Hassan al Banna. Each *usroh* consisted of eight to fifteen members, who were obliged to help each other, study Islam and enforce Islamic law within their group. They were told that 'Pancasila and the Constitution should be replaced by Islamic law, that it was idolatrous for Muslims to salute the national flag, that Muslim women should wear headscarves, and that according to Islamic law the punishment for theft was amputation of the hand'. At some meetings it was said that 'only those people who took the oath were the real followers of the Prophet and that anyone who died before taking such an oath would die a heathen's death'.[15]

Within months of their release from prison, it was obvious that Sungkar and Bashir were heading for another showdown with the regime. Suharto had made it illegal to question the state ideology,

Pancasila, with a new law requiring every organisation in Indonesia to adopt the official credo as its 'sole ideological basis'. Islamic groups were outraged, condemning the new policy in religious study groups and mosques around the country.

Their anger erupted in September 1984, when a prayer meeting in Tanjung Priok in Jakarta turned into a protest and government troops opened fire, leaving dozens of people dead. In the brutal crackdown that followed, more than 200 people were arrested, some of them dragged from hospital beds with bullets still lodged in their bodies.

Amnesty International reported the experience of a 16-year-old ice-seller: 'He was eating fishball soup at a foodstall when he heard the crowd and went to see what was going on. He was not shot but fell on the ground when the shooting started, he said. An official reportedly stepped on him and said to his commander, "What do we do with this one?" The commander said to kill him . . . so the official hit him with a rifle until he lost consciousness. He was treated for wounds at the army hospital for ten days. He reportedly was beaten and threatened while under interrogation and agreed to anything his interrogators wanted him to say.' The young ice-seller was jailed for a year.[16]

'The bloody events of Tanjung Priok', as Sungkar and Bashir called them, only hardened the pair's resolve — and motivated more of their followers to turn to violence. In the wake of the massacre, the famous Buddhist temple at Borobodur in Central Java was damaged by a bomb blast and separate bombs went off in a bus and a Christian church. Another of the teachers at the Ngruki school — the same one who had authored the book urging Muslims to wage war against the enemies of Islam — was later convicted of supplying the explosives and sentenced to fifteen years in jail.[17]

Over the next two years, dozens of Bashir's adherents would be rounded up and jailed. The acts of violence committed by a handful of their followers were never definitively linked to Sungkar and Bashir. Most were arrested simply for belonging to Bashir's *usroh* groups. They were charged under the same anti-subversion laws used to incarcerate hundreds of government critics and jailed for up to fifteen years. Amnesty International classified them as 'prisoners of conscience, detained for their non-violent religious activities or their non-violent views about government policies'.[18] The sole case that made it to appeal was dismissed by the normally compliant Supreme Court, on the basis that it was never proved that *usroh* activities amounted to subversion.

Suharto's ferocity only fortified the conviction of his Muslim opponents that they must be willing to suffer for their faith. One activist, jailed for thirteen years for daring to publish the court documents from Bashir's case, declared at his trial: 'I definitely know that this judgement is evil, tyrannical and full of injustice. But I have no need for pity. Because thirteen years is very small. I would be happy if I were sentenced to death, so that I could die a real martyr's death.'[19]

In February 1985, the Indonesian Supreme Court upheld the government's appeal against the reduced prison terms already served by Sungkar and Bashir. Their original sentence of nine years was reinstated and the court ordered their rearrest to serve the remaining five years. But the two militants from the Ngruki school were not going back to jail.

At daybreak on 1 April, as the dawn call to prayer echoed out across the Ngruki compound, Abu Bakar Bashir stole out of the schoolyard on his black Yamaha motorbike. He met up with Abdullah Sungkar and a small band of their most loyal disciples, mainly teachers and students from their school. Then, as Muklas put it, 'it might be said that they ran away, the two Ngruki clerics who were going to be tried in court ran away.'

Bashir saw it differently: 'I came to the conclusion that the political trials were just for show and could not be justified. I then decided to reject the decision of the Supreme Court and fled to Malaysia with Abdullah Sungkar, because in my opinion the decision was tyrannical, so I was unwilling to accept it on the basis of Islamic law.'[20]

It was a small group of about ten men who fled that day, leaving wives and children behind. 'Nobody knew we set off for Malaysia that dawn,' said one of the group.[21] Some had false passports already prepared, others went with no documents at all. They travelled for nearly 2000 kilometres across the archipelago to the western-most Indonesian island of Sumatra and from there across the Strait of Malacca by boat.

In the eyes of Bashir and Sungkar their journey was no furtive escape but an epic voyage. They likened it to the legendary *hijrah* — migration — of the Prophet Muhammad fourteen centuries before, when Islam's founder fled persecution in his home town, Mecca, for refuge in Medina, from where he waged war for eight years until he finally defeated the unbelievers and established the first Islamic state.

The Ngruki preachers characterised their own escape as 'strategic evasion' and saw it as a crucial step in their long struggle to replicate the Prophet's original Islamic state. The pair would remain in exile for the next thirteen years working towards that dream and building the support base they hoped would achieve it — the militant network that became known as JI.

❧

CHAPTER FOUR

EXILE

BASHIR AND HIS BAND OF EXILES arrived on the shores of southern Malaysia in April 1985 and headed for a village on the outskirts of the capital, Kuala Lumpur. A safe house had been prepared where they would stay in hiding until new identities and documents could be arranged.[1]

Their hideout was facilitated by a fellow Indonesian who had fled into exile in the 1960s after the original Darul Islam rebellion was crushed. Abdul Wahid Kadungga had escaped after his father-in-law, a revered Darul Islam commander, was hunted down and shot by the military.[2] Kadungga had travelled to Germany and then the Netherlands where he was given political asylum and later citizenship, styling himself as a globe-trotting holy warrior.

'I'm an international activist,' Kadungga boasted. 'I travel from Europe to the Middle East and to Asia. I establish contacts with Islamic fighters everywhere. I dream of an Islamic empire.'[3] Kadungga was a crucial contact for Sungkar and Bashir. While studying in Cologne, he had helped set up the Muslim Youth Association of Europe, travelling and forging links with Islamic groups worldwide. His connections with militants from Southeast Asia to the Middle East would eventually go right to the top, according to a profile in an Indonesian Islamic magazine in October 2002: 'Occasionally he's in the Netherlands, then he's talking with top officials of PAS (the Opposition Islamic party in

Malaysia) . . . and not long after, he's conversing with Osama bin Laden in the depths of Afghanistan.'⁴ Kadungga would help arrange Sungkar and Bashir's entrée to the ranks of like-minded Islamic extremists around the world.

Within a few months of arriving in Malaysia, the fugitives began rebuilding their group. They held a series of secret meetings in late 1985 to plot their course. They decided to raise funds by asking their *jemaah* (community) back home in Indonesia to recruit volunteers to come and work in Malaysia and then donate 20 per cent of their salaries to the group. The volunteers would be employed by 'sympathetic Malaysian businessmen' who supported their cause and could use the cheap Indonesian labour. Former students were used as couriers to send instructions back to Solo, to carry funds from Indonesian donors, and to escort the volunteers who came to bolster the new *jemaah* in Malaysia.⁵

By the second year of their exile, Sungkar and Bashir had re-established themselves with new names and identities as preachers and itinerant traders, as Bashir later told the police: 'In 1986 after I had been in Malaysia for a year I applied for and obtained an identity card under the name of Abdus Samad, resident of the Kuala Lumpur district. I then moved to the Kuala Pilah district . . . I had a business dealing in honey and cumin oil . . . I also taught religion in a number of places, with an average congregation of 20 people.'⁶

Sungkar and Bashir had found a powerful protector willing to give them refuge. Hashim Abdul Ghani was a veteran of Malaysia's independence struggle and a man of some influence according to Bashir, because of his support for Prime Minister Mahathir Mohamed's party, the United Malays National Organisation (UMNO).⁷ Ghani ran his own Islamic boarding school in the valley town of Kuala Pilah, 250 kilometres southeast of Kuala Lumpur. Known locally by the honorific *ustad*, meaning teacher, and described as a man of 'good manners and a noble character', Ghani's patronage was a godsend for the two refugees. According to one newspaper report, 'Ustad Hashim welcomed Bashir and his group as fellow Muslims and opened up his home to them. Sungkar and Bashir could not refuse the offer. They were running out of money and had with them only a few pieces of clothing. The host let them use one of his houses as their temporary lodging.'⁸

The plywood shack loaned to the exiles by Hashim Abdul Ghani became the destination of a procession of young Indonesian radicals who made the trip across the Strait of Malacca to escape the iron rule of Suharto and join the new *jemaah* in exile. One of the first to join them was the former goatherd from Tenggulun, Muklas, who had graduated as a student and then spent four years as a teacher at their Ngruki school.

With Suharto's clampdown continuing and his old Ngruki classmates heading off to go jihad in Afghanistan, Muklas had grown anxious to join the exodus, but his superiors at the Ngruki school were reluctant to let their bright young teacher go. 'I wanted to go on to Saudi Arabia and Pakistan. I sent off applications but there was no reply. I sent them again and still there was no reply. So in 1985, because I had been teaching there for such a long time, I got a bit pushy. I insisted on quitting . . . I was very enthusiastic about the whole thing . . . I also sent applications to Yemen — still no reply. I even applied to Libya.'[9]

Tired of waiting for admission to an Islamic school in the Middle East, Muklas finally pestered his superiors at Ngruki to let him leave for Malaysia instead to join Sungkar and Bashir. He was convinced it was ordained by God. 'I prayed and asked for Allah's guidance and even in that prayer I had a dream. I remember feeling very touched because I dreamed I saw the Prophet Muhammad . . . He advised me to go ahead, to continue walking — because I had a noble goal and was walking on the paths of the prophets, of the holy and devout. It was a long dream, it had lots of meaning. In short, I was blessed because I was on the good road.'

After getting himself a passport and cadging some money from one of his brothers, Muklas made his way by train, bus and boat to Kuala Lumpur. 'I didn't really know where to go so I went to the mosques, expecting that I would somehow be assisted and I was.' He eventually tracked down his mentors at their new base in Kuala Pilah, where he swore the *bai'at* to Sungkar, vowing to give his all for their struggle.[10]

Back in Tenggulun, the escapades of Muklas's brother Amrozi were continuing to cause headaches for his parents, Nur Hasyim and Tariyem. His mother was forever on the phone to Muklas, wringing her hands. 'My mother was always crying at me [about Amrozi] because at the time I was away, either in Solo at the boarding school or elsewhere,' Muklas later recounted.

Amrozi was oblivious to his mother's angst. 'Back then I had one of those huge motorcycles, those KE–250 trail bikes, which I often used to ride around on,' Amrozi boasted. 'Also I let my hair grow long and loose, so people might have been deceived and thought I was a kid.'

The youngest brother, Ali Imron, a teacher's pet like Muklas, was fed up with Amrozi's juvenile ways. At fifteen, Ali Imron was a diligent student who had been nagging his father for some time to let him follow his older brothers to the Ngruki school and he blamed Amrozi for stopping him. 'I wanted to join the boarding school in Ngruki but my father wouldn't allow me, because Muklas was already there and Amin Jabir [another brother] was already there. There was no-one at home — Amrozi was hardly ever home, he just fooled around most of the time. So that was it, I wasn't allowed.'

Bored and idle in tiny Tenggulun, Amrozi was itching to leave home as well, though not to study Islam. Amrozi headed off to Malaysia in search of work on the country's booming construction sites. He got a job with a road construction firm, using explosives to blast away hillsides to make way for bitumen roads. He said later that his boss was an Australian, whom he referred to during his court case as 'my friend' but never identified by name. The other foreigners he worked with made his blood boil with their stories of holidays in Bali, drinking and chasing the local women. 'When I was with the foreigners they were talking about Indonesia and they did not know I was Indonesian,' he said later. 'They wanted to destroy Indonesia and I hated them for that.'[11]

To Ali Imron's dismay, Amrozi was soon back from his sojourn abroad. 'He was only there for six months. He didn't want to work, didn't do anything and then he returned — more nasty than ever.' Aged twenty-three, Amrozi married a local girl, but his family's hopes that he would settle down were short-lived. He and his wife had a daughter but the marriage lasted only two years, Amrozi blaming his bride's parents for their divorce. 'It seems that after they learned the truth [about me] my in-laws felt deceived ... Perhaps they realised that there was nothing to me — they must have been so upset,' he said later, making light of his break-up. 'The in-laws came up with various lies, just to separate us. In the end they succeeded. They tried several times to take my child away — that's how it ended.'

Amrozi went back to high school but dropped out a second time. Once again bored and idle, he amused himself by vandalising graves in the village, apparently inspired by his father's disapproval of the Javanese tradition of grave worship.

'When there was a grave that was considered sacred, I dug it up, I burnt it. People always got jittery about it. Since way back I guess it's

fair to say that I liked it when I could make other people upset . . .
These were graves that were considered sacred, like the ones belonging
to those clerics who spread religion to Indonesia, the ones people make
monuments of . . . Sometimes even after I had burnt it, they would
rebuild it, then I would dismantle it, and they would still build it again
. . . There was often fabric laid out on graves considered to contain
special powers, right? I would sometimes take away those pieces of
fabric, and eventually when they keep on putting the fabric back,
sometimes I would shit on it.' Amrozi told this story to the BBC,
laughing gleefully at his old pranks, adding 'Sorry, but that was what I
often did!'

Amrozi's vandalism eventually landed him in the local police lockup.
After torching the grave of a respected village elder he was detained for
a week,[12] to the mortification of his family.

While Amrozi was off on his high jinks, young Ali Imron remained
stuck at home. With one troublemaker on their hands already, his
parents grew alarmed when their youngest son started losing interest in
his schoolwork and his grades began to fall, as Ali Imron himself
admitted. 'Once I reached puberty it was a problem. My diligence
greatly eroded. I started to ride on my brother Jafar's motorbike . . . I
was out of control — I was almost like Amrozi . . . The only difference
is I don't fool with girls, what's the term — dating? Well I don't date.
Who'd date with me? This was back then, I was small, who would want
to date a small boy? . . . I think my parents started to realise that their
refusal to put me through the Islamic boarding school had created
problems. My parents thought that I was going to turn out like Amrozi.'

A family tragedy would soon shock Ali Imron out of his indolence.
It occurred during an expedition to Mount Lawu in Java by a group of
amateur climbers from the Ngruki school, among them Ali Imron's
brother Amin Jabir, the second youngest in the family. The climbers
were lost when bad weather closed in. 'It was pure miscalculation by
those leading the climb,' Ali Imron reflected bitterly. 'They had too
much faith but not enough work and preparation was done. So they
emphasised only faith — and ran out of everything while high up the
mountain. There was a storm and heavy fog. They had no water, no
nothing. So when they were told to descend, they had nothing left and
therefore they were lost. Sixteen people died.' Ali Imron struggled to
reconcile the climbers' blind faith with the tragic result but was assured
it was God's will. 'Thank God, eyewitnesses said that their deaths were,

God willing, a holy death, because they died while preparing for strength.'

After the tragedy, Ali Imron's father finally relented and allowed him to take his late brother's place at the Ngruki school. Determined not to disappoint his grieving father, Ali Imron vowed to change his ways. 'I wanted to change because I didn't want to turn out to be a scoundrel. I didn't want to be Amrozi. It's such a danger, a disgrace, to have another Amrozi.'

From their base in Kuala Pilah, Sungkar and Bashir began building an international network. They travelled widely, to the Middle East and Pakistan, to Singapore, the Philippines and later to Australia. They encouraged their followers in these countries to build up individual *jemaah*, which answered directly to the leaders in Malaysia, spread their teachings and raised money for their cause. As the two provincial preachers expanded their overseas contacts, their horizons broadened and they increasingly saw their fight for an Islamic state in Indonesia as part of a global struggle for Islam.

The pair turned to their foreign connections to finance their growing network and, like Islamists the world over, found a lucrative source of funds in Saudi Arabia. The Saudi kingdom was willing to bankroll Muslim extremists anywhere, as long as they subscribed to its orthodox brand of Islam known as Wahhabism, named after the eithteenth-century theologian Muhammed ibn Abd al Wahhab. A leading philosopher of the movement sometimes referred to as 'fundamentalism', Wahhab had spearheaded the campaign to renew and purify the Islamic faith by returning to the fundamentals of the Koran and the Prophet Muhammad's teachings, rejecting all 'new' interpretations since the time of the Prophet. Wahhab was the dogmatist behind the rise of the House of Saud, which adopted his doctrine as its state creed. Since the oil boom of the 1970s, the Saudis had been pouring their petro-dollars into promoting Wahhabism around the world, to shore up their own moral and political legitimacy and as a bulwark against the rival Shiites in neighbouring Iran.

Sungkar and Bashir's own beliefs mirrored the Wahhabi world view, so much so that Sungkar was nicknamed 'Ustad Wahhabi'.[13] Sungkar took part in the hajj pilgrimage to Mecca in Saudi Arabia each year, an occasion he used to meet up with fellow militants from around the world.[14] Saudi funding would later underwrite the training of a generation of JI fighters.

The men from Ngruki also became acquainted with the writings of one Saudi citizen who would soon become an icon of the Islamist cause. 'In Malaysia I once read a book written by Osama bin Laden about why he opposes America,' Bashir said later. 'In the book it was explained that he opposes America because he is carrying out the final decree of the Prophet Muhammad who ordered that Muslims should evict all Jews and Arabs from the Arabian Peninsula . . . From reading this, I felt an obligation to support the struggle to the extent to which I was capable.'[15] Bashir would later laud bin Laden as a 'true Islamic warrior', declaring 'I am not a member of al Qaeda. However I really praise the fight of Osama bin Laden, who has dared to represent the Islamic world to combat the arrogance of the US and its allies.'[16]

In between their travels, Sungkar and Bashir steadily built a new following in Malaysia. They avoided mosques and public gatherings, instead preaching and giving lectures in private homes, at first in Kuala Pilah and then further afield. Word steadily spread of the courageous dissidents from Indonesia who called themselves the Darul Islam Association and invoked the memory of their hero, Kartosuwiryo, and his fight to the death for Islam.

Sungkar was the more political of the two, a gifted demagogue who would gesticulate vehemently, his voice rising to a shout as he denounced the tyranny of Suharto. Bashir was softly spoken and preached about faith, exhorting his listeners to join their holy struggle. Anyone who wished to do so was asked to swear the oath, pledging to 'stand united in support of their leader and [to] faithfully implement the leader's teachings.'[17]

One day a businessman from Kuala Lumpur came to hear them preach. His name was Faiz bin Abu Bakar Bafana. Born in Singapore, Bafana was a slight, fine-featured man with spectacles and a neat goatee. Apparently a typical, law-abiding Singaporean, Bafana had completed a diploma in civil engineering then moved his family to KL and set up a construction company to cash in on Malaysia's galloping economy. Dr Mahathir's vision of transforming Malaysia into a developed nation by

2020 was well on the way to becoming reality, and for entrepreneurs like Bafana, business was booming. But for Bafana, like many people, the dizzying changes caused by economic growth and modernisation had left a spiritual void. In Malaysia, as in Indonesia, Muslims were returning to their religion to fill the vaccum. Bafana was one of them.

'I first became acquainted with Abdullah Sungkar and Abu Bakar Bashir in 1987 while attending religious lectures in Kuala Lumpur,' Bafana later testified. 'These lectures . . . were on the subjects of religious proselytising, Islam, the Jihad and the history of Darul Islam.'[18] Bafana was immediately captivated and became especially devoted to Abu Bakar Bashir. Bafana's business skills would prove crucial to JI when he was made treasurer of its central branch, Mantiqi 1, covering Malaysia and Singapore, and a member of its regional *shura*, or council.[19]

Years later, Bafana would be the first senior JI leader to be captured and provide detailed evidence of the structure, role and activities of the organisation and its leaders. He would appear via video-link from Singapore as the star witness in Bashir's trial in 2003, teary-eyed and trembling as he was called to testify against his beloved *ustad*. 'I considered him to be like a father to me,' he told the judge, when asked why he was upset. At the end of his testimony, which detailed Bashir's role in planning a string of bombings, Bafana declared: 'No matter what, I love you, Ustad.'

Throughout the 1980s, a steady stream of Muslim militants flowed across the Malacca Strait, fleeing Suharto's Indonesia for refuge in Malaysia. One of them was a brilliant young ideologue named Encep Nurjaman, a short, moon-faced young man just past twenty, stockily built and wearing round, wire-rimmed glasses. He was quietly spoken, 'a gentle person' by the account of one of his colleagues,[20] but grimly obsessed with his cause. He would later take the nom de guerre Hambali and become operations chief of JI.

'I know Mr Hambali, he is a businessman . . . and a religious teacher,' Bashir recounted later. 'He is short with a long beard . . . He comes from West Java and sells kebabs.'[21] Hambali was a salesman, that much is true, and kebabs weren't all that he sold. He could apparently sell just about anything. He flogged traditional medicines and sarongs, religious books and carpets and the box-shaped hats called songkoks typically worn by Malay men.

And Hambali sold jihad. The secret to his success as a salesman was the same power of persuasion that would make him an exceptional recruiter for JI. 'Everyone we've spoken to who has met Hambali says he's a quiet person but that when he speaks he's very convincing,' said one Malaysian security official in 2003.[22] But it was Hambali's genius as a strategist that later made him indispensable as Bashir's closest aide and JI's operational chief.

Hambali was born in April 1964 in the lush, volcanic rice belt of West Java, a region blessed with so many streams and rivers that every second place name begins with *ci*, meaning water, like Hambali's home town, Cianjur. Hambali would later bemoan the fact that everything in his village was green, even the food, the village so poor and so waterlogged that they only ever ate vegetables, never meat.[23]

Hambali was the second of eleven children in a family of Muslim scholars. His great-grandfather had founded a local pesantren; his father ran a school in Cianjur and was the imam (religious leader) at the local mosque; while his mother taught religion as well. Hambali's aunt reportedly still leads a religious study group in his village, her voice crackling out through the loudspeaker at the mosque as she calls the local women to study the Koran.[24]

As a chubby child growing up in the village, Hambali apparently didn't stand out. 'He was just a quiet kid. He studied and went straight home,' recalled a former classmate who now teaches at his great-grandfather's school.[25] 'He was very religious, but also very quiet, aloof and reserved,' said his mother, Eni Meryani, to whom Hambali was devoted.[26] While Hambali was a diligent pupil, there were no early signs of brilliance and certainly no clues to his later obsession, according to his old schoolmate. 'When we heard reports about him on the news we were confused and surprised. Usually people who are following hard-line Islam like to preach . . . But he was nothing like that. On the other hand, he said something about not being able to totally follow the Koran.'

Hambali's birthplace was in the heartland of radical Islam in Indonesia. West Java had been the seat of the first Javanese Muslim state, the Sultanate of Demak, where legend has it that the warriors who guarded the Sultan would plunge weapons into their bodies without drawing blood, defying the pain through the strength of their faith. It was the same kind of fervour that gave birth to the Darul Islam rebellion two and a half centuries later. Hambali's village had been part of Kartosuwiryo's Islamic state under the banner of Darul Islam. For more than a decade, until Kartosuwiryo was executed and his state dismantled two years before Hambali's birth, the villagers had lived under Islamic law. The dream of reviving the Abode of Islam lived on in the district, and still does. In 2001, the voters of Cianjur elected a new local leader on a platform of 'upholding goodness' through Islamic law with measures that included banning gambling dens and obliging female students to wear the veil to school.[27]

From the time he was a tubby, poker-faced pre-schooler, Hambali was educated exclusively in religious schools. He joined a Muslim youth group and in 1984, after finishing high school, applied for a scholarship to study Islam in Malaysia, but failed to make the grade. He spent the next two years idle, unable to find a job. What he did find in this time was a passion for Islamic politics. According to one of his neighbours, it was the Tanjung Priok massacre in Jakarta in 1984 that stirred Hambali to anger over the treatment of Muslims and made him a vocal opponent of the Suharto regime.[28]

Hambali eventually set out for Malaysia to find a job to help support his family. He travelled to the port of Klang on the Malacca Strait, the main harbour servicing Kuala Lumpur and a place teeming with Indonesians in search of work. He got a job at a market slaughtering chickens, before discovering his calling as a salesman, hawking rugs and religious books and kebabs. Hambali would eventually secure Malaysian permanent resident status in 1989.

Hambali stayed in a share house in Klang with a group of fellow Indonesian workers, who would go out at night carousing while their earnest young housemate stayed in to study the Koran. By one account, Hambali complained that 'his fellow countrymen had loose morals . . . his housemates were bringing home their girlfriends and this greatly upset Hambali.'[29]

Hambali soon left behind his loose-living compatriots, eventually moving 20 kilometres south to a more secluded spot in a village named Sungai Manggis, meaning mangosteen river, for the lush fruit trees shading the creek that winds around the town. Set back from the main road that runs between the port of Klang and the town of Banting, Sungai Manggis is a short drive to the Malacca Strait where speed boats shuttle passengers between Indonesia and Malaysia without the inconvenience of immigration procedures.

The kampung where Hambali lived is little more than a huddle of tin-roofed, wood-plank shacks along a potholed dirt track stretching into a grove of banana trees. His landlord there was Mior Mohammed Yuhana, a stern-looking man with a face full of creases, who owns the collection of ramshackle huts including the one marked 86G in which Hambali stayed, on and off for a decade, for 100 Malaysian ringgit (A$35) a month.

'Hambali kept himself busy by selling kebabs and traditional medicines,' according to Mior.[30] While earning his keep as a salesman, the portly Indonesian dressed like a cleric, in long white robes and cap. He kept largely to himself, but hosted many visitors in his modest home. 'He would sometimes bring foreigners who looked like Arabs or Africans,' recalled Mior. 'He said they were students but when I told them my name they didn't introduce themselves.'[31]

The huddle of huts in the banana grove became home to a growing band of Indonesian émigrés. All the men wore white, while the women wore full black burkahs and were forbidden from speaking to men other than relatives. The villagers called them 'the Wahhabis'. But they were good tenants for landlord Mior: 'They and their families used to come to my house for Eid [end of Ramadan] parties. We even posed for pictures.'

Another of Mior's tenants was a gregarious former youth leader from Yogyakarta in Central Java named Fikiruddin but better known as Abu Jibril. He had been among the original group who had fled Indonesia with Sungkar and Bashir in 1985. It was Abu Jibril's brother who had been sentenced to thirteen years' jail for publishing the documents from their trial. A fiery orator, Abu Jibril later starred in a JI recruitment video, brandishing a Koran and a gun and declaiming: 'No one can fight a jihad without the holy hook in their left hand and a weapon in their right hand.' Abu Jibril was a key recruiter and JI lieutenant until his arrest in Malaysia in 2001.

Eventually Abu Bakar Bashir would move to Sungai Manggis as well, moving into a blue-painted timber bungalow with a red tin roof next to Hambali's. Their twin shacks among the banana trees would become the new headquarters for the expanding *jemaah* in exile, as people converged from nearby towns and villages to hear them preach. 'Abu Bakar Bashir was the most aggressive,' said one man who joined them. 'He kept talking about how we needed to participate in the jihad.' Hambali, the strategist, preferred to work behind the scenes, building up their support base and making plans. 'He talked about how to keep secrets, how to not just talk to anybody, how to be careful. He was preparing us for battle.'[32]

The preparations would take place, not in some dusty prayer room in Malaysia, but on a real-life battlefield 5000 kilometres away. Afghanistan was embroiled in a long and ferocious guerilla war against the occupying Soviet forces, a cause that had become a rallying point for Muslim militants all over the world. In the mid-1980s, Sungkar and Bashir decided to send recruits from their *jemaah* to join the jihad to build up their group's military strength. Afghanistan would become the training ground for an entire generation of Islamic extremists, among them the men from JI, and the crucible for the global holy war they would join.

CHAPTER FIVE

THE BATTLE OF LION'S DEN

IN LATE 1985, THE FIRST volunteers from Bashir's *jemaah* set off for Afghanistan. They were a small band of fewer than a dozen men, the vanguard of several hundred Indonesians who would have their baptism of fire on the battlefields of Afghanistan over the coming decade. These were no raw recruits but highly disciplined devotees. Many of them were second- and third-generation Muslim activists whose fathers and grandfathers had fought and died for an Islamic state in the Darul Islam rebellion of the 1950s and 1960s.[1] The 'Afghans', as they called themselves, would become the next generation of leaders, ideologues and commanders of JI.

Among the early volunteers was Muklas, the lanky young scholar from Tenggulun who had quit his job as a teacher at Bashir's Ngruki school to follow the exiles to Malaysia. Muklas was one of the first to put his hand up to 'go jihad', which he described as 'the utmost form of religious service.'[2]

The 5000-kilometre journey to Afghanistan was just the beginning of a long and testing ordeal. 'I flew to Pakistan, I was alone, it was winter, I had nothing to eat for a week when I first arrived in Karachi,' said Muklas. 'I finally hooked up with the Arabs. They were there because it was 1986, it was the peak time for the jihad.'[3] The 'Arabs' that Muklas referred to were the thousands of Muslim volunteers who were flocking to Afghanistan from all over the Islamic world to join the fight against the Soviets. Muklas joined them on the long trek northwards to the jihad base camps in the desolate mountains of the Pakistan–Afghanistan border.

Muklas and his fellow travellers were the latest in a procession of warriors and religious crusaders who have traipsed through Afghanistan's harsh chiselled mountains seeking to vanquish or convert those who came before them. As the Pakistani author Ahmed Rashid wrote, conquerors have 'swept through the region like shooting stars'.[4] Alexander the Great, the fearsome Genghis Khan, the mighty Tatar warrior Tamerlane; all stormed through Afghanistan leaving death and destruction in their wake. The British statesman and writer Lord Curzon, back in the nineteenth century, called it 'the cockpit of Asia'.

As the Soviets were learning in the 1980s, the quest to conquer Afghanistan is not for the faint of heart. For one thing there's the treacherous terrain; and then there are the legendary Pashtun, the black-turbaned tribesmen who inhabit the godforsaken mountain wilderness that straddles the Pakistan–Afghanistan border. The Pashtun live and die by their code of honour, Pashtunwali, which obliges a man to avenge any insult or challenge to his *zar, zan* or *zamin* — gold, women or land.[5] And woe betide any woman who doesn't know her place: a local proverb decrees that 'women belong in the house or the grave'.[6]

The perils of taking on the Pashtun had been well learned by the British in Lord Curzon's time, during the contest between Britain and Russia known as 'the Great Game', when Afghanistan and its neighbours were mere 'pieces on a chessboard upon which is being played out a game for the domination of the world'.[7] The British Imperial Army was chased out of Afghanistan twice, an entire garrison save for its doctor slain in the Khyber Pass, in one gruesome retreat lamented by the imperial historian of the time. 'In the military history of this country there is no darker page . . . Dr Brydon reached Jellalabad alive, the sole [British] survivor of 4,500 fighting men and 12,000 camp followers.'[8] Lord Curzon was forced to acknowledge: 'In the history of most conquering races is found some spot that has invariably exposed their weakness like the joints in armour of steel. Afghanistan has long been the Achilles' heel of Great Britain in the East.'[9]

The British never did subdue the Pashtun. Instead they carved off a strip of what was then British India, called it North West Frontier Province and gave it back to the Pashtun to control. Now part of Pakistan, the tribal areas of the province running along the Afghanistan border are to this day the realm of the Pashtun. The laws of Pakistan are enforced along the main road; step off it and the ancient code of Pashtunwali applies. As for the border created by the British between Afghanistan and Pakistan, known as the Durand Line, it remains unmarked and unmonitored for much of its length and is nothing but a line on a map to the Pashtun people living on either side.

By the 1970s, Afghanistan was once again a pawn in a new game of world domination: the Cold War between the Soviet Union and the United States. Lavish aid from Moscow had transformed Afghanistan into a satellite state of the Soviets. In April 1978, a clique of Moscow-trained Marxists in the Afghan army staged a bloody coup and established a communist government in Kabul. Afghanistan's *mullahs*, or religious leaders, declared that the atheist communists must be fought and declared a jihad. Thus, Afghanistan found itself at war again.

The Afghan resistance quickly won the backing of the United States. In July 1979, 'President Carter signed the first directive for clandestine aid to the enemies of the pro-Soviet regime in Kabul,' as later revealed by Zbigniew Brzezinski, the then national security adviser. Brzezinski boasted of his role in persuading Carter to do it. 'I wrote a note to the President in which I explained to him that, in my opinion, this aid would result in military intervention by the Soviets . . . We didn't push the Russians to intervene, but we consciously increased the probability that they would do so.' Brezinski's strategy was revealed in another memo: 'Now we can give the USSR its own Vietnam war.'[10]

Just as Brzezinski had predicted, in December 1979 the Soviets invaded Afghanistan to reassert their control. The mujahideen forces, funded and armed by the United States, would keep the Soviets bogged there for ten years in a war that left more than one million Afghans dead and five million of them refugees — one-third of the population. The Soviets' fateful invasion and the US support for the Muslim resistance have reverberated through history ever since — through the collapse of the Soviet Union, the rise of the fanatical Taliban and the torrent of Islamist terror that would later crash back on the United States itself.

Brezezinski was asked once if he regretted having provoked the war. 'This secret operation was an excellent idea,' he responded. 'Its effect was to draw the Russians into the Afghan trap. You want me to regret that? . . . Which was more important in world history — the Taliban or the fall of the Soviet empire? A few over-excited Islamists or the liberation of Central Europe and the end of the Cold War?'

꧁꧂

The CIA was tasked with funnelling money and military support to the mujahideen. In the course of a decade, the motley lot of tribal factions that made up the Afghan resistance would be bankrolled to the tune of at least US$3 billion by the United States[11] and transformed into a fearsome though divided army. The former CIA station chief who ran the covert program from Pakistan, Milton Bearden, has said that the US military assistance added up to 'several hundred thousand tons of weapons and ordnance'.[12]

The United States was anxious 'to maintain plausible deniability', in Bearden's words, so it ensured the weapons it supplied were mainly models made in the Soviet bloc. When these ran out, an old arms factory in Egypt was cranked up and converted to produce 'bogus Russian weapons', which were then delivered by US cargo planes to the mujahideen bases in Pakistan near the Afghanistan border. In the interests of deniability, US Special Forces trainers were sent to Egypt to train Egyptians to train the mujahideen.[13]

America's funding was matched by its ally Saudi Arabia, which jumped at the chance to further expand its influence and counter the rival Shiites led by the revolutionary Ayatollah Khomeini, who had recently seized power in Iran. It was Saudi money that would finance the training of the young Indonesians sent to join the jihad by Bashir and Sungkar.

America's other key ally, Pakistan, provided the launchpad for the anti-Soviet resistance and the conduit for the US-funded training and arms via its powerful Inter Services Intelligence Agency. Pakistan had its own agenda — to instal a compliant regime in neighbouring Kabul and to resolve in its own favour the long-running border disagreement in the Pashtun lands once and for all.

By the mid-1980s — the time Muklas arrived and which he called 'the peak time for jihad' — the Soviets were mired in their own Vietnam, just as Brzezinski had hoped. The reformist Soviet president Mikhail Gorbachev came to power in 1985 and, the following year, described Afghanistan as 'a bleeding wound'. Gorbachev gave the Soviet army a one-year deadline to win the war. That year would be the bloodiest of the long campaign.

As the Soviets intensified their efforts, the United States stepped up its support to the mujahideen. In another fateful decision, the US

Congress decided to supply the Afghans with US-made Stinger anti-aircraft missiles to shoot down Soviet planes. Over the next two years, 900 of these state-of-the-art weapons would be handed over to the Muslim resistance. 'We were handing them out like lollipops', one US intelligence official said later.[14] The Stingers became an indispensable weapon in the Afghan armoury, as confirmed by the mujahideen commander, Ahmad Shah Massoud: 'There are only two things the Afghan must have: the Koran and Stingers.'[15]

It was during the war's bloody climax that the first band of Indonesians from Sungkar and Bashir's *jemaah* arrived at jihad headquarters in Peshawar, capital of Pakistan's wild North West Frontier Province. A medieval bazaar town at the eastern end of the Khyber Pass, which leads from Pakistan to Afghanistan, Peshawar was the main hub of the Afghan resistance, described by one journalist as 'an Asian Casablanca, awash in spies, journalists, aid workers and refugees'.[16] Turbaned warlords sporting AK-47s roared around the city's ramparts in jeeps paid for with US greenbacks or Saudi riyal, or with the money the warlords made from the opium trafficked out of Afghanistan on the same supply convoys that took the US-financed weapons and fighters in.[17]

Peshawar was head office for the leaders of the seven main mujahideen groups fighting the Soviets, some of whom hated each other as much as they despised the Russians. Chief among the warlords was the legendary Tajik commander, Ahmad Shah Massoud, who was later assassinated by al Qaeda agents on the eve of the September 11 attacks on the United States. The other key mujahideen leader was Massoud's arch-rival, the ruthless Pashtun commander, Gulbuddin Hekmatyar. Because of his close links with Pakistan, Hekmatyar was the main recipient of America's largesse.

The leader of the smallest mujahideen group, but the most important for the arriving Indonesians, was Abdul Rab al Rasul Sayyaf, a former associate professor in the Faculty of Sharia Law at Kabul University, who now headed the Islamic Unity Party. Sayyaf was an old friend of Abdullah Sungkar, one of the fellow militants that Sungkar would meet up with during his trips to Mecca for the annual hajj.

Although his group was the smallest, Sayyaf received generous funding from Saudi Arabia because of his links with the Saudi establishment and his support for its Wahhabi creed. One of his contacts was Osama bin Laden, the Saudi tycoon's son who had come to

Afghanistan to help underwrite the jihad, and who worked closely with Sayyaf because of their common Saudi connections.

When the Indonesian recruits arrived in Peshawar, it was Sungkar's friend Abdul Rasul Sayyaf who took them under his wing.[18] From Peshawar, the Indonesians were dispatched to the training camp where Sayyaf drilled his new recruits, a site called Camp Saddah located near the town of Parachinar, directly west of Peshawar in the rugged Pashtun lands along the Afghanistan border. It was here that Muklas and his fellow JI recruits were taken in 1986. The remote desert camp would be their home for the next three years.

Muklas and the other pioneers prepared the ground for the hundreds of Indonesians who would follow them to Afghanistan. A detailed account of these early days has been compiled by Sidney Jones of the International Crisis Group based on interviews with Afghan veterans:

'Initially they had planned to construct a separate military academy near Peshawar, but the area was too crowded with refugees, and they got an offer from Sayyaf to conduct their training within Camp Saddah. Sayyaf provided the land, arms and food; the Indonesians had to build the dormitories, a large kitchen and training facilities, including an obstacle course . . . Camp Saddah was divided into *qabilah*, the Arabic word for tribe. The South East Asians were considered one tribe, so Indonesians, Filipinos, Thais and Malaysians trained together, with a combination of Malay and English as the languages of instruction.'[19]

The full Camp Saddah training program lasted three years but after an initial crash course the recruits were sent to the frontlines for a taste of jihad. As Muklas told it, 'I departed from *baitul khodamat* [the house of services], which was a transit house for mujahideen from all over the world who wanted to enter Afghanistan. These *baitul khodamat* were all along the border between Afghanistan and Pakistan, and as far as I know they were all financed by Sheik Osama bin Laden.'[20]

Osama bin Laden had arrived in Peshawar back in 1980, within weeks of the Soviet army marching into Afghanistan. 'I was enraged and went there at once', he told a journalist in 1993.[21] His contribution was his zeal for the cause and his family's immense wealth.

Bin Laden was the son of Saudi Arabia's richest construction tycoon, Mohammed bin Laden, who had been minister for public works in the Saudi Government and whose firm was known as King Fahd's private contractor.[22] Bin Laden senior was a deeply religious man whose status was confirmed when he won the contract to refurbish the holy cities of Mecca and Medina. In keeping with his prestigious position, Mohammed bin Laden had numerous wives who bore him fifty or so children, so many that he reportedly became confused about which children belonged to which wife. Despite bin Laden senior's personal piety, his family enjoyed a splendid lifestyle. While holidaying in Europe, Osama's siblings were famously photographed posing in the latest 1970s Western fashions in front of an ostentatious American stretch sedan.

The seventeenth son, young Osama was an unassuming child, eager to impress his father. 'Osama was rather shy, reserved and perhaps a little afraid of making mistakes,' the boy's former English teacher told the BBC.[23] The ten-year-old Osama was shattered when his father was killed in a plane crash. Bin Laden junior vowed to live up to his father's name, as he told a Pakistani journalist in 1998: 'My father was very keen that one of his sons should fight against the enemies of Islam. So I am the one son who is acting according to the wishes of his father.'[24]

Osama went on to study economics and public administration at Saudi Arabia's King Abdul Aziz University, a leading hub of the Islamic intelligentsia. His teachers included the radical scholar Muhammad Qutb, brother of the pioneering ideologue Sayyid Qutb, who was executed in Egypt in 1966 and whose writings provided the philosophical underpinning of the jihadist movement. Another teacher was the renowned theologian Abdullah Azzam, a Palestinian with a doctorate in Islamic jurisprudence who had fought against Israel in the 1967 war and was a lifelong enemy of the Jewish state. Azzam became a powerful mentor and father figure to the young bin Laden with his motto 'Jihad and the rifle alone: no negotiations, no conferences and no dialogues.'[25]

Osama bin Laden was still at university when the Soviets invaded Afghanistan, presenting the earnest young Saudi with the opportunity to live up to his father's wishes. He arrived in Peshawar just twenty-two years old, by all accounts a serious and reserved young man with not much to say. Dressed in white robes, white turban and green camouflage jacket, he cut an imposing figure, physically at least. 'Thin and tall, he is six feet five inches, with long limbs and a flowing beard; he towered above his contemporaries who remember him as a quiet and pious individual but hardly marked out for greater things.'[26]

This impression of bin Laden in his early days as unremarkable was widely shared by those who knew him, including his brother-in-law and friend Mohammed Jamal Khalifa, who went to Afghanistan with him. 'He was very humble, very simple, very polite,' Khalifa reflected later. 'I am surprised to hear about what he is doing now because it's not in his personality [to lead] . . . Even at prayer time he would say "You lead the prayers."'[27] The head of Saudi intelligence, Prince Turki al Feisal, who was in charge of Riyadh's war effort and worked closely with bin Laden, had a similar view: 'He seemed to be rather a shy and reticent individual who spoke very little and when he did he spoke in a very soft voice.'[28]

After arriving in Peshawar, bin Laden sought out his old professor from Jeddah University, Abdullah Azzam, who was by then running the offices of the World Muslim League and the Muslim Brotherhood, the key bodies recruiting foreign fighters for the jihad. Bin Laden volunteered his family company's money, equipment and expertise. He brought in engineers and machinery to carve roads, depots and supply tunnels into the jagged mountains of the Pashtun lands for the mujahideen. The elaborate underground complexes would later provide bin Laden himself with a safe haven against the bunker-busting bombs of the United States after — as he put it — 'I discovered that it was not enough to fight in Afghanistan, but that we had to fight on all fronts, communist or Western oppression.'[29]

Bin Laden and Azzam teamed up to establish the Afghan Services Bureau, known in Arabic as the Makhtab al Khidmat, or MAK, the main office for processing the thousands of foreign volunteers. Because of their Saudi connections, the pair worked most closely with the Saudi-funded mujahideen leader, Abdul Rasul Sayyaf, the warlord who was training the Indonesians in Camp Saddah. Bin Laden became well known to the rookies from Indonesia. They were all processed through his bureau and many of the early arrivals met bin Laden personally.

Thanks to the United States and Saudi funding pouring in to support the resistance, 25,000 foreign Muslim fighters received combat training during the course of the Afghanistan war, according to former CIA station chief Milton Bearden. Others have said the total was higher still, perhaps up to 35,000 from forty-three countries.[30] The numbers of foreigners who actually took part in the fighting was much smaller; most were there simply to train. They were known as the 'Arab Afghans', even though none of them were Afghans and many were not Arabs either.

For many of them 'going jihad' in Afghanistan in the 1980s was a rite of passage. Travel agents conducted two-to-three-week 'jihad tours' during school holidays for Muslim students eager for a piece of the action.[31] While the 'Arab Afghans' would later boast of having helped to defeat the Soviets, the interlopers were regarded by some Afghan commanders as simply a nuisance with their inexperience, naivety and foreign ways. The CIA's Milton Bearden said: 'The Afghans thought they were a pain in the ass.'[32]

For the young Indonesians like Muklas, their three straight years in the harsh Pashtun border lands were like nothing they had ever known. They sweltered in the summer heat of the desert and froze in the sub-zero winter temperatures of the mountain camps. 'The snow was very thick, up to two metres,' Muklas later recalled with awe.[33] Others reported: 'They were miserably homesick, spoke poor Arabic, were unaccustomed to the harshness of their surroundings and the weather, hated the food and experienced "diarrhoea as a way of life".'[34]

The instruction regime in Camp Saddah included extensive religious training and study of 'military sciences', as it was described by Muklas. 'To summarise, I guess there were four elements of these "sciences". The first related to weapons of all sorts, from regular or light weapons all the way to rockets, both theory and practice. And all sorts of bombs — 19 kilograms, 20, 80, 60, thanks to Allah, we were able to try them all. The second science is about tactics — how to go to war, every type of battle — in an open field, a village, a city, in a building, out in the jungle, and so on. We had to learn about all of those. We also learned about map reading. And the last was field engineering — how to make bombs and so on.'[35]

The instructors in Camp Saddah were some of the most seasoned militants in the jihad, at first mostly Afghans, Pakistanis and Arabs, though later as they rose through the ranks the Indonesians became trainers themselves. One instructor remembered with awe by the Indonesians was an Egyptian, Muhammad Sauwki al Istambuli. He was a leader of the Egyptian Islamic Group, one of the core groups that joined al Qaeda. His brother was one of the killers of Egyptian President Anwar Sadat, assassinated in 1981 for making peace with Israel. Al Istambuli was such a ferocious instructor that, according to one Indonesian veteran, 'even the toughest among the Indonesian mujahideen ended up vomiting and fainting when they were trained by him.'[36]

Convinced of the holiness of their struggle, the young Indonesians relished their war. Muklas later waxed lyrical about his tour. 'It is the sort of pleasure that can't be described, let alone understood by those who have never experienced it. I have had a wife, I have had my first night — but the pleasure is nothing, not even close, compared to the pleasure of war. It was very, very delightful. Especially when we see our friends who bravely died a holy death. They smelled fragrant, they were smiling, and it often made me wonder — why is it not for me to die such a peaceful, contented death?'[37]

In 1987 while Muklas was in his second year in Afghanistan, Sungkar and Bashir sent their third batch of recruits for training in Camp Saddah. Among the new arrivals was the stocky kebab-seller from Cianjur known as Hambali. He was accompanied by his neighbour from Sungai Manggis, Abu Jibril, the firebrand preacher and later star of JI recruitment videos.

Hambali distinguished himself in Camp Saddah, reportedly graduating with honours in both the military and religious components of the course.[38] In between classes and practice sessions, he began to develop the network of contacts he would later utilise as operations head of JI.

Chief among these was Khalid Sheik Mohammed, later to become the senior operational planner for al Qaeda and principal architect of the September 11 attacks on the United States. When he was finally captured, a scowling mug shot of Khalid Sheik Mohammed — grubby, unshaven and paunch protruding from a wrinkled t-shirt — would be splashed on front pages across the world, his capture hailed in the United States as 'equal to the liberation of Paris in the Second World War'. This was not Mohammed's best shot. The picture that emerges from what we now know about him is that of a highly sophisticated man.

In the words of the July 2004 report of the 9/11 Commission, 'No one exemplifies the model of the terrorist entrepreneur more clearly than Khalid Sheik Mohammed . . . highly educated and equally comfortable in a government office or a terrorist safe house.' Mohammed was of Baluchi origin but grew up in Kuwait, where he joined the Muslim Brotherhood at the age of sixteen, taking part in youth camps in the desert and becoming 'enamoured of violent jihad'.

Eager for a solid education, his affluent family sent him to a Baptist school in North Carolina in the United States, and then to a North Carolina university to study mechanical engineering. From there Mohammed went straight to Afghanistan and began working for the warlord Abdul Rasul Sayyaf, who trained him in Camp Saddah. He went on to later work for Osama bin Laden's mentor and co-founder of al Qaeda, Abdullah Azzam.

Hambali and Khalid Sheik Mohammed were both brilliant strategists. Mohammed's prodigious talents earned him the alias Mukhtar, meaning 'the Brain'. From their first encounter in Camp Saddah, the two men went on to form a close personal and professional bond.

Another of the Indonesian 'Afghans' who excelled in Camp Saddah was one of Muklas's old classmates from the Ngruki school in Solo. The boy Muklas had known as Aris Sumarsono was now known by his nom de guerre, Zulkarnaen. He had been among the very first group of Indonesians to blaze the trail to Afghanistan and became a protégé and star pupil of the fearless Eygptian trainer al Istambuli.[39] By 1987 Zulkarnaen was running the training program himself in the Indonesian section of Sayyaf's camp. He would spend eight years in Afghanistan and later be promoted to the role of military chief of JI.

Muklas, Hambali, Abu Jibril, Zulkarnaen. The names of the Indonesians who served in Afghanistan reads today like a roll call of the top ranks of JI. And there were many more: Abu Rusdan, who would eventually replace the imprisoned Abu Bakar Bashir as emir of JI; Mustafa, who would head Mantiqi 3; Mustaqim, later the commander of JI's own Islamic Military Academy in the southern Philippines; the list goes on. These early arrivals would be followed by successive new waves of recruits, men whose names became equally synonymous with JI — names like al Ghozi, Ali Imron, Dulmatin, Azahari and Samudra. The Indonesian 'Afghans' would later be dubbed 'Group 272', referring to the number thought to have trained in the Afghan border camps.[40]

In the classrooms and practice fields of Camp Saddah, the Indonesians rubbed shoulders with Muslim fighters from all over the world. Their shared ordeal in the Afghan jihad would persuade them that their separate struggles, from the Middle East to Indonesia, Malaysia and the Philippines, were all part of a single holy war, to be waged against those who would oppress the forces of Islam.

While Muklas and his countrymen were in Camp Saddah, Osama bin Laden was beginning to emerge as an iconic figure, a symbol of the devotion and sacrifice needed to win the holy struggle. What he lacked in charisma, bin Laden made up for with money, dedication and willingness to eschew his billionaire's lifestyle for the privations of a life of jihad.

Bin Laden's status was cemented during his brief but legendary tour of duty on the frontlines, where some of the Indonesians went into battle under his command, Muklas among them. 'I met with Sheik Osama bin Laden at Jaji,' Muklas recounted. 'At the time the Jaji territory was under fierce attack by Russian soldiers and the snow was very thick . . . When the mujahideen prepared to hold an attack on Jaji I joined them. The leader of the mujahideen at Jaji and also the camp owner was Sheik Osama bin Laden.'[41]

The encounter described by Muklas was known as the Battle of Lion's Den. It became part of jihad folklore, apparently because it was one of the few battles in which bin Laden actually fought. Muklas and the fifty-odd men bin Laden was commanding endured a week of bombardment in the snow by the Soviet army in which about a dozen of their comrades were killed before they were finally forced to retreat.[42] It was no victory, but in their own eyes they had made a heroic stand.

From this, in the words of the CIA's Milton Bearden, 'the military legend of Osama bin Laden was born'. It owed as much to his self-denial as it did to his courage under fire. 'He was a hero to us because he was always on the front line, always moving ahead of everyone else,' said one veteran. 'He not only gave us his money, but he also gave himself. He came down from his palace to live with the Afghan peasants and the Arab fighters. He cooked with them, ate with them, dug trenches with them. This is bin Laden's way.'[43]

The exploits of the tycoon's son dug into the trenches of Afghanistan made good copy for the Arab journalists based in Peshawar covering the war, and their daily dispatches about bin Laden's bravado were published widely in the Middle East.[44] Bin Laden himself was happy to embellish the legend during later interviews with journalists from around the world. 'Once I was only 30 metres from the Russians and they were trying to capture me,' he told Robert Fisk of the *Independent*. 'I was under bombardment, but I was so peaceful in my heart that I fell asleep.' Bin Laden liked to boast that the old Kalashnikov he always carried had been taken from the corpse of a dead Russian soldier.[45]

Bin Laden's image was enhanced by the tales of his ascetic lifestyle, like this account from a visitor to his home in Saudi Arabia: 'When I observed his house and his way of living, I couldn't believe my eyes. He had no fridge at home, no air conditioning, no fancy car . . . The house was nothing. People were sleeping on the ground.'[46] Bin Laden increasingly exuded the aura of a holy man, though he had no credentials as an Islamic scholar. The fatwas, or Islamic decrees, he would later issue had no legal or religious authority, a mere technicality to his growing legions of followers.

In jihad mythology, the Battle of Lion's Den became the turning point in the mujahideen struggle; and in the minds of young fighters like Muklas, bin Laden — the same man described by his brother-in-law as having no leadership qualities — became the man who won the war: 'During that time he was leading the war, he led the war against Russia, he led the war by himself,' said Muklas. 'One of his strengths was that he went to the battlefield with all his wealth . . . He's a real leader. He is one human being that I very much adore in this life.'[47]

In reality, the war had already been won. President Gorbachev's forces had missed his one-year deadline for achieving victory and Afghanistan was still a 'bleeding wound' for the Soviets. More than the efforts of bin Laden and his 'Arab Afghans', America's Stinger missiles had helped turn the tide of the war in favour of the mujahideen. At the end of 1986, Gorbachev decided to withdraw, though it would be another three years before the last Soviet troops would leave.

For Afghanistan, the end of the war against the Soviets only heralded the beginning of a vicious new struggle, as the rival mujahideen groups, now flush with US and Saudi cash and weapons, went to war against each other for control of their ravaged country. That civil war would drag on for six years, ending with the rise of the fanatical Taliban, who would subject the Afghan people to five more years of misery with their vicious brand of Islam. They would also provide a save haven for bin Laden to turn his holy war against the West.

In the United States, the defeat of the Soviets was hailed as a victory for freedom and democracy over communism. As the Soviets finally departed, the CIA threw a party at its headquarters in Langley, Virginia.[48] Within months the 'evil empire' of the Soviet Union would collapse and the West would claim a historic victory.

But for the holy warriors of the mujahideen, their result was a triumph of Islam over the forces of oppression which had sought to subjugate Muslims; a victory they would now seek to replicate all over the world. For Osama bin Laden, this was just the beginning of his life's work. Bin Laden and his old professor, Abdullah Azzam, were determined to capitalise on their success and now set out to organise the foreign volunteers they had recruited into a global network of warriors that would continue fighting for oppressed Muslims everywhere.

Abdullah Azzam called it 'a vanguard . . . to achieve victory for this ideology'. Its role was to keep the jihad alive and to take it from Afghanistan to the rest of the world, to carry the flag of Islam 'all along the sheer, endless and difficult path'. Azzam called his vanguard *al Qaeda al Sulbah* — meaning the solid base.[49] After Azzam's death in 1989, bin Laden took over 'the base', which became known as simply al Qaeda.

For the trained and battle-hardened Indonesians returning home from Afghanistan, the defeat of the Soviets was an electrifying event. They now saw themselves as fighters in a global struggle, part of the 'vanguard' that would carry the flag of Islam 'all along the sheer, endless and difficult path'. If the Soviets could be defeated, there was no limit to what could be achieved. As bin Laden himself put it, 'The myth of the superpower was destroyed.'[50]

CHAPTER SIX

BE BRAVE IF YOU'RE RIGHT

A few months after the last Soviet tank rumbled out of Afghanistan, Muklas headed for home. After three years away from his family, he didn't want to return empty-handed. 'We're all human — I was ashamed to go home with no keepsakes for my family. So I stopped by Malaysia, wanting to look for work.'[1] His search for work took him to the rubber and palm-oil estates of Malaysia's southernmost state, Johore, where there were jobs aplenty in the plantations and the processing plants that service them. Muklas got work as a labourer and found lodging in a village called Ulu Tiram. 'I thought that after two or three months I'd be able to earn some money and then I'd head home. But Allah had different plans. I was looking for a job — but Allah found me a wife.'

The girl that Muklas met was the sister of Nasir bin Abas, one of his fellow trainees from Afghanistan, a Singaporean who would later become the leader of JI's Philippines branch, Mantiqi 3. Nasir's father was a former army officer from Singapore, who had moved to Malaysia and joined a religious study group led by Sungkar and Bashir. Among his other five children, Abas had a daughter named Farida, described as a 'highly cosmopolitan and well-educated young woman,'[2] who was studying at an Islamic university in Malaysia. Farida was of marrying age and Abas thought highly of the handsome young religious teacher just back from Afghanistan.

'One day he called on me, after I was there for about two months,' Muklas recounted. 'He asked me to ride in a car with him and he said "Ustad" . . . well no, actually he just called me by my name, he said "I want to marry you to my daughter." I was startled, shocked — Is this gentleman joking? He said "OK, I'll give you three days to think about it."' Muklas had turned down marriage proposals before and this one was odder than most. 'This gentleman posed a peculiar condition — "Before you answer yes, you cannot meet my daughter. Only after you've answered yes you may see her."'

Muklas went home and prayed for guidance and after a day and half his prayers were answered with an apparition. 'In those dreams I saw her skipping with ropes, wearing a school uniform — blue and white, and she wore a headscarf. When I prayed that was the image I saw. When I eventually got to meet her she was just like that.'

Muklas said yes to Abas but he still had to win the favour of Farida herself — not to mention her brother Nasir and the rest of his family, who admired Muklas's credentials as a Muslim warrior but thought they could find a better match for Farida than the former goatherd from Java. 'At first my wife was not interested, mainly because Indonesians at that time didn't have the best of reputations, they were [thought to be] thieves — bad reputations, very bad. So her entire family objected, they didn't want to accept me. Their position was they would do all they could to prevent it, to not have this Indonesian as a member of their family.'

Farida's father, Abas, invited Muklas to Singapore to meet the rest of the family and talk them around. One of Farida's brothers confronted Muklas. '[He said] "You — Indonesian — what do you want messing with my sister?" That's what he said, that's what he thought. I told him, "I came here because I wanted to meet you, to meet the older members of the family." We then went to her house. I was interrogated for more than three hours. Then, perhaps because I answered his questions satisfactorily he turned into my second staunchest supporter.'

Farida, too, finally succumbed. 'Praise be to Allah, my wife gave in,' said Muklas. 'She was defeated, so to speak, perhaps she thought that she's a girl and she shouldn't be rebelling against her parents' will. So she gave in, she surrendered.' Farida would eventually bear Muklas six children, the youngest a baby born after his father's arrest over the Bali bombings and named Osama in honour of Muklas's hero. Farida's brothers, who had so resisted Muklas's advances, became his firm friends and went on to form the core of the Singaporean branch of JI.

Muklas and Farida settled in Ulu Tiram, a community of mostly plantation hands and factory workers located amongst the palm-oil estates of Johor. Muklas worked days as a labourer and in the evenings taught Arabic and Islamic law. While seemingly secluded, Ulu Tiram is just 30 kilometres from the state capital, Johor Bahru, and a half hour drive to the causeway that links Malaysia with Singapore. Also close by is the grandly appointed University of Technology, Malaysia, an intellectual engine of Malaysia's Islamic resurgence, and later a rich recruiting pool for JI. 'Ulu Tiram has always attracted radical Islamic teachers,' said the village headman was reported saying. 'As far back as I can remember there have always been madrasahs [religious schools] here that were started and later abandoned.'[3]

In Ulu Tiram, Muklas was given a crucial new assignment by his leaders Abdullah Sungkar and Abu Bakar Bashir. Now in their sixth year in exile in Malaysia, Sungkar and Bashir had decided to establish a new Islamic boarding school modelled on their famed Ngruki school in Solo. Their trusted alumnus was tasked with setting up the pesantren. 'Ustad Sungkar told me to do this because I had experienced life at the school at Ngruki and in Malaysia an Islamic boarding school teaching the Quran and Sunna was badly needed, especially by our children, the children of the Indonesians living in Malaysia.'[4]

The new school was funded by donations from supporters in Malaysia and Singapore. A local benefactor provided 11 hectares of agricultural land at the end of an isolated road running through a government-owned plantation. 'There were many children around the area,' the donor said later. 'I thought they were illiterate in religion and a number of them were school drop-outs. They probably didn't know how to read the Koran. I also thought they probably didn't have a chance to go to a government school. So I was very happy that a madrasah could be built where the children could get together and enrich their knowledge and at the same time I could perform a good deed.'[5]

The old plantation buildings were transformed into dormitories, classrooms and offices, along with living quarters and a small mosque. Soon the sound of young voices chanting Koranic verses rang out across the oil palms. The Luqmanul Hakiem Islamic boarding school would become a major new focal point for Sungkar and Bashir's group, indoctrinating a new generation in their radical creed.

Today the school that Muklas built lies abandoned, the jungle slowly creeping in to reclaim it. The air was dank with humidity and thick with hungry mosquitoes, the day I went there with a *4 Corners* crew in January 2003. We clambered through a tangle of undergrowth to a vantage point at the top of a small hill, from where the school was barely visible in the valley below, save for the odd glimpse of tin roof or timber outhouse through the canopy. Down in the valley we found a bitumen track leading to a dead-end with a steel boomgate and a rusting padlock. The two-storey concrete administration block was closed and shuttered and a sign warned off trespassers. The scrawny trees were wilting and weeds had conquered the lawn.

Next door in a clearing among the oil palms we came to a dilapidated wooden house on stilts with the sounds of a Malaysian daytime soapie blaring from a TV inside. The inhabitants came out to greet us. Yusof bin Usman, a man of about forty, his skin tanned black and leathery from labouring in the tropical sun, was at first too taken aback by a group of strangers showing up with a TV camera to say much at all. His wife, Nor Aishah, a loquacious young woman with a big smile, a single brown tooth and a baby perched on her hip, was happy to regale us with stories about their strange neighbours at the Luqmanul Hakiem school.

'They wouldn't mix with women who didn't wear the head scarf,' Nor told us. 'If we wanted to mix with them, we couldn't go in there if our head was not covered. We weren't allowed to talk loudly, weren't allowed to laugh, we had to look serious . . . We're friendly, we like socialising and then they come here and tell us we're not allowed to do anything . . . weren't allowed to watch TV, weren't allowed to listen to radio. We're used to TVs and radios. I like watching music shows but they said we couldn't do any of that. They said it's forbidden by Islamic law. Everything was forbidden by Islamic law.'

Yusof showed the way across the clearing to the deserted classrooms where Muklas taught his pupils. Chairs were stacked neatly on old wood-and-iron desks. A gecko sidled up a blackboard. A sign on a wall spelt out a motto in Malay, which our local guide translated: 'Be scared if you're wrong — Be brave if you're right.'

In its heyday, according to Nor and Yusof, the school had 400 students, ranging from five-year-olds in kindergarten to teenagers doing the equivalent of senior high. By day it seemed like an ordinary school; after nightfall, reported Yusof, there were all sorts of goings-on. 'They took their students out walking, even at night. They walked up here to the field. They didn't go anywhere, just went round and round at night . . . The boys did training, they were told to run and all that but they didn't wear uniforms like soldiers, just school clothes.' As for the style of Islam being taught there: 'You could call them fanatics,' said Yusof. 'It wasn't simple Islam. I don't like Islam like that.'

Most of the teachers, students and followers who came to join the school community were outsiders, many of them from Indonesia or Singapore. They lived commune-style, the land divided into lots and sold off to members of the *jemaah* to build houses of their own and the proceeds channelled back into the school. 'I suspected something was not right at that school,' the village headman said later. 'They lived and prayed apart . . . They never mixed with other villagers.'[6]

Abdullah Sungkar moved to a house nearby to supervise the running of the school, while Bashir and Hambali both commuted from their shacks in Sungai Manggis to give lectures to the students. According to the benefactor who donated the land, Muklas set the tone for what was taught. 'He did influence the teachers by embedding in them the spirit of holy war in Afghanistan and Osama bin Laden.' Bashir later acknowledged the teachings at the school were opposed by most of the community and 'its followers were branded Wahhabis'.[7]

According to authorities in neighbouring Singapore, Muklas's school became a new training site for JI, and a meeting place for a cell of militants that plotted havoc in the island state. It was the investigations by the Singaporean authorities that first exposed the existence and activities of JI — more than a decade after Muklas set up the new school. 'They decided to have military training or operational training, I believe, in 1998, because they wanted to carry out some terrorist activities,' Singapore's Minister for Home Affairs, Wong Kan Seng, told me in 2003. 'The groups of Jemaah Islamiyah members which we have in Singapore as well as those in Malaysia have been to the school for training . . . The training was conducted in the jungle and in other remote places . . . They learn how to do reconnaissance, for example. They learned how to avoid detection. And they learned how to shoot, how to fire weapons and how to make bombs.'

∘✵∘

Back home in Tenggulun, Muklas's two younger brothers Amrozi and Ali Imron were still floundering about, figuring out what to do with their lives. After his spell in the local lockup, Amrozi had given up his hobby of torching and defecating on graves. He had married for a second time but, like his first marriage, it only lasted two years. 'He was just like a kid, going out all the time,' his second wife complained.[8]

The youngest brother, Ali Imron, had finally got his wish to go to the Ngruki school in Solo. But on his first trip away from his parents, the eighteen-year-old baby of the family was homesick and out of his depth. 'I only managed to stay for one month. I didn't feel at ease, I didn't feel at home with the teachings. Even during that one month I felt I couldn't bear it any longer. I wanted to go home. Those teachers at Ngruki, they taught extreme lessons.' Apparently not cut out for a life of jihad, Ali Imron had to lie to get home. 'I pretended to be ill, so my family came to fetch me.'[9] His parents enrolled him as a day student in a local boarding school to finish his studies.

With nothing much to keep him in Tenggulun, Amrozi decided to head off to Malaysia again, this time to seek out his brother Muklas, who had been away now for more than ten years. By this stage, the delinquent of the family claimed, he had seen the error of his ways. 'After I left my village for the second time I already intended to change all my bad habits and behaviour . . . I no longer smoked, I also no longer watched movies and there was no more bad talk.'

Amrozi made his way to Muklas's pesantren at Ulu Tiram to seek out his long-lost sibling, only to have his idolised older brother turn him away. 'I wanted to go to this place, this brother of mine's place, to Muklas, but I wasn't accepted. He didn't believe in me. Perhaps he was afraid that I would just create trouble.' The rejection was a bitter blow. 'So I just worked, I did construction work, for around two or three years . . . but somehow my heart was no longer in it.'

After two years labouring on construction sites all over Malaysia and praying five times a day to become a good Muslim, Amrozi decided to try again. 'Eventually I plucked up my courage and went back to Johor. I just stuck it out. I didn't have his permission, I just went to his place. When I finally got there I guess there was hope in this heart of mine. It was as if I was there to seek, what would you call it — to seek Allah's blessing.' Finally Muklas took pity on his wayward brother and took him in.

'I was still a bachelor then so I stayed at the kids' dormitory,' recalled Amrozi. 'I was mostly with the small children so I would clean up the kids, help them wash their clothes, everything. If there was any construction work that needed to be done I would help with that . . . In the end I felt very comfortable at that place . . . I felt very much at home.'

Amrozi swapped his jeans for a Muslim tunic and his unkempt hairdo for a skullcap and wispy beard. At the age of almost thirty, he had finally won the favour of the older brother he adored. 'At that point he trusted me, it was like, how would you say, finally I was worthy of sitting here.'

Still at home in Tenggulun, it was now young Ali Imron who was at a loss. Since his brief stint at Ngruki, he had lost interest in studying and was skipping classes and bringing home school reports with ordinary grades. 'I often stayed up late, roamed around in motor cars here and there and just hung around outside . . . That's all, it was just a teenage phase . . . I figured as long as I could pass the final exams, I would be OK.'

Forever living in the shadow of his older brothers, Ali Imron didn't want to bring shame on his family but couldn't work out what to do, until one day he attended a religious meeting arranged by some students at his school. The meeting was addressed by a preacher from Jakarta who was a veteran of the separatist struggle in Aceh and a proponent of the teachings of the Muslim Brotherhood from the Middle East. He showed videos of Palestine and Afghanistan and spoke about the oppression of Muslim brothers worldwide. Ali Imron would later describe this experience as 'the beginning of my true conversion'. But he also admitted he simply didn't want to be 'another Amrozi', especially as now even the former delinquent of the family had reformed. 'After that meeting I didn't want to do anything except to change my ways,' he recounted. 'And there was no better way to change than to move to another place, as far away as possible. I had to go across the sea if necessary . . . to change from what I call that period of idle, wasted existence.'

Ali Imron headed straight for Malaysia to find Muklas. 'I was still confused. What mattered to me was that I had to go to Malaysia . . . I just needed to get out . . . Amrozi was already in Malaysia — so Amrozi changed for the better sooner than I did.'

Arriving in Kuala Lumpur, Ali Imron rang Muklas who sent one of his in-laws to fetch his little brother and bring him to Johor. Ali Imron planned to find a job on a construction site, as Amrozi had done. But Muklas had other plans for him. He sent Ali first to Singapore to get a visa for Pakistan, and then to Sungkar and Bashir to be inducted into their group, which at this stage they still called Darul Islam.

It all happened so quickly that Ali Imron barely knew what was going on. A farewell ceremony was held at Sungkar and Bashir's base, where the teenaged Ali was sworn in with two other new recruits. One of his fellow novices was another young Indonesian by the name of Fathur Rahman al Ghozi, an old schoolmate of Ali Imron's from the Ngruki school, whose father had been jailed for links to the so-called Komando Jihad, formed by Sungkar and Bashir in the 1970s. Al Ghozi junior would go on to become a top bomb maker for JI.[10]

'Right before we left we made an agreement,' Ali Imron recounted. 'That agreement was to read a text and shake hands with Ustad Abdullah Sungkar. We praised Allah and said "By Allah's grace I will follow Allah and the Prophet's instructions to the best of my capacity" . . . Then we shook hands. That was it.'

Ali Imron and his two companions then headed off to 'continue their studies', as he put it. By his own account, Ali Imron didn't even know where he was headed, let alone how he felt about going. 'Well [I felt] pretty elated, although at the time I wondered — where will I be going to school? What school started at the end of September?' Ali Imron's destination was the school of jihad in the radical madrasahs and mujahideen training camps of Afghanistan and Pakistan, where he would spend the next three years.

By the time Ali Imron was bundled off to Afghanistan, the Muslim world had found itself at war again. In August 1990 the forces of Iraqi dictator Saddam Hussein had invaded Kuwait, provoking the United States and a coalition of its allies to declare war on Iraq. This new war would galvanise the veterans of the Afghan jihad afresh and provide a new focus for their fury: America and its partners in the West.

The Gulf War began at 2 a.m. on 2 August, when Iraqi troops stormed across the border to seize control of Kuwait's immense oil wealth and its ports and shipping lanes through the Persian Gulf. Saddam Hussein was bent on extending his influence in the Middle East and considered tiny Kuwait, which had been part of Iraq under the Ottoman empire, to be fair game. Saddam also felt emboldened by the backing he had received during his ten-year war with Iran, when he had secured arms from France and the Soviet Union and intelligence about Iranian manoeuvres from the United States, which saw the dictator in Baghdad as a lesser evil than the fanatical Shiites in Teheran.

The invasion alarmed the Arab world just as it did the West. There was little sympathy for Saddam and his brutal secular regime in the Middle East. Arab liberals viewed him as a thug, while radical Muslims saw him as — even worse — an apostate, someone who has abandoned his faith.

Saddam's eviction of the Kuwaiti royal family prompted panic next door in the House of Saud, which feared it might be next. As the Saudi royals fretted over their future, their still loyal subject Osama bin Laden came up with a plan. Bin Laden had returned to his homeland a hero after the Afghan war. His public lectures on the oppression of Muslims attracted huge crowds and cassettes of his speeches sold in the hundreds of thousands.[11] Bin Laden now offered his assistance to the Saudi Government; he would rally the network of mujahideen he had assembled under the banner of al Qaeda and send an army of holy warriors to evict the Iraqis from Kuwait.

To bin Laden's horror, his plan was rejected by the House of Saud, which believed a surer way of guaranteeing its survival was by turning to its old friends in Washington for protection. On 7 August, the first US forces landed in Saudi Arabia to launch Operation Desert Shield, backed by troops from seven Arab states. By the following January there would be 500,000 US soldiers on the Arabian Peninsula and another 200,000 sent by America's allies.

The stationing of US forces in his homeland would later be cited by Osama bin Laden as the catalyst for his holy war against the West, when he announced it was time to drive out 'the American soldiers of Satan and their allies of the Devil'. For bin Laden, the presence of US troops in Saudi Arabia, the holiest land of Islam, was 'the greatest disaster since the death of the Prophet Muhammad'.[12]

In the dramatic rhetoric of his later fatwas, he would portray it as the final insult after centuries of Western victimisation of the Muslim world. 'Since Allah spread out the Arabian Peninsula, created its desert and drew its seas, no such disaster has ever struck as when those Christian legions spread like pests, crowded its land, ate its resources, eradicated its nature, and humiliated its leaders.'[13]

To many Western eyes, especially since the events of September 11, these read like the words of a madman. But to many Muslims, even some who abhor bin Laden's actions, his words ring powerfully true. They feel cheated and aggrieved by the impoverishment and backwardness of much of the Muslim world; they believe Islam has been humiliated and subjugated; and some believe the West is to blame. To trace the history of this profound sense of grievance it is necessary to delve back 1500 years, to the life and times of the Prophet Muhammad and the rise and fall of the glorious empire that he founded on the Islamic faith.

CHAPTER SEVEN

STRIVING IN THE PATH OF GOD

IN THE YEAR OF THE ELEPHANT, more or less, a boy was born in a sandy settlement in the Arabian desert just inland from the Red Sea. The chronicles of the time are so sketchy that we can't be certain, but it was around 571 — the year the viceroy of Yemen marched from the tip of the Arabian Peninsula all the way to Mecca with a large army and an elephant — the first elephant the amazed residents of Mecca had seen.

Mecca was just a collection of mudbrick houses gathered around a well, in a barren valley amid the rocky wilderness peopled by the nomadic Bedouin. But the settlement was flourishing as a stopover for the trading caravans that criss-crossed the deserts from Yemen in the south to Syria in the north. It was in Mecca that the boy was born.

They named the child Muhammad. His father died around the time of his birth and his mother passed away when he was only six years old, so the orphan was left to be raised by his grandfather and uncle, the leaders of the Hashim clan, part of the ruling tribe, the Quraysh. Muhammad travelled with the menfolk and their caravans as they traversed the Arabian peninsula with cargoes of frankincense, Indian spices and silks. The boy would mind the camels when the caravan stopped to rest.

Muhammad was marked out early as a special child. Legend has it that as he tramped under the blazing desert sun, a small cloud would hover above him so he could walk in shade. One day a hermetic monk reputed as a visionary told his uncle: 'Go back home with your nephew and keep an eye on him . . . for he is going to be a very big man.'[1]

Despite its harsh setting, Muhammad's birthplace, Mecca, was already considered holy because of its ancient box-shaped shrine known as the Kabaa, or cube, to this day the holiest building in the world for Muslims. A flat-roofed edifice of stone and marble, the Kabaa had been built in the sand by the prophet Abraham, according to Islamic lore, after the angel Gabriel led him and his son Ishmael to the desert site, where they prayed to the Almighty to 'put in the hearts of men kindness towards them, and provide them with the earth's fruits, so that they may give thanks,' (Koran 14:37).

God answered Abraham's prayers and the community at Mecca thrived. It became a place of pilgrimage, as the people of Arabia flocked to pay homage at its shrine. In Muhammad's time, the Meccans still prayed to Abraham's God — the same God worshipped by the Jews and the Christians — only they called him Allah.

Little is known about Muhammad's childhood and youth, but in his twenties he was employed by a wealthy widow and merchant named Khadijah, to act as her agent on a caravan travelling north to Syria to buy Byzantine merchandise for sale in the Meccan markets. Twice married and fifteen years Muhammad's senior, Khadijah was so taken by her young salesman's acumen and charisma that she soon proposed marriage. Muhammad and Khadijah became husband and wife and she bore him four girls and two boys, though his sons died in infancy. Muhammad was devoted to Khadijah, describing her as the best woman of her time and saying 'he would live with her in paradise in a house built of reeds, in peace and tranquillity.'[2] They remained married for more than twenty years, during which time Muhammad took no other wives.

Muhammad was a sensitive man, and, although a businessman himself, he was pained by the unbridled greed of Mecca's new merchant class. The growth of commerce had eroded the social customs that had governed tribal life, such as the obligation to care for the poor and needy and orphans, such as he himself had been. The religious life of the settlement had also declined. Many Meccans had lapsed back into pagan worship, praying to a pantheon of idols including three female deities known as 'Allah's daughters'.[3] A religious man, who once helped to rebuild the sacred Kabaa with timber retrieved from a shipwreck after the shrine was destroyed by flood, Muhammad was aggrieved at the pagan rituals being practised in Abraham's temple.

Muhammad would often retire to a cave in the rocky hills to pray and meditate alone, away from the troubles of the settlement. It was during these solitary vigils at about the age of forty that he began to have vivid dreams and visions. A glorious being appeared before him, as later described in the Koran: 'He stood on the uppermost horizon; then, drawing near, he came down within two bows' lengths or even closer, and revealed to his servant that which he revealed,' (53:7).

The being who appeared to Muhammad was the Angel Gabriel, the same messenger who had first been sent to the prophet Abraham to bring him the word of God. The Angel now proclaimed to Muhammad: 'Recite!' And Muhammad replied: 'What shall I recite?' The Angel instructed him: 'Recite in the name of your Lord who created, created man from clots of blood. Recite! Your Lord is the Most Bountiful One, who by the pen taught man what he did not know,' (96:1–5). After the angel vanished, Muhammad said these words were 'inscribed upon his heart'.

And so began the revelations 'sent down' to the Prophet Muhammad over a period of twenty-two years. It is these revelations, collected and transcribed later, that comprise 'the recitation' or, in Arabic, the Koran — the holy book of Islam.

The central message of the revelations was encapsulated in the word that defines the faith — 'Islam' — meaning surrender or submission. The message was that the Meccans must abandon their false idols and submit to *the one and only* God, who had revealed his word to Abraham and was now calling on Muhammad to return his flock to the true path. Those who did so were called *muslimin* — or Muslims — meaning those who surrender or submit.

In surrendering to 'the God' — *Al-lah* in Arabic — the Meccans were instructed to abandon their worship of commerce, to spurn excessive wealth and pride, and to care for those in need, as Muhammad himself had been. 'Did He not find you an orphan and give you shelter? Did He not find you in error and guide you? Did He not find you poor and enrich you? Therefore do not wrong the orphan, nor chide away the beggar. But proclaim the goodness of your Lord,' (93:6–11).

Muhammad's God in these early days was lenient to those of other faiths, famously decreeing: 'Unbelievers, I do not worship what you worship, nor do you worship what I worship . . . You have your own religion, and I have mine,' (109:1). His revelations urged tolerance towards 'People of the Book', the Jews and Christians who had received the word of God earlier but who were judged to have strayed from the true path. 'If the People of the Book accept the true faith and keep from evil, We will pardon them their sins and admit them to the gardens of delight . . . There are some among them who are righteous men; but there are many among them who do nothing but evil,' (5:65). This emphasis on tolerance lessened with time and the revelations became sterner towards those who still refused to submit, warning: 'The unbelievers among the People of the Book and the pagans shall burn for ever in the fire of hell. They are the vilest of all creatures,' (98:5).

As the Prophet repeated the revelations to his family and friends, a growing circle of admirers was captivated by his message of charity, humility and social reform. But Muhammad was shunned by Mecca's elite, who resented the challenge to their mercenary ways. The Prophet was ostracised by his tribe, the Quraysh. Some said he was possessed by evil spirits, or that he was mad or motivated by personal ambition; others dumped their rubbish on his doorstep.

Muhammad's tribulations worsened when his beloved wife, Khadijah, and his powerful uncle both died. Bereft of his soul mate and his protector and spurned by his tribe, Muhammad decided to leave his home town of Mecca and take refuge in the town of Medina, 300 kilometres to the north, where a group of supporters had offered him a base.

Muhammad's journey from Mecca to Medina, known as the *hijra*, or migration, was a historic flight. He travelled north across the desert with a band of followers, on a journey that has been invoked ever since by Muslims fleeing persecution and oppression in order to practise their religion and spread it further afield. It was the *hijra* of the Prophet that inspired Abdullah Sungkar and Abu Bakar Bashir, centuries later, on their escape from Indonesia to Malaysia.

As Muhammad fled his enemies in Mecca for sanctuary in Medina, a crucial new revelation was 'sent down'. Previously, fighting to spread the faith had been forbidden by God. Now, Muhammad announced that God had revealed: 'Permission to take up arms is hereby given to those who are attacked, because they have been wronged,' (22:39). This was strengthened with another revelation: 'Fight for the sake of God those that fight against you, but do not attack them first. God does not love aggressors,' (2:191). And for those who refused to heed God's message: 'When the sacred months are over, slay the idolaters wherever you find them. Arrest them, besiege them, and lie in ambush everywhere for them,' (9:5).

Waging war in the name of Islam was now allowed, but there were conditions attached. For example people unable to offer resistance, like women, children, the old, blind or handicapped, could not be killed. But exactly how and when the use of violence was sanctioned has been debated vigorously by Muslims ever since.

Muhammad's arrival in Medina with dispensation to use force to defend Islam was the turning point for the Prophet and his new faith. A deal known as the Constitution of Medina was struck with Muhammad's local supporters, in which they agreed to form one *umma*, or community, and accept his rulings in disputes between their rival tribes and clans. Thus far, Muhammad had not been motivated by power, but as one historian has commented: 'When power came to him at Medina, he did not shrink from it, but regarded political leadership as having been thrust upon him by God.'[4]

Having founded his new Islamic *umma*, Muhammad set about laying down its rules. The revelations he delivered, such as those relating to women, reflected the social mores of the patriarchal society he lived in, as did Muhammad's own life; after the death of his beloved Khadijah, he went on to have ten more wives.

'Men have authority over women because God has made the one superior to the other, and because they spend their wealth to maintain them,' Muhammad revealed. 'Good women are obedient. They guard their unseen parts because God has guarded them. As for those from whom you fear disobedience, admonish them, forsake them in beds apart, and beat them. Then if they obey you, take no further action against them,' (4:34). Women were urged to 'draw their veils over their bosoms and not to display their finery,' (4:31), while men seeking the ear of the Prophet were advised 'if you ask his wives for anything, speak to them from behind a curtain,' (33:53).

In his new role as political and military leader, Muhammad set out to expand the territory under Islamic rule. He led raids on neighbouring settlements and on camel caravans sent out from Mecca. One by one the tribes of Arabia were defeated or surrendered, Muhammad's realm growing ever larger and enriched by the spoils. After eight years of warfare, Muhammad finally conquered his former home, Mecca, as well.

By the early seventh century, Muhammad's sway extended the length and breadth of the Arabian Peninsula. Then suddenly, in the year 632, aged not much over sixty, the Prophet grew ill and died. His closest followers quickly convened and chose his good friend, Abu Bakr, to succeed him as the first *caliph*, or deputy. Some of the opponents whom Muhammad had vanquished saw his death as heralding the decline of Islam, and the Prophet's successors had to resort to military force to reimpose Islamic rule on the tribes of Arabia. Thus, under Abu Bakr and the caliphs who succeeded him, Muhammad's empire would flourish and expand for centuries.

In the years after Muhammad's death, the caliphs embarked on the task of compiling his revelations into a book, commissioning a group of experts to do so. It was a huge undertaking, collecting and sorting the mass of edicts that Muhammad had delivered orally and his acolytes had memorised and recited over the decades. Some of them had been written down on stones, palm-leaves or bits of leather or bone; others committed purely to memory. Eventually the revelations were collated into the 114 *suras*, or chapters, that make up the Koran.

The Koran is a splendid book, regarded by Muslims as a masterpiece of classical Arabic prose. It is also an opaque and mysterious text, precise meanings of which are often hard to divine. It was originally transcribed in an arcane script, with no indication of vowels and in which many consonants look the same. Unlike the Christian Bible, the Koran has no central narrative to provide context and no beginning, middle or end. The suras were arranged, not in chronological order, but in descending order of length, from longest to shortest, one effect of which is to obscure the logical connection with Muhammad's life and thus deepen the mystery over exactly what they mean.

To fill in the gaps and further illuminate the revelations, Muhammad's followers set out to collect first-hand accounts of what the Prophet had said and done in his lifetime. These recollections of Muhammad's companions, wives and relatives were known as the *hadith*, or Prophetic reports. The task of collecting them was even more arduous than compiling the book itself; it went on for two centuries after Muhammad's death and ended with some 600,000 accounts of the Prophet's deeds and sayings collected by one scholar alone. A test was devised to separate the true stories from the false, and ultimately the vast majority failed the test; only some 3000 hadith were deemed to be sound, though arguments over their reliability persisted.[5]

The *hadith* that were sanctioned by the early Islamic scholars provided a comprehensive picture of the way in which Muhammad lived his life, known as the *sunna* — or customary behaviour — of the

Prophet. The *sunna* was afforded its own sacred status, just below that of the Koran itself. From a combination of Koran and *sunna*, Islamic scholars and jurists then extracted an entire belief system and set of rules to govern how Muslims should live, known as the Islamic 'way', or *sharia,* and often referred to as Islamic law.

The vigorous contention over the meanings and practice of Islam has continued ever since. But one sticking point has divided Islamic and Western scholars. The question is posed by the Professor of Middle Eastern Studies and Religion at New York University, Frank Peters, as this: 'Who composed the Koran, God or Muhammad?' The answer, he says, 'is precisely the difference between Muslims and non-Muslims'.[6] While the issue may exercise Western scholars, it is a question that doesn't arise for Islamic readers of the Koran. For Muslims there is no doubt — the Koran is not the work of Muhammad but the pure, unadulterated word of God.

∝✕∾

For centuries after the death of Muhammad, the civilisation he had founded — now known as the *caliphate* — was the greatest military and economic power on earth. It stretched for more than 7000 kilometres from Pakistan in the east, across Central Asia, the Middle East and northern Africa, to Spain and Portugal in the west. In the view of the caliphate's inhabitants, 'beyond its borders there were only barbarians and infidels'.[7]

The golden age of Islam lasted beyond the twelfth century. The caliphate imported slaves and gold from Africa and exported innovations like Arabic numerals to Europe.[8] It was at the forefront of science, medicine and the arts. Having conquered them, it tolerated other 'People of the Book', whom, the histories record, lived peaceably and prosperously alongside their Muslim neighbours:

'In the Islamic lands, not only Muslims but also Christians and Jews enjoyed the good life. They dressed in fine clothing, had fine houses in splendid cities serviced by paved streets, running water and sewers and dined on spiced delicacies served on Chinese porcelains. Seated on luxurious carpets, these sophisticated city dwellers debated such subjects as the nature of God, the intricacies of Greek philosophy or the latest

Indian mathematics. Muslims considered this Golden Age God's reward to mankind for spreading His faith and His speech over the world.[9]

The empire of Islam had no separate nation states, only one vast community of Muslims united by their faith, as the twentieth century Islamic philosopher Sayyid Qutb reminisced: 'In this great Islamic society Arabs, Persians, Syrians, Egyptians, Moroccans, Turks, Chinese, Indians, Romans, Greeks, Indonesians, Africans were gathered together — in short, peoples of all nations and races. Their various characteristics were united, and with mutual cooperation, harmony and unity they took part in the construction of the Islamic community and Islamic culture. This marvellous civilisation was not an "Arabic civilisation", even for a single day; it was purely an "Islamic civilisation". It was never a "nationality" but always a "community of belief".'[10]

The two linchpins that held the empire together were faith and military might. The early Islamic jurists divided the world into two sides. The caliphate was the 'Abode of Islam' — in Arabic *Dar ul-Islam* — while the rest of the world was the 'Abode of War', the heathen lands which had not yet submitted to the word of God. In theory the two were seen to exist in a permanent state of warfare, which could only be resolved when the infidels surrendered to Islamic rule.[11]

The concept of defending the faith by force if necessary was central to the Islamic world view. It was encapsulated in the Arabic word *jihad*, meaning striving or effort. It is a word which appears often in the Koran, most commonly in the phrase *jihad fisabilillah*, which means 'striving in the path of God'.

Jihad has many forms. It can be fulfilled 'by the heart, the tongue, the hand and the sword'.[12] There are essentially two interpretations of the word, depending on the context in which it appears. The first interpretation — and the one preferred by moderate Muslims — is that jihad refers to the personal struggle of all believers to overcome sin and temptation and to live virtuous lives. The second — the one favoured by many radicals — is that jihad means the duty to go into battle to defend and uphold Islam when the religion is under threat.

Both types of jihad are clearly sanctioned in the Koran. The early revelations sent down at Mecca focused more on moral striving, while the later ones at Medina tended towards the militaristic view: 'God has exalted the men who fight with their goods and their persons above those who stay at home. God has promised all a good reward; but far richer is the recompense of those who fight for Him,' (4:95–96).

Exactly how jihad should be interpreted has been the subject of centuries of debate. The argument has centred on which is the 'greater' and which is the 'lesser' form of jihad. The interpretation preferred by moderates was bolstered by a famous and often-quoted *hadith*, which recounts a comment made by Muhammad on his return one day from battle: 'We have all returned from *jihad asghar* [the lesser jihad] to *jihad akbar* [the greater jihad].' His companions asked: 'What is *jihad akbar*?' And Muhammad replied: 'Jihad against the desires.'[13] Throughout the history of Islam, this has been taken by many peace-loving Muslims to mean that the personal struggle against sin and temptation is the true meaning of jihad.

But this view was bitterly contested over time, by militant Islamic jurists who favoured the concept of jihad as war. After Muhammad's death, the source who related the story of the Prophet's comment was systematically attacked: 'He often adulterates, is very weak and narrates unknown hadith,' claimed one jurist; while another declared: 'He is a known liar and forger of hadith.'[14]

The notion of jihad as warfare was steadily strengthened, as the caliphs relied on military conquest to defend and expand the Islamic empire. 'Jihad is your duty under any ruler, be he godly or wicked,' declared one famous *hadith*. 'A day and a night of fighting on the frontier is better than a month of fasting and prayer. The nip of an ant hurts a martyr more than the thrust of a weapon, for these are more welcome to him than sweet, cold water on a hot summer day. He who dies without having taken part in a campaign dies in a kind of unbelief . . . Learn to shoot, for the space between the mark and the archer is one of the gardens of Paradise. Paradise is in the shadow of swords.'[15]

The conviction that armed force must be used to defend Islam was fortified by the series of bloody holy wars launched by the Christians of Europe against the Abode of Islam in the eleventh century. The attacks mounted to recapture the holy places of Jerusalem from the Muslims were referred to in Latin as the *peregrinatio in armis*, or armed pilgrimages, and later known as the Crusades.

'The Crusaders were spectacularly severe in capturing Jerusalem in 1100,' wrote the Australian scholar, Professor Amin Saikal. 'They not only brutalised and humiliated the Arab Muslim citizens of Jerusalem, but also made the Jewish inhabitants of the city suffer to the extent that many of them felt they had more to fear from the Christians than from their traditional Muslim rulers.'[16] The Muslims eventually retook

Jerusalem and repelled the holy warriors from Europe. But the series of battles created a powerfully symbolic enemy that would later loom large in the minds of modern jihadists — the Western Christian 'Crusader' intent on humiliating and subjugating the Muslim world.

By this time the once harmonious Islamic empire was beset by divisions within. The ancient clashes between warring tribes and clans still flared, alongside new conflicts between rival sultans who ruled in separate parts of the empire under the figurehead of the calilph. There was also a bitter divide between the mainstream *Sunni* Muslims, named after the *sunna* of the Prophet, and a splinter group known as *Shiites*, who were followers of Muhammad's cousin Ali and believed that only the Prophet's descendants should be appointed to rule over his empire.

By the thirteenth century, the caliphate was also under siege from the Mongols of Central Asia, who captured and sacked its then capital, Baghdad. It was at this time of crisis for the Abode of Islam that the elevation of armed struggle as the highest form of jihad reached its zenith. Its greatest exponent was the fourteenth-century jurist, Ibn Taymiyya, whose works remain a major inspiration for modern-day militant jihadists. 'Jihad against the disbelievers is the most noble of actions, and moreover it is the most important action for the sake of mankind,' Ibn Taymiyya decreed.[17]

The Mongol invasion created a new dilemma for the jurists. The Mongols had converted to the Islamic faith, raising the question: could invaders who were also Muslims could be fought? The issue was resolved by the renowned hawk, Ibn Taymiyya, with a fatwa, or legal ruling, declaring that the Mongols were not true believers because they still lived by their own pagan law, and therefore jihad could be waged against them. This historic fatwa has been invoked by militants ever since to justify declaring war on fellow Muslims who are deemed to have abandoned their faith — such as the House of Saud, according to Osama bin Laden, or the secular government of Indonesia, according to the followers of Abu Bakar Bashir.

The reign of the Ottomans from the fourteenth century brought new glory days for the caliphate, even though many Arabs, as the original recipients of Islam, resented being ruled by the convert Turks. One history chronicled the expansion: 'The Ottoman armies continued their conquest of Europe and reached the gates of Vienna in the 1530s. The sultans now ruled a massive empire, with superb bureaucratic efficiency, unrivalled by any other state at this time.'[18] The Ottoman empire would endure for 600 years, but as the centuries passed it was weakened by internal decay, imperial over-reach and its inability to keep up with Western innovation.[19] The various Christian armies of Europe began to inflict defeat after defeat on the Islamic realm, steadily pushing back its borders.

As the Abode of Islam grew more embattled, its energy devoted to the defence of its territory, a profound conservatism set in. 'From the end of the Middle Ages, there was a dramatic change,' wrote the British historian Bernard Lewis. 'In the Muslim world, independent inquiry virtually came to an end, and science was for the most part reduced to the veneration of a corpus of approved knowledge.'[20] Where once there had been spirited intellectual inquiry, now 'knowledge was something to be acquired, stored, if necessary bought, rather than grown or developed'.

This conservatism extended to the religion as well. Since the time of Muhammad, a lively debate over the meanings of the Koran and *hadith* had continued using a principle called *ijtihad*, meaning personal initiative or interpretive powers. But in a historic turning point for Islam designed to end disunity in the *umma*, it was declared that 'the gates of ijtihad' were closed — in the eyes of the conservative jurists the Islamic way was effectively set in stone.[21]

Just as extraordinary advances were being made in the West, Islamic civilisation stalled. The Muslim *ulama*, or learned experts, whose role was to preserve Muhammad's legacy, opposed the import of innovations from the heathen West. And so in the Islamic world, the Renaissance, the Reformation and the Industrial Revolution passed virtually unnoticed. European literature was spurned, none of the works of Shakespeare or Dante translated into Arabic or Turkish.[22] 'The failure of Muslims to catch up with many of these transformations,' in the words of Professor Amin Saikal, 'enveloped the domain of Islam in the cloth of conservatism.'[23]

Increasingly weak and stagnant, the lands of the Abode of Islam were picked off by the rising Western powers, until finally the Ottoman empire was defeated by the European Allies at the end of World War I. The long struggle between Islam and the West had — for now — ended for Muslims in a crushing defeat.

The Islamic caliphate was formally abolished six years later by the government of the new Turkish Republic on 3 March 1924 — a day of infamy in the annals of the Islamic faith. It was this historic setback that was later invoked by Osama bin Laden when he railed against the 'humiliation and disgrace' suffered by Islam for 'more than eighty years'.[24]

In the aftermath of the Great War, the provinces of the conquered Islamic empire were carved up by the Western victors, given new names and new borders, and turned into 'mandates' under British and French control. Iraq and Palestine (later divided to create Jordan) were handed to the British, while Syria (divided to create Lebanon) was given to the French. Thus vanquished, the lands of the Middle East — and the massive oil wealth contained within them — remained under European control for almost thirty years until the end of World War II, when the Arab states were granted independence.

But as one era of domination ended, another began, with the rise of the new world powers, the Soviet Union and the United States, and the advent of their Cold War. Eager for oil and strategic advantage, the US moved into the vacuum left behind by the European colonial powers in the Middle East. As Moscow and Washington competed for clients, the US found a firm ally in the House of Saud, which was happy to swap access to its huge oil reserves for American support against its domestic and regional opponents.

The US also cultivated the Shah of Iran, whose credentials as a democrat were as unimpressive as those of the Saudi sheiks. When Iran's popular new prime minister Dr Mohammad Mossadeq nationalised the oil industry to get control of it back from the British, the CIA and British intelligence engineered a campaign of destabilisation that eventually saw Mossadeq arrested for treason. This event is often cited by America's critics as a typical example of US intervention in the Middle East. The one-time national security adviser Zbigniew Brzezinski has acknowledged: 'American involvement in the Middle East is clearly the main impulse of the hatred that has been directed at America.'[25]

Anti-US resentment was fuelled further by America's support for the new state of Israel, established in 1948 as a homeland for the Jewish people after the genocide of World War II. In the eyes of aggrieved Muslims, the formation of a Jewish state right in the middle of the Abode of Islam was yet another humiliation. To this day the creation of Israel is referred to by Arab historians as *al nakba*, meaning the catastrophe. Muslim anger was exacerbated in the 1960s when Israel waged and won a series of wars against its Arab neighbours, seizing large slabs of Egypt, Syria and Jordan, including almost all of the territory earmarked for the Palestinians, who have been fighting ever since for their own state.

It was during this time of 'humiliation and disgrace', in the decades after the end of the caliphate, that the Islamic resurgence began to take hold, eventually sweeping all the way to Indonesia. The Muslim Brotherhood and organisations like it sprang up across the Islamic world, preaching their modernist mantra of social and economic reform and a return to the fundamentals of the Koran. Islam became increasingly an ideology of resistance against the West.

By the 1970s and 1980s, it seemed that finally the tide of history might be turning once again, in favour of the Abode of Islam. The Arab states, grown rich and powerful on oil, fought back against Israel. The Palestinians began to rebel. In Iran, the Ayatollah Khomeini and his Shiite revolutionaries swept to power. And in Afghanistan, the Soviets were defeated by the holy warriors of the mujahideen. It appeared that Islam's era of humiliation might be coming to an end.

Then, in 1990, came the arrival of the 'infidel' US army in Islam's holiest land, Saudi Arabia, to oust Iraqi troops from Kuwait. While there was little sympathy for the thuggish Saddam, there was also deep unease over inviting in the Americans to wage war on a fellow Arab state. Iraq was, after all, a Muslim country and Baghdad had been the seat of the Islamic empire for half a millenium. Islamic militants invoked the memory of the Christian Crusades, and even to many ordinary Muslims it seemed that history was being repeated. As one Saudi scholar put it: 'What is happening in the Gulf is part of a larger Western design to dominate the whole Arab and Muslim world.'[26]

The stationing of US forces in Saudi Arabia was reluctantly sanctioned by the country's *ulama*, under pressure from King Fahd. They agreed on the condition, promised by the US Defense Secretary Dick Cheney, that the Americans would not be there 'a minute longer than they were needed'.[27] The secular dictator Saddam was quick to employ the language of jihad to garner support for his cause, declaring 'Bush's brute and infidel force, even if it is redoubled to several times what it is now, will not weaken the determination of the men of faith and jihad in great Iraq . . . When the deaths and dead mount on them, the infidels will leave.'[28]

From its base in Saudi Arabia, the US-led coalition waged war on Iraq for forty-three days, until President Bush announced on 28 February 1991: 'Kuwait is liberated. Iraq's army is defeated. Our military objectives are met.'[29] Saddam's troops were evicted from Kuwait and, soon after, the bulk of the US forces went home. But a rump of US troops was left deployed on the Arabian Peninsula and has remained there ever since.

For Osama bin Laden, this was an intolerable affront, especially as his own offer to rally his al Qaeda mujahideen to fight Saddam's forces had been rejected by the House of Saud. Bin Laden wrote in a letter to King Fahd: 'Oh King, it is unconscionable to let the country become an American colony with American soldiers with their filthy feet roaming everywhere. Those filthy infidel Crusaders must not be allowed to remain in our Holy land.'[30]

Bin Laden's fury was echoed by his devotees around the world. Among them were the followers of Abu Bakar Bashir, who were by now fanning out across Southeast Asia ready for jihad; men like Muklas, then in southern Malaysia setting up his new Islamic school for JI.

Many years later, Muklas would be asked by the Indonesian police: 'When was the first time you began to discuss a jihad to retaliate against the interests of the United States and its allies?' He responded, 'Since the Gulf War, when the United States attacked Iraq and placed hundreds of thousands of its soldiers in the Arab peninsula.' It was this, Muklas claimed, that persuaded him that 'Muslims must take part in the jihad against the US and the Jews . . . just as the mujahideen fought the Russians in Afghanistan.'[31]

⚜

CHAPTER EIGHT

THE FIELD COMMANDER

A PROMISING FUTURE BECKONED for a bright-eyed nineteen-year-old named Abdul Aziz, who had graduated top of his class in 1990 from high school in Serang, West Java. A gifted student and bookworm, Abdul Aziz was a whizz with computers and electronics, a skill he had learned from his father. He also had a flair for Arabic and had been offered a government scholarship to study Arabic language and literature in the provincial capital, Bandung.

But Abdul Aziz had other plans which involved abandoning both his studies and his given name. 'I use an alias to keep myself safe while I do my work in this world,' he explained later. 'What I mean is the work that I do when I carry out jihad.'[1] Abdul Aziz would become famous by his alias, Samudra, as the field commander of the Bali bombings.

The eighth of eleven children, Samudra was born in 1971 in the village of Lopang in the market town of Serang, on the far northwestern tip of Java. He grew up in a working-class family in a shabby part of town, where his mother worked as a seamstress making clothing while his father repaired electronic equipment. An older brother drove trucks carting wood from the nearby forests to the timber mills of Jakarta.

Samudra's grandfather had been a well-to-do tobacco merchant whose shop was 'the best in town'. But he had gone bankrupt, leaving the family with no money to spare. 'There were no happy times,' recalled Samudra's older sister Aliyah. 'We were always poor. Misery came after misery. We always lived in misery. We always had hard times — but I consider this a test of Allah.'[2]

Young Samudra was a skinny kid, fretful and intense according to his sister. 'He studies a lot, is very calm and prays every day. But when he was a child, he easily got upset and cried a lot.' His siblings called him *cengeng*, meaning crybaby. 'I always had to carry him when he was a baby. He would cry very easily at the smallest thing.'[3]

Samudra was a loner as a child. While growing up he would often spend his days at the nearby port town of Merak, the main terminus for the ferries and cargo ships that shuttle between Indonesia's main island of Java and the island of Sumatra to its west. Samudra would while away hours at the harbour on his own. 'I liked to hang out by the sea, just hang out . . . I liked to watch construction workers and watch the ships.'[4]

Despite his petulance, Samudra was smart, so smart that his parents fudged his age to enrol him early in school. 'Those times in elementary school were fun for me,' he said later. 'I think it wasn't just coincidence but also Allah's will that I was often top of the class, number one in my class.' Samudra was a member of the school poetry team and took part in competitions with other schools. At this, like most things, he excelled, according to his own later boasts. 'I was top of the class, top in poetry, top in general knowledge, also top in chess. All the way through sixth grade. In grade five I took part in a contest for exemplary students and, thanks to Allah, I won.'

Samudra's parents were followers of the Indonesian organisation, Persatuan Islam (Islamic Union), or PERSIS, which adhered to the Saudi Wahhabi school of Islam.[5] Each day after regular classes, Samudra was sent off to a local pesantren for religious instruction. But he found reciting Koranic verses no match for regular school. 'I was not so motivated with the Islamic schooling system. I often skipped class . . . Once it got to about two o'clock in the afternoon I would feel sleepy. It was also boring. Elementary school was different — it was lots of fun.'

When the time came for high school, Samudra ranked fourth out of 240 students who took the entrance exam. He joined the Muslim Boy Scouts and the student association, but more than anything Samudra loved to read. 'My love for reading was at its peak in eighth grade. I was always in the school library. I gradually lost the friends I had hung out with.' As he grew older and more headstrong, he increasingly preferred

learning by himself to being part of a class. 'I've never really liked —
never really enjoyed — anything that's formal in nature. Whenever the
teachers taught I would listen, I heard what they said, I did hear — I
even respected them. But the truth is I didn't really like it. Because for
me, personally, I prefer reading. I prefer to be reading on my own than
to listen to others talk.'

After attending an 'express religious course' run by local Islamic
groups when he was in ninth grade, Samudra's boredom with his
religion came to an end. He spent hours in the library devouring
everything he could find on Islam, from the treatises of the Muslim
Brotherhood to the writings of the executed Darul Islam leader
Kartosuwiryo, whose short-lived Islamic State of Indonesia had
flourished in Samudra's home province. He even read the works of the
radical African-American Muslim leader Malcolm X. 'I enjoyed reading
Malcolm X's thoughts. I liked to read about the history of the black
Muslims. I've read them all.'

Samudra took all of his reading to heart. 'In ninth grade I started to
experience more conflict,' he reported. 'The tendency to practise what I
had read in books grew stronger and stronger . . . At that time I had
already started to preach, to teach religion in classes. But most of my
peers didn't connect, they had no idea what I was talking about . . . 99
per cent of them couldn't relate.'

When he was sent, at seventeen, to the local state Islamic High
School, Samudra finally found someone with whom could 'relate'. It
was a teacher named Kyai Saleh As'ad, a former Darul Islam rebel and
commander, who had fought under the legendary Kartosuwiryo before
his capture and execution.[6] Two decades after his death, the tales of
Kartosuwiryo's bravado were the stuff of local legend in the schoolyards
of West Java. And despite Suharto's ongoing crackdown, the Darul Islam
movement was spreading underground. Under the wing of his new
teacher, Samudra became a zealous initiate of the Darul Islam cause.

By his later years in high school, the teenage bookworm had grown
into an opinionated and domineering young man, with a snappy
tongue, a fiery temper and an unswerving belief in the rightness of his
views. Samudra commanded a following even at school. He became
vice president of the student union and was chosen to lead a provincial
association of religious schools.[7] He held a religious study group known
as a *halaqah*, or circle, where young believers would sit in a circle and
talk longingly of jihad. 'I kept on praying that I could put into practice

what I had read in those books . . . I would often cry and pray to Allah asking that one day I could be delivered to Afghanistan. That's what I wanted.'

After graduating with top honours from his Islamic high school in 1990, Samudra applied for scholarships to the State Islamic Institute and the Saudi-funded Institute for the Study of Islam and the Arabic Language. He was accepted into both but said later, 'I didn't want to continue to study locally, I wanted to go abroad.' He had been fired up by the books he had read on the Afghan resistance, in particular one book called *The Pleasure of Being a Syahid*, or Islamic martyr.

Samudra began attending religious study sessions at a mosque run by the Islamic Propagation Council, an organisation known for its hostility toward Christians and its strong Wahhabi line.[8] There he met a fellow traveller named Jabir, who became a crucial new contact. 'When I met Jabir I felt that Allah had answered my prayers by bringing me together with someone who shared the same views as me.'[9] Samudra's new friend would be his entrée to the network run by Abdullah Sungkar and Abu Bakar Bashir and the global jihad that he was so desperate to join.

Jabir was a former student of Sungkar and Bashir's Ngruki school in Solo. His father had been a Darul Islam fighter and his brother had been jailed for involvement in the old Komando Jihad.[10] Ten years Samudra's senior and also from the Darul Islam heartland of West Java, Jabir had been in the Indonesian 'class of 1987' sent to Afghanistan. He had trained and fought alongside Hambali, who was by now a firm friend. Jabir had returned to Indonesia obsessed with what he saw as the dangers of 'Christianisation' and was now a recruiter for the cause.

'Jabir asked me about my intentions. I told him that I was absolutely ready for jihad,' Samudra recalled. He didn't have to wait long. 'I remember him saying "Come on, you want to go to Afghanistan, don't you? There is a departure this year. Do you want to join?" It was just like that.'[11]

The system for sending new recruits to Afghanistan for indoctrination and training was by this time well in place. Everything was arranged by the network. 'To obtain a passport all I had to do was give them my photograph. Everything else was prepared by Jabir. The passport I got at the time, if I am not mistaken, was issued by the North Jakarta Immigration Office, but I don't even remember the address because someone took care of it for me.'[12]

All Samudra had to do was cover his own fare across the Malacca Strait, which meant lying to his family to get the cash. 'Jabir asked me to look for my own money for travel expenses from Jakarta to Malaysia. So I asked my mother for some travel money, using college as an excuse, because Jabir had told me never to reveal to anyone my plans to go on jihad.'

Before leaving, Samudra swore the *bai'at* to Jabir whom he called *ustad*. Samudra's account, like others, suggests the wording of the *bai'at* varied depending on who was doing the swearing in. 'Ustad Jabir and I were leaving for Afghanistan. The *bai'at* was as follows: that I will obey the command of Allah and his Prophet to the best of my ability, heed and obey my leaders as long as they do not deviate from the command of Allah and the Prophet, always place Jihad in the path of Allah before my personal interests, those of my family or any other group, and reprimand my leader when he errs.'

Samudra and Jabir set off first for Malaysia, island-hopping from Java to Sumatra and then travelling by ferry and bus to Malacca on Malaysia's west coast. Their initial destination was a kind of orientation camp in the forest. 'Once I got to Malacca we continued by taxi towards some woods about fifteen minutes' walking distance from the main road. I don't remember the name of the place, but at that place there was a mosque made of wood and also a library. I saw about 15 men in the mosque . . . The activities there mainly consisted of memorising the Koran and physical training.'

After a few days in the camp, Samudra and Jabir took a bus to Kuala Lumpur and then a plane to Pakistan. They were met by an intermediary named Sofyan and taken to a house in Karachi for a final indoctrination session and a grilling for Samudra. 'I was questioned repeatedly about my plans to take part in jihad — was I doing this for Allah or to gain popularity?'

Samudra evidently passed the test because after a short stay in Karachi, they began the final leg of their journey, a bus trip to the Pakistan–Afghanistan border, escorted by the intermediary. 'It took about seven hours. When we got to the border, I was asked to cross to Afghanistan through a back road and Sofyan arranged [for] someone who had lived in Pakistan for a while to show us the way . . . And so we travelled on foot to Khost.'

The mountain fortress of Khost in eastern Afghanistan, with its underground labyrinth of arms depots, bunkers and command posts, was a major stronghold of the Afghan mujahideen. The Khost area was now the main training ground for Muslim militants from all over the world — an estimated two to three thousand of them at the time Samudra was there.[13]

It was also where Abdullah Sungkar's old friend, the Pashtun warlord Abdul Rasul Sayyaf, was now training his own fighters and the recruits sent by Sungkar and Bashir. He had moved his camp across the border from Pakistan following the Soviet withdrawal in 1989. His new camp was not far from where Osama bin Laden had commanded Muklas and his fellow fighters in the legendary Battle of Lion's Den.

For the next two years the Sayyaf camp would be home and school for Samudra, the place where he finally got to practise what he had been reading about for all those years. 'I did target practice with Kalashnikovs, M16s, handgun shooting, anti-tank grenade practice, grenade throwing and making bombs.'

He also got to mingle with leaders and proponents of the groups whose teachings he had devoured. 'In Afghanistan I met and was exposed to Islamic movements from all sorts of countries. I wasn't stuck with what you could call the parochial nature of the local Islamic movement, thanks to Allah. I met with the Muslim Brotherhood, the Egyptian Islamic Group, the Egyptian Jihad Group, and so on. They were all in Afghanistan.'

By this time in the long-running Afghan conflict, there wasn't much fighting to be had for new arrivals like Samudra. 'I was in the camp for about seven months before they sent me to the front,' he reported. It was a year since the Soviet army had beat its retreat. By now the mujahideen were on the verge of another victory, against the puppet regime of President Najibullah, installed by the Soviets. The Afghans didn't need any more foreign volunteers; newcomers like Samudra were there simply to train.

The dispatching of new recruits from the Darul Islam group for training in Afghanistan had escalated steadily since the pioneers like Muklas and Hambali had gone in the mid-1980s. By 1991 Bashir and Sungkar were sending dozens of new trainees off each year. Among the rookies in Camp Saddah when Samudra arrived were Muklas's brother Ali Imron and his travelling companion, Fathur Rahman al Ghozi. Also there was the bespectacled Kuala Lumpur businessman, Faiz bin Abu Bakar Bafana, who would become the treasurer of JI.[14]

The 'class of '91' in Afghanistan also included a contingent from Sungkar and Bashir's flock in Singapore.[15] The tightly run nanny state of

Southeast Asia had produced a band of educated, professional, middle-class extremists who would prove a valuable asset to JI. The Singaporean trainees included Bafana's younger brother, Fathi, and the former army man, Abas, whose daughter Farida had married Muklas. Also in the group was one of Farida's brothers, Hashim, a core member in Singapore. Their departure for Afghanistan was a big occasion for the fledgling Singapore branch; they were farewelled personally by Sungkar and Bashir, who travelled to Kuala Lumpur airport to see them off.[16]

Some of these Afghan alumni from the 'class of '91' would reunite more than a decade later in Bali. Samudra and Ali Imron were among them. Another was a pale, serious young man from Central Java named Djoko Pitono, but better known by his alias, Dulmatin. A prize-winning maths student, he had reportedly quit school after arguing with a teacher who insisted he stay in class when he wanted to attend Friday prayers.[17] In Afghanistan, Dulmatin found another subject at which he excelled — making bombs. After topping his explosives class he became an instructor, passing his skills on to the other Indonesians in Camp Saddah.

Another classmate was a friend of Ali Imron's called Mubarok, who lived next door in Tenggulun and had also been to the Ngruki school. Yet another in the class was a young man from the island of Flores, east of Bali, called Abdul Ghoni. It was in Afghanistan that this group learned to make bombs from potassium chlorate, sulphur and aluminium powder, a recipe they would later use to devastating effect.

Ali Imron's travel companion, Fathur Rahman al Ghozi, was among the most adept of them all when it came to explosives. Like Dulmatin, al Ghozi became a trainer himself, first in Afghanistan and then in Mindanao in the Philippines. He would later help engineer and execute JI's first campaign of bombings. (He would also severely embarrass the Philippine Government by escaping with ease from his prison cell in July 2003 on the same day that Australian Prime Minister John Howard was in Manila to sign an anti-terrorism pact.)

In between explosives and weapons classes, Samudra and his classmates pored over the works of the Islamist philosophers whose writings provided the intellectual fuel for the jihad. Among the ideologues whose teachings were drilled into the trainees at Camp Saddah were Osama bin Laden's mentor and co-founder of al Qaeda, Abdullah Azzam. 'You are like a detonator that will set off the explosives in your country,' Azzam had preached before his death in 1989. 'Jihad guarantees the spread of this religion ... Without jihad, without the sword it would be impossible for this religion to get its position in the world. It would be impossible to block the power of the infidels except by war.'[18]

They were also indoctrinated in the writings of the fourteenth-century militant, Ibn Taymiyya, the jurist who had elevated the so-called 'lesser jihad' of armed combat to the highest form of struggle for Islam. 'Jihad implies all kinds of worship, both in its inner and outer forms,' Taymiyya wrote. 'More than any other act it implies love and devotion for Allah ... And the individual or community who participates in it finds itself between two blissful outcomes: either victory and triumph or martyrdom and Paradise.' On the subject of dying for Islam, Taymiyya had ruled: 'The death of a martyr is easier than any other form of death. In fact, it is the best of all manners of dying.'[19]

Samudra would later cite the works of Ibn Taymiyya as a profound influence on his 'perceptions of Islam'. He was particularly enthralled by the spectre of dying for the cause, although it was not his own death that he would finally arrange.

While Samudra and his cohorts were in Afghanistan, serious cracks were emerging in the ranks of the old Darul Islam leadership, which was now scattered across Indonesia and Malaysia. These divisions would later lead Sungkar and Bashir to finally split from the Darul Islam movement and form their own separate group.

The exiles in Malaysia had fallen out with another Darul Islam veteran named Masduki, who had stayed on in Indonesia when the men from Ngruki had fled. Sungkar and Bashir accused Masduki of being weak and influenced by the renegade Shiite and Sufi streams of Islam, which they saw as heresy.

The tension erupted in 1992 when Sungkar moved to challenge Masduki's pre-eminence in the Darul Islam movement, according to the JI specialist Sidney Jones, whose account is based on interviews with JI veterans who were there at the time. 'The rift spilled over into Afghanistan, when Sungkar flew to the Sayyaf camp to ask those there to choose between him and Masduki. Everyone chose him, save for one who abstained — Imam Samudra.'[20]

The lone wolf Samudra had no particular allegiance to Sungkar and Bashir. Samudra had been recruited through the old Darul Islam network in Indonesia and had not sworn the *bai'at* to the exiles in Malaysia. At the age of twenty, the self-taught Samudra had his own very firm views; among other things he believed Abdullah Sungkar was too soft. 'His views and mine are not the same,' he said later. 'He is always talking about *dakwah* [proselytisation], the goodness of the followers of Islam and the socialization of Islam, and never about anything that is direct or frontal in nature.' Samudra's belief, as he put it, was that 'jihad has to be executed first'.

While the tensions within the Darul Islam leadership continued to fester, Samudra was sent home from Afghanistan early as punishment for abstaining from the vote for Sungkar, according to his fellow trainees interviewed by Sidney Jones. Samudra apparently shrugged off the rebuke, returning to his village in Serang, West Java, still intent on a life of jihad. 'He had seen his Muslim brothers slaughtered and he wanted revenge,' his sister later claimed.[21] If Samudra had seen any slaughtering, it was probably Afghan Muslims killing each other in the deepening civil war between the rival mujahideen. But, inspired by his two years of training, Samudra was determined to find a struggle to carry on.

In the meantime he found himself a wife. The girl he chose, Zakia, was an old childhood sweetheart and fellow poet from primary school. 'She was the chair of the student body and I was her deputy,' Samudra recounted fondly. 'She was the girl champion for poetry and I was the boy champion.'[22] The daughter of civil servants who worked for the Department of Labour, Zakia had gone on to study medicine at university, but took leave in her final semester to become Samudra's wife.

Samudra and his bride left Serang and headed for Malaysia to join the community of Indonesians in exile. The newlyweds shifted to the village of Sungai Manggis, the secluded kampung in the banana grove south of Kuala Lumpur, where Hambali had lived on and off for years. Hambali was now back from Afghanistan as well, living in his shack under the mangosteen trees, working as an itinerant preacher and hawking his various wares.

'Hambali was my neighbour in Sungai Manggis,' said Samudra. 'He went around on his big motorbike selling medicine and textiles at the places where construction workers stayed.' Samudra and his wife moved into a house nearby where Zakia soon fell pregnant with the first of their four children. 'Abu Bakar Bashir was [also] my neighbour . . . He frequently gave sermons at a small mosque near my house.'

Despite their wanted status in Indonesia, the presence of Bashir and his cohorts was tolerated in Malaysia, even as they became steadily more open and well known. Bashir had obtained a government permit enabling him to work as a freelance preacher. He even sermonised once a month at the Grand Mosque in Kuala Lumpur and, according to the respected Indonesian news magazine *Tempo*, was invited to preach before the Malaysian Special Forces.[23]

Hambali travelled around on his motorbike bike from Sungai Manggis to towns and villages around Kuala Lumpur spreading their militant message in religious study groups. 'At these discussions . . . the members were instilled with the spirit of jihad and *mati syahid* [martyr's death] to fight infidels and to set up an Islamic state by force,' according to one report.[24]

Bashir and Hambali both travelled regularly from Sungai Manggis south to Johor, to lecture at the pesantren on the palm-oil plantation being run by Muklas. Abdullah Sungkar was living nearby, supervising the running of the school. Samudra began commuting there too, first as a student and later as a teacher. It was there that Samudra first met Muklas and his brother Amrozi, who now had a job fixing motorbikes in Ulu Tiram and also helped out at the school.

Already a generational shift was taking place within Sungkar and Bashir's network. The young militants from Afghanistan — like Samudra, Hambali and Muklas — were rising fast up the ranks, bringing with them their cataclysmic version of jihad, which would become JI's main article of faith.

For the exiled preachers, the main aim was still achieving an Islamic state in Indonesia; but the young Afghan veterans had embraced a more revolutionary goal: the restoration of an international caliphate, uniting all Muslim lands into one mighty Islamic state. And they believed that armed struggle was the only way to achieve it. As Samudra put it: 'Jihad has to be executed first.'

❦

CHAPTER NINE

THE JEMAAH

FIFTEEN KILOMETRES AS THE crow flies north of Sydney, six lanes of highway wend their way through a string of flat seaside suburbs en route to the millionaires' beachfront havens further out of town. Flanked by used-car yards and surf shops, video barns and homeware mega-stores, it's a strip of Aussie suburbia by the sea. Past the KFC and Barbeques Galore, the signs in the real estate agents' windows announce your arrival in 'Dee Why the delightful' — a suburb boasting sparkling green surf, a laidback lifestyle and '$5 schnitzels on Thursdays' at the pub.

A world away from the jungles of Malaysia and the battlefields of Afghanistan, this stereotypical slice of Australia became, in the 1970s and '80s, home to a sizeable community of Indonesians in exile. Some of them were fleeing repression under Suharto, others were simply after a better life. Many were illegal immigrants, arriving on short-term visas then melting into the community.

Today the Indonesians are inconspicuous among the Asian and Pacific faces that crowd the shops and eateries on Dee Why's main drag. 'People here don't care about different beliefs or cultures,' one Indonesian told me. 'That's why we like it.' After the poverty and persecution of Suharto's Indonesia, Dee Why was a sanctuary by the sea, with its easy lifestyle, cheap accommodation and plenty of factory jobs in the industrial estates off the highway. It also became a haven for the émigrés who eventually formed the Australian branch of JI.

Zainal Arifin was one of the Indonesians grateful for the refuge offered by Australia in the 1980s. A short, chubby man with a wispy beard, Arifin arrived in 1988 with a suitcase and a tourist visa, applied for refugee status and was joined by his wife and two children three months later.

In Jakarta, Arifin had been a religious teacher and member of a radical Islamic youth group, Remaja Islam, which was an opponent of the Suharto Government and its compulsory state ideology, Pancasila. Arifin's group had taken part in the rally at Tanjung Priok in Jakarta in 1984, when government troops shot dead dozens of protestors and arrested scores more, including some of Arifin's friends and colleagues. 'Anyone who criticised [Suharto], he just shot or put in jail,' Arifin recounted to me when I met him in 2003.

After escaping to Sydney, Arifin moved in with a friend in North Manly just south of Dee Why and got a job making air-conditioners in a local factory. Welcomed into Dee Why's 'little Indonesia', Arifin became the community's imam, presiding over Friday prayers in their makeshift mosque. 'It was an interesting time, I was always busy with lectures, I was very happy,' Arifin says today.

By the early 1990s, the Indonesian community on Sydney's northern beaches numbered around 500. On Fridays they would pitch in and hire 'the Tongan church' in Dee Why, an English-style clinker-brick chapel used by the local Tongan community. Under its mock stained-glass windows they would congregate for the weekly communal prayers led by Arifin. On special occasions they booked out the nearby North Curl Curl community centre to celebrate events like the Muslim festival Eid, to mark the end of the fasting month of Ramadan.

With the nearest mosque more than an hour's drive away at Lakemba in the southwestern suburbs, the Indonesians were eager to build a mosque of their own. Arifin and his friend Mohammed Baluel, who had also arrived from Jakarta in 1988, began raising money to buy a block of land. They put a collection box at the door of the Tongan church at Friday prayers and everyone gave $10 a week. To raise extra money, Mohammed Baluel did a weekly meat run to a halal butcher shop in the southwest, charging $5 per family for delivery, which also went towards the mosque.

It took about two years to raise enough money to buy the land, a block with a disused Uniting church riddled with asbestos. It was so old, the Indonesians simply tied a rope around the roof and pulled it down. Later, after the mosque was built, the proud new owners would hold an open day and a sausage sizzle to welcome their non-Muslim neighbours. 'We wanted to be Aussie-style in Dee Why,' said Mohammed Baluel.[1]

One day in January 1991, Zainal Arifin was at work at the factory when he got a phone call from an old friend. It was an acquaintance from his days in Jakarta — an Indonesian by the name of Abdul Rahim Ayub. Arifin hadn't seen Abdul Rahim for years, not since their days back in Indonesia when Abdul Rahim and his twin brother had been students in Arifin's religious study group. Abdul Rahim had migrated to Australia as well and was now living in Melbourne.

'When Abdul Rahim rang, he said, "I just come from Malaysia, I've got two guests, they came from Malaysia, they want to meet you,"' said Arifin. The news about the two important guests from Malaysia was quickly passed around. Another migrant recalled being phoned and told that 'a big *ustad*' was here and wished to meet the leaders of the local community. The talk was that the two VIPs were renowned Muslim activists who had been jailed and forced into exile for standing up to Suharto.

That night Arifin and a select group of invitees converged on a block of flats in Flora Street, Lakemba, just around the corner from the Haldon Street shops in Sydney's Muslim heartland. It was a week night and the men from Dee Why had hurried home from work, bolted down dinner, then driven for an hour to get there. It was 9 p.m. by the time they traipsed upstairs to the modest two-bedroom apartment where the two honoured visitors were waiting to receive them.

The small living room was redolent with sweet-smelling smoke from the clove-scented cigarettes being chain-smoked by the older of the two guests. The smoker was a large man with pale skin and a long beard, wearing a white skullcap. 'He looked like a sheik,' said one of the men who was there.[2] Clearly the more senior, the 'big *ustad*' was introduced as Abdul Halim.

His companion was a thinner man, bearded, bucked-toothed and wearing large spectacles, also in his early fifties and similarly attired. He was softer spoken and deferential, evidently the *ustad*'s trusted confidant and aide. He was introduced as Abdus Samad. These were the aliases adopted by Abdullah Sungkar and Abu Bakar Bashir after fleeing Indonesia for exile in Malaysia six years before.

The meeting went late into the night — 'talking, talking, a long time, till midnight,' said Zainal Arifin. For Arifin, it was a reunion of sorts. He had met Sungkar and Bashir briefly in Jakarta in about 1983, when the two preachers had visited the small mosque where he held religious classes. It was not long after their release from jail, after their imprisonment for subversion. They had returned to the Ngruki school in Solo, where Bashir was promoting the formation of his *usroh* groups to implement Islamic law. The pair had also started up their own Islamic study group in Jakarta and they wanted Arifin and his followers, who numbered around forty, to join their group. Arifin declined, wary of trouble with the Suharto Government and preferring to remain a free agent. Arifin and the men from Ngruki had gone their separate ways, Sungkar and Bashir escaping to Malaysia, Arifin migrating to Australia. He hadn't seen them since.

Eight years later, on the night they were reintroduced in Sydney, Arifin at first didn't recognise Abdullah Sungkar, who was suffering from diabetes and had aged beyond his fifty-three years. It didn't stop him puffing away throughout the evening on his clove cigarettes, as he and Bashir quizzed Arifin and the others on life in Australia. They were keen to know how the Indonesians were treated and how easy it was to get refugee status. Then they came to the reason for their visit. 'They wanted us to support them,' recalled another man who was present. 'They wanted to have a group overseas to help promote their opposition to the Indonesian Government.'[3]

As he had been back in Indonesia, Zainal Arifin was wary about throwing his lot in with Sungkar and Bashir. 'I said I didn't want to join a group with strict rules,' Arifin told me. 'Abdullah Sungkar said, "No, don't worry, we [will do it] together. When we got problem, we solve it."' Reassured by Sungkar that decisions would be made on a consensual basis, this time Arifin agreed to join their following, as did the other men in the smoke-filled flat in Lakemba. It seemed safe enough; after all, they were in Australia now and weren't likely to be thrown in prison for supporting an Islamic state; and anyone who was fighting the dictator Suharto deserved support. 'After that,' said Arifin, 'we agreed to join together to teach and preach in Australia.'

The arrangement was formalised when Sungkar and Bashir returned to Sydney some six months later. A second meeting was called with much the same group of men at a house in Campbelltown, on the city's southwestern outskirts. Sungkar and Bashir were keen to cement the relationship. 'They said that to fight Indonesia we had to have a group,' said one of those who attended this meeting. 'We had to form a group, so we formed the Darul Islam group in exile.'

This time it was clear that this was to be no casual alliance. Sungkar and Bashir demanded a 100 per cent commitment from those who agreed to join them. Arifin and his companions were asked to take the *bai'at* to the men from Ngruki. In a small ceremony each man grasped the hand of Abdullah Sungkar and swore to follow the Koran and sunna of the Prophet and do their utmost to uphold Islam. But they knew it meant more than that. 'The doctrine of Sungkar was you have to take *bai'at* because then people are more loyal to the group and the struggle,' said one man. At least one one of those invited to take the *bai'at* declined, because, as he told me later: 'Whatever the leader said, that's it. You have to be loyal.'

And so began the Australian branch of what would later become JI. At this stage, Sungkar and Bashir were still using the banner of Darul Islam, or sometimes Negara Islam Indonesia (NII), harking back to Kartosuwiryo's old Islamic State of Indonesia. The tensions between the Ngruki pair and others in the Darul Islam movement, which had emerged in Afghanistan were still brewing, but had not yet led to a final split.

As with the other branches of Sungkar and Bashir's network, their followers in Australia referred to themselves as simply the *jemaah* (community). They would eventually number around 130 in Sydney, Melbourne and Perth, with about thirty of them thought to have sworn the oath of loyalty.[4] Their role in these early days was to provide financial and moral support for the struggle against Suharto. The two leaders would visit Australia every six to twelve months. Zainal Arifin and his community would pay for their visits, raise money for their activities and recruit new supporters. They would also submit to their complete authority. As Arifin put it: 'Abdullah Sungkar and Abu Bakar Bashir is our leader. We make agreement in Sydney so everything that goes on in Australia, must get permission from this emir.'

The role of heading the Australian group and reporting back to the emir in Malaysia was assigned to Abdul Rahim Ayub, the former student of Zainal Arifin in Jakarta, who had brought Sungkar and Bashir to Sydney and called the first meeting at Lakemba. Abdul Rahim was to play a crucial role, later becoming leader of the Australian branch of JI, known as Mantiqi 4.

Abdul Rahim is a diminutive man with tousled hair, a scrap of a beard, a mischievous smile and dimpled cheeks. He is described by those who know him with a mixture of fondness and respect. 'He's a good guy, likeable but tough,' said one former follower. 'He's a bully, he likes bullying people. He's very commanding, a born leader.'[5]

Abdul Rahim was born in Jakarta in October 1963, the second of twin boys. Their parents chose their names from the opening line of the Koran: 'In the name of God, the most Beneficent, the most Merciful.' The first-born twin was called Abdul Rahman, meaning 'slave of the most Beneficent'; the second, Abdul Rahim, 'slave of the most Merciful'. The twins lived with their mother and siblings in a small house in central Jakarta. Their father, a soldier in the Indonesian army, died when the boys were still small and the family later moved to their mother's home village of Depok near the city of Bogor, south of the capital.

Like many of their generation, at high school the twins were caught up in the rising student resistance to Suharto. Student groups were at the forefront of dissent against Suharto's new law forcing every organisation in the country to adopt the state credo, Pancasila, as its 'sole ideological basis'. The twins joined the religious study group held by Zainal Arifin, one of many such groups opposed to the new law. They attended every day after high school. As Arifin explained: 'A lot of young people were turning to Islam at the time, [because] Suharto very bad for Muslims.'

Recently released from prison, Abdullah Sungkar and Abu Bakar Bashir were gaining a name in Jakarta for their fearless opposition to Suharto. Bashir's *usrob* groups were spreading through towns and villages across Java, their members instructed to follow only Islamic law and refuse to salute the Indonesian flag. Sungkar's new study group in Jakarta was exciting the interest of student radicals and activists in the capital, like the brothers Ayub.

The teenaged twins became dedicated followers of the two preachers from Ngruki. According to their own evidence later to the Refugee Review Tribunal in Australia, they were 'closely involved with the leaders of NII since 1985' and 'swore an oath to pursue the cause of an Islamic state and overturn the five principles of Pancasila.'[6]

The younger twin, Abdul Rahim, was the less fanatical of the two. After finishing high school, he enrolled at the Jayabaya University in Jakarta to study economics while continuing to attend Abdullah Sungkar's religious study group in the capital. Abdul Rahim had taken a shine to another of Sungkar's followers who was highly conspicuous in their class — a vivacious young Australian woman from Mudgee in New South Wales named Rabiyah.

Rabiyah was apparently quite a girl. She had been 'a Nimbin type', by one description, a young woman with a keen sense of adventure from 'an alternative lifestyle background'.[7] She had gone to Bali on holidays and loved it so much that she stayed, got married and had a child. But she later spurned the carefree Balinese Hindu lifestyle and embraced life as a strict Muslim instead, taking to it with her characteristic verve.

Rabiyah had moved from Bali to Java with the daughter from her earlier marriage and joined Abdullah Sungkar's religious study group. Although she wore the full face-covering burkah, she was a woman of obvious charms and 'very fanatic' by one account. People who knew her say she was desperate to go to Afghanistan to fight the Russians but the menfolk wouldn't allow it.[8] In any event, three of Sungkar's followers wanted to marry her, including the 21-year-old economics student, Abdul Rahim. 'Abdul Rahim was the youngest, and he was quite handsome — pale skin and green eyes. So she chose him,' revealed Zainal Arafin, who knew them both at the time.

The union received Abdullah Sungkar's blessing, and Abdul Rahim and Rabiyah were married by Sungkar at Ngruki in Solo in 1984. The following year, when Sungkar and Bashir fled into exile in Malaysia, Abdul Rahim migrated to Australia with his new wife. 'I think it was because Abdullah Sungkar wanted him in Australia,' one follower told me. 'So he sent the other twin off to jihad and sent Abdul Rahim to Australia.'[9]

Abdul Rahim lived for a while in Darwin then moved to Melbourne, where he completed a diploma in computer science and applied physics at the Victoria University of Technology. He obtained permanent residency, thanks to his Australian wife, and on 20 April 1988 was granted Australian citizenship. Abdul Rahim and Rabiyah later separated and he married again. He and his second wife, and Indonesian, had six children.

While the younger Ayub twin was settling in Australia, his brother had taken a very different course. After completing high school,

Abdul Rahman enrolled in the Saudi-funded Institute for the Study of Islam and the Arabic Language. Abdul Rahman later told the Refugee Review Tribunal in Australia that his studies were 'a front' for his activities as an organiser in Jakarta for Sungkar and Bashir's group.

After completing his course in Arabic and Islamic studies, Abdul Rahman took off to join the jihad. He spent five years in Afghanistan and Pakistan and later boasted of having fought alongside Osama bin Laden.[10] He also fought with Hambali, the future operations chief of JI, and took up arms with Muslim rebels in the jungles of Mindanao in the southern Philippines. 'I asked him once how many people he had killed,' one man who knew him told me. 'He said he didn't know but that he had no issue with killing people — he said that was "a warrior's point of view".'[11]

Abdul Rahman returned from Afghanistan to Indonesia to become a key lieutenant in Sungkar and Bashir's network. He described his role later to the Refugee Review Tribunal as 'propagator of activities for the district of Jakarta' and said he worked to a man called Ibnu Taib, whom he named as 'the leader in Indonesia'.[12] Ibnu Taib is an alias of Abu Fatih, who was the leader of JI's Indonesian branch, Mantiqi 2. Abdul Rahman would later be reassigned to join his brother in the Australian branch, Mantiqi 4.

By the time Sungkar and Bashir made their first visit to Australia together in 1991,[13] the junior Ayub twin, Abdul Rahim, was well ensconced in Melbourne and the natural choice to become the emir of the Australian branch. 'Everything that happened in Sydney or Australia, Abdul Rahim was in charge,' recounted Zainal Arifin. The congregation at Dee Why had to report regularly to Abdul Rahim and send the money they raised to Melbourne, from where it would be forwarded on to the leaders in Malaysia, along with Abdul Rahim's regular reports on the activities of the jemaah. Nothing happened in Dee Why without the say-so of Sungkar and Bashir.

Throughout the 1990s, Abu Bakar Bashir visited Australia eleven times, travelling under his alias Abdus Samad Abud. Abdullah Sungkar made ten visits using his pseudonym Abdul Halim. They were welcomed into the homes of their followers in Dee Why and Lakemba, sometimes staying three or four weeks at a time, lecturing at mosques, universities and private houses in Sydney, Melbourne and Perth. They came so often their supporters suggested they seek refugee status. But the two leaders didn't want to live in Australia; they saw it instead as an important support base and lucrative source of funds.

As opposition to Suharto mounted within Indonesia, Sungkar and Bashir were increasingly renowned in Muslim circles in Australia as courageous advocates of a popular cause. Sungkar would rage in his sermons: 'We have to oppose this government! Because this government is opposing Muslims!' 'He can scream,' said one Indonesian who witnessed him preach in Sydney.

'When he come to Australia, he get to speak freedom — not like in Indonesia or Malaysia,' noted Zainal Arifin. 'He can talk anything — about politics, about religion, anything he wants in Australia.' When Sungkar was occupied, his deputy, Bashir, would speak in his place. While the delivery was less commanding, the message was the same; as one follower described it to me: 'Suharto bad, Suharto bad.'

Indonesian Australians flocked to hear them, drawn by their cachet as political dissidents and their passion for Islam. Followers like Muchsin Thalib of Dee Why were honoured to host Bashir in their homes. 'I was living with two flatmates and we'd move into one room and give the other room to him,' said Thalib. 'It was not a problem at all. He always ask us to have good behaviour to the Australian community . . . Don't show any bad things, try to help each other, consider your neighbours, be helpful to them, that is the main thing they say.'[14]

Another who joined their congregation was an Indonesian known as Wandi, who had moved to Australia in 1974. Wandi worked sixteen hours a day running a halal butcher shop and driving a taxi to support his wife, six children and mortgage. As Wandi told it, he barely had time for his religion until, one day, he heard an impassioned sermon in Sydney by Abu Bakar Bashir: 'Before that I was empty. I said "Wow!" I never heard it before, you know, I never heard it before.' From there, said Wandi, he became a devotee. He would later become deputy leader of the JI branch in Australia, Mantiqi 4.[15]

Bashir preached to his Australian followers that the struggle for Islam — nothing less than a life or death mission — had to be waged down-under as well as in Indonesia. This message was spelt out in one speech Bashir gave in Sydney in 1993 which was taped by a follower:

'Scholars of our faith give this advice: in order that your life has meaning, you must live nobly or take your life. And how can we live a noble life? Clearly a noble life is one that is regulated 100 per cent by God's law, namely, life in an Islamic state. If we do not yet have an

Islamic state then a noble life has not yet been achieved. Therefore, how can we bring this into being? By working hard to undertake jihad, to uphold the rule of God's law. There is no other way apart from this.'

Bashir told his audience that alternative beliefs practised in Australia, like capitalism and nationalism, were all 'the same sin' — just as bad as the state doctrine of Pancasila in Indonesia — because they were rival creeds to Islam. 'It is abasement for a Muslim to live in a non-believing nation, it is forbidden . . . And if we do not live in an Islamic state, then we must do all we can to bring one about.' The message to his local followers was this: 'The Islamic faithful in Australia must endeavour to bring about an Islamic state in Australia, even if it is 100 years from now.'[16]

In his 1993 sermon in Sydney, Bashir expounded on one of his favourite themes, the same mantra he would return to in Solo in October 2002 just after the Bali bombings. 'The world is divided into two sections,' he told his Sydney audience. 'One section is called Hizbullah, namely God's party. The second section is Satan's party. The devoted followers of Islam comprise God's party — Muslims whose faith is pure. Meanwhile there are 1001 parties of Satan.'

It was clear that in Bashir's mind, a large chunk of the Australian population belonged to the party of Satan. 'What types of people follow Satan's party?' he asked his audience. 'Communists, capitalists, perhaps also those who take half their teachings from Islam, some from Christianity, some from Buddhism, some from their ancestors, that is the path of Satan . . . What then is the path of God? Pure Islam, in accordance with God's will.' Although the wording was slightly different, Bashir's message to the followers of Satan in Sydney was the same one he would repeat almost a decade later in the silver-domed mosque in Solo: 'Between you and I there will forever be a ravine of hostility and hate, until you choose to return to belief in God.'

At the end of his sermon, Bashir closed with a word of encouragement to his loyal followers in the local jemaah. 'May God bless the struggle of our brethren in Australia who have demonstrated such loyalty, despite being surrounded by nonbelievers.'

However far-fetched Bashir's goal of an Islamic state in Australia might seem to non-Muslims, his followers were in no doubt that he was serious. As Zainal Arifin put it, 'They got the intention to make, to establish an Islamic state everywhere — even in Australia.' Said another follower: 'They had some greater plan for Australia . . . They would have liked to have seen an Islamic state established in the whole of Southeast Asia. Why just go for Indonesia, when you could take the rest with them?'[17]

But, for the time being, the jemaah in Australia was primarily for fundraising. Members were obliged to donate a per centage of their weekly incomes to the group. It started at 2.5 per cent and later rose to 5 per cent. By one account, the sum raised in Australia and sent to the leaders in Malaysia added up to around $15,000 per year.[18] The members of the jemaah never knew exactly how the money was spent; Zainal Arifin told me they thought it went to 'many hungry people and many poor people'.

On one visit, Sungkar brought with him a brochure on poultry farming and told his followers he wanted to set up a chicken farm as a business venture in Malaysia to help fund their activities. The Australian followers were asked to donate $500 each. More than thirty of them willingly did so, raising about $16,000, which was handed over to the emir. Sungkar assured them that once the business was up and running they would get their money back. But on his next visit to Australia, recounted Zainal, 'he give us bad news, the chicken is not really good, so better you make intention for charity.' The contributors wouldn't be seeing their $500 again.

While Sungkar and Bahir's following flourished, some Muslims in Dee Why were dismayed at the blatant politicking in the house of God. 'They made the mosque a forum for opposing the Indonesian Government. When they gave sermons they were always calling for jihad against the government,' one listener complained. Some Indonesians feared it would land them in trouble if they went home; others simply believed the mosque was no place for politics.

Eventually, the complaints would see Sungkar and Bashir banned from making political speeches in the Dee Why mosque. Elections for the local Islamic Society, which ran the mosque, became hotly contested affairs between candidates standing for the jemaah and those who objected to their radical politics. 'The majority were against the group because they didn't want the mosque used for political purposes,' related one critic.

As time went by there were growing rumblings within the jemaah as well. The relentless demands for money were increasingly resented. 'They wanted to push us,' said Arifin's friend Mohammed Baluel. 'They wanted all our money. We wanted to send some to our families in Indonesia as well. They would say, for example, we want 75 per cent of your income. We'd say we'll give you a third and send the rest to our family.'

Some people fudged their earnings so they didn't have to pay as much, while others refused to donate to the special appeals for more funds. There was constant argument over finances, complaints from Abdul Rahim that money collected in Dee Why wasn't being forwarded to Melbourne, and frequent accusations of theft. When it was discovered that money from the jemaah was being used to bribe immigration officials in Indonesia to help get people's relatives into Australia, the man who had approved it in Dee Why was sacked by Sungkar and Bashir from the group and accused of stealing the funds. Sungkar declared that under Islamic law his hand should be chopped off, but since that couldn't be enforced in Australia the offender, instead, should be cut off from the community.

The growing tensions exacerbated long-standing divisions among the Indonesian Australians, between those of Middle Eastern background and those of Javanese descent. The followers of Sungkar and Bashir, who both hailed from Yemen, were referred to by some as 'the Arab group'. As with any organisation there were personality clashes as well, with insults traded, including the Indonesian epithet *ular*, meaning snake, and the more familiar Aussie term of abuse 'gutless wanker'.

A more serious source of friction was the tight control exerted by the leaders in Malaysia over their followers in Australia. Everything that went on in Melbourne and Sydney was reported back to Sungkar and Bashir by Abdul Rahim Ayub. 'When somebody get married or someone goes somewhere, [they] must get permission from Malaysia, from the leader,' Zainal Arifin complained. Some, including Arifin and his friend Mohammed Baluel, became increasingly disenchanted. As Mohammed put it, 'We wanted to be Aussie-style. We don't want to be in charge from outside.'

The last straw came for the imam, Arifin, when a young man in the Dee Why jemaah wanted to marry the daughter of a man who had been thrown out of the group, the same man accused by Abdullah Sungkar of stealing funds. The match had been agreed on, the wedding was arranged and Arifin and Mohammed Baluel were to officiate at the ceremony. But from head office in Malaysia, Sungkar decreed that the wedding must not take place. Because the father of the bride had been expelled from the jemaah, Sungkar declared that he was 'not a Muslim any more'. The same went for his daughter, who was judged by the leaders to be a kafir because she chose not to wear the veil. Abdul Rahim passed on the message from the leaders with a warning that if the wedding proceeded, anyone who took part in it would be punished.

Zainal Arifin was incensed at this harsh intervention in the life of the Australian community. He sat down at his typewriter and tapped out a thirteen-page letter, arguing 'with the proof of the Koran and *sunna*' that the pronouncements from Malaysia were not in accordance with Islamic law. He informed Bashir and Sungkar in writing: 'I want to resign from now until the day of judgement.' About ten others, including his friend Mohammed Baluel, resigned with him. After that, said Arifin, Abdullah Sungkar issued an 'instruction to all the followers to boycott Zainal and hate Zainal because Zainal doesn't follow the jemaah any more'.

Still in its infancy, the Australian wing of Sungkar and Bashir's network had split in two. In the wake of the resignations, their main man in Australia, Abdul Rahim Ayub, was ordered to move from Melbourne to Sydney to take over and restore order in the jemaah. Abdul Rahim's flat in Pacific Parade, Dee Why, with its aqua roller doors and pink hibiscus, would become the new headquarters for the Australian group.

'They were very secretive and radical after that,' recalled one of those who had quit. 'They met separately from us. Everybody would go to Abdul Rahim's house, because [now] he was their leader . . . When we led prayers, they would leave the mosque.'

The tensions in the Australian group would only deepen as time went by, to the later consternation of the leaders overseas. But for the moment, Bashir and Sungkar had much more pressing concerns. The cracks between the exiles in Malaysia and their rivals in the Indonesian leadership of Darul Islam had opened up into a chasm. The men from Ngruki now moved to formally renounce the old Darul Islam movement and establish a separate organisation of their own, named Jemaah Islamiyah.

CHAPTER TEN

The Islamic Military Academy of JI

A COURIER WAS DISPATCHED from Sungkar and Bashir's base to deliver the news of their formal severance from the Darul Islam movement back to Indonesia. The emissary who was sent to make the announcement later testified about this historic event during the trial of a senior JI member. 'On 1 January 1993, Jemaah Islamiyah separated itself from Darul Islam . . . but even earlier, I had delivered a letter from Malaysia, written by Abdullah Sungkar, to this effect.'[1]

The formation of the new group, Jemaah Islamiyah, was announced to their followers in Australia during a visit to Dee Why in February 1993. 'They said they were not Darul Islam any more — that's when they became JI,' one of their followers told me. The way Bashir explained it to the Australian jemaah was that he and Sungkar felt it was no longer appropriate to use the term coined by the Darul Islam pioneer Kartosuwiryo for his Islamic state. 'Bashir said that to be Darul Islam you need to have a place, some land, but they didn't have a place or any land, so the view was that the group shouldn't be named as a state any more but should just be named after the group or community.'[2]

The date of JI's formation was confirmed in a document headed 'Official Statement from Jemaah Islamiyah', which was drafted by JI in Indonesia in 2003 but never formally released. The document, obtained by Sidney Jones of the International Crisis Group, was intended to rebut assertions that JI did not exist and to publicly explain its aims.

'Jemaah Islamiyah indeed exists and has consistently carried the mandate of Allah as the standard-bearer of al Haq [truth], the bringer of hope, victory and glory for all Muslims,' it proudly declared. 'It continues to position itself as the opponent of oppression and arrogance of anyone who prevents mankind from following the path of Allah. Jemaah Islamiyah was founded by Ustad Abdullah Sungkar, Allah's mercy be upon him, on 1 January 1993, with one lofty goal — that is to uphold the word of Allah.'[3]

Thus the organisation Jemaah Islamiyah was born. Where previously Sungkar and Bashir had used the phrase as a generic term for their separate communities of followers, it was now adopted as the formal name of their group.

Jemaah Islamiyah's first emir, Abdullah Sungkar, later outlined his conception of JI in an interview with the Sydney-based magazine, *Nida'ul Islam* (The Call of Islam) in 1997. Sungkar said the Islamic movement in Indonesia largely took two forms: Islamic political parties and educational and social organisations, which he described as being 'cooperative' and 'easily dictated [to] by the authorities'. A third form, which he described as 'non-cooperative' was his own group, Jemaah Islamiyah. He said its aim was to use 'three strengths' — faith, brotherhood and military strength — 'to establish Dawlah Islamiyah [an Islamic state] by means of jihad'.[4]

The next step after JI's formation was to continue building its military strength in preparation for the jihad to come. So Sungkar and Bashir decided to set up their own training facility, the grandly named Islamic Military Academy of Jemaah Islamiyah.[5]

The new facility would be established in the jungles of Mindanao island in the southern Philippines, home of the Moro Islamic Liberation Front (MILF), which had been fighting since the 1970s for a separate Islamic state. Recruits from Sungkar and Bashir's group had been training and fighting alongside the MILF's men in Pakistan and Afghanistan for years and the two groups were already closely linked. The MILF had its own long-established training ground known as Camp Abubakar, deep in the jungles of Mindanao. It was there that JI would set up its new training ground.

It was also there that JI would strengthen its alliance with Osama bin Laden's network, al Qaeda. Bin Laden saw the local militant groups in Southeast Asia as natural partners in the global struggle and their region as a new theatre of operations for al Qaeda. Bin Laden's headquarters would provide training, military expertise and ideological backing for JI and the MILF. They, in turn, would become willing combatants in al Qaeda's war against the West.

❦

The man al Qaeda chose for the assignment in Southeast Asia was a tall athletic Kuwaiti, with the looks and build of a Middle Eastern movie star. Mustachioed and in his early twenties, his name was Omar al Faruq — or at least that's the name he went by.

Like many in al Qaeda's ranks, Faruq's real identity was blurred. He travelled on a forged passport and had several aliases. The Americans said he was from Kuwait, while the Kuwaitis claimed he was an Iraqi. Faruq was trained in one of bin Laden's principal camps, the Khalden camp near Khost in eastern Afghanistan. He was there for three years and was so dedicated that he was singled out by Abu Zubaydah, a senior bin Laden lieutenant in charge of recruitment and liaison with foreign terrorist groups. Abu Zubaydah put Faruq through an intensive course in explosives and then assigned him to his first post, the Philippines.

Faruq's own account of his role was later summarised in a report by the CIA. 'During a custodial interview on September 9 2002 Faruq stated that he was Al Qaeda's senior representative to Southeast Asia and was initially sent to the region . . . to plan large-scale attacks against US interests in Indonesia, Malaysia, Philippines, Singapore, Thailand, Taiwan, Vietnam and Cambodia.'[6] Faruq's mobile number was found in Abu Zubaydah's phone when he was captured in Pakistan and, according to US intelligence, Zubaydah 'confessed that Faruq was the senior al Qaeda rep in Southeast Asia'.[7]

Faruq arrived in the Philippines in early 1994, travelling on false documents supplied by Abu Zubaydah. He was accompanied by another trusted al Qaeda operative, his friend al Mughira al Gaza'iri, who was the emir of the Khalden camp in Afghanistan. Their destination was the southern island of Mindanao and the sprawling jungle training ground, Camp Abubakar, operated by the MILF. Their mission: 'to conduct jihadist training.'

Faruq was welcomed in the Philippines by Hashim Salamat, founder of the MILF, the largest of several rebel groups that operate in the country's south. The MILF's campaign for a Muslim state enjoys widespread popular support in Mindanao and the Sulu islands, where the people were Muslims for some 300 years before the Spanish conquistadors arrived in the sixteenth century to convert the Philippines to Christianity. The Spaniards called the country's Muslim south 'Moro', after the Moorish Muslim invaders who had occupied Spain centuries before. Hashim Salamat viewed the Philippine Government as just another occupying force, like the Spanish and the American colonisers who came after them, and portrayed the MILF's insurgency as a legitimate struggle for self-determination, calling it 'the longest and bloodiest in the entire history of mankind'.[8]

A graduate of the prestigious Al Azhar University in Cairo, Salamat had long-standing connections with the Afghan mujahideen network, most notably through his old university contemporary, the mujahideen leader Abdul Rasul Sayyaf.[9] Like his counterparts in Indonesia and Malaysia, Salamat used Afghanistan as the training ground for his fighters. In the very first year of the Afghan jihad, Salamat reportedly sent about 1000 Filipinos to train and fight against the Soviets.[10] Many more followed them, including the head of the MILF's special operations group, Muklis Yunos, who trained in Abdul Rasul Sayyaf's Camp Saddah in 1987, alongside the early JI trainees like Muklas and Hambali.

Now al Qaeda was sending its expertise to the MILF at home and, in the process, bringing Camp Abubakar into the fold of bin Laden's expanding training infrastructure. Al Qaeda's men, Faruq and Al Gaza'iri, conducted explosives courses in Camp Abubakar for the MILF and for the growing contingent of Arab fighters who were being sent there for training from the Middle East.[11]

Al Qaeda's role in the running of the MILF camp was further strengthened a year later when, after briefly returning to Afghanistan, Faruq and another commander from bin Laden's Khalden camp were assigned as emir and deputy emir of Camp Abubakar. According to Indonesian intelligence, 'Faruq became the liaison between the Arabs in the camp and the leader of the MILF, Hashim Salamat.'[12]

Camp Abubakar would become even more integral to al Qaeda's decentralised training system after the US bombed bin Laden's camps in Afghanistan in 1998. In the aftermath, bin Laden and his lieutenant

Abu Zubaydah would phone the Philippines to ask the MILF to set up new camps there for its Arab fighters.[13] At this stage, Omar al Faruq was made the commander of a new site called Camp Vietnam where, according to Philippine intelligence, 'Arab nationals, including Kuwaitis, Saudis, Moroccans and Algerians conducted training on terrorist tactics.'[14]

Once the training had been organised, al Faruq could begin focusing on the second part of his assignment — planning 'large-scale attacks'. His first plan, according to the later CIA report, was 'to get flight training to blow up a commercial plane', but, he told his interrogators, he failed to get into flight school. Another idea was to get a scuba-diving licence in Indonesia to make use of his al Qaeda training in planting explosives under water.[15]

During his eight years in Southeast Asia, Omar al Faruq made many such plans. Only later when he was reassigned to Indonesia would Faruq's plans take concrete shape, in partnership with the MILF's comrades in JI.

It was soon after Faruq's arrival at Camp Abubakar that Sungkar and Bashir moved to shift their own training to the MILF's jungle base in Mindanao. A seasoned veteran of the Afghan jihad and member of the JI extended family was chosen to set up the Islamic Military Academy of Jemaah Islamiyah.

Mohammed Nasir bin Abas was a brother-in-law of Muklas, one of the siblings who had resisted Muklas's advances toward their sister Farida before finally accepting the young suitor from Tenggulun into their family. Born in Singapore but a Malaysian national, Nasir had been among the earliest trainees in Afghanistan and had then become a trainer himself, teaching younger recruits like Samudra and Ali Imron. Nasir would later be made leader of the JI branch responsible for the Philippines, Mantiqi 3. Much later when he was captured he would give a crucial insider's description of the running of JI.

Like Omar al Faruq before him, Nasir was well received at Camp Abubakar. The MILF leader, Hashim Salamat, was an old friend of Abdullah Sungkar. The two men used to meet at the hajj pilgrimage in Mecca along with mujahideen leaders from all over the world.[16] The MILF chief was happy to do a deal, providing space in his extensive camp in return for JI's offer of funding and operational assistance. One fighter described it as 'a standing agreement wherein the MILF will accommodate JI fighters in the former's camps and in return JI will help MILF guerrillas in conducting bombings in any targeted area until such time that Mindanao can attain its independence.'[17]

The result of this agreement was the establishment, within the bounds of Camp Abubakar, of JI's own separate training area. It was named Camp Hudaibiyah, after the historic site near Mecca where the Prophet Muhammad had signed a truce with his tribal enemies, the Quraysh, allowing him to preach the Islamic faith.

'I helped establish Camp Hudaibiyah in Moro in 1994 by the order of Abdullah Sungkar,' Nasir later confessed. 'Funding came from Abdullah Sungkar. I was given 2000 Malaysian ringgit [A$700].'[18] After the startup was paid for with the cash sent by Sungkar, the running costs were covered by money wired by JI's treasurer, Abu Bakar Bafana, through a Malaysian bank.[19]

Camp Hudaibiyah in Mindanao became the training ground for a new generation of JI recruits. Some of JI's top graduates from Afghanistan were sent there as trainers, among them Muklas, Hambali and Fathur Rahman al Ghozi, who took over from Nasir in 1996. According to Muklas, the Academy's officer cadet training course ran for four semesters over two years.[20] Trainees were required to be between eighteen and twenty-three years of age, unmarried and to have graduated from an Islamic high school.[21] The course was modelled on the training programs used in Afghanistan and included self-defence, leadership, regular warfare and guerrilla tactics, map reading, field engineering, weapons training, demolition and bombing. According to JI's treasurer, Bafana, more than 1000 Indonesians were trained in Camp Hudaibiyah.

At the end of the course, trainees underwent a series of examinations. The results were outlined in detailed reports submitted from the Military Academy to JI's leaders. The following sample from the weapons training examination in which the recruits used Colt pistols, M16s and Belgian FN battle rifles, gives a snapshot of the rigorous training and testing regime:

1. Describe the following:
   a) calibre
   b) effective range
   c) muzzle velocity
   d) zeroing
   e) categorisation of small arms and their uses.
2. What do you know about the following working system and the kinds of weapons used in this system?
   a) gas operation system
   b) blow back system
   c) recoil system
   d) delayed fuse in hand grenade
3.
   a) What is the difference between a rifle and a machine gun?
   b) How to dissect and assemble the .45 pistol?
   c) How to carry out zeroing of AK47
   d) How to dissect and assemble M60
   e) How to carry out zeroing of M16.[22]

The recruits were tested in similar detail on topography, orienteering, explosives and 'the nine principles of war', including surprise, cover, concealment, camouflage and ambush. They were required to learn the chemical properties and methods of production of all the ingredients used in bomb making. They also had to 'write an operational plan' for an attack on an armed and guarded enemy post.

The first formal graduation ceremony at JI's Military Academy took place in 1999 and was presided over by Abu Bakar Bashir, who made a speech congratulating the course graduates.[23] JI's new setup in the base run jointly by the MILF and al Qaeda further entrenched the links between Bashir and Sungkar's organisation and the global jihad network being nurtured by Osama bin Laden.

Bin Laden had been cultivating his connections in Southeast Asia for years, starting back in the 1980s with his first foray into the Philippines. In 1988, the same year that al Qaeda was founded, bin Laden sent his brother-in-law, Mohammed Jamal Khalifa, to Manila. A smooth-talking charmer with an easy smile and perfect English, Khalifa was well suited to his job as regional front man for the Saudi charity, the International Islamic Relief Organisation, which built schools and hospitals, channelled funds to the mujahideen in Afghanistan and was later identified as a financer of terrorism.[24]

The peripatetic Khalifa has had a long and varied career. In the mid-1980s, while bin Laden was helping run the Afghan Services Bureau in Peshawar, his brother-in-law was heading up the nearby branch office of the Saudi Muslim World League, another body involved in dispatching foreign volunteers to the jihad. At last report Khalifa was back in Saudi Arabia running the Sultana Seafood Restaurant in Jeddah and reminiscing with foreign journalists about his old friend, bin Laden.

'Osama was my best friend, more than a brother, I love him very much, even now,' Khalifa told one reporter. 'He was very humble, very simple, very polite. I never heard him say a bad word against anybody.' As for Khalifa himself, 'I was someone who was focused on changing the situation of poor people in the Philippines and in the end I was accused of supporting terrorists! I really loved charity work. When you make someone smile and change their situation from bad to good, it gives you a happiness you can't find anywhere else.'[25]

After marrying a Filipina and setting up an import-export firm dealing in rattan furniture, Khalifa set about charming Manila society to raise money for his causes. Urbane, well-travelled and garbed in the pristine white robes and headdress of a Saudi sheik, Khalifa schmoozed his way into the Philippines' mainly Catholic establishment. He was described in a later police report as 'rich, influential and close to Filipino Muslim leaders'; these included a provincial governor and a senator married to the Philippine ambassador to Saudi Arabia.[26]

Khalifa incorporated the International Islamic Relief Organisation (IIRO) in the Philippines with himself as its president, and started an orphanage, a clinic and a university in Zamboanga in Mindanao. Thanks to his tireless efforts as a fundraiser, there was plenty of money to spare for his other causes.

Khalifa oversaw two important projects in the Philippines for his brother-in-law bin Laden in the early 1990s. The first was setting up an al Qaeda franchise in the southern Philippines, a brutal new offshoot to be called the Abu Sayyaf. The second was financing plans for what was to have been al Qaeda's first catastrophic attack — a diabolical campaign of hijackings and bombings code-named Operation Bojinka.

Bin Laden assigned a promising young operative named Ramzi Yousef to work with Khalifa on these two jobs — the same Ramzi Yousef who is currently serving 240 years in a US prison for the first attack on the World Trade Center in 1993.

Yousef was born in Kuwait, where his father worked as an engineer with Kuwaiti Airlines, earning enough to send his son to Oxford to learn English and then to Wales to study computer-aided electrical engineering.[27] But like many of his contemporaries, Yousef found a career in jihad more alluring than a highly paid job as an engineer. From the West Glamorgan Institute of Higher Education, Yousef made his way to the Pakistan–Afghanistan border and enrolled in Camp Saddah, the training ground run by the Afghan mujahideen leader Abdul Rasul Sayyaf. Yousef had a personal entrée to the camp: his uncle was Sayyaf's secretary, Khalid Sheik Mohammed, the man who would later become chief operational planner for al Qaeda. It was in Sayyaf's camp that Yousef acquired the knack with explosives that earned him the nickname 'the Chemist'.

During his stay in Camp Saddah, Yousef befriended a young Filipino named Abdurajak Janjalani. He was a zealous and ambitious young jihadi from Basilan island near Mindanao who believed the MILF was too soft and wanted to go home and set up his own rebel outfit. The two trainees were reportedly introduced by bin Laden himself,[28] who assigned Yousef to help Janjalani set up his new group, named in honour of their patron at Camp Saddah, the Abu Sayyaf.

Yousef and Janjalani travelled back to the Philippines together and set up camp on Basilan island. There 'the Chemist' passed on his explosives skills to Janjalani's recruits, a ragtag band in bandanas and blue jeans from the ghettoes of the Philippines' dirt-poor southern islands.

'The rebels came . . . and someone asked if I wanted to join them,' said one nineteen-year-old. 'I was fascinated with guns so I figured joining the Abu Sayyaf is the best thing to do to realise my dream to own a gun.' As an added incentive — 'we were given food and clothes'.[29]

According to Philippine intelligence, bin Laden's man in Manila, his brother-in-law Khalifa, provided the funds for the Abu Sayyaf's first operations in the early 1990s, including a hand-grenade attack on a church in Jolo, the assassination of an Italian missionary and the bombing of a public market on Basilan island.[30] The Abu Sayyaf group later made its trademark the kidnapping and beheading of Western tourists and Filipinos when the ransoms it demanded were not paid.

After training the Abu Sayyaf group, Ramzi Yousef returned to Peshawar and then flew via Karachi to New York. 'The Chemist' was impatient to put his skills to the test. On 26 February 1993, Yousef eased his way through the rush-hour traffic of New York, in the passenger seat of a yellow Ford van. It was heading for the twin skyscrapers of the World Trade Center, the towering symbol of US financial might.

Yousef had recruited a friend to drive the van while he navigated. 'In the middle of a major street we stopped at a traffic light,' the driver later told police. 'He [Yousef] said "Go to the right from here" in the direction of an underground tunnel. I did and went down underground . . . He said, "Park here."'[31] Inside the World Trade Center carpark, Yousef pulled out a cigarette lighter and lit four fuses attached to the massive bomb in the back of the van, then jumped in a getaway car with his friend and sped away.

On his way to the airport, Yousef stopped briefly on the waterfront opposite Manhattan to admire his handiwork, as smoke billowed from the twin towers where six people lay dead and more than 1000 injured. He would later confess to being disappointed that the towers remained standing. 'They wouldn't be if I had enough money and explosives,' he told an FBI agent years after the event.[32] Yousef's aim had been to topple one tower into the other, sending both of them crashing to the ground. To most people at the time, his vision would have seemed like sheer fantasy.

Yousef continued on his way to the airport and took a first-class flight back to Pakistan. He lay low for a while in an al Qaeda safe house until he was confident the FBI was not yet on his trail, then returned to the Philippines to begin work on another grandiose attack — the plot code-named Operation Bojinka.[33]

Ramzi Yousef was accompanied to the Philippines by his uncle Khalid Sheik Mohammed. Even after his years in Afghanistan, the US-educated Mohammed 'was not considered a typical jihadi member by Western authorities because of his kind-hearted nature and constant smile,' according to a terrorist profile later published in the West. Mohammed had taken time out from his job in Qatar, where he worked as a project engineer with the Ministry of Electricity and Water.[34]

In the Philippines with his nephew, he cut quite a flashy figure in the karaoke joints and five-star hotels he frequented. Mohammed posed in many guises. Sometimes he was a wealthy sheik, lavishing gifts including airline tickets and clothing on bar girls with names like Precious and Rose. At other times he said he was a businessman who exported plywood, or even 'a practicing Christian and a former Catholic priest'.[35]

Reports of his sojourn in the Philippines have Mohammed out on the town in a white tuxedo, scuba diving at a beach resort and packing condoms in his luggage as backup for his story that he was travelling around 'to meet women'. He certainly set out to impress them. Ramzi Yousef told a story of Mohammed chartering a helicopter and flying it over a dental clinic where a girl he was dating worked, then ringing her on his cellphone while he hovered overhead.[36]

The bar girls were apparently all part of the plan. One of them told police about an incident involving another girl, after an evening at a downtown karaoke bar: '[Mohammed] proceeded to his room upstairs. Before he left, he asked Rose secretly if she could help him deposit money in a bank.' The girl called Rose agreed and went with Mohammed to the bank next day. There 'she was advised to fill up application forms and deposit money, all activities using her name. The issued bankbook was held by Sheik Mohammed and was never given to her. After that they bought a cellular phone . . . also in her name [which] was taken by Sheik Mohammed.'[37] For her trouble, Rose got a blouse, a skirt, a plane ticket and spending money for a week on the resort island of Cebu.

Meanwhile, back at the apartment that Mohammed and his cohorts had rented a few blocks from the red-light district, his nephew, Ramzi Yousef, was hard at work at his laptop on the blueprint for Operation Bojinka. He used code names for the operatives who would carry out the intricate plot:

'Zyod flies from Bangkok to Tokyo on a United flight, placing a bomb set to explode over the Pacific as the flight nears Los Angeles. He flies to Taipei via Seoul and places a bomb on a second United flight before flying back to Bankgok on a United flight and placing a third bomb. He escapes to Karachi while the second and third planes are set to explode on their way to the US.'[38]

Simultaneously, four other operatives would be planting eight more bombs on separate flights, resulting in twelve passenger jets blowing up in mid-air. To cap off what they called their '48 hours of terror', they planned to assassinate the Pope and US President Bill Clinton during their visits to Manila.

Mohammed and Ramzi Yousef had assembled a cell to carry out their planned attack. One of their recruits was an old al Qaeda hand, an Afghan named Wali Khan Amin Shah. 'We were good friends,' Osama bin Laden said of him later. 'We fought in the same trenches against the Russians.'[39] The second recruit was a former classmate of Yousef's from high school, Abdul Hakim Murad, who had got himself a commercial pilot's licence in the United States and dreamed of crashing a plane kamikaze-style into the headquarters of the CIA. Murad had been the one to first suggest targeting the World Trade Center in New York, because 'it is one of the tallest buildings and the most famous commercial centre in the world'.[40]

In the throes of Operation Bojinka, Mohammed turned to one of his old Indonesian contacts from Afghanistan for help. It was a former comrade from Camp Saddah, from back in the days of the Battle of Lion's Den, who had since become a firm friend and close colleague. The man Mohammed turned to was Hambali, the former kebab-seller marked out as chief of operations for JI.

Hambali had long since returned from Afghanistan and was living back in his shack in the banana grove in Sungai Manggis, south of Kuala Lumpur. Hambali commuted between the kampung and the capital, KL, where he had begun setting up a web of companies as fronts and fundraisers for JI. One of these was a trading firm called Konsojaya, incorporated in Malaysia in June 1994. It would be used as a vehicle to channel funds for Mohammed's project.[41]

The documents filed when Konsojaya was incorporated said its business was 'exporting all kinds of products from Malaysia and the Asia Pacific region' to the Middle East. The company's founding directors included Hambali (using the name Riduan Isamuddin) and his Chinese Malaysian wife, Noralwizah Lee. Another director and holder of half of the company's 6000 shares was bin Laden's old comrade from the trenches of Afghanistan, Wali Khan Amin Shah. The other directors were all based in the Middle East.[42]

Hambali's role was only uncovered much later by Manila's top anti-terrorism cop, Rodolfo Mendoza, a barrel-chested colonel with slicked-back hair, whose men click their heels to attention and salute when he passes. Back in the early 1990s, Mendoza headed the Special Operations Group of the Philippine National Police, at a time when the rising 'chatter' of intelligence indicated a dramatic upturn in suspected terrorists moving in and out of the country.

'During that time, the Philippines served as the command centre for al Qaeda's regional operations,' Mendoza told me when we met at his headquarters outside Manila in 2003. 'Specifically the operations for the implementation of Operation Bojinka. You know they assembled their best operatives in Manila to execute that plan.'

Mendoza's investigations revealed that, as early as 1993, al Qaeda and JI were working together, using Hambali's company, Konsojaya, as the conduit for funding Operation Bojinka. 'My analysis is that Konsojaya was formed for the purpose of terrorist activity . . . Konsojaya was the nerve center, not only for business, but also for operational supervision.' His analysis is supported by Australian investigators, who have described Konsojaya as 'a cover to get money from Al Qaeda and Saudi sources into Malaysia'. The funds were transferred through a Hong Kong bank, supposedly to cover shipments of goods like palm oil, ghee and lambswool from Afghanistan.[43] Electronic surveillance by the Philippines police revealed that Hambali was in regular contact with bin Laden's brother-in-law and local financier, Mohammed Jamal Khalifa, at this time; the calls between their offices in Malaysia and the Philippines monitored by Mendoza's team.

After months of preparations, Khalid Sheik Mohammed and Ramzi Yousef were ready for a final test-run of their plan. They had already tried out combinations of chemicals in a series of small experimental blasts and successfully smuggled bomb components through airport security on a trial run.

In December 1994, Ramzi Yousef took a Philippine Airlines flight from Manila bound for Tokyo. He assembled a bomb in the plane's toilet, then placed it in a life-jacket under his seat, before disembarking on a stopover in Cebu. The bomb exploded on the next leg of the flight, blowing a hole in the fuselage and leaving one man dead and eleven people injured. Australian investigators believe that by this time Hambali was playing a hands-on role in the plot, rather than just arranging the finance; they believe it was Hambali who ordered the test bombing of this flight.[44]

It was now time to execute Operation Bojinka. But one night while Ramzi Yousef and his co-conspirators were mixing chemicals, black smoke was seen billowing from a window of the flat they rented in the Dona Josefa apartment block. Yousef and his former schoolmate Murad were making their getaway just as the fire brigade arrived. 'What happened to your room? There's a reported fire alarm,' asked a fireman. 'Don't worry, we were just playing with firecrackers,' the bombers replied. After a quick check of the flat, the firemen declared 'There's no fire after all, no fire, so let's go home.'[45] The plotters fled, their plan was aborted and Operation Bojinka and its architects very nearly went undetected.

But the next day Yousef sent Murad back to retrieve the laptop containing his elaborate blueprint. By this time the police had the apartment staked out, suspecting that its Middle Eastern tenants might be connected with a plot to kill the Pope, about which Philippines intelligence had received a tipoff.

Murad was grabbed and placed in the hands of the redoubtable Rodolfa Mendoza, renowned for his persistent interrogation techniques. Mendoza knew exactly how to make Murad talk — forty-eight hours of sleep deprivation and then, as Mendoza related: 'I told him I would turn him over to the Israeli Jews and the FBI.' Murad quickly revealed all, spilling the story of Operation Bojinka as well as evidence that would later help convict Ramzi Yousef over the earlier bombing of the World Trade Center in 1993.

While Murad was being interrogated, the others in the group had scattered. Assisted by Hambali, Ramzi Yousef fled to Pakistan, but was captured a month later and deported to the United States, where he was tried over the World Trade Center attack and jailed for 240 years. Wali Khan Amin Shah was arrested in Manila but escaped and fled to Malaysia, where Hambali provided him with a new identity and a hideout on the resort island of Langkawi. Wali Khan was eventually captured as well and convicted over the Bojinka plot with Murad and Yousef in a US court in 1996.

Bin Laden's brother-in-law and financier, Mohammed Jamal Khalifa, had already left the Philippines and flown to the United States, on a business trip, he later claimed. He was arrested on arrival at San Francisco airport. In his luggage customs officials found a document outlining 'the institution of jihad', under the headings 'The Wisdom of Assassination and Kidnapping; The Wisdom of Assassinating Priests and Christians; The Wisdom of Bombing Churches and Places of Worship; and The Wisdom for Operations and Martyrdom'.[46]

Khalifa was held for four months in the United States but finally released, as there was no evidence he had committed any crime there.

He was extradited to Jordan instead, to face charges over a plot to blow up a cinema. Khalifa was sentenced to death, one witness testifying that the smooth-talking Saudi had given him $50,000 to finance bombings and assassinations. His conviction was overturned on appeal.

Tracked down at his Sultana Seafood Restaurant in Jeddah in 2003, Khalifa was still protesting his innocence — and demanding to know why the Australian Government had cancelled his visa in December 1994, spoiling his plans to holiday in Australia. 'They said I was a threat to national security. Believe me, I was shocked. Wow! Me? A threat? I ran to the mirror to take a good look at myself.'[47]

The mastermind of Operation Bojinka, Khalid Sheik Mohammed, returned to his base in Pakistan, to become the head of al Qaeda's military committee and its chief operational planner. He was eventually indicted in absentia for his role in the Philippines plot. But at the time the Philippine and US authorities had no inkling of Mohammed's or Ramzi Yousef's connections to bin Laden's al Qaeda. 'The Brain' would continue to work on his masterplan for the next six years, adapting it and finally honing it to perfection in September 2001.

The bond between Khalid Sheik Mohammed and his comrade Hambali would strengthen with time. Their personal and professional alliance became the pivot for the connection between al Qaeda and JI. Already well known to al Qaeda's chiefs from his tour in Afghanistan, Hambali became a trusted insider in bin Laden's hierarchy, as Mohammed himself later confirmed.

'In 1996 I invited Hambali to Afghanistan to meet Osama,' Mohammed later revealed. Hambali spent three or four days with the al Quaeda chief, according to Mohammed's account, and was given a new car, mobile phones and a computer. In the course of their discussions, the partnership between JI and al Qaeda was formalised. As Mohammed told it: 'It was agreed that al Qaeda and Hambali's organisation would work together on targets of mutual interest.'[48] This historic agreement would soon be implemented, to deadly effect.

❦

CHAPTER ELEVEN

A BIT OF A MAD BUGGER

IN THE SOUTHERN STATE OF Johor in Malaysia, a short drive from the JI school at Ulu Tiram, the road sweeps up and around through the oil palms to a guardpost and a grand concrete archway two storeys tall. Atop the arch is an emblem in gold and maroon bearing a flask, a crescent and an open book, symbolising science, Islam and the Holy Koran. The motto emblazoned around it reads, 'For God and Mankind'. This imposing gateway is the entrance to the University of Technology, Malaysia, known as UTM — the alma mater of the men who became the brains trust of JI.

Beyond the archway, the road winds through 1200 hectares of neatly cropped grounds, carved out of the rubber and palm-oil estates that surround the campus. Where plantation workers once laboured, book-laden students scurry between classes or stroll along the neat pathways that link the university's eight live-in student villages. The Malay-style A-framed roofs on the cement-block dormitories are among the few concessions to tradition in this monument to Muslim modernity.

The centrepiece of the campus is the Sultan Ismail Mosque, a shimmering palace topped by six soaring minarets and a gleaming dome. The mosque took four years and 19 million ringgit (A$7 million) to build and its prime position symbolises the philosophy of UTM proclaimed on its website: 'The divine law of Allah is the foundation for science and technology . . . The mosque is sited right at the centre of the campus . . . in line with the concept of Islamic learning in which the mosque is the source for the acquisition and dissemination of knowledge.'

From the gateway, the road winds up past the mosque and the library to the Faculty of Geoinformation, Science and Engineering, which houses the Department of Property Management and Valuation. For much of the 1990s, the office on the second floor near the stairwell was occupied by an affable extrovert with a PhD from Britain, a passion for fast cars and a photo album full of happy snaps of his student days in Australia. He wore thick glasses, a droopy moustache and a grin that showed off a mouthful of crooked teeth. His friends called him Azari; to his students he was Associate Professor Dr Azahari Husin.

Dr Azahari was an irrepressible joker of a man — the life of the faculty staffroom and 'a bit of a mad bugger', in the words of a former friend and fellow UTM staffer, John Cooper. Not at all what you'd expect for an academic whose specialty was statistics and who lectured in valuation and property management. 'He was bright, cavalier, not very serious on the surface,' said Cooper. 'He seemed to have a healthy disrespect for authority. He was a bit incorrigible in some ways.'[1]

John Cooper was new on the staff at UTM. An Australian who had grown up in the Blue Mountains west of Sydney, Cooper had been teaching valuation at the University of South Australia when he was headhunted by UTM. Azahari had seen a paper Cooper had written on using statistical models to value property and had persuaded the head of the faculty to lure Cooper to set up a masters course at UTM. Cooper arrived in Malaysia in mid-1991 and he and Azahari eventually became friends.

'He had a very strong presence,' recalled Cooper when I contacted him in 2003 to talk about his old colleague. 'Not in a serious way — he was happy-go-lucky . . . He was not the typical public-servant lecturer. He liked to play around, buck the system if necessary. In meetings he was always making some crazy comment. He was the guy who would always make people laugh.'

A lean, athletic man, Azahari was mad on sports. His favourites were soccer and sepak takraw, a Malaysian game in which teams of players kick a rattan ball over a net. He even had a poster of the American basketballer Michael Jordan adorning his office wall.

Azahari loved to talk of his student days in Australia and show off snapshots of his travels across the Australian outback. John Cooper recalled one of Azahari's proudest shots. 'It was a picture of a big smiling

Azahari, with his hands on the handlebars of some big motorbike, with nothing behind him but the wide blue yonder.' This was Azahari crossing the Nullarbor Plain, on a trip he made from Adelaide in the 1970s with a group of his Malaysian student friends.

Azahari came to Australia as a 17-year-old on a student visa in January 1975. He stopped briefly in Sydney before flying on to Adelaide, where he was enrolled at Norwood High School to do his final year of secondary school before going on to university. Norwood High was a popular choice for Malaysian students wanting to matriculate in Australia in preparation for university studies. The school had a large Malaysian student body and even provided a prayer room.

After high school, Azahari went on to Adelaide University where he studied mechanical engineering for three years. He lived in a student share house, in a big pink block of flats near the showgrounds in suburban Goodwood. Funny, bright and gregarious, he settled into his new Australian lifestyle with ease. According to John Cooper, 'He thought Australians were great.'

Azahari got himself a 500cc motorbike and set out to see as much of the countryside as he could. 'He was young then, smart and adventurous. I guess it's only natural that he would love Australia and her ruggedness,' another old UTM friend, 'Dani', told me.[2] More devoted to enjoying student life down-under than qualifying as an engineer, Azahari never did get his degree. He told John Cooper he didn't finish his course because he was having too much fun. According to 'Dani': 'He flunked.'

Azahari returned home to Malaysia in January 1979 and enrolled at UTM to knuckle down and finish his degree. His friend 'Dani' said he had done so poorly in Adelaide that 'he was lucky to be accepted into UTM'. After his easy-going student days in Australia, life on the UTM campus must have come almost as a culture shock.

UTM was established by the Malaysian Government to stimulate education and development in Johor, one of the country's poorest states, and to create opportunities for the impoverished ethnic majority, the Muslim Malays. The UTM campus became a showcase of the Islamic revival that swept Malaysia from the 1970s. It was primarily a homegrown movement driven by the poverty and backwardness of the Muslim population, whose resentment towards the relatively affluent Chinese community sparked the race riots of 1969, in which approximately 200 people were killed.

The emotions of the time were voiced by the then Muslim youth leader Anwar Ibrahim. 'We were impatient and angry about the plight of the Malays, their education, rural development, rural health . . . We were very angry, disgusted and critical of the government. There seemed to be no moral foundation and no spiritual guidance. We turned to Islam to fill this vaccuum and to look for solutions.'[3] Inspired by the Iranian revolution and the worldwide Islamic resurgence, Islam became the major ideology of dissent.

To improve the lot of Muslim Malays and head off further racial tensions, the Malaysian Government established university quotas for Malay students under its New Economic Policy. Thousands of young Muslims were given the opportunity to study abroad, the cream of them sent off to universities in Britain. For many, the strangeness of life in Britain only strengthened their identification with Islam and radicalised them even further.

On the campuses of their British universities, they were exposed to the teachings of the Muslim Brotherhood and other radical groups. They joined Muslim youth clubs and began to campaign for an Islamic state, denouncing the Malaysian Government with its Western style of administration as 'un-Islamic'. Their view was: 'The West is no longer a source of emulation or the fount of solutions for Malay backwardness . . . Islam now holds all the solutions to society's ills.'[4]

Concerned at being outflanked by the rising tide of Islam, Malaysian Prime Minister Dr Mahathir Mohamed embraced it instead, with his own policy of 'Islamisation'. He promoted Islamic institutions and introduced a compulsory course called 'Islamic civilisation' in universities. UTM, with its motto 'For God and Mankind', became a hub of the Islamic renewal and a centre of radical Muslim politics.

Life on the UTM campus began at 4.45 a.m., when students were woken by the call to prayer crackling out through the dormitory loudspeakers. Female students were housed in a separate compound, where headscarves and modest attire were obligatory. At graduation ceremonies, females sat on one side of the aisle, males on the other. The university canteens could serve only Muslim halal food, despite the protests of the large non-Muslim Chinese student body. Living on campus was mandatory and students had to be checked in and out by security at the front gate; only those with good reason could leave and they had to be back in their dormitories in time for lights-out.[5]

Despite the constraints of his new surroundings, the 21-year-old Azahari hadn't changed since his days in Adelaide, according to his UTM friend 'Dani'. 'He was fun loving, rowdy, happy-go-lucky and joked like any "ex-Oz" would do.' But by this time he had found a subject that intrigued him — enough to apply himself seriously to his studies. Azahari's new passion was valuation. A mathematician at heart, it was the science of it that he loved, in particular the use of statistical models, rather than subjective judgement to arrive at valuations. Azahari dumped engineering for valuation, and statistics became his specialty.

Having found his calling, Azahari excelled at it. He graduated at the top of his class in 1984 and was immediately appointed as an assistant lecturer at UTM. He worked for a spell as a valuer with the Property Services Office in Malacca, then went on to Reading University in England for three years. His aim was to do a masters degree, but according to his friend 'Dani', 'He never got his masters, because he's too smart.' Reading put him on its PhD program instead, which he successfully completed in 1990.

Azahari obtained his PhD with a thesis entitled 'The Construction of Regression-based Mass Appraisal Models: a Methodological Discussion and an Application to Housing Submarkets in Malaysia'. It's an arcane subject; since Azahari wrote it, only ten people have taken his two-volume tome off its shelf in the Reading Library. Nobody has taken it out since 1995.[6]

Written in English, Azahari's thesis might as well be in a foreign language for those not versed in the jargon of valuation. But it does provide a snapshot of the brain of the man. 'To determine the appropriate functional form, the study compares the performance of the conventional linear form to other functional forms,' Azahari wrote. 'The findings show that the popular conventional linear form is not the appropriate functional form. The log–log or semi-log functional form is a more appropriate functional form for regression-based appraisal models. As to multicollinearity, the results indicate that the widely employed pairwise correlation and variance inflation factors are not adequate multicollinearity detection measures.' And so it goes, for more than 400 pages.

Azahari applied his startling intellect with equal intensity to any subject that caught his interest. He would spend hours working at a problem until he had it solved, whether it be a statistical equation or one of his other passions, his share portfolio and fast cars. 'I've always known him to be a bit obsessed with things,' said his uni friend 'Dani'. 'When he developed a craze for fast, sporty cars he would be at it like no other. When he was in college, problems regarding computer programming would render him sleepless nights and sometimes he wouldn't sleep until he managed to crack it.'

After completing his PhD in Britain, Azahari returned to UTM in 1991 and was promoted to Associate Professor in the Department of Valuation and Property Management. His proudest new possession was not his weighty thesis or his new title, Doctor of Philosophy, but a gleaming midnight-blue Audi 5-cylinder sports sedan, which he had imported duty-free from the UK.

The car was a conspicuous luxury in Johor, although Azahari was not the first UTM academic to take advantage of this tax-free perk on his return from overseas. It was barely a five-minute drive from UTM to Azahari's home, a modern terrace in a brand-new estate filled with mock Tudor and Spanish-villa style facades. Compared with his car, Azahari's home was simple — a small house with ceramic floor tiles, basic furnishings and white walls, adorned with a simple banner in Arabic extolling the greatness of God.

Although he didn't make a show of it, Azahari applied his characteristic intensity to his faith as well. His parents were devout Muslims who had both made the hajj pilgrimage to Mecca and whom Azahari thanked in the acknowledgements in his thesis 'for their spiritual guidance'. His colleague John Cooper remembers: 'He always went to the mosque on Fridays with all his fellow lecturers. He seemed to observe all of the main principles of the faith and showed no indication at all that he was not a true believer.'

The other part of his life that Azahari took seriously was the woman he thanked in his thesis and described as 'my beloved wife', Wan Noraini Jusoh. Azahari's wife, Noraini, also taught valuation at UTM. But in contrast to her exuberant husband, she was a gentle, soft-spoken woman, who always wore a brown or black *hijab*, the Malaysian style head covering, and full-length robe.

Noraini was an Indonesian from the ravaged province of Aceh, where Muslim rebels had been fighting for a separate state since the 1970s. Her family was said to have been descended from the Muslim sultans who ruled Aceh until the nineteenth century, when it was occupied by the Dutch.[7] Noraini's family had fled the Suharto

Government's brutal crackdown on the Free Aceh Movement (GAM), to find refuge in Malaysia. Azahari was devoted to his wife, whom he acknowledged in his thesis 'for her constant encouragement and support [and] her forebearance, especially in her moments of less than perfect health'.

Noraini's soft-spokenness was not only due to her gentle manner. Azahari's wife had developed throat cancer while they were in Britain and it steadily grew worse. She had a series of operations but gradually lost her voice. 'She was forced to speak in little more than a whisper but was so dedicated to teaching that she would not give up,' John Cooper recalled. To add to their worries, Azahari and Noraini had been trying to have children for years but could not conceive, a fact that clearly pained them. They prayed to be blessed with a family.

While working at UTM, Azahari began making regular trips to Indonesia, where his faculty was running an offshore masters course. The real-estate conglomerates formed by Indonesian companies in partnership with big foreign firms would send their managers and staff along to be taught valuation and property management. In Jakarta, Azahari was headhunted by SGT-Hillier Parker, a joint venture between the well-known British firm and a local operation run by a prominent Jakarta businessman, who, according to John Cooper, had family connections to the Suharto Government.

Azahari and Noraini took leave from UTM and moved to Jakarta for a year. Azahari's job was to do market analysis and evaluate proposals for property development and investment. It was 1996 and Indonesia's economic frenzy was at its height, just before the Asian crash. The hours were long but the position was high powered and well paid. And Azahari was no ascetic. 'The money that he made and the luxury that he got to enjoy — car with driver, fancy hotels and so on and so forth. He sort of began to enjoy the good life,' his friend 'Dani' later observed.

Highly paid job, fast car, fancy lifestyle, loving wife — Dr Azahari seemed to have it all. His friends could later only guess at what may have changed him. 'His experience in Indonesia would have exposed him to extremes of social division,' said his friend and colleague at UTM John Cooper. 'You don't have to think too seriously as a Muslim to conclude that most Muslims are getting ripped off. It must be easy to get emotional and lose reason. The rich get obscenely rich, the poor are very poor — like in Indonesia. That's what Azahari would have seen.'

Another thing he would have seen was the Suharto Government's ruthless suppression of the Muslim separatists in his wife Noraini's home province of Aceh. By the end of the 1990s, the crackdown would leave an estimated 10,000 people dead and many thousands more tortured or maimed.

Despite all the trappings of his expat lifestyle, one thing Azahari still didn't have that he was desperate for was a child. By this time, he and Noraini were so anxious for a family that they sought the help of a traditional Muslim faith healer, known as a *dukun*. The healer probably told them that they must put all their faith in God if ever they were to be blessed with children. After twelve years of marriage, Noraini quickly conceived and later gave birth to a girl, the first of their three children. After so many years of trying, it must have seemed like a miracle. John Cooper believes this 'pushed Azahari closer' to his faith.

After their year in Jakarta, Azahari and Noraini returned to UTM in Malaysia. On the surface nothing had changed. 'When he came back he still digs fast cars and share investments so I don't reckon [his time in Indonesia] had any profound effect,' said his old friend 'Dani'. Azahari resumed teaching at UTM and he and Noraini had their second child, a boy. But Noraini's throat cancer had advanced further. She finally lost the power of speech and was reportedly forced to give up teaching.[8]

It was around this time that Azahari began to take greater solace in his faith. He started attending religious meetings in Johor, held at the home of one of his colleagues. The weekly sessions were a popular event among staff and students at UTM. They promoted the same 'modernist' principle espoused in UTM's motto — that science and technology should be pursued in tandem with the pursuit of faith.

'The emphasis in all the classes was towards how to educate people in both science and mathematics, technology and religion,' said Azahari's friend 'Dani', who also attended these sessions. 'The message was more about being true to oneself and [increasing] one's efforts to be closer with the creator. There was no mention whatsoever about waging war or the like. In fact, the "jihad" that was discussed was more towards the educational effort, so that one's knowledge in both religion and other worldly knowledge like science, technology, management and so on could be enhanced.'

Azahari's colleague who held these classes was another UTM lecturer named Wan Min bin Wan Mat, a fellow Malaysian who taught project management in the same faculty as Azahari. Wan Min had studied in Britain as well, earning a masters degree in science construction from the University of Manchester.

Wan Min was in his thirties, married and a father of six — 'skinny and quiet, but always smiling', as John Cooper recalled. He was more serious than Azahari and not as sharp. 'Wan Min was an average person academically but very dedicated to his work ... He was a bit conservative, inferior and to a certain extent easily influenced. Nonetheless, he was a kind person and easy going,' according to 'Dani', who also worked with Wan Min.

Wan Min was from Kelantan, Malaysia's most devoutly Muslim state and a stronghold of the opposition Islamic party, PAS. Like many overseas-educated Muslims, Wan Min had a love–hate relationship with the West — admiring its economic progress and standards of education but shunning what he saw as its immoral and decadent ways.

Wan Min was a fervent believer in the concept of Islamic schooling, believing that secular education was a key reason for the corruption and degeneracy of the West. This is a common view among Islamist scholars, one of whom described it this way: 'While people in secular societies are being educated, they are also being morally and ethically degenerated. The education of an immoral human being gives him or her the tools to be more wicked and destructive in this world.'[9] Wan Min shared the view that Muslims must live and learn according to Islamic law.

It was this interest in Islamic education that brought Wan Min and his colleague Dr Azahari into the orbit of Jemaah Islamiyah. The connection was through the JI school Luqmanul Hakiem, run by Muklas among the palm-oil plantations at Ulu Tiram, a short drive from UTM.

By the mid-1990s, Muklas's school was a key meeting place for the leaders and followers of JI. Muklas and his brothers Ali Imron and Amrozi were living at Ulu Tiram, as was Dulmatin, the explosives instructor from Afghanistan. Bashir, Hambali and the young zealot Samudra all commuted regularly to the JI school from Sungai Manggis to lecture the students. Abdullah Sungkar was living closer, supervising the school. Other JI veterans had enrolled their children there, among them the battle-hardened future military chief of JI, Zulkarnaen, back after eight years in Afghanistan.

Muklas later told the Indonesian police how the crucial connection between JI and the UTM academics was made. 'I first met with Wan

Min around 1995,' said Muklas. 'He came to visit my school. Because Wan Min was from Kelantan he was interested in the Muslim boarding-school education system. The state of Kelantan is famous for having many such schools. From that first meeting, Wan Min was sympathetic and interested . . . Then, because Wan Min has expertise in certain fields, such as education, administration, government matters and buildings, eventually I invited him to take part directly in organising my school. Wan Min was willing. So, with the agreement of our teachers, I appointed him chairman of the school foundation.'[10]

Wan Min was instantly drawn to the passionate young preacher from Tenggulun. He invited Muklas to speak at the prayer sessions that he held at his home in Johor and urged his fellow staff and students from UTM to come along to hear him.

At one of these sessions Dr Azahari was introduced to the men from JI. Muklas described how he met Azahari 'in the home of Wan Min in Johor in a praying event'. Islam had become Azahari's new obsession. 'He's a real born-again Muslim,' a Malaysian security official later remarked.[11] Fired by his growing disillusionment about the plight of Muslims, Azahari became a passionate convert to the revolutionary brand of the religion that Muklas preached.

UTM provided a pool of new recruits for JI. Another academic who joined, a lecturer with a PhD in robotics, said later: 'I was instructed to assist in religious sermons in Johor. So several lecturers and I conducted classes for UTM students and for some outsiders. We conducted sermons for the public every week.'[12]

Another recruit was a science graduate who was studying for his masters, Noor Din Mohammed Top. He also attended the sessions at Wan Min's home. Noor Din became a teacher at the JI school, tutoring in maths and geology, and later replaced Muklas as the school's director when Muklas was promoted to the job of leader of JI's Mantiqi 1.[13]

The men from UTM would form the intellectual and administrative powerhouse of JI. Wan Min Wan Mat was appointed to the board of the Luqmanul Hakiem school and was made the head of JI's top *wakalah*, or branch, in Johor. He was later 'appointed chair for the groups in Malaysia and Singapore', according to Muklas. An Australian police report called him 'possibly the CEO of JI'.

While Wan Min was sent for military training in the Philippines, his role was administrative rather than operational. 'My tasks after I replaced Muklas were to give religious training to members via *usroh*; run the education program at Luqmanul Hakiem; run the *dakwah* program and recruit new members; and give a training program for new members.'[14]

Wan Min's account to the police after his capture illustrated the highly compartmentalised structure of JI. 'The jihad operations were run by a special team that was not directly connected with *wakalah* activities. These were all done in secret, and even though I was head of Wakalah Johor, I wasn't part of the operations team. The details of the jihad operations were never explained to me. If my people were needed, I was only told that certain personnel were going to be used, I wasn't told for what purpose. This was to protect security.'

Dr Azahari was also appointed to serve on the board of the Luqmanul Hakiem school. But unlike Wan Min, Azahari's role would end up very much on the operations side. As time went on, Azahari developed another obsession — the chemical composition and construction of bombs. He was later sent to Afghanistan for an advanced course in explosives and returned to write the bomb manual for JI, which he did with the same precision and attention to detail as he used in his thesis, only in language much easier to understand. 'It is better when leaving the bomb factory that the bomber turns the bomb's first safety switch to the "on" position,' wrote Azahari. 'When the bomber sees the target, the second safety switch is turned "on". The bomber is then ready to push the detonating switch. When the vehicle hits the target, the detonating switch is activated.'[15]

Azahari would eventually become so hellbent on his new obsession that he would abandon everything that had been most dear to him. It happened one evening at the end of 2001, when he took an urgent phone call at home in Johor. The news was bad — the Malaysian Government was onto JI and there had been a wave of arrests. 'He was told that his name was on the list of those that would be rounded up by our authorities and decided to flee,' his friend 'Dani' told me. Azahari already had a small overnight bag packed and ready to go. He turned to his beloved wife, Noraini, and said, 'I have a greater cause in life. It is to serve God.' And then he was gone.

While the men from UTM were signing up to join JI in Malaysia, thousands of kilometres away in Afghanistan, Osama bin Laden was on the verge of issuing his Declaration of Jihad against the United States. It was 1996 and bin Laden was on his way back to Afghanistan, where the fanatical turbaned warriors known as the Taliban had swept to power. Their revolution would provide new impetus to Islamic extremists all over the world — and a launchpad for bin Laden's war against the West.

The Taliban roared into Kabul in their Toyota pickup trucks, brandishing AK-47s and declaring, 'We want to recreate the time of the Prophet. We want to live a life like the Prophet lived 1,400 years ago and jihad is our right.'[16]

Their first act was to seize the former President Najibullah and beat him senseless, then drag him behind a jeep for several laps around the palace, before shooting him dead. The bodies of Najibullah and his brother, who just happened to be visiting, were strung up from a post in Kabul's main square.[17] Cigarettes were wedged between their fingers and Afghani notes stuffed in their pockets, to signify the fate awaiting anyone the Taliban viewed as decadent or corrupt.

The Taliban — from the word *talib*, meaning religious student — were the children of the Afghan jihad, many of them orphans and refugees, raised in the camps and militant madrasahs that sprang up along the Pakistan border during the decade-long struggle against the Soviets. After the ensuing seven years of bloody civil war between the rival mujahideen groups, the Taliban saw themselves as Afghanistan's new saviours, the 'cleansers and purifiers of a guerrilla war gone astray, a social system gone wrong and an Islamic way of life that had been compromised by corruption and excess'.[18]

The initial hopes that the Taliban's arrival would bring an end to Afghanistan's years of misery soon turned to dismay at their draconian interpretation of the Koran. 'Thieves will have their hands and feet amputated, adulterers will be stoned to death and those taking liquor will be lashed,' announced Radio Kabul, after the Taliban arrived.

'In shops, hotels, vehicles and rickshaws, cassettes and music are prohibited,' proclaimed another Taliban decree. 'If any music cassette [is] found in a shop, the shopkeeper should be imprisoned and the shop locked.' Flying kites and keeping pigeons were banned, along with dancing at weddings and playing drums. For men there would be no shaving or growing long hair. 'To prevent the British and American hairstyle, people with long hair should be arrested and taken to the religious police department to shave their hair.' As an extra disincentive: 'The criminal has to pay the barber.'[19]

The restrictions on women were far more severe: 'You should not step outside your residence. If you go outside the house you should not be like women who used to go out with fashionable clothes, wearing much cosmetics and appearing in front of every men.' Under the Taliban, women could be seen in public only when swathed in the tent-like burkah, covering everything but their eyes. For those who transgressed: 'They will be cursed by the Islamic Sharia and should never expect to go to heaven.' They could also expect to be beaten by the enforcers from the Department for Promoting Virtue and Preventing Vice, who waited on street corners armed with sticks and with scissors to cut the hair of offending men.

To the most militant Islamists, Afghanistan under the Taliban was the perfect Islamic state. The leaders of Jemaah Islamiyah watched in admiration from afar. The head of JI's Singapore branch sent a letter of support to the Taliban leader, Mullah Mohammed Omar, saying: 'I am glad to inform you that some of our brothers are ready to extend their help for the cause of Islam and Muslims,' and enclosing a $1000 donation.[20]

JI later sent a delegation to Afghanistan to observe the Taliban's style of government first-hand. The two delegates sent from Singapore were deeply impressed, their leader writing again to ask Mullah Omar whether he should now be considered the new caliph, or leader of all Muslims, and if so: 'Is it compulsory upon Muslims in non-Muslim countries to migrate to Afghanistan? In what way can they do so? If all Muslims are required to migrate, what would happen to the mosques, Islamic institutions and other Islamic affairs in their countries? If only some of them are required to migrate, who are these people?'[21]

For Osama bin Laden, the Taliban's Afghanistan provided a perfect new sanctuary. Bin Laden had fled Saudi Arabia in 1991, after being placed under house arrest for turning against the House of Saud. He had then taken refuge in Sudan, as the guest of Hassan al Turabi, leader of the country's National Islamic Front. But after five years and under pressure from the United States, which was growing alarmed at bin Laden's support for Islamic militants in Pakistan, the Sudanese authorities had finally asked him to leave. It was time for bin Laden to find a new home.

Arriving with his coterie of three wives and numerous children, bin Laden was welcomed by the Taliban as an honoured guest, for his role in having helped to defeat the Soviets seven years before. Just as Sungkar and Bashir had done on their flight from Indonesia to Malaysia, bin Laden likened his return to Afghanistan to the seventh-century *hijra* of the Prophet Muhammad from Mecca to Medina, to escape his persecutors for refuge among his followers and to wage war in the name of Islam.

The Saudi multimillionaire set up camp in a cave in the Hindu Kush mountains, where he occasionally received visiting journalists, one of whom described his typically ascetic base: 'It was not comfortable. His quarters were built in an amateurish way with the branches of trees. He had hundreds of books, mostly theological treatises. I slept on a bed underneath which were stored many grenades . . . At night it was very cold, fifteen degrees below zero.'[22]

Bin Laden's cave may have been basic but it did have all the mod cons he needed, like satellite phones and an Apple Mac computer on which he reportedly composed his manifesto of jihad against the West. In August 1996, he issued the first of a series of decrees, entitled 'The Declaration of Jihad on the Americans Occupying the Country of the Two Sacred Places: A message from Osama bin Laden to his Muslim brethren all over the world, and towards the Muslims of the Arabian Peninsula in particular'.

The declaration of jihad was an eloquent and vitriolic litany of the centuries of grievances felt by Muslims, which he blamed on the West. 'The people of Islam have suffered from aggression, iniquity and injustice, imposed upon them by the Zionist/Crusader alliance and their collaborators, to the extent that the Muslims' blood has become the cheapest in the eyes of the world and their wealth has become as loot in the hands of their enemies.'

Bin Laden railed against the spilling of Muslim blood in Palestine and Iraq, in Tajikistan and the Philippines, in Somalia and Chechnya. All of this, he said, 'the world watched and heard' and 'did not respond'. The wrongs he cited culminated in the ongoing presence of US troops in Saudi Arabia, six years after they had landed there to drive the Iraqis out of Kuwait. 'The latest and greatest of these aggressions incurred by Muslims since the death of the Prophet is the occupation of the land of the two Holy Places, the foundation of the house of Islam . . . by the armies of the American Crusaders and their allies.'

The al Qaeda chief signalled that his retribution would be no conventional war. 'Due to the imbalance of power between our armed forces and the enemy forces, a suitable means of fighting must be adopted, using fast-moving light forces that work under complete secrecy. In other words, to initiate a guerrilla warfare, in which the sons of the nation and not the military forces take part.'

The declaration ended with an emotive appeal to Muslims everywhere. 'Your brothers in Palestine and in the land of the two Holy Places are calling upon your help . . . They are asking you to do whatever you can, with your own means and ability, to expel the enemy, humiliated and defeated, out of the sanctities of Islam . . . O you horses of Allah, ride and march on. This is the time of hardship, so be tough.'[23]

Bin Laden's call to arms would inflame militants all over the world, rousing them to rise up against the forces they believed were oppressing them. For the thousands of trained fighters who had returned from Afghanistan to their homelands sworn to carry on the struggle, the new enemy had now been named — the United States and its allies. Bin Laden's cry for jihad resonated from the Middle East to Europe and the United States, and across Southeast Asia from Indonesia and Malaysia to Australia, where the men of JI were getting ready to answer the call.

CHAPTER TWELVE

MANTIQI 4

'USING THESE WELL ORGANISED and methodical concepts of struggle, Jemaah Islamiyah is determined to take the noble steps of collecting, fostering and building strength for the sake of Muslims to re-establish the caliphate and the supremacy of Islamic law in all corners of the earth . . . May Allah bless this jemaah so that it can play a greater role in bringing the Islamic community closer to its aim, which is establishing the caliphate and freeing all slaves from slavery, so that they are enslaved by Allah alone.'

So proclaim the *General Guidelines for the Struggle of Jemaah Islamiyah*, the official bible of JI. The JI book is an impressive piece of work — twenty-four pages of densely typed text in Indonesian, Arabic and a smattering of English, which outlines the group's structure, rules and objectives and its preparations for jihad.

'Human life is only to worship God,' the Guidelines state at the outset, before going on set out the ten principles of JI. These include: 'Our love is for Allah, the messenger and the faithful . . . Our enemies are demonic spirits and demonic human beings . . . Our practise of Islam is pure and total.'

Aside from the ominous rhetoric, the Guidelines read in some parts like a modern human-resources tool for any large organisation. Education and training are described as 'the most important part of personnel development'. The Guidelines state: 'Education and Training is a process which begins with selection, recruitment, training and instilling discipline, and culminates in supervised trials in the field for the purpose of obtaining personnel who are skilled, loyal and able to work effectively and efficiently.'

It could almost be a management primer for McDonald's or Coles Myer — until it comes to the section entitled 'Jihad'. Under the sub-headed 'Functions' is the following list.

1. To smash the forces that continually prevent Islamic proselytising.
2. To get rid of tyranny.
3. To ensure the continued existence and honour of Muslims and to help the weak.
4. To humiliate and terrify the enemies of Allah and prevent their crimes.
5. To differentiate and separate Muslims and infidels and to open the way for a martyr's death.'

Volume 1 of the Guidelines was endorsed by the JI leadership on 17 December 1995. A second volume, which added a JI constitution, was sanctioned at a meeting at Muklas's Luqmanul Hakiem school in Johor on 30 May 1996. The guide book was first uncovered by the authorities when a copy of it was seized, along with Dr Azahari's bomb manual and other texts, in a raid on a JI command post in December 2002. It was one of the few copies preserved. Wan Min told the police that after September 11 'all the books were destroyed'.[1]

The Guidelines detail a strict hierarchy of control. JI is ruled by its emir in conjunction with a Central Leadership Council, which he appoints, known by its Arabic name the Qiyadah Markaziyah. Under this central council are five subsidiary councils with separate tasks. The first is an advisory council known as the *majelis syuro*, made up of 'experts' from the ranks of the jemaah. The others are a *fatwa* council, which issues rulings under Islamic law; a *hisbah* council, which enforces discipline; and a *mantiqi* council and *wakalah* council, responsible for JI's four separate territories and the individual branches, or *wakalahs*, that come under them. The book outlines procedures for appointing council members and for removing the emir if he dies, becomes infirm, is 'proved to have behaved like an infidel' or is deemed 'too weak to manage the organisation'. It also provides rules for setting an annual budget, swearing in members and scheduling meetings, and forbids communications between the various councils and branches, except when approved by the emir.

JI is divided into four *mantiqis*, an Arabic word meaning territorial organisations. Mantiqi 1 was headquarters in Malaysia and included Singapore; Mantiqi 2 covered most of Indonesia, JI's heartland and main area of operations; Mantiqi 3 was the southern Philippines, including Camp Hudaibiyah in Mindanao, along with the Malaysian state of Sabah and the Indonesian provinces of East Kalimantan and North and Central Sulawesi. Finally, there was Mantiqi 4, the last to be established and the least developed. Mantiqi 4 was Australia. It also covered West Papua and, by some accounts, the Maldives as well, and came under the control of JI's Indonesian branch.[2]

The JI Guidelines were distributed among the leaders of the mantiqis, according to Muklas. They were sent with instructions to each branch leader, to educate their members in the Koran, implement Islamic law, collect donations and 'conduct physical and basic training to be ready for jihad.'[3]

⊗

In Australia, the *Guidelines for Struggle* was delivered to the Sydney home of Abdul Rahim Ayub, the man who had hosted Abdullah Sungkar and Abu Bakar Bashir on their first visit to Australia and called the original meeting in Lakemba where the Australian jemaah was formed.

Abdul Rahim's flat in Dee Why, just up from the Go-Lo supermarket, became the headquarters of Mantiqi 4 and Abdul Rahim was officially named its leader.[4] A long-time trusted intimate of Sungkar and Bashir, Abdul Rahim was now also a ranking member of the leadership of JI. His position as a mantiqi head earned him a place on its Central Leadership Council, the Qiyadah Markaziyah. Abdul Rahim was highly regarded by others in this elite group, one fellow mantiqi leader describing him admiringly as a skilled long-term strategist.[5]

As well as dispatching regular reports to the leaders in Malaysia and hosting Sungkar and Bashir's visits to Australia, Abdul Rahim travelled frequently to Indonesia. He made trips to his homeland in 1991, 1992, 1993, 1995 and 1998, staying for three months each time. While little is known about the precise purpose of these trips, on one visit he is known to have met up with the leader of JI's Indonesian branch, Mantiqi 2.[6] He is also known to have attended at least one of the regular twice-yearly meetings of the Central Leadership Council, in the hill-town of Puncak, Bogor, south of Jakarta, where the mantiqi heads gave reports on the activities of their jemaah, such as fundraising, recruitment and training.[7]

Abdul Rahim's deputy was the Australian Indonesian known as Wandi, who ran a halal butcher shop and drove a taxi in Sydney. According to Australian investigators, Wandi trained in the early 1990s in Afghanistan, where he met Abdul Rahman Ayub. Wandi was well known to key leaders in the JI hierarchy in Malaysia. A fellow JI member later testified that Wandi 'knew Hambali well'.[8] Australian investigators have said that Wandi underwent further training in Selangor, Malaysia, attached to a JI cell under Hambali's command named *fiah yarmuk*.

Wandi was also well acquainted with JI's treasurer, Abu Bakar Bafana, with whom he was a co-founder of a company called the Mawashi Corporation. Established in Malaysia in the early 1990s, its interests included halal meat wholesaling and construction. According to Australian investigators, the firm was a key front company for JI, used to channel funds for its activities and provide jobs for its members. A paper trail of dozens of receipts and invoices was later found connecting the Mawashi Corporation with JI members in Australia and Southeast Asia.[9] The company was later sold and today operates as a legitimate corporation with no connections to JI to the author's knowledge.

Abdul Rahim's skills as a long-term strategist were the key to building up Mantiqi 4, steadily and patiently over time. But the job of recruiting in a country like Australia, where Indonesian Muslims are a small minority, was a challenge, made harder still by the schism within the community at Dee Why.

Five years had passed since the split in the jemaah, when the imam Zainal Arifin had quit over Sungkar and Bashir's boycott of the wedding of one of their followers. The local community remained divided between the mainstream group that ran the mosque and the rival group led by Abdul Rahim.

Since the transition from Darul Islam to Jemaah Islamiyah, Abdul Rahim's group had become more clandestine. He and his followers mostly stayed away from the mosque, instead cramming into his two-bedroom flat to meet. 'They were very secretive towards us,' a former member who had quit the jemaah told me. 'They claimed there were enemies everywhere. Anyone who didn't join them or who left their group was the enemy.'[10]

Abdullah Sungkar and Abu Bakar Bashir visited often to supervise the development of Mantiqi 4. They always came together except for one trip each, when they came alone. They generally visited once a year, sometimes twice, though in 1994 they arrived three times — in January, May and December — spending a total of three months in Australia in the space of just over a year. They would typically stay for three to five weeks at a time, often arriving in Melbourne and departing via Sydney or vice versa. The records show they went to Perth once, in 1997.

Discussion of the affairs of Jemaah Islamiyah was confined to the private homes of their followers. In their public appearances at mosques and universities, Sungkar and Bashir denounced the tyranny of Suharto and called for an Islamic state, but made no mention of JI. Their bravado and conviction continued to win them respect in Muslim circles, well beyond the Indonesian community and their own congregation. The imam of the Tempe mosque in Sydney, Sheik Amin Hady, later praised one 'courageous' speech by Sungkar. 'He didn't ask us to take up arms — rather we should express concern that the regime was a dictator . . . and very much against Muslims.'[11]

But in Dee Why, Sungkar and Bashir's highly political sermons were a source of consternation among some mosque-goers who were not followers of JI. 'There were some complaints,' recalled Romzi Ali from the local Islamic Society, 'particularly about Abdullah Sungkar, who spoke quite a lot about politics, especially about the political issues in Indonesia. So some people complain that we shouldn't talk about politics at all in the mosque.' The complaints were conveyed to Sungkar and Bashir. 'We informed the two of them not to talk about anything else but religion in the mosque. If they [want to] speak something about politics — maybe outside the mosque, not inside the mosque.'[12] When the complaints continued, on a subsequent visit Sungkar and Bashir were banned from speaking at the mosque.

On their visits to Sydney the two preachers would often stay in a chocolate-brown block on busy Pittwater Road, Dee Why, next to the wildlife refuge. The location was also a sanctuary for members of their flock. For nearly a decade, unit number seven was used as a safe house for visiting members of JI.

The flat was leased by an Indonesian named Ahmad, who had permanent residency in Australia. He was a member of Sungkar and Bashir's following in Sydney, one of the men who had joined them at that very first meeting in Lakemba. 'Ahmad was the housing guy,' reported another follower. 'That's where everybody stayed.'[13] For two bedrooms, an internal laundry and lockup garage, Ahmad forked out $175 a week, always paid on time and in cash at the real-estate agent's office in Dee Why's main drag.

The agent recalled Ahmad as 'a good bloke' who liked a chat; he spoke English well and dressed like a typical Australian. On weekends, Ahmad liked to go to garage sales to pick up old pieces of crystal tableware to send home to his mother in Indonesia. Unknown to the agent, Ahmad didn't live in the flat himself, but kept it as a halfway house for new JI recruits and visiting VIPs. 'It was known all over Jakarta and Indonesia,' said another follower. 'If you're going to Australia and you want a place to stay, just contact Ahmad.'

The modest two-bedroom unit was home to up to a dozen young men at any given time, mostly new arrivals from Indonesia sent to bolster the ranks of Mantiqi 4. With so many people, there was barely room for furniture, just a coffee table, a TV, a pair of sofas and a dozen sleeping mats stacked neatly against the walls. 'They always wore skirts,' said a neighbour. 'That's how you could tell the new ones.'

Ahmad would pop by most days to check on his young charges, telling the other residents, 'Any problems, just let me know.' But the newcomers kept to themselves. 'They never had any women there,' observed a man from another unit. 'That was strange.' The only complaint the neighbours had was the thumping sounds sometimes heard at night, which prompted one resident to knock on their door to ask them to keep it down. 'They were in there wrestling!' he found to his surprise.

To help pay their expenses, the Indonesians did piecework for a local factory, assembling springs for baby bouncers — 500 springs a week at 30 cents apiece. It was all arranged by Ahmad, who oversaw the assembly work done in the flat and dropped into the company's office in Dee Why to pick up the weekly cheque. The factory owner knew only Ahmad by name; the others he called 'the Arabs'. An employee named Peter would go by the flat once a week to drop off the parts and pick up the assembled springs. While the van was being loaded, Peter would be invited in for a coffee and often got talking to the young men, or at least those of them who could speak English.

'They were very into radical Islam,' Peter told me. 'They said Australia was a good country, and one day it was going to be part of an Islamic state. I said, "You've gotta be joking!" They believed the northern part of Australia belonged to them. They said that historically they had more right to be here than us Westerners. They said that northern Australia used to be part of their fishing and hunting grounds. I said, "You'll have to kick out the rest of the population." And they said, "No, we'll convert them to Islam."'

Mostly in their early twenties, the Indonesians said they were students. One said he was doing business studies, another economics, a third 'religious instruction, while another told Peter, 'We're here to study Western culture.' They said the bearded man in the wall poster that took pride of place in the living room was their teacher; Peter recognised the face later as that of Abu Bakar Bashir.

'I asked them one day, "What's this jihad that you're always talking about?"' said Peter. 'They said, "It's our holy struggle to convert the rest of the world to Islam." I said, "How are you going to do that?" And the guy said, "Either by the book or by the sword."' Peter asked the young Indonesian what he meant. 'He just smiled and said, "It's all symbolic." He said "It is a war, but it's not a war with tanks, it's a war between people."'

The arch-enemy in their 'war' was the dictator, Suharto, according to another man who used to visit the flat for meetings. 'It was always understood that they wanted to kill Suharto or to overthrow him. It was discussed many times . . . It wasn't a matter of how they were going to do it. It was just that that's what they were going to do.'

∽∾

One day a big, overweight stranger lumbered in to the Dee Why mosque. Compared with the Indonesian regulars, the Aussie newcomer with the North Yorkshire accent was a bear of a man, nearly 2 metres in height and weighing close to 100 kilograms. Though physically imposing, the stranger was serious, quietly spoken and obviously sad. He just wandered in, apparently looking for something. 'He had just got divorced from his wife. He was very depressed,' one mosque-goer recalled. 'He started talking to us about it and we gave him some advice.'

The newcomer's name was Jack Roche.[14] 'I had a couple of failed marriages, mainly due to alcohol, or should I say my abuse of alcohol,' Roche told me, years after the event. 'I had lost track of who I was as a person and what my direction and purpose in life was.'[15]

Mired in a mid-life crisis, Roche had got talking to some Indonesians at the factory where he worked. A heavy drinker, he would come in each morning bleary-eyed and hung-over. His teetotal Muslim workmates would ask, 'Why do you do this to yourself every day?' They soon got onto the subject of religion. Roche had always been a sceptic but he was desperate to fill the void in his life; he did some reading and one day he drifted along to a mosque. Suddenly, as Roche told it, 'an alternative lifestyle presented itself — namely Islam'. Within months, Jack Roche had converted. He would later become a crucial member of JI, and much later again, its only member in Australia to be charged with terrorism.

Jack Roche was born in the industrial town of Kingston-upon-Hull, in Yorkshire, England, in 1953, 'Biggest baby of the week, so I'm told, 9 lb 3 oz [approximately 4 kg],' by his own account. His father was in the Royal Air Force and the family was constantly on the move. 'When I was approximately four years old my father was posted to Malta. We all set sail on, if memory serves me correctly, the SS *Uganda* and arrived in Valetta some days later.'

The young Jack attended a school run by nuns and enjoys 'good memories' of this time. But after a year there the family moved again, this time to Scotland — Jack and his three brothers in tow. 'My mother was raised Roman Catholic and made it a point to have us attend Sunday school,' he told me. The Sunday school teacher was a strict Scotsman whose approach, to quote Roche, was 'Dinnae firget te rispect yer elders.' As for his father, 'I later understood that my father's beliefs were to be found at the bottom of a pint glass!'

The family was soon off again, with Roche's father posted to Sarawak and his mother and the four boys shifting to a different town in Scotland, then back to England and yet another new school. The older Roche got, the more troubling his family's unsettled life became. 'The move upset me as I had made many friends and I was very aware of just up and moving. I felt like something had been stolen from me and after that I was reluctant to get especially close to anyone.'

When Roche was thirteen, his mother died. His father remarried a year or so later and was reposted to Germany. Roche became a boarder at the Dukes Grammar School for Boys where, he said, 'All the kids were misfits — I suppose I was one myself . . . I lasted about two years in the boarding part of the school but was "asked to leave" for not adhering to the boarding-school regime.' Roche went to live with his father in

Germany, but, as he recounted, 'By this time I was rebelling against any form of authority . . . When I was almost eighteen, I left home.'

Roche returned to England to look for a job but couldn't find one so he joined the army instead. That didn't work out either. After a few months working odd jobs around England, he hit the hippy trail, travelling to Morocco, Greece and ending up in West Berlin, where he lived for three years.

At twenty-four, Roche upped stumps again, landing this time in Sydney in 1978. He picked up work as a labourer and driving forklifts at factories and warehouses in the city's western suburbs, switching jobs often. After marrying an Australian girl, he got Australian citizenship and had a son, Jens, born in 1980. Roche divorced, remarried, had two more kids and divorced again, all the while drinking himself into near oblivion. He had an unpaid tax bill and was on the verge of bankruptcy. Near rock bottom, he finally found Islam in 1992: 'It offered strong principles upon which to base my life, and clear direction and purpose.'

Roche took to his new-found faith with zeal. He adopted a Muslim name, Khalid Sayfullah, meaning eternal sword of Islam. Eager to explore his new religion, Roche paid a visit one day to the Dee Why mosque. There he met the Indonesian Abdul Rahim Ayub. This was back in the early days of the jemaah, in mid-1993; Abdul Rahim was still living in Melbourne but travelling regularly to Sydney to keep tabs on the congregation at Dee Why. Roche at the time was living in Marrickville.

Always on the lookout for new recruits, Abdul Rahim took a keen interest in the convert Khalid. 'You can't stay there on your own,' the diminutive Indonesian told the burly Yorkshireman. 'You should move to Dee Why, there's a big Muslim community here.' Roche did as he was urged and soon became a regular at Dee Why.

After a lifetime as a loner, Roche found himself warmly welcomed into a tight-knit group, which became his new family. 'Those "friends" I had had before embracing Islam all but disappeared, especially since the bond of alcohol we shared no longer existed,' reflected Roche.

Encouraged by his new friends in Abdul Rahim's jemaah, Roche decided to go to Indonesia 'to learn more about Islam' and to find himself a new wife. 'Oh, you're going shopping?' his friends joked. He left in 1994 and spent two years in Jakarta. He got work as a 'native speaker of English' in a privately owned English language school with more than two dozen branches in Indonesia; all he had to do was speak so the students could hear how English was pronounced. Roche picked up Indonesian as he went and became a fluent speaker.

'In my spare time I was visiting friends recommended to me by my friends in Sydney. All were Muslim and I was learning about Islam from them,' said Roche. In Jakarta, he met a bright young woman from a strict Muslim family, who had studied law but become disillusioned with the secular court system. She had quit her job as a legal assistant and gone to work as a secretary in a furniture export company. She and Roche married in September 1994 and the following year Roche returned to Sydney to be joined later by his bride.

After his return to Australia in November 1995, Jack Roche moved back to Dee Why and got a job in the same factory as Abdul Rahim, assembling wall panelling for offices. The following year, Roche met the two leaders of Jemaah Islamiyah during one of their visits to Sydney. 'I originally met Abu Bakar Bashir in 1996 . . . I liked what he was saying. It was very clear, it all made sense. And I joined a group of people who were actually the organisers of his visits to Australia. I would go and visit him not just at the lectures but at the places he was staying at . . . I was certainly part of the entourage when he came. I certainly went to all his lectures when he was here, or all that I possible could.'[16]

In 1997 Jack Roche was formally inducted into JI, when he swore the *bai'at* to Abdullah Sungkar at Dee Why. Roche believes he was the only Caucasian to do so. His swearing-in took place during a small ceremony in the home of a man who worked as the librarian at the Dee Why mosque. Witnessed by his host and Abdul Rahim Ayub, the large and now bearded Australian known to his new friends as Khalid Sayfullah grasped Sungkar's hand and swore to join the struggle.

Roche thus became a fully fledged member of Mantiqi 4 and one of Sungkar and Bashir's inner circle in Australia. As a native English speaker fluent in Indonesian, Roche was given the task by the two leaders of translating their speeches and other JI texts into English for dissemination within Mantiqi 4. Roche's nom de plume, Khalid Sayfullah, appears on a series of JI lectures and papers published in Australia.

The first piece that Roche translated appeared in October 1996, before his formal induction into JI. It was an article by Bashir entitled 'Indonesia, Democracy, Priests, Parliament and Self-Made Gods'. While it began as a typical tirade against Suharto, its main thrust was to denounce the rival Indonesian Democratic Party of Struggle, headed by the emerging opposition leader, Megawati Sukarnoputri. Bashir's message was that democracy was not the solution to Indonesia's ills; in fact, it was just as bad as dictatorship.

'Within Islam, the creation of laws which regulate the life of man are absolutely in the hands of Allah,' Bashir pontificated. 'Whereas democracy — in accordance with the meaning "sovereignty of the citizens" — is made up of laws and decrees passed by institutions . . . Thus, democracy assumes the form of a new *deen* [way of life] which is placed above the beliefs of the citizenry and by doing so deprives them of Allah's rightful authority.'

While it focused on events in Indonesia, there was a clear meaning in Bashir's article for his congregation living in democratically governed Australia as well: 'There is no doubt any more that, in truth, this situation constitutes *shirk* [disbelief] towards Allah and is an open declaration of disbelief.' To his devotees down-under the message was that they must follow the laws of Islam alone and, if necessary, ignore the laws passed by Australia's elected governments, because, as Bashir put it, 'is prohibited.'

⟞⟝

In Australia, JI's leaders found a willing and widely read outlet to propagate their views. Bashir's denunciation of democracy was published in the militant Islamic magazine, *Nida'ul Islam*, or The Call of Islam, based in Lakemba. This fortnightly magazine of around seventy pages, printed in Arabic and English and complemented by a website, describes itself as 'amongst the best sources of authentic Islamic literature'. It also claims a readership of 4000 in Australia, Europe, North America and elsewhere.[17]

Nida'ul Islam is put out by a group of radicals at Lakemba who call themselves the Islamic Youth Movement (IYM). They congregate at an office in Haldon Street, behind an unassuming shopfront with a sign soliciting donations for 'needy and orphan sponsoring,' and worship at an expansive private prayer room upstairs. The IYM prayer room has been closely monitored by the Australian Security Intelligence Organisation (ASIO) for years because of the vitriolic anti-Western views expressed by some of the men who frequent it.

The IYM's key members were once followers of Australia's senior Muslim leader, the Grand Mufti, Sheik Taj el Din al Hilaly, who has himself been called an extremist. Sheik Taj was almost deported in the 1980s for his virulent and anti-Semitic views. In 1988, in a speech caught on home video, Sheik Taj ranted: 'The present continuing struggle with the Islam nation is a natural continuation of the Jews' enmity towards the human race as a whole . . . Jews try to control the world through sex, then sexual perversion, then the promotion of espionage, treachery and economic hoarding.' He would later call the September 11 attacks on America 'God's work against oppressors'.

Some of the younger firebrands in Sheik Taj's congregation adopted an ideology even more extreme than his own, espousing the puritanical Salafi stream of Islam — similar to Saudi Arabia's Wahhabism[18] — and embracing the militant dogma of the international jihadist movement. A key figure in this was Bilal Khazal, who migrated to Australia in 1987 from Lebanon, where he had been a member of the radical Islamic Tawhid movement.[19] After settling in Lakemba, Khazal became a founding member of the Islamic Youth Movement, whose 'principal activity', according to a 2003 Spanish court document, is 'the recruitment of mujahideen in Australia.'[20]

In the mid-1990s, violence broke out between members of the Lakemba-based IYM and the rival Islamic Charitable Projects Association, based at Bankstown in Sydney's southwest. The series of clashes included a shooting and a stabbing. Sheik Taj eventually expelled the troublesome IYM from the main Lakemba mosque, declaring later in an interview with *4 Corners* that their ideology was 'more dangerous than the AIDS virus'. The renegades split off and established their own separate prayer room, to spread their message to Sydney's Muslim youth, whom they describe on their website as 'the fuel for the Islamic movement in general and the jihad stream in specific'.

While working as a baggage handler for Qantas and running the IYM magazine and website, Bilal Khazal travelled frequently to the Middle East, organising hajj trips to Mecca, until his passport was confiscated by the Australian authorities in 2002. In 2004, Khazal was facing charges of making documents likely to facilitate terrorism, over a book posted on the internet which allegedly outlined how to carry out a range of terrorist acts.

Under Khazal's stewardship, *Nida'ul Islam* was able to obtain a rare interview with Osama bin Laden, just after his Declaration of Jihad in

1996. The article expounded on 'the necessity for armed struggle . . . in order to repel the greater Kufr [infidels]', and quoted bin Laden decreeing that 'terrorising the American occupiers is a religious and logical obligation'. The magazine also ran interviews with the British-based cleric Abu Qatada, accused of heading al Qaeda in Europe; the famous 'blind sheik', Omar Abdul Rahman, imprisoned in the United States over his role in Ramzi Yousef's 1993 bombing of the World Trade Center; and the MILF leader in the Philippines, Hashim Salamat.

The IYM's spiritual leader in Australia is the head of the Ahlus Sunnah wal Jama'ah Association, Sheik Mohammed Omran, who is known by his followers as Abu Ayman. Sheik Omran is an erudite and charismatic man, who is well-connected in international Islamist circles; among his friends he counts the British-based Abu Qatada, whom he hosted on a speaking tour of Melbourne and Sydney in 1994.[21]

Bashir met Sheik Omran personally during his first visit to Melbourne when, according to Omran, they met at the Preston mosque in the city's northern suburbs in 1998. Sheik Omran described Bashir as 'a very peaceful man'.[22] Sheik Omram's followers in the Islamic Youth Movement were happy to give Sungkar and Bashir a forum in their magazine, *Nida'ul Islam*.

The members of Mantiqi 4 became regulars at the IYM's Haldon Street prayer room. Abdul Rahim Ayub and his followers would make the long drive from Dee Why to Lakemba to attend meetings and lectures there. (At one point, Abdul Rahman moved to Lakemba himself, but later shifted back to Dee Why.) The Indonesians were welcomed into the fold, Sheik Omran later declaring, 'They are very lovely people.'[23]

But the men from JI now wanted their own permanent base. Still shunned by the mainstream community at Dee Why, for years they had been forced to hold their meetings and prayer sessions in the cramped confines of Abdul Rahim Ayub's two-bedroom flat. They needed a more auspicious headquarters for Mantiqi 4. And Abdul Rahim had just the place in mind — the brand new mosque being built at Dee Why.

After nearly a decade of collecting donations at Friday prayers and saving up the proceeds from their halal meat runs, Imam Zainal Arifin and his friends in Dee Why were ready to realise their dream. They had already bought a block of land in South Creek Road, Dee Why, and pulled down the old asbestos-riddled Uniting church they had been using as a makeshift mosque. Finally they had enough funds to start building their new place of worship — the first proper mosque in Sydney north of the Harbour Bridge.

But despite the excitement of the project, the community was still bitterly divided. Since the split in the early 1990s when Arifin and his supporters had resigned from Sungkar and Bashir's jemaah, relations between the two groups had remained hostile. Arifin was now vice president of the local Islamic society and his group was in charge of constructing the mosque.

Everyone was pitching in, with working bees held on weekends to level the site, lay cement, cart bricks and build foundations. But the tensions between Arifin's group and Abdul Rahim's jemaah were simmering. 'On Sundays people would come and work voluntarily on the mosque — if one group came, the others wouldn't come, and vice-versa,' recalled a former official of the local Islamic society.[24]

The tensions had worsened since the arrival in Australia of Abdul Rahim's twin brother, Abdul Rahman. The older twin flew in from Indonesia on a false passport using the name 'Mr Abdullah' on 2 December 1997. He was accompanied by his wife and three children, then aged twelve months, two and four years. A fourth child would be born in Australia a year after their arrival.

Abdul Rahman Ayub was a formidable character — physically identical to his twin brother but with poorer English, less amiable and more reserved. The stories of his exploits in the holy war soon had others in the jemaah in awe. 'Well, he had been on jihad in Afghanistan for five years,' remembered Ibrahim Fraser, 'and that's where he had fought alongside Osama bin Laden . . . He always impressed me as a fearless sort of person.'

During his five years in Afghanistan and Pakistan, Abdul Rahman had become a significant figure in the al Qaeda network. He was on first-name terms with top al Qaeda leaders, including bin Laden's military chief, Abu Hafs.[25] Abdul Rahman was a specialist in knife fighting and martial arts. Australian investigators believe that he helped to write the al Qaeda manual on warfare, in particular the section on combat with knives.[26]

Abdul Rahman was also an old comrade of Hambali. They had trained together in Afghanistan and had met again in the Philippines and in the Malaysian state of Sabah, a key transit point for mujahideen travelling from Malaysia and Indonesia to JI's training site, Camp Hudaibiyah, in Mindanao. Abdul Rahman and Hambali knew each other well; by one account they both married in the Philippines at the same time. But it seems there wasn't much love lost between them. Abdul Rahman would always 'kick up a stink' when Hambali's name was raised, according to the JI insider Jack Roche. 'He used to say, "I'm more senior in status than Hambali. He was only there for two years, I was there for five years."'

After arriving in Australia, Abdul Rahman lodged an application for refugee status, claiming he feared persecution or imprisonment if he returned to Suharto's Indonesia, where scores of Muslim activists had been jailed for their beliefs. The evidence given to back his application provides a first-hand version of the activities of the brothers Ayub.

Abdul Rahman listed the grounds for his bid for a protection visa as 'Belief in Islamic state; member of NII' — referring to Negara Islam Indonesia, the alternative name used by JI's forerunner, Darul Islam. He said he had been a member of the *usroh* movement started by Abu Bakar Bashir in the 1980s, when Bashir had set up small communities of his followers to implement Islamic law. Abdul Rahman stated in his application that he wanted to overthrow the Indonesian Government and its state creed, Pancasila.

In support of his application, Abdul Rahman gave a detailed account of his recent activities and how he had been sent to Australia by Abdullah Sungkar and Abu Bakar Bashir. After five years in the Afghan jihad, he had returned to Indonesia as 'a senior cadre of that organisation' and 'propagator of activities for the district of Jakarta'. It was in this testimony that he revealed working under the man he called Ibnu Taib, whose real name is Abu Fatih, the leader of JI's Indonesian branch, Mantiqi 2. Abdul Rahman said that he was 'on the next rung of the hierarchy, in charge of the group's activities in Jakarta'.

Abdul Rahman claimed he had been arrested in Indonesia in a new government crackdown in 1996 and jailed for three months. He then fled to Malaysia to join Sungkar and Bashir, intending to stay with them there in exile. But the emir and his deputy had other plans. As Abdul Rahman told the Refugee Review Tribunal: 'The leaders advised him that he would be better off fleeing for Australia.' He was sent back to

Indonesia to train up a new leader for his Jakarta branch, then flew to Sydney in December that year.

A letter from Abu Bakar Bashir was presented to the Refugee Review Tribunal to support Abdul Rahman's bid for protection. Bashir's letter was headed 'Declaration' and stated:

> With this, I,
> Name: Abu Bakar Ba'syir
> Address: lot 56, Jalan Bawah, Sungai Manggis . . . Malaysia
> declare that Mr Abdul Rahman Ayub is a member of the 'Usroh Movement' group which I, together with Ustad Abdullah Sungkar, established in 1984, in Surakarta, Central Java.

Bashir's letter said that Abdul Rahman's role in Australia was to provide 'guidance' to others in the group. It ended: 'I submit this declaration in order to state the truth. Malaysia, 3rd March, 1998' and was signed by Bashir. A separate letter was provided from Abdullah Sungkar, stating that Abdul Rahman 'acts as a co-ordinator' of the group in Australia. A third letter vouching for the fact that he was Abdul Rahim's brother was provided by JI's translator, Jack Roche.

The tribunal's summary of Abdul Rahman's evidence read: 'Soon after his arrival in Australia, the leaders came from Malaysia and appointed [Abdul Rahman] as the leader of the NII in this country.' This account of Sungkar and Bashir's visit is supported by immigration records which show the two leaders flew into Australia using their aliases in December 1997 — just three days after Abdul Rahman arrived — and stayed for a month. However, the claim that he was appointed 'as the leader' was clearly an exaggeration designed to boost his case, just like his claim of imprisonment, which the tribunal later found to be 'concocted'.

According to JI followers, the younger twin, Abdul Rahim, who had been in Australia since the 1980s, remained the emir of the Australian branch, now assisted by his brother. A handwritten note found much later in the home of one of their members supports this. The note, written in Indonesian, was seized with other documents from a house raided in the wake of the Bali bombings. It is headed 'Ko Organisasi Mantiki Australia IV'. 'Ko Organisasi' is an abbreviated term meaning organisational command. The note listed Abdul Rahim as *ketua* (leader) and his twin Abdul Rahman as *penasehat* (adviser). It named the halal butcher known as Wandi as *wk ketua*, an abbreviation for deputy leader.

While he waited for the verdict on his visa, Abdul Rahman, his wife and three children moved in with his brother, Abdul Rahim, and his family in their now very crowded two-bedroom flat. As well as being an 'adviser', the would-be refugee, Abdul Rahman, became the imam for Mantiqi 4.

An Arabic speaker who had studied the Koran in Pakistan, Abdul Rahman was regarded as an authority on Islam and on jihad. With his five years of combat and training in Afghanistan, Abdul Rahman was also seen as more of an action man than his twin: 'Abdul Rahim had never been to jihad himself — he was just a great talker,' said one former follower. But the brothers shared the same militant views: 'Abdul Rahim and Abdul Rahman always both said the Abu Sayyaf were the greatest Muslims — "These are true Muslims" — that's what Abdul Rahim said.'[27]

With Abdul Rahim's affable manner and skills as a strategist and leader combined with his brother's status as an Afghan veteran, the Ayub twins made a formidable pair. 'Both the Ayub brothers were likeable. Their charisma was strong,' their colleague Jack Roche told me. 'They were very strict in their beliefs . . . However, below the surface they were very singled-minded and determined, through fair means or foul, to have things their way.'

The presence of the older twin, Abdul Rahman, deepened the divide in Dee Why between the JI jemaah led by the Ayub brothers and the mainstream group headed by Zainal Arifin, which was in charge of building the new mosque. Abdul Rahman's appointment as imam for the jemaah was a recipe for further tension.

'There was [now] two imams in the area,' reported Gabr el Gafi, a local businessman who was overseeing construction of the new mosque. 'One was Abdul Rahman and his group and the other was Zainal and his group, so there was two imams in the area or two leaders of two separate communities . . . They did not get on. They still came, some of them [the Ayubs' group], to Friday prayers, but you could tell from their faces they were not happy.'

Keen to ensure the division didn't disrupt work on the new mosque, Gabr el Gafi went around to Abdul Rahim's place one day to try to sort things out. 'I asked him, "What's your group?" He said their leader was an imam in Malaysia and that they took instructions from him and followed his orders.' A newcomer to the politics of the jemaah, el Gafi was amazed. 'He told me personally that they were taking instructions from overseas . . . I was shocked. I said, "We don't take instructions from anybody."'[28]

The Ayub brothers now began a campaign to get rid of Zainal Arifin and instal Abdul Rahman as the main imam for Dee Why. The push won the support of some moderates who were not JI members but believed Abdul Rahman to be better qualified for the job. From JI's standpoint, having its man appointed as imam would have been a major boost for the Australian branch, delivering control of the new mosque and a brand-new headquarters to Mantiqi 4.

The hostilities would later end up in court, with a complaint and summons issued under the Crimes Act in the name of Zainal Arifin, identifying the Ayub twins as 'members of a faction within the Mosque which is strenuously opposed to the beliefs of the complainant and his friends in respect to the administration and running of the Mosque'. The summons said: 'The complainant has been threatened many times . . . The defendant [Abdul Rahim Ayub] and his brother have initiated those threats. These have included death threats.'

The rival camps finally came to blows one Saturday during a working bee at the mosque. The twins had been there that morning labouring on the site along with half a dozen of their group, including the burly Australian convert, Jack Roche. When Zainal Arifin turned up for a scheduled meeting of the management committee, he was furious to find the Ayub brothers there. 'We didn't want anyone to come if they were not a member of the committee,' complained Zainal. 'It was a committee meeting. We told Abdul Rahim you can't bring your group because it's not a general meeting, it's a committee meeting.'

By the account of one witness, 'Zainal pointed at Abdul Rahim and said, "You get out!" It looked like Zainal was going to assault him. That's when the punch-up started.' The twins and their supporters moved in. 'Abdul Rahim was swearing very badly,' said Arifin. 'Abdul Rahman was very upset and angry . . . he just bashed me in my face, and many people just come, just grab me and somebody punch me on the front.' Jack Roche claimed it was Arifin who threw the first punch, while another witness said Arifin provoked the fight by making threatening gestures but that Abdul Rahim struck out first. Arifin's complaint to the court started: 'The defendant and his brother made threats to kill the complainant and then proceeded to assault him in company with six other men.'

The brawl was reported to the local police. At their suggestion, Arifin took out Apprehended Violence Orders against the Ayub twins, claiming he feared further threats and assaults. Abdul Rahim was summonsed to face the Manly Local Court and ordered not to go within 100 metres of Arifin's home or workplace for three months or 'engage in conduct that intimidates the protected person'. Abdul Rahman, who was summonsed for a separate hearing, failed to show up in court, perhaps fearing that the case might put a swift end to his bid for refugee status in Australia. An AVO was issued against him in his absence, prohibiting him from going near Arifin for twelve months.

Since Arifin was the imam and vice president of the mosque society, the Ayub twins were now effectively barred from the new mosque. Their hopes of a takeover were dashed. They would have to look elsewhere for a permanent headquarters for Mantiqi 4.

Within weeks of the punch-up, the Ayub brothers and their families would pack up their belongings in Sydney and move to Perth to set up a new base. JI's leaders would eventually become impatient with the slow progress in Australia. But right now their attention was on Indonesia, where far more dramatic events were unfolding.

CHAPTER THIRTEEN

∿

TEAR THEM TO SHREDS

THE DICTATOR LOOKED GREY and somehow shrunken as he stepped up to the microphone in the Presidential Palace in Jakarta. It was just after 9 a.m. on 21 May 1998 when Suharto appeared on national television to utter these historic words: 'I have decided to declare that I cease being the President of the Republic of Indonesia, effective from the time of this statement.' After thirty-two years in absolute power, it was all over in a minute. The thousands of students gathered around TV sets in the national parliament building erupted, dancing and screaming in the corridors, their fists punching the air; they banged drums and cavorted like children in the ornamental pond; many of them simply wept.

Suharto was swept from the presidency just as he had seized it, on a wave of bloody violence. Fuelled by the collapse of the economy in the Asian economic crisis of the late 1990s, then ignited by the shooting of six student protesters, an explosion of rioting and looting had left hundreds of people dead and thousands of homes, shops and offices destroyed. Students had occupied the parliament, vowing to stay there until Suharto resigned. When he finally did, the TV pictures showed students falling to their knees and praying out loud, arms outstretched, giving thanks to Allah.

Suharto's resignation was greeted with jubilation in Malaysia by Abdullah Sungkar and Abu Bakar Bashir. They immediately began making plans to return to their homeland to seize this new opportunity to push for an Islamic state. 'When Suharto fell, myself and Abdullah Sungkar put out a leaflet, calling for the struggle to establish Islamic law to be intensified,' Bashir said later.[1]

The document they released was more than just a leaflet. It was a major political manifesto, entitled 'The Latest Indonesian Crisis: Causes & solutions', which set out plainly their vision for Indonesia post-Suharto. It was translated into English in Australia by Jack Roche and published in the Islamic Youth Movement's magazine, *Nida'ul Islam*.

'Whoever leads Indonesia, we must realise that the struggle to come must be directed towards smoothing the way for strengthening the laws of Islam,' the JI leaders declared. 'We must understand that this nation is a gift from Allah and it must be based on the Quran and the Sunnah, without exception. Only this will save Indonesia from the crisis.'

This time, for the men from Ngruki, there would be no turning back. Their treatise contained a stark ultimatum to those who would rule Indonesia: 'We have two choices before us:

'1. Life in a nation based upon the Quran and the Sunnah, or

'2. Death while striving to implement in their entirety laws based upon the Quran and Sunnah.'[2]

Five years after JI's creation, the rhetoric of its leaders increasingly echoed in language and tone the pronouncements of the jihadist icon, Osama bin Laden. After their long years in exile, the two preachers had firmly embraced the international Islamist view that their own struggle in Indonesia was part of a much larger campaign to end the 'humiliation and disgrace' of Muslims worldwide.

'In truth,' declared Sungkar and Bashir, 'the disaster which has befallen the Islamic *umma* [community] in this 20th century commenced with the fall of the [Islamic caliphate] in the month of March 1924. This event was the starting point of the crisis which has befallen the Islamic community throughout the various nations of the world . . . The reasons for the crisis [in Indonesia] were because we neglected and failed to be thankful for the blessings of Allah.'

As the two dissidents prepared to return to their homeland, they stepped up their campaign to enlist support — for their cause and bin Laden's — sending letters to dozens of fellow clerics in Indonesia urging them to join the struggle. The letters, some of which were intercepted by Indonesian intelligence, reportedly contained a message from bin Laden: 'The most important obligation for Muslims nowadays

[is] to work hard in order to free the Arabian lands from the grip of the enemy of Allah, [especially] the American Christians and Jews.' The message reportedly urged them to 'prepare for a jihad against the Americans'. For those who wished to meet the al Qaeda chief personally, the JI leaders said they were 'willing to show the most secure way to visit Osama whenever the Islamic prominent figures would like to do so.'[3]

Bin Laden's war against the United States and its allies was about to begin. Since returning to Afghanistan and issuing his original Declaration of Jihad in 1996, the al Qaeda chief had spent two years marshalling his forces for the holy war to come. In February 1998, he had issued a second fatwa, which signalled that hostilities were about to begin.

Bin Laden's public announcement from his mountain lair in Afghanistan was a dramatic affair. Journalists were summoned to a camp near Khost for the occasion, which one of them described: 'I could see a plume of dust coming and then I saw three cars coming and these hooded guys escorting Osama. Then Osama came out of the car and the moment he stepped out there was shooting, you know, frenzied shooting. And these guys firing RPGs — rocket propelled grenades — at the mountains.'[4]

Flanked by masked gunmen with military assault rifles, bin Laden took centre stage at a table set up with microphones. To his right sat his trusted adviser and personal physician, Ayman al Zawahiri, whose Egyptian Jihad Group had been one of the first to join forces with al Qaeda. On bin Laden's left sat his other key lieutenant, al Qaeda's then military chief, Muhammad Atef, also known as Abu Hafs al Masri.

Bin Laden and his deputies were there to announce the inauguration of the World Islamic Front for Jihad against the Jews and the Crusaders, a coalition of Islamist groups from Egypt, Pakistan and Bangladesh, under whose banner his war against the West would be conducted. Also present were two sons of the Egyptian Sheik Omar Abdul Rahman, who was by then serving a life sentence in a US jail for his role in the 1993 bombing of the World Trade Center. The two sons handed out a laminated card with a picture of their father praying and a message from him in Arabic to all Muslims: 'Divide their nation, tear them to shreds, destroy their economy, burn their companies, ruin their welfare, sink their ships and kill them on land, sea and air . . . May Allah torture them by your hands.'[5]

Bin Laden's new fatwa flagged to his followers exactly how the jihad should be waged. 'We hereby give all Muslims the following judgement: The judgement to kill and fight Americans and their allies, whether civilians or military, is an obligation for every Muslim who is able to do so in any country . . . In the name of Allah we call upon every Muslim who believes in Allah and asks for forgiveness to abide by Allah's order by killing Americans and stealing their money anywhere, any time and whenever possible.'

Nine weeks later, simultaneous truck bombs destroyed the US embassies in Kenya and Tanzania. The explosions killed 224 people and injured hundreds more. It was al Qaeda's first major attack, timed for the eighth anniversary of the arrival of US troops in Saudi Arabia. Bin Laden told a Pakistani journalist: 'Tell America the war has just begun.'[6]

United States retaliation was swift but clumsy. US cruise missiles aimed at al Qaeda camps in Afghanistan killed sleeping villagers and only a handful of his troops, while an attack on a supposed chemical weapons plant in the Sudan destroyed a pharmaceutical factory that produced half the nation's medicines. 'Whoops! What a Cock-up!' was the headline in one British newspaper.

America's bungled revenge coincided with President Clinton's disingenuous denials of his sexual tryst with the White House intern Monica Lewinsky. The timing only compounded the outrage in the Muslim world. 'The US President made a gross mistake when he thought he could divert attention from his sexual and ethical scandal through barbaric, unjustified missile attacks against Sudan and Afghanistan,' railed one Islamist group in London.[7]

The ill-aimed US strikes on impoverished Sudan and Afghanistan elevated Osama bin Laden from a figurehead among Islamic extremists to a popular hero throughout much of the Muslim world. Bin Laden's friend, the Sudanese Muslim leader Hassan al Turabi, chortled: 'Now — ho, ho! — You raised him as the hero, the symbol of all anti-West forces in the world. All the Arab and Muslim young people look to him as an example.' Turabi warned that America's own actions would 'create 10,000 bin Ladens'.[8]

In 1999, after fourteen years in exile, Abdullah Sungkar and Abu Bakar Bashir went home. 'When I arrived in Solo, I stayed at my parents-in-laws' house ... for about five months,' Bashir recounted. 'I then returned to the Al Mukmin school in Ngruki.'[9]

By the time they got back to Solo, Indonesian politics had descended once again into disarray. The self-described 'crazy scientist' and former Suharto deputy, Dr B.J. Habibie, was now in the presidential palace. A committed secularist like his predecessor, Habibie had no time for talk of an Islamic state. Determined instead to be remembered as the man who brought democracy to Indonesia, the pint-sized aerospace engineer educated in Germany had embarked on a frenzy of reform.

While *reformasi* had been long called for, the loosening of control after thirty-two years of dictatorship had unleashed long-suppressed tensions between Muslims and Christians in the provinces. Violence had erupted in Ambon in the Maluku islands and in Sulawesi as well. And the Catholic-dominated province of East Timor had begun its slide towards chaos, after Habibie's impetuous decision to call a referendum on independence.

After returning to Solo, Sungkar and Bashir established a new base at the Mahad Ali Islamic University.[10] Its campus had become a centre of support for the dissidents during their years in exile. Several former staff from their Ngruki school had gone on to teach there and one of the university's directors, Abu Dujanah, would later be identified as first secretary and treasurer of the JI Leadership Council, the Qiyadah Markaziyah.[11]

JI's new headquarters in Solo now became a new hub for Sungkar and Bashir's disciples, as the men who had followed them into exile flowed back to Indonesia to resume the struggle on their home soil. Among the first to return was Muklas's reformed younger brother Amrozi. After several years living and working at JI's Luqmanul Hakiem school in southern Malaysia, Amrozi arrived home in his village of Tenggulun, about two hours' drive from Solo, with a new wife — the former cook from the JI school[12] — and another child. 'We had a daughter named Khaulat and we came back with her towards the end of 1999,' Amrozi confirmed.[13]

The Amrozi who came back to Tenggulun was a very different man from the one who had gone away. His oily jeans had been replaced by a Muslim tunic and cap; he sported a wispy beard, while his new wife wore a full-face burkah. One of the wives he had left was stunned at the change: 'His clothes were all different and his attitude was very different when he returned . . . He was not the same man at all.'[14]

The family which had once despaired of Amrozi could finally be proud of its formerly recalcitrant son, according to the oldest brother, Khozin: 'Before going to Malaysia he talked about driving fast, hanging out with friends, but after coming back he talked about *ulamas* who preach Islam. Before he went to Malaysia when he heard the call to prayer he would keep working, but after Malaysia he would stop to pray.'[15]

The youngest brother, Ali Imron, had returned to Tenggulun earlier, to become a teacher at the family's Al Islam school in the village, where he was busy passing on the lessons he had learned in Afghanistan. 'When I returned I was an Afghan alumnus, so I just thought it was, well, fitting for Afghan alumni to be dealing with jihad matters . . . While I was teaching students at the boarding school I continued to plan the concept of jihad. I planted my radical thoughts on those students, both boys and girls . . . Wherever I went, whatever was being discussed, I preached about jihad.'[16]

Ali Imron was so caught up with jihad that he missed the birth of his first child, a girl born prematurely in 1999. After a few days at home the infant's condition deteriorated and Ali Imron had to rush her to hospital by ambulance where she was hooked up to tubes and intravenous drips. After two months, they decided to turn off the life support and take the baby home. She died on the way. 'There wasn't any sadness,' Ali Imron later told the BBC. 'It didn't reduce my intensity or [cause me to] reconsider my well-charged spirit for jihad. That remained the same. That was how it was. Losing a child wasn't enough to change me.'

Amrozi, who had never been to Afghanistan, was keen to join the ranks of the jihadists, but, as always, had to wait for someone else to give him direction. 'I had been back at home for nearly a year, it had been a year and I had started to think about what job I should do. At about the same time that I was thinking about this, I ran into some friends I had met in Malaysia, the ones who had been to Afghanistan. We were reunited and began to meet.'

Amrozi's meeting up with his old friends from Malaysia was no fluke. In the political flux after the fall of Suharto, JI was regrouping in Indonesia. One of the key figures who had returned to Solo, was the hardened JI veteran Zulkarnaen, who had spent eight years in Afghanistan and been chief instructor of the JI trainees. After JI's formation, he was made a member of its Leadership Council and given the powerful position of *askary* chief, head of its military wing.[17]

In June 1999, Zulkarnaen summoned his fellow Afghan veterans to a meeting at Bashir's new base at the Mahad Ali University in Solo. His purpose was to remind them that the reason they had gone to Afghanistan was so they could come home and wage jihad.[18] There were reportedly some twenty men present. Amrozi and Ali Imron were there, along with Ali's classmate from Afghanistan, Mubarok, who was also teaching at the Al Islam school in Tenggulun. Also there was Amrozi and Ali Imron's older brother, Muklas, who by this stage had handed over the running of the JI school in Johor to the UTM graduate, Noor Din Mohammed Top, in order to focus on JI activities in Indonesia.

A year had passed since Suharto's fall and Indonesia was no closer to achieving an Islamic state. Militants like Zulkarnaen and the brothers from Tenggulun were impatient for action. 'This society is already so corrupted that it cannot be cured simply through preaching,' Muklas explained later.[19] He and his confreres wanted jihad now.

But not everyone shared this view. In the aftermath of Suharto, divisions were emerging within Jemaah Islamiyah over how to carry on the struggle. While the exiles fresh back from Malaysia believed it was time for armed rebellion, there were moderates as well in JI's ranks, mainly in the Indonesian branch, Mantiqi 2. Those who had stuck out the years of repression under Suharto took a long-term strategic view and resisted the immediate resort to force. The divide has been documented by the International Crisis Group's Sidney Jones:

'When Suharto fell, JI's Malaysia-based central command decided that Indonesia was ripe for jihad ... Abdullah Sungkar asked Achmad Roihan, a Mantiqi 2 leader, why it had not yet begun. Roihan, reflecting the views of the more cautious Mantiqi 2 leaders, said that human resources were insufficient and there were no clear operational targets. JI needed to step up education and training inside Indonesia and get a stronger local support base before it could act ... Mantiqi 2 leaders also questioned whether there was a clear enemy to fight in Indonesia ... They believed it would be a mistake to expend scarce resources on waging a jihad under such circumstances and argued instead for a long-term strategy to build up cadre and a target date of 2025 for establishing an Islamic state in Indonesia.'[20]

This conservative view was anathema to hotheads like the brothers from Tenggulun, and the divide erupted dramatically at the meeting called by Zulkarnaen in Solo. The head of Mantiqi 2, Abu Fatih (also known as Ibnu Taib), was 'reportedly lambasted by several of those present', according to Sidney Jones. His critics included Amrozi, Ali Imron and their friend Mubarok, who blasted the Indonesian branch leader for being 'too slow and bureaucratic'.

Zulkarnaen and his supporters, including the brothers from Tenggulun, were tired of waiting for orders from Mantiqi 2. They were ready to join their own holy war — and they had just the place. As Amrozi put it later: 'Everyone wanted to do jihad in Ambon.'

The long-simmering strife between Muslims and Christians in Ambon had boiled over into a raging civil war. It was as good as a new Afghanistan for the men from JI. Zulkarnaen and his group agreed to send a team of jihadists to join the fight, and divided up tasks such as recruiting, fund-raising and sourcing weapons. Amrozi was given the job — not for the last time — of buying explosives to make bombs.

As the arguments continued over how to carry on the struggle, JI convened a seminar to decide on a strategy. The theme of the conference was headlined in a JI document called the Seminar Report, which outlined in detail the agenda for the gathering and the matters that were discussed. It was entitled: 'Looking at the Future of Jihad staged by Jemaah Islamiyah in the ASEAN region: Evaluating the development of the JI movement in Mantiqi 2'.[21]

The Seminar Report does not state where or when the conference was held but it was clearly in the aftermath of Suharto's resignation and aimed at mapping out a plan of action for the new Indonesia. The seminar was attended by officers, cadets and trainees. It identified Mantiqi 2, Indonesia, as 'the main operational ground of Jemaah Islamiyah' and stated for the record: 'Islamic jihad is an aim which we will pursue.' It also stated: 'We need to expand our operations in ASEAN.'

The delegates held a free-wheeling discussion on the 'obstacles, impediments, challenges, threats and opportunities' facing Jemaah

Islamiyah. They were presented with a report on the strengths of the enemy versus the strengths of JI. Under the heading 'Enemies' Strength', it listed the 'rapid political changes after the fall of Suharto, marked by the emergence of new political parties'; the dominance of non-Islamic media; the strong grip still held by the military; and the country's worsening economic crisis, rising poverty and national debt. This section ended on a positive note: 'Actually the situation is an open opportunity for everyone who has an interest against the ruling regime.'

Under the next heading, 'Our Own Strength', was this summary of JI's membership in Indonesia: 'We have more than 2,000 members (plus 5,000 trainees)', stating that these were spread across nine separate branches around the archipelago. There was also a report on training in the Islamic Military Academy of JI, including samples of the examinations undertaken by trainees.

The report listed JI's 'handicaps', such as the distance between branches 'hindering speed and flexibility'; the lack of funding and facilities; and noted 'our quality and quantity compared to our enemies in the region are far from adequate'. Another obstacle mentioned was being surrounded by Muslims with 'weak religious devotion', their practice of Islam eroded by 'the influence of TV, various ideologies, secular lifestyles, radio, etc, which degrades morals'.

The Seminar Report posed a range of alternative strategies for JI. The first option was 'to topple the government of Indonesia.' This was rejected, on the basis that 'the people are not ready, thus the bearer of truth may be antagonised by the society, or Islamic sharia [may be] perceived as a burden'. The second option was 'to take over parts of Indonesia as Qoidah Aminah', an Arabic term meaning a secure base; while the third option was described as 'movement with command forces'. The Seminar Report concluded that the 'expected pattern' that JI would follow was a combination of options two and three, namely taking over parts of Indonesia 'to secure Qoidah Aminah', a secure base from which to conduct 'military operations'.

This was JI's ambitious plan — to take over parts of Indonesia as its own 'secure base', while preparing the population for its eventual Islamic state. It was already clear which parts of Indonesia JI would target first — the flashpoints like Ambon and Sulawesi, where sectarian conflicts were raging. These home-grown holy wars would become a new crucible for the jihadists of JI.

The mustachioed Kuwaiti slipped into Indonesia hardly noticed amid the turmoil surrounding Suharto's demise. He came on a false passport and moved around to avoid detection, eventually settling south of Jakarta, in a village of luminous green rice paddies and thatch-roofed concrete houses.

'He said he was from Ambon, he didn't have any parents — that's all that I know,' said the woman in the black burkah who answered the door of his house. The stranger had claimed he was a businessman, that he sold handicrafts and pearls. In fact he was 'the senior al Qaeda rep in Southeast Asia', Omar al Faruq, reassigned from the Philippines to Indonesia in 1998.

The woman in the burkah was Mira Augustina. It was October 2002 when I knocked on her door with a team from *4 Corners*. The first thing I noticed was Mira's sorrowful brown eyes; they were all I could see of her, peering through the slit in her billowing black shroud.

Mira hesitated then let us in and showed us to a purple satin sofa next to a tank of wriggling orange fish in her lounge room. Mira sat, her hands emerging from the garmet to fidget with the folds of heavy cloth. (Even her feet were covered for modesty's sake in socks and thongs.) Clutching a chubby toddler, she reluctantly answered my questions about the total stranger she had married four years before.

'I met him in the morning at nine o'clock, for only a short time, and he said, "I want to marry you. Would you like to or not?" And after evening prayers I decided yes.' Unknown to Mira Augustina, her betrothed was about to be thrown out of Indonesia unless he could find a wife. While Faruq's role with al Qaeda remained undetected, his arrival as an illegal immigrant had been picked up and he was facing deportation.[22] Faruq needed someone to marry — and Mira's father, a mujahideen commander in Ambon, had been happy to help.

'It's not possible that my father would have married me to a terrorist, it's just not possible,' Mira told me, her eyes welling with tears. 'And I would never dream of marrying a terrorist because I would have to consider my children and myself.'

The toddler that Mira jiggled in her lap as she spoke was Faruq's daughter, a cute three-year-old, though uncommonly chubby for a child in rural Indonesia. I wondered if it was all the foreign TV crews plying her with lollies, as we did that day. Mira's child would never see her father again, unless perhaps at the local newsstand on an old copy of *Time* magazine, which splashed Faruq's picture across its cover after his capture in June 2002.

Until his arrest made world headlines, the man from al Qaeda had been barely known in his village in Bogor. 'Faruq was quite solitary,' the village leader told us. 'He didn't mix with his neighbours. As far as the citizens here went, they really only met him in the mosque at prayer times . . . He was the sort of person who spoke little, he rarely socialised and only met with his neighbours in the street. At the most he would say, "Peace be with you," that sort of thing.'

Faruq initially based himself in Makassar on the island of Sulawesi in Indonesia's northeast, just as street fighting between Christian and Muslim gangs was flaring into full-scale sectarian warfare in late 1998. Faruq's first contact there was an old comrade from the Khalden camp in Afghanistan, an Indonesian named Syawal Yasin, the son-in-law of JI's leader, Abdullah Sungkar.[23] Yasin had returned to his home town, Makassar, to recruit Muslim fighters for this new provincial jihad.

Faruq's second key contact was another Indonesian, Agus Dwikarna, a close associate of Abu Bakar Bashir. Dwikarna ran the local branch of an Islamic 'charity' called Kompak, which made recruitment videos to entice young Muslims to sign up for the local jihad, and then helped to train them. Dwikarna was also the Indonesian representative for the Saudi charity, Al Haramein.

Faruq's own explanation of his activities and how he worked with these local operators was later summarised by US intelligence: 'Faruq was taking over the Indonesian mujahideen community to prepare for al Qaeda's terrorist acts in Southeast Asia.'[24] By Faruq's account, he was funded by a bin Laden lieutenant named Rashid, who sent money via Dwikarna's Saudi charity. 'Faruq said that Al Haramein was the funding mechanism of all operations in Indonesia. Money was laundered through the foundation by donors from the Middle East . . . Faruq was given orders by Rashid to get money transferred to the foundation's office in Jakarta.'[25]

Al Faruq and Agus Dwikarna used al Qaeda's money to set up a new militia group known as Laskar Jundullah, or Army of Allah, to fight

Christians in the provinces. The militia was described by US intelligence as the 'paramilitary wing' of Bashir's Indonesian Mujahideen Council, which was formed later, in 2000. Faruq's role was providing 'technical expertise' from al Qaeda. Laskar Jundullah grew to have six separate divisions and a fighting strength of 2000 men.[26] It later merged with a group recruited earlier from the ranks of JI, which called itself Laskar Mujahideen. (The most notorious militia group, Laskar Jihad, headed by Jafar Umar Thalib, was formed later and quite separately from JI.)

These militias were central to the strategy adopted by JI's leaders, according to the confessions of al Faruq, as summarised by US intelligence: 'Bashir continues to envision a separate Islamic state and he encourages the escalation of a religious war between Muslims and Christians in Indonesia. In a lecture to Ambon community leaders, TNI [army] officers and the Indonesian police in 1999, Bashir preached the killing of as many Christians as possible and praised the TNI and police massacres of Christians in the province.' Bashir even ordered the bombing of a mosque in Jakarta in 1999, according to al Faruq, and 'blamed Christians for the act to foment sectarian strife'.

It was all part of the JI game plan, developed in consultation with al Qaeda and funded from the Middle East, by Faruq's account. 'Faruq said that Al Qaeda encourages Bashir's goal to spark a religious civil war in Indonesia, in order to achieve his vision of a pure Islamic state under Islamic law. Bashir's plan of training jihadists and massing weapons and ammunition has been coordinated with "Rashid", a senior lieutenant of Osama bin Ladin. "Rashid" also acts as a representative of Gulf-state sheiks who are Al Qaeda financiers and who have committed ample funds, weapons, ammunition and computers to support this war.'[27]

❧

By 1999 another troubled province, East Timor, was spiralling into anarchy. After twenty-four years of brutal Indonesian occupation, the referendum on independence, hastily called by President Habibie, was set down for the end of August. Australia had played a central role in this historic decision. After backing the occupation for two decades in the face of public protest, the Australian government had sensed the chance for change after Suharto's fall, and thrown its support behind the push for self-determination.

'It made Pak Habibie angry because it came from Australia,' the Foreign Minister Ali Alatas claimed later. 'Why should Australia get involved?'[28] Ignoring Australia's entreaties for a slow and gradual handover, the petulant Habibie had announced the East Timorese could go free when they wished, dismissing the province as 'a millstone' and 'nothing but rocks'.

The shift in policy infuriated the Indonesian armed forces, TNI, which had run East Timor as their own political, economic and military realm, using the province's natural resources like coffee and timber to bankroll their occupation and the resistance movement to blood their troops. As the vote drew nearer, the military began forming and arming local militia groups to intimidate and terrorise independence supporters. Australian Prime Minister John Howard lobbied to send in peacekeepers, to which Habibie responded: 'No, no, no . . . I can't allow foreign troops into Indonesia.'[29]

On 30 August 1999, the people of East Timor voted 78.5 per cent in favour of independence. Unleashed by the armed forces, the militias embarked on a vicious retaliatory rampage, killing an estimated 1500 civilians, and destroying 70 per cent of buildings in the province. The atrocities caused a wave of public revulsion in Australia and demands for intervention. Canberra's push to send peacekeepers won US support, President Clinton declaring on the south lawn of the White House: 'the Australians have been with us every step of the way for decades now.' Habibie finally had no choice.

A convoy of Hercules C130s lumbered in three weeks after the vote and disgorged a company of Australian troops kitted out in full battle gear, with instructions to 'capture' the Dili airfield. 'We went in like it was a war,' recalled one soldier who was there.[30] They were the first of 4600 Australians, who made up three-quarters of the international force sent to restore peace. And restore it they did, overseeing East Timor's painful transition to nationhood in three years' time.

Canberra's belated support for the East Timorese was applauded at home and abroad. But in Indonesia it sparked a furious backlash — against both President Habibie and Australia. Molotov cocktails were hurled at the Australian embassy and there was talk of cutting trade and diplomatic ties.

'People are no longer really focusing on what happened in East Timor, but on how Indonesia has been insulted,' said Habibie's adviser, Dewi Fortuna Anwar. 'There's always been a suspicion of white people in general, which is understandable because of the long experience of colonialism. Indonesia has always been very touchy about being pushed around by outside countries.'[31]

Even moderates like Abdurrahman Wahid, head of the Muslim organisation NU, lashed out at the sending of Australian troops. 'Let's wait several months from now, when the East Timor integration people begin to kill them. We know it will happen. When ten of them are hit, that will change public opinion in Australia.'[32]

Extremists like Sungkar and Bashir were even more enraged, depicting the 'loss' of East Timor as part of an international conspiracy against Islam. Sungkar railed against 'the community of the cross in East Timor' and 'the other kafir groups which are behind all of these issues'.[33] In the eyes of the two fanatical clerics, the presence of Australian and other foreign troops in Indonesia was comparable to the US forces stationed in Saudi Arabia — yet another deliberate humiliation of the Muslim world. To the leaders of Jemaah Islamiyah, Australia had joined the ranks of the enemies of Islam.

The backlash over East Timor coupled with the urge for a clean break from Suharto soon swept Habibie from power. In an upset victory, the maverick, half-blind cleric and NU leader Abdurrahman Wahid became president, with Megawati Sukarnoputri as his vice president.

For Sungkar and Bashir the election of such a moderate Muslim deeply committed to secular government was yet another defeat. 'Leadership by a Muslim applying secular principles . . . will lead the followers of Islam to hell,' Bashir warned in one speech. Politicians who pass laws against Islam are 'not Muslims', according to Bashir, and should be 'expelled from Islam'. Muslims living in a secular state are 'obliged to fight [with] all their might'. If not, 'they will be drowned in a lifetime of evil.'

The fact that the deputy president was a woman was a further affront to the leaders of JI. 'A nation led by a woman won't be successful — that's what the Prophet said, and this becomes my opinion,' Bashir told a journalist. 'A woman should be put in the right place . . . Don't be the country's top leader because she will never succeed.'[34]

Within months of their return from exile, Sungkar and Bashir were on a new collision course with the Indonesian state. With the demise of the dictator Suharto, the country's long-awaited secular democracy had become the new enemy and target of their struggle.

Megawati Sukarnoputri was quickly identified as a target in the holy war to be staged in Indonesia, according to US and Indonesian intelligence reports based on the confessions of the al Qaeda operative, Omar al Faruq. The plot Faruq outlined would have convulsed Indonesia's brittle democracy had it succeeded. 'Faruq confessed his plan to kill Megawati in 1999, when she was a presidential candidate, and 41 other Indonesian figures,' reported Indonesian intelligence, on the basis of Faruq's account.[35] The other figures named as potential targets included the former head of the Indonesian armed forces Benny Murdani.

The intelligence reports say Faruq identified three co-conspirators in this elaborate plot, among them Abdullah Sungkar's son-in-law, Syawal Yasin.[36] Faruq was 'assigned as the trigger man', while Yasin was to get the guns. The plot came to nothing, Indonesian intelligence reporting: 'Yasin went to Malaysia and the Philippines to buy guns but said he couldn't get them back into Indonesia. It was suggested by JI that he stole the money.' A second plot to kill Megawati also reportedly failed 'when the assassin blew off his leg in a premature detonation at the Atrium mall.'[37]

The assassination plan was reportedly hatched at Faruq's home in Bogor, with his wife Mira translating notes of the meeting into Arabic. Mira denies it, claiming she knew nothing of any of the activities outlined in Faruq's extensive confessions. 'I am deeply hurt and shocked,' said Mira, 'I feel like the most violated person on earth. If they were true, it means that I have been lied to all of this time.'[38]

꧁꧂

A few months after the fugitives' return to Indonesia, the first emir of Jemaah Islamiyah, Abdullah Sungkar, died, aged sixty-two, apparently from a heart attack. He had suffered from diabetes for many years. The obvious choice to succeed him was his long-time faithful deputy, who had been increasingly hands-on in the running of the organisation.

'I heard that Abu Bakar Bashir had been appointed the new emir of JI from Mustapha and from Hambali, because they both contacted me by mobile phone and told me.' This account of Bashir's appointment was provided later by the captured leader of Mantiqi 3, Mohammed Nasir bin Abas, who at the time of Bashir's elevation was in charge of the JI Military Academy at Camp Hudaibiyah in Mindanao. 'I was told to convey the news of Abu Bakar Bashir's appointment to all the JI members under me . . . I also told the Hudaibiyah Camp.'

But Bashir's succession caused rumblings in the ranks of JI. The Young Turks of the organisation, like the Afghan-trained fanatic Samudra, saw Bashir as too soft. The always outspoken Samudra, who had earlier been punished in Afghanistan for failing to support Sungkar, now made no bones about his views of Bashir.

'Ever since Ustad Abu Bakar Bashir returned from Malaysia, he has become more "open",' Samudra complained later. 'Bashir leans towards dakwah and the socialisation of Islam, while I realise that society's needs go beyond that.'[39] Samudra believed that JI could only operate 'underground' and, as he was fond of telling his colleages, that 'jihad has to be executed first.'

'Many of Sungkar's Indonesian recruits, particularly the more militant younger ones, were very unhappy with the idea of [Bashir] taking over,' wrote Sidney Jones of the International Crisis Group. 'They saw [Bashir] as too weak, too accommodating, too easily influenced by others.'[40] The dissenters reportedly also included Hambali, Muklas and the military chief, Zulkarnaen, who had all been together in Afghanistan.

The criticism of Bashir would intensify when he later formed a public lobby group, the Indonesian Mujahideen Council in 2000, to campaign openly for the introduction of Islamic law. As Bashir wrote letters to the US president and demanded talks with Indonesia's leaders, his public agitating angered some of his troops, who believed that negotiating with the infidels was a betrayal. More seriously, they were alarmed that it could compromise the secrecy of JI. One of those who took this view was Hambali.

Hambali was becoming an increasingly powerful figure in JI. A brilliant recruiter and strategist with close personal connections to al Qaeda luminaries like Khalid Sheik Mohammed, Hambali was revered by the younger militants. Since their days as neighbours in Sungai Manggis, the former kebab-seller had exerted increasing influence over Bashir.

Now, even as Bashir was assuming the role of emir, Hambali moved to take operational control. Bashir would take on the role as JI's political and spiritual leader, but it was Hambali as operational chief who would make the key decisions from now on, though he would do it with the imprimatur of the emir. And Hambali's operations would take over from Bashir's *dakwah* as the central strategy in JI's campaign.

Hambali moved immediately to step up JI's preparations for jihad. Recruitment and military training were accelerated while less core activities were wound down, according to a White Paper issued by the Singapore Government based on the later interrogations of JI detainees:

'Hambali had instructed that all JI groups (missionary work, economy, etc) be converted into operations cells and that as many members as possible be sent for training in Afghanistan or Mindanao. In compliance with this instruction, the Singapore JI network disbanded its *dakwah* (missionary) and other non-operations cells/units and deployed its members for training. In Malaysia the JI training also changed from fitness type training to terrorism related training.'[41]

Just weeks after the death of Sungkar, Hambali and Bashir summoned mujahideen leaders from all over Southeast Asia to a summit on Hambali's turf, the Malaysian capital Kuala Lumpur. The purpose of the meeting was to implement the strategy decided upon at the recent JI seminar: 'to expand our operations in ASEAN.' One of those who attended, the JI treasurer, Abu Bakar Bafana, said the idea was to set up a forum 'to promote co-operation between Islamic organisations from Indonesia, Aceh, South Sulawesi, Singapore, Burma, Thailand and the Philippines.'[42]

The two dozen men who gathered at the International Islamic University in KL at the end of 1999 were a who's who of radical Islamists in Southeast Asia, a group whose faces would later dominate wanted lists across the region. The core group from JI included Bashir, Hambali, Muklas and the moderate leader of Mantiqi 2, Abu Fatih. There was a contingent from the old Darul Islam group and representatives from the MILF in the Philippines and the Free Aceh Movement, GAM. There to represent Malaysia's radical Islamists was Nik Adli, son of the leader of the Opposition Islamic party, PAS. The head of the militia group Laskar Jundullah, Agus Dwikarna, was present. There were two men from the Thai rebel group, PULO, along with representatives from two separate Islamist groups in Burma.[43]

At this elite gathering, the leaders of militant Islamic groups from across Southeast Asia agreed to join forces for the first time, to form what they called the Rabitatul Mujahideen, or Mujahideen League. One intelligence report described the RM as 'the JI military arm'.[44] But it is probably more accurate to describe it as Southeast Asia's own equivalent of al Qaeda, a regional version of bin Laden's World Islamic Front for Jihad. It united a collection of once disparate militant groups with separate domestic agendas into a united front determined to struggle together to achieve Islamic law across the Muslim lands of Southeast Asia.

⚜

CHAPTER FOURTEEN

THE SPRINGBOARD

NAME: KHALID AL MIHDHAR. Date of birth: 16 May 1975. US multiple entry visa, valid till April 2000.

To the passport control officer at Kuala Lumpur International Airport, the name on the 24-year-old Saudi's travel document rang no alarm bells. And in any case he was only in Malaysia for a short stay, before heading to the United States. The passport was stamped and its owner waved through, to make his rendezvous in KL.

Unknown to Khalid al Mihdhar, he was being watched from the moment he arrived — the CIA knew he was coming, even though they weren't sure exactly who he was. All they had was his first name and the fact that, before flying in from Yemen, he had been at an al Qaeda depot linked to the 1998 bombing of the US embassies in Africa. In the words of one CIA officer, 'a kind of tuning fork buzzed' when they got intelligence that al Mihdhar was on the move.[1]

After al Mihdhar had passed through Immigration, a copy of his passport was handed on to the CIA. His full name still didn't mean anything to them but they were sure he was with al Qaeda. The CIA asked Malaysian intelligence to put him under surveillance.

Al Mihdhar met up with another Saudi named Nawaf, who had flown in from Pakistan a few days before. The Americans were onto him as well, although, like al Mihdhar, they only had his first name and the fact that he was from al Qaeda. It was enough for the CIA to tag them both as 'terrorist operatives' and send a cable warning that their trip may be 'in support of a terrorist mission'.[2] Their visit was viewed as 'a potential source of intelligence about a possible Al Qaeda attack in Southeast Asia', in the words of the then CIA director, George Tenet.[3]

Al Mihdhar and his Saudi friend Nawaf al Hazmi were trailed to a condominium on the outskirts of KL, the Evergreen Park Kondo, a gated compound of high-rise towers in Tuscan terracotta and white, with a figure-eight shaped swimming pool fringed by palm trees and pruned frangipanis. The security guard seated in the plastic pool chair by the boomgate would have let the two strangers through without further question when they told him they were the guests of Mr Sufaat in building B2.

Their host, Yazid Sufaat, was a Malaysian biochemist trained in the United States. He had graduated from California State University in 1987, then come home and joined the army, becoming a captain and serving as a lab technician. His wife was a biochemist too, with two degrees from Cal State. Sufaat was a born-again Muslim, who reportedly took up religious studies after his mother-in-law complained that he had strayed from his faith.[4] He had become a zealous convert and joined JI. According to the CIA, Sufaat had been 'directed by a terrorist leader to make his apartment available' for the KL meeting.[5] The terrorist leader who had so directed him was his boss, Hambali.

Al Mihdhar and al Hazmi stayed for three days in KL, spending most of their time at Sufaat's condo. They did no business and no sight-seeing and often used public telephones and internet cafes, behaviour the CIA called 'consistent with clandestine activity'. They were videotaped and photographed by Malaysian intelligence coming and going with a number of other men.

One of the men caught on camera was the person who had arranged the gathering, Hambali.[6] Another was a swarthy foreigner conspicuous for his missing leg, who was also staying at Yazid Sufaat's condo. This was an operative known as Khallad, real name Tawfiq bin Attash, an al Qaeda fighter who had lost a limb in Afghanistan and who had arranged the 'special training' the two Saudis had undertaken in Afghanistan before heading for the United States via KL.[7]

The CIA didn't know it then but the men visiting Kuala Lumpur had been handpicked by Osama bin Laden for what was then known as the 'planes operation', to be executed in the United States. Khallad, the two Saudis and a fourth man who accompanied them to Kuala Lumpur had completed advanced training at an elite al Qaeda camp in Afghanistan, before being sent to Karachi for personalised tuition with the al Qaeda mastermind nicknamed 'the Brain'.

Khalid Sheik Mohammed was by now in charge of all operations outside of Afghanistan for bin Laden. In Karachi, Mohammed had taught the four operatives how to read phone books and airline timetables, to communicate in code, make travel reservations and use the Internet. They had spent hours playing flight simulator games on Mohammad's computer and watching Hollywood movies featuring hijackings, though only after Mohammed had edited out the shots of female characters.[8] At the end of their training Mohammed had sent his operatives off to his old friend Hambali in Malaysia, for the next part of their assignment.

The one-legged Khallad had arrived in Kuala Lumpur first, his job: 'to study airport security and conduct casing flights.' As Khallad explained later to his interrogators, 'Malaysia was an ideal destination because its government did not require citizens of Saudi Arabia or other Gulf states to have a visa [and] Malaysian security was reputed to be lax when it came to Islamist jihadists.'[9] Khallad's cover was that he was in Malaysia to get a new leg, at a KL clinic that reportedly specialised in prosthetic limbs for Afghan veterans wishing to disguise their injuries. Hambali picked Khallad up at the airport and took him first to his home and then to the clinic.[10]

While staying in Kuala Lumpur, Khallad took a flight to Bangkok and back, to study the plane's layout for a hijacking and to test whether he could get box cutters on board in his carry-on bag; the airport security staff checked his toiletries kit, saw the contents and let them through. Back in KL, Khallad met up with the two Saudis, al Mihdhar and al Hazmi, when they arrived. According to the 9/11 Commission Report, based on the interrogation of Khallad, they 'spoke about the possibility of hijacking planes and crashing them or holding passengers as hostages'.

At this stage, the team in KL was to be involved in two separate attacks. The first was the 'planes operation' against the United States, for which al Mihdhar and al Hazmi had been personally chosen by bin Laden as suicide operatives. The two had been so inspired by the death of their cousin in the suicide attack on the US embassy in Nairobi in 1998 that they had gone straight out and got themselves US visas. The other operation was what Khalid Sheik Mohammed referred to as his 'second wave' of attacks, for which Khallad was doing the casing. Under this plan, which was a refinement of Mohammed's former Operation Bojinka plot in the Philippines, US airliners taking off from Asian airports would be hijacked and blown up in mid-air. By Khallad's account, they looked at commandeering planes originating from Thailand, South Korea, Hong Kong or Malaysia, to be exploded simultaneously, possibly using shoe bombs.[11]

At the end of their visit to Kuala Lumpur, the two Saudis and their colleague Khallad, with the help of Hambali, bought tickets to Bangkok. They flew out together seated side by side, then parted ways. Khallad returned to the Middle East to help orchestrate the bombing of the USS *Cole* in Yemen, which killed seventeen American sailors on 12 October 2000. It was only after that attack, when the CIA reviewed its surveillance shots of the KL meeting and identified Khallad as the one-legged man in the photos, that the Americans became concerned about what the two Saudis with the US visas might be planning next. As one CIA officer put it, 'Something bad was definitely up.'[12]

Al Mihdhar and al Hazmi were put on a watch-list in the United States but by that time they had already flown into America and vanished. They were never tracked down. The two Saudis accomplished their mission on September 11, 2001, when they seized the controls of American Airlines Flight 77 and slammed it into the Pentagon.

It is now known that the summit in Kuala Lumpur in January 2000 was one of the sessions in which planning of the USS *Cole* bombing and the September 11 strikes against America occurred. The US Congressional committee that investigated the disaster identified Malaysia as one of 'the springboards' where 'the operational planning for the September 11 attacks took place'.[13] This was all thanks to the good offices of Hambali, JI's operations chief and al Qaeda's main man in Southeast Asia.

This was not the last time that Hambali's Kuala Lumpur headquarters would be used as a service centre for al Qaeda. A few months after the two Saudis flew out, another al Qaeda operative arrived in KL. The new visitor was Zacarias Moussaoui, a French national of Moroccan descent, trained by al Qaeda in Afghanistan, selected by bin Laden as a suicide pilot, and sent to Hambali by Khalid Sheik Mohammed.

Once again, the hospitable Malaysian biochemist and JI member Yazid Sufaat played host, putting Moussaoui up at his condo and providing him with letters of introduction to help him gain entry to the United States. On the letterhead of his wife's company, Infocus Technology, Sufaat wrote that Moussaoui had been hired as the firm's marketing consultant[14] in the US, the UK and Europe, on a retainer of US$2,500 a month plus $35,000 up front.

Moussaoui met in KL with Hambali and the JI treasurer, Abu Bakar Bafana. The Frenchman told them about his 'dream' of flying a plane into the White House, according to evidence later given by Bafana. While they admired his ambition, Moussaoui struck the two JI men as odd. Bafana said he demonstrated 'paranoid behaviour', insisting on leaving Bafana's home during some discussions in case of electronic surveillance, yet speaking freely about his plans to hijack and crash a plane. Bafana and Hambali decided that Moussaoui was 'cuckoo'.[15]

Despite their misgivings, Hambali sent Moussaoui off to the Malaysian Flying Academy in Malacca. But the school didn't offer the simulator training he needed to pilot wide-bodied planes. So Moussaoui travelled on to the United States where he enrolled first in the Airman Flight School in Oklahoma and then the Pan Am school in Minnesota, to learn to fly a Boeing 747, paying cash up front from the money given to him by the JI men in Malaysia.

However, the Pan Am staff became suspicious of the fact that Moussaoui had no aviation background, no flying licence and no intention of becoming a pilot; he told them he 'simply wanted to learn the most challenging elements of flying, taking off and landing a 747, which he referred to as an "ego-boosting thing".'[16] One of the staff rang the FBI and Moussaoui was taken in for questioning in August 2001.

Moussaoui was later charged with being the missing '20th hijacker' from September 11. Khalid Sheik Mohammed has claimed instead that he was one of the trainee pilots recruited for the 'second wave' of attacks, in which US aircraft originating in Asia would be hijacked and blown up.

According to Mohammed, Moussaoui was one of three potential pilots recruited for this 'second wave'. The others were a Canadian and a JI member from Malaysia named Zaini Zakaria, who had been instructed by bin Laden's military chief, Abu Hafs, to enrol in flight training in 2000. According to the 9/11 Commission Report, Zakaria and the Canadian both got cold feet and pulled out. In any event, the 'second wave' was called off by bin Laden in 2000, because he believed it would be too difficult to coordinate with the attacks on the United States.[17]

⚘

From early 2000, Hambali's base in Malaysia was the operational headquarters of JI and a crucial link in the al Qaeda chain of command. Since 1996, Hambali had been the head of JI's main branch, Mantiqi 1, which covered Malaysia and Singapore. He also ran its regional *shura* (council), which was based in Kuala Lumpur.[18]

After Sungkar and Bashir's return to Indonesia, Hambali had stayed on in his bungalow in the banana grove in Sungai Manggis, commuting regularly to the capital. While Solo in Indonesia was JI's main political and spiritual centre, it was Hambali's HQ in Malaysia where the operational decisions were made.

Hambali's chief assistant in Kuala Lumpur was JI's long-time treasurer, the former Singaporean developer Abu Bakar Bafana. His other aide was a Malaysian accountant and businessman named Zulkifli Marzuki, described by Muklas as Hambali's 'business partner'. Marzuki ran a home-security business called MNZ and Associates and a 'charity' named by Muklas as the the Al Ihsan Foundation, which raised money for Muslims in conflict zones like Afghanistan and Ambon.[19] Marzuki also set up and administered a web of front companies for JI.

Hambali's ascendancy solidified the connections with al Qaeda forged earlier by Sungkar and Bashir. Pivotal to this relationship was the close bond between Hambali and his old friend 'the Brain', Khalid Sheik Mohammed. The friendship forged in Afghanistan at the time of the Lion's Den battle and in the Philippines in the days of Operation Bojinka had gone from strength to strength.

In 1996 Mohammed had paid a visit to Hambali's Malaysian base to 'personally observe Hambali's recruitment operations', as he later put it. He observed that Hambali was a skilled recruiter whose trainees were 'loyal and well-prepared' and that Hambali himself was 'extremely charismatic and popular'.[20] It was after this that Mohammed had invited Hambali to Afghanistan to meet Osama bin Laden and the two groups had struck their historic deal, to work together on targets of mutual interest.

The agreement reached between al Qaeda and JI for future operations was later revealed by Hambali under interrogation and summarised in the 9/11 Commission Report: 'JI would perform the necessary casing activities and locate bomb-making materials and other supplies. Al Qaeda would underwrite operations, provide bomb-making expertise, and deliver suicide operatives.'

Having already taken the *bai'at* with Abu Bakar Bashir, Hambali never swore allegiance to bin Laden, but he became as much al Qaeda as he was JI. As Hambali described it, he 'received his marching orders from JI, but al Qaeda would lead any joint operation involving members of both organisations.' His friend Mohammed regarded him as an al Qaeda member working in Malaysia, and later claimed credit for causing Hambali to switch JI's focus from pursuing its regional aims in Southeast Asia to mounting attacks aimed at the United States and its allies.[21]

Hambali became so close to Khalid Sheik Mohammed and al Qaeda that, at one stage, the operations chief earned himself a rebuke from his emir. Abu Bakar Bashir was an enthusiastic supporter of bin Laden's cause, but he didn't want Hambali getting too distracted from JI's main game, according to an account from Khalid Sheik Mohammed recorded in the 9/11 Commission Report. 'According to KSM, his close personal relationship with Hambali prompted criticism from Bashir, the JI leader, who thought Hambali should focus more directly on Indonesia and Malaysia instead of involving himself in al Qaeda's broader terrorist program.'

But Bashir and Hambali were as one when it came to joining bin Laden's jihad against the West. In the wake of the al Qaeda chief's famous 1998 fatwa authorising the killing of civilians, Hambali issued an edict of his own, with the imprimatur of Bashir. It was described by the former Mantiqi 3 leader, Mohammed Nasir bin Abas:

'I heard there was a decree brought down by Hambali that was passed onto him by Abu Bakar Bashir. The decree was allegedly from Osama, urging Muslims to defend themselves from the Americans. The Americans had persecuted Muslims all over and had even killed the Muslims. The decree said it was alright to kill Americans even though they were not armed. We were also told that we could kill women and children and other civilians. The decree was given to all the Mantiqis.'[22]

Hambali's fatwa, issued with Bashir's approval, was the source of great consternation within JI. While everyone agreed that armed struggle was an essential element of jihad, the killing of innocent civilians was another thing. 'I personally read a photocopy of the decree and felt something was not right and could not accept such a decree,' said Mohammed Nasir. 'That is why I did not read the decree to my followers. I asked myself why we should attack the innocent when it is the American leadership that we are after. The other reason was that the civilians could be Muslims.'

As with the earlier fatwas from bin Laden — who has no real authority to issue them — the use of Islamic rulings to justify acts of violence and terrorism was the subject of intense debate. '[Fatwas came] mostly from Hambali and also from Muklas,' recalled another member. 'Muklas, for instance, said in his fatwa that you can rob a bank. At that time I heard there was a robbery of a Southern Bank . . . So when I had the opportunity to meet him I asked him about the robbery and whether JI members were involved. He said it was all right . . . I didn't agree. The money kept in the bank belonged to the public, to a lot of people. That was what I said.'[23]

This new dispute exacerbated the old divisions that had already emerged between JI's militants and the moderates in charge of its Indonesian branch, Mantiqi 2. 'Mantiqi 2 leaders argued that these fatwas were inappropriate for Indonesia,' wrote Sidney Jones of the ICG. 'They also were reportedly irritated that Mantiqi 1 seemed to be ignoring JI's own fatwa council, which was rarely convened.'[24] The moderates were also concerned that attacking US targets would squander JI's resources. The military chief, Zulkarnaen, responded that JI would not have to use its own money, as funds for such attacks would be forthcoming from al Qaeda. The issue of finance was easily solved; but the discord over the morality of killing civilians in the name of Islam would continue to divide the organisation.

Hambali was unmoved by this debate. Impatient with the years of preparation and planning, his view was — let the jihad begin. Hambali was ready to mount an operation of his own — the first JI–al Qaeda joint venture, using Hambali's operatives with al Qaeda's funding, expertise and logistical support. And if his colleagues in Indonesia didn't yet have the stomach for action, then Hambali would choose another branch and another theatre for his attack. The arena he chose was Singapore, which as part of Mantiqi 1 was under his own direct command.

✧

Hambali's man in Singapore was an operative he knew he could trust
— Hashim bin Abas, one of the brothers-in-law of Muklas. Clean-
shaven with a crew cut and spectacles, Hashim was an electrical
engineer with the German-owned high-tech industrial machinery
maker, Bystronic Asia; typical of the educated, middle-class professionals
who made up JI's Singapore branch. Hashim was the branch secretary
and treasurer and had been among the group waved off on their way for
training in Afghanistan by Abu Bakar Bashir. Unlike his brother Mantiqi
3 leader Mohammed Nasir, Hashim apparently had no qualms about
killing civilians in the name of Islam.

Hashim's offsider was Mohammed Khalim bin Jaffar, one of JI's
earliest recruits in Singapore and the leader of its first cell, known as *fiah
ayub*. Thirty-nine years old, with spiky hair and a close-cropped goatee,
Khalim's day job was running a printing press in Chinatown, where
workmates described him as 'a quiet, thrifty worker who ate packed
lunches and was well-liked by his boss'.[25]

Beneath Khalim's mild exterior, there seethed a loathing of America,
nurtured by his years of indoctrination with JI. He lived with his family
near the Mass Rail Transit (MRT) station at Yishun, the northernmost
stop on the line, not far from the US naval base at Sembawang Wharf.
A regular shuttle bus ferried the US military personnel and their
families between the wharf and the MRT, and Khalim used to bristle
with hatred seeing the busloads of Americans in uniform pass by his
home. His plan was to bomb the MRT station just as a crowd of
Americans was getting off the bus.

Khalim and Hashim had already spent months in 1999 casing the
MRT site. Khalim drew up maps and Hashim did video surveillance,
taking his kids along so the recce looked like a family day out. While
Khalim acted as lookout, Hashim filmed the MRT station and its
surrounds, zooming in on spots where explosives could be planted. He
later edited the tape, deleting the shots of his children and adding a
running commentary in English, delivered with deadpan calm and
chilling attention to detail.

'This is the place where US military personnel will be dropped off
from a bus and they will walk towards the MRT station . . . After they
alight from the bus, they will move towards the MRT station — as you

can see from the far left, the people walking towards the MRT station, they will walk the same way.' Synchronised with Hashim's voiceover, the video pans across a crowd of commuters and zooms in on scores of parked bicycles, whose owners will be coming and going as the bomb goes off. The narration goes on:

'This is the bicycle bay as viewed from the footpath that leads towards the MRT station. You will notice that some of the boxes placed on the motorcycles, these are the same type of boxes that we intend to use . . . That is the entrance of the temple where many vehicles parked there so it will not be suspicious to have a motorcycle or a bicycle there. The pillars of the MRT track are very very solid. You will notice that there is a drainage hole, it might be useful.'[26]

The surveillance tape was packaged up with maps, sketches and explanatory notes and passed on to Hambali in Kuala Lumpur. Hambali then dispatched his assistant and treasurer, Abu Bakar Bafana, to take the tape and supporting documents to Afghanistan to get al Qaeda's approval.

In Afghanistan, Bafana took the tape to bin Laden's military chief, Abu Hafs. After viewing the surveillance footage and supporting documents with Bafana, Abu Hafs endorsed the idea and 'instructed [Bafana] to procure the explosives and short-list men to execute the attack'.[27] The edited tape with Hashim's voiceover would later be found in the rubble of Abu Hafs' home, after the US bombing of Afghanistan.

Bafana returned to Kuala Lumpur to inform Hambali that the bombing had got the green light from al Qaeda. The Singaporeans were instructed to continue the preparations.

A few months later, Khalim bin Jaffar went to Afghanistan himself for training and took the opportunity to update Abu Hafs personally on his bombing plan. According to the Singapore Government White Paper based on interrogations of JI detainees: 'He briefed the al Qaeda leaders (in English because they did not speak Malay and Khalim's command of Arabic was limited) and provided notes and diagrams of the location of Yishun MRT station to explain his plan.' Once again, Abu Hafs gave the nod.

Southeast Asia had been chosen as a new frontline in al Qaeda's war against the West, thanks again to the assistance of Hambali, operations chief of JI. Osama bin Laden was so impressed with the level of support for the jihadist cause in the region that he reportedly considered shifting his entire operation to Indonesia. Bin Laden sent his two trusted lieutenants on a tour of inspection in 2000. Their visit was described in a report by one of the intelligence agencies in the region:

'Ayman Al Zawahiri, the Egyptian close to Osama bin Laden, and Mohammad Atef aka Abu Hafs, the military leader of bin Laden's organisation, travelled to Indonesia to explore the possibility of OBL's relocation there. At the time the security situation in Afghanistan was too difficult . . . This visit was part of a wider strategy of shifting the base for OBL's terrorist operations from the subcontinent to South East Asia.'[28]

The men from al Qaeda travelled widely in Indonesia, visiting conflict zones including Ambon and West Papua. They were assigned two local escorts to show them around. One was the Kuwaiti operative Omar al Faruq, the other his close associate, Agus Dwikarna, head of the militia group Laskar Jundullah.[29] The al Qaeda chiefs held talks with local militant leaders in the provinces and also with representatives of the Philippines groups, the MILF and the Abu Sayyaf.

Bin Laden's deputies travelled to Aceh as well, 'to explore the possibility of assisting the Aceh separatist group's struggle,' according to Omar al Faruq. By Faruq's account, this was 'never followed up, as al Qaeda considered the Aceh struggle not in line with its mission'.[30] This was apparently because backing a separate Muslim state in one province could undermine the broader campaign for a single Islamic state covering all of Indonesia.

Al Zawahiri and Abu Hafs reported back to bin Laden that the conditions in Indonesia were ideal for al Qaeda. 'Both of them were impressed by the lack of security, the support and extent of the Muslim population and the obscurity provided by the density of the forests.'[31] The proposed relocation never went ahead, presumably because of the daunting logistics involved.

The bombing of the MRT station in Singapore did not go ahead either, for reasons that have never become clear. But the Singapore branch would continue its preparations for a bombing. Hambali, meanwhile, was turning his attention to JI's southernmost branch — Mantiqi 4 in Australia.

❧

CHAPTER FIFTEEN

THE ENEMY'S PLOT

A CHOCOLATE-BROWN BRICK-VENEER house with a paling fence and white lace curtains, in Perth, Western Australia, was now the headquarters of JI's Mantiqi 4. The house in suburban Thornlie was where the group's leader, Abdul Rahim Ayub, had settled after leaving Sydney in mid-1998, following the brawl at the Dee Why mosque and the apprehended violence orders taken out against him and his twin, Abdul Rahman.

Perth was a perfect new base — just over four hours' flying time to Jakarta, and with a large well-ensconced Indonesian community. Abdul Rahim and his wife and six children were barely noticed when they moved into their rented house near the Thornlie mosque.

'I never met him until I had been here about fourteen months. He asked me if I had just moved in,' the next-door neighbour, Peter Wenn, told me in 2003. 'We had a little bit of a chat and he told me about his kids — if they were noisy to just let him know and I said they were quite fine . . . He says he'd ask me over for a meal one day and I said, "Oh yeah, that'd be nice." But then I never heard from him after that.'[1]

Abdul Rahim enrolled his children at the Al Hidayah Islamic school in suburban Bentley. With his dimpled grin and affable manner, Abdul Rahim became a well known and popular figure at the school, often trailed around by his two boys, aged about seven and nine. 'He loved the school and the kids loved him,' remembered Al Hidayah's administrator, Umar Abdullah, an Australian convert to Islam.

Not long after Abdul Rahim's arrival, the school's religious teacher announced that he was leaving to go home to Kuwait. 'The principal said to me, "We need a new teacher and Abdul Rahim is available — I've talked to him and he seems good,"' Umar Abdullah recalled. So 'We asked him to work for us on a volunteer basis as a teacher of religion.'[2]

The Al Hidayah school wasn't fussed by Abdul Rahim's lack of teaching qualifications and didn't ask for references; his obvious devotion to Islam was enough. At Al Hidayah, each school day is extended by an hour, to allow more time for religious instruction without cutting the time spent on the mandatory government curriculum. The school claims consistently above-average results for Western Australia, even though most of the students come from homes where English is the second language.

After starting as a volunteer Abdul Rahim was later taken on as a paid employee, teaching religion two to three days a week on a salary of $500 a fortnight. He was so well regarded that within a year of his arrival he was invited to attend a meeting of the Al Hidayah board, as the school later explained: 'He was being considered as a potential board member because he had earned the respect of his supervisor and co-workers in the performance of his duties as a teacher, and his level-headed and calm approach, when invited to participate in discussions regarding school matters in general, had been noted by some members of the Board. He had also demonstrated that he clearly understood the necessity of following the School's mainstream approach in Religion Studies given the very diverse nature of the Muslim Community of Perth, and that he was a supporter of the School's aims and objectives.'[3]

The school knew nothing of the punch-up at Dee Why, the accusations of death threats and assault, or the apprehended violence orders taken out against Abdul Rahim and his twin. It certainly had no inkling of their roles in JI. Abdul Rahim betrayed no sign of radical politics, except for the occasional comment about the plight of Muslims in his homeland, according to Umar Abdullah. 'His only grievances were the situation in Indonesia, places like Aceh, and the persecution of Muslims. It really upset them.'

The Ayub twins reminded Umar Abdullah of a book he kept on his shelf called *The Ideal Muslim*. 'You know, how you're supposed to behave, how you're supposed to react to certain things, in terms of

'Between you and us there will forever be a ravine of hate.' Abu Bakar Bashir in the silver-domed mosque in Solo, October 2002. COURTESY *4 CORNERS*

LEFT The repentant Ali Imron at his trial. AFP/NEWSPIX
RIGHT 'Never underestimate a tiny kindness, even if it's only to show people your happy face.' Muklas, controller of the Bali bombings. RENEE NOWYTARGER, NEWSPIX

Amrozi welcomes the death penalty: 'There will be a million Amrozis to come.'
RENEE NOWYTARGER, NEWSPIX

Former student poet and high-school honours graduate Samudra, JI's field commander for the Bali bombings. RENEE NOWYTARGER, NEWSPIX

The kebab-seller turned JI operations chief, Hambali.

JI's co-founder and first emir, Abdullah Sungkar, replaced as emir by Abu Bakar Bashir in 1999.

Osama bin Laden with his deputy, Ayman al Zawahiri (left), and military chief, Abu Hafs (right). The trio fronted a 1998 press conference in Afghanistan to announce the formation of the World Islamic Front for Jihad. AFP/NEWSPIX

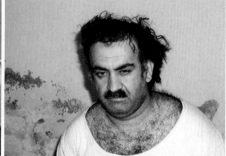

LEFT Two of the many guises of al Qaeda's Khalid Sheik Mohammed. RIGHT After his capture in March 2003.

The author (and translator) in Tenggulun with Zakaria, principal of the Al Islam religious school, run by the family of Muklas, Amrozi and Ali Imron. COURTESY *4 CORNERS*

'I can't believe my father would have married me to a terrorist.' Mira Augustina and her daughter – the wife and child of al Qaeda's 'senior rep in Southeast Asia', Omar al Faruq.

The family home in Tenggulun, East Java, where village chief Nur Hasyim raised his sons Muklas, Amrozi and Ali Imron. COURTESY *4 CORNERS*

JI's Luqmanul Hakiem school among the palm-oil plantations of Johor, southern Malaysia. Its motto: 'Be scared if you're wrong – Be brave if you're right.' COURTESY *4 CORNERS*

The home in suburban Denpasar where the Bali bombs were made and where an accidental explosion nearly gave the game away. COURTESY *4 CORNERS*

Abu Bakar Bashir photographed in Australia. On the right is Mantiqi 4 leader Abdul Rahim Ayub.

The talkative Jack Roche goes public on ABC TV news before his arrest in November 2002.

Reformed amphetamines addict Asman Hashim, sent to Australia to conduct 'jihad training' for the members of Mantiqi 4, pictured during a training camp in the NSW Blue Mountains in 1999.

An unidentified paintball warrior poses for a photograph during one of the Ayub twins' weekend expeditions near Myalup, south of Perth, WA.

A young Osama
fan in Indonesia.
COURTESY *4 CORNERS*

The Sari Club,
14 October 2002.
COURTESY *4 CORNERS*

controlling temper and courtesy and showing respect and general demeanour and so on. [Abdul Rahim] presented as someone who understood these principles and applied them, and that goes for his brother, Abdul Rahman. They were people that you couldn't help liking and respecting.'

Abdul Rahim's twin, who had moved to Perth with him, was also a regular at the school, where his reputation as a preacher and scholar of Islam were much admired. Abdul Rahman was often asked to give a sermon on Fridays and to lead the school prayers. Unlike his brother, the Afghan veteran's English was poor, so his sermons were delivered in Arabic, which most of the children couldn't understand, and a teacher would stand by to read a translation in English afterwards. The older twin was never employed at the school, as Umar Abdullah explained. 'We couldn't hire Abdul Rahman because he was a refugee.'

In fact, by this time, Abdul Rahman's claim for refugee status had been refused and the Ayubs were locked in a legal battle with the Immigration Department to head off his deportation. Abdul Rahman's application for a protection visa had been heard by a delegate of the Immigration Minister in early 1998. His claim to have been imprisoned in Indonesia had been contradicted by his wife in her evidence, leading the Minister's delegate to find that 'the account of his arrest was concocted'.[4]

Abdul Rahman's appeal to the Refugee Review Tribunal was listed for hearing while the Ayub twins were living in Perth. In a letter to the tribunal dated 28 October 1998, obviously penned with assistance, Abdul Rahman wrote in his faltering English: 'I have explained to you my hardship situation that I can not wait any longer for the RRT decision without having the right visa class that allowed me to seek for a job and to help my family in Australia.'[5]

Abdul Rahman was living in the home of a JI loyalist, David Suparta, who had been the group's treasurer in Sydney before moving to Perth ahead of the Ayubs. Suparta had children of his own, and Abdul Rahman pleaded with the Tribunal: 'It is the time for me to live separately because he has a big family to support and the house is too crowded with children. The [living expenses] too dear that I cannot afford on borrowing money all the time. There are many other things to state that I am in hardship situation.'

Making the most of his entitlements as an asylum seeker, Abdul Rahman had applied for a Medicare card to get free health care for his family and had asked the Red Cross for financial support. His letter to the RRT ended: 'I live in danger in Indonesia and I have hardship situation in Australia which is both of the situations do not support me to live normally as human. Thank you for your co-operation.' It was signed: 'Yours faithfully, Abdullah' — the false name under which he had come to Australia and lodged his refugee claim.[5]

While Abdul Rahman was doing battle with the Immigration Department, his twin, Abdul Rahim, made another visit to Indonesia. It was his fifth trip since being appointed head of the Australian jemaah of JI. He flew out in November 1998, at the end of the school year, and spent two or three months away, according to his later testimony to the Refugee Review Tribunal, where he mentioned the trip as evidence of his and his brother's political activities in Indonesia. Abdul Rahim told the Tribunal that he had met up with Ibnu Taib, also known as Abu Fatih, the leader of JI's Indonesian branch, Mantiqi 2, whom Abdul Rahim said was under surveillance at the time.[6]

Abdul Rahim's visit came amid the escalating dispute within Jemaah Islamiyah over how jihad should be waged in Indonesia. It was at the time when Abu Fatih was being hammered by the militants over the lack of action in Mantiqi 2. Abdul Rahim would have taken part in this debate and, from what his colleagues have said about him, it is likely that he would have taken Abu Fatih's side. Accounts from some of his colleagues indicate that Abdul Rahim was not among the militants of JI. The moderate Mantiqi 3 leader, Mohammed Nasir bin Abas, an outspoken opponent of Hambali's fatwa in favour of killing civilians, has praised Abdul Rahim as a long-term thinker and strategist, differentiating him from the revolutionaries in the Hambali camp who advocated violence.[7]

Abdul Rahim was back in Perth in time for his brother's hearing before the Refugee Review Tribunal in February 1999 and fronted up to give evidence, along with three men from among the Ayubs' local followers in Perth. The witnesses included Abdul Rahman's host, David Suparta, and another Indonesian migrant, Jan Herbert, both of whom had been followers of Sungkar and Bashir in Dee Why before moving to Perth. The witnesses swore that they were all followers of Negara Islam Indonesia (NII) and supported an Islamic state in Indonesia. They said the group had about thirty members in Australia and that its activities consisted of holding religious services in their homes and collecting money for the needy. David Suparta swore that Abdul Rahman had been sent to Australia to become the group's local leader, evidence intended to bolster Abdul Rahman's claim.

Despite his supporters' testimony, the Refugee Review Tribunal rejected Abdul Rahman's claim, upholding the earlier finding that he had lied in sworn evidence about his supposed arrest. And, in any case, it judged that since the fall of Suharto, Abdul Rahman would be unlikely to be persecuted if he returned to Indonesia. He was informed by letter: 'The Tribunal has decided that you are not a refugee ... The Tribunal's file on your case is now closed.'[8]

Abdul Rahman would eventually be forced to leave Australia, flying out with his family in February 2002. But for the moment, the Ayub twins weren't about to give up. They lodged another appeal, this time to the Federal Court and hired the law firm Minter Ellison to fight it, along with a barrister to front up in court. By now the case was causing a serious drain on Mantiqi 4's funds and a cause of fresh tension among its members. 'People were pissed off with the twins because they were using the jemaah's money on Abdul Rahman's case,' said one former follower back in Sydney.[9]

The incessant demands for money from head office were increasing as well. Hambali needed more funds for the operations he was planning — and the relatively affluent members of the Australian branch were ordered to contribute. A letter was sent by Abu Bakar Bashir to the Australian branch to this effect. It was written under the letterhead 'Jemaah Islamiyah Markaziyah' — JI headquarters — and addressed to 'the brother, Abdul Rahim, Co-ordinator of the Australian Leaders'.

Bashir's letter gave the following instruction to Mantiqi 4: 'It is the obligation of the Australian brothers to immediately send funds to the value of 16,000 Malay ringgit (A$6,000) to the account of Brother Hambali.'[10] Bashir's undated letter, forwarded as an attachment by email, is believed to have been sent in late 1998. It was later found on the computer hard drive of one of JI's Australian members. No record was found of the money having been sent, but it is likely that such a demand from the emir would have been obeyed.

Money was always a sore point in the Australian branch. The jemaahs in Sydney and Melbourne were now supposed to send the funds they collected from their members to Perth, so the Ayub twins could forward them on to Bashir. But the members interstate were so annoyed at the twins wasting their money on Abdul Rahman's court case that they began bypassing the Perth office and sending their donations directly to Bashir. This infuriated the Ayubs.

'On one occasion they made a snap visit to Sydney in order to chastise — if not physically attack — the members in Sydney and Melbourne (who happened to be there at the time) over their refusal to send moneys collected directly to Perth,' according to the JI convert, Jack Roche. As the costly court case dragged on, the grumbling intensified about JI's money being used 'to wholly support Abdul Rahman's existence in Australia', said Roche.[11]

Despite the rows over money and their troubles with the Immigration Department, the Ayub twins were steadily building a new following in Perth. Abdul Rahim held regular prayer sessions and lectures in his suburban home, attended by fifteen to twenty men. He and his brother gained a name as fundamentalist firebrands among Perth's close and mostly moderate Muslim community.

'His group was more revolutionary,' said Abdul Jalil, imam of the suburban Rivervale mosque. 'They had a view that, to establish the Islamic state, they have to make every effort — sometimes we just call it jihad. Jihad literally means to struggle in different ways, not necessarily in battle. But these people — they may take the harsh or maybe the violent method to achieve their goals.'[12]

Abdul Rahim also gave lectures to Muslim students at Curtin University, its large and relatively affluent Indonesian student population seen as a potential pool of recruits, as one former follower explained: 'The opportunity to approach Indonesian students of wealthy parents was [there] . . . and they're the ones you'd want to target because they're the ones with the money and power in Indonesia.'

It wasn't only students that the Ayubs were targeting, according to Jack Roche: 'When they came to Perth they began recruiting converts.' Just as Roche had been embraced into the jemaah in Sydney, the Ayub twins welcomed Australian converts in Perth into their fold. Two of the men they befriended were a bus driver and a mechanic at the Al Hidayah school, who were invited along to the prayer sessions and meetings at Abdul Rahim's home.

The bus driver, John Bennett, became part of the Ayub twins' circle. 'He struck me as being their bodyguard,' Jack Roche would later testify. 'Wherever they went, he was there.' Bennett agreed in court that he saw the twins regularly and that they were 'reasonably close'. On one occasion, Bennett travelled with the twins to Sydney for a week, staying at Jack Roche's home and attending religious classes and meetings with the Ayubs' Sydney followers.[13]

In Perth Bennett would invite the twins for weekend paintballing sessions in the bush near his property at Myalup, south of the city. The Ayubs and their friends would load up a van and trailer with a stack of paintball guns that one of the men had imported and set off into the bush with up to twenty men. But Bennett later scoffed at suggestions that he was targeted for recruitment by the Ayubs. 'Surely they'd want some kind of a loner? I lead a pretty busy life with my family [and] six children . . . We moved to Perth two years ago so our kids could get a good education . . . All we ever did was play paintballing games . . . It is just ridiculous to suggest it was any kind of terrorist training.'[14]

Umar Abdullah was also invited on the paintballing exercises but declined. 'A group of brothers for twenty years have been going down south somewhere to engage in paintball as a recreation activity, as a lot of other people do. I mean, I was invited to go once or twice and I just thought I was a bit old to be rolling around, barrel-rolling around the bush, you know, spraying paintballs everywhere . . . but it was purely as recreation — "A bunch of us are going down in a bus or a van and, you know, you want to come along?" — "No thanks, I'll give it a miss."'[15]

Photographs taken by the paintballers suggest they took their hobby seriously. One photo shows Abdul Rahim Ayub demonstrating the workings of a paintball gun to a roomful of enthusiasts. Another snap shows a man decked out in camouflage gear posing with a paintball gun and full face mask on a dusty road outside Perth.

Jack Roche, who never attended the outings, said later that the paintballing was 'a guise' and that the war games in the bush were for physical training. Another former follower, who didn't go either, called them 'jihad training'.[16] Paintball sessions were also held by the Ayub brothers for JI members in Sydney and in Melbourne as well, with paintball camps held near the Victorian towns of Moama in 2001 and Blackwood in 2002. Australian investigators say that the Perth paintball sessions also included training with real weapons, overseen by the Afghan veteran Abdul Rahman Ayub.[17]

While for some participants the bush jaunts may have been mere recreation, at least one of the Australian converts who took part in these sessions did so with serious intent. His name was Abu Ishmael, at least that was the name he had adopted after converting to Islam. A roofing contractor with his own business and a block of land in the same subdivision as John Bennett's, Abu Ishmael was so conscientious about the bush training sessions that he was singled out by the local leaders of JI, according to his fellow convert, Jack Roche: 'He was chosen by the Ayubs because he was keen to go on jihad.'

In 1999, Abu Ishmael was sent by the Ayub brothers to undergo proper jihad training with JI. He travelled from Perth to the Philippines, his destination the Islamic Military Academy of JI, within the Camp Abubakar complex in the jungles of Mindanao. The roof tiler from Perth spent six weeks in the JI camp, training alongside recruits from all over the world. On his way either to or from the Philippines, he stopped over for a meeting with Hambali. The operations chief was evidently impressed, because later when Hambali decided that he needed an Australian, it was Abu Ishmael that he asked for first.[18]

The training of Australians in Camp Abubakar was corroborated by regional intelligence agencies at the time. The camp was under surveillance by the Philippine authorities, while the government held on and off negotiations with the MILF. The existence of Jemaah Islamiyah was, at this stage, still unknown. Australian intelligence was aware that some Indonesians were training in Camp Abubakar, but thought they were called the 'Indonesian Islamic Liberation Front'.[19]

Philippine authorities had detected Australians among the steady flow of Indonesian and other foreign fighters arriving at Camp Abubakar to train with the MILF's Filipino fighters. This was documented in one classified report: 'It was noted in 1999 that Indonesian trainees came in smaller number and they were mixed with other nationalities.' The authorities knew of the existence of Camp Hudaibiyah, but didn't realise it was a JI camp. They also knew that foreign instructors were being flown in from overseas to conduct training, including two veterans of the Algerian Islamic Front, who arrived from Paris. 'The two participated in the training of about 40 mujahideen at Camp Hudaibiyah from October to December 1999 . . . The trainees were allegedly composed of Indonesian, Malaysian, Singaporean, Australian, Syrian and South African nationals.'[20]

As well as the flow of fighters, regional intelligence agencies were detecting large amounts of money being sent from Australia to Muslim rebels in the Philippines. Another intelligence report documented a payment made in January 1999 to the MILF: 'US$1.07 million dollars in the form of a foreign commercial Letter of Credit from Australia through the Hong Kong and Shanghai Bank.' According to the same classified document: 'It was also reported that MILF supporters in Australia, the Middle East and Germany are funding an MILF arms factory at Camp Abubakar that allegedly produces homemade RPGs (rocket propelled grenades) and grenade launchers.'[21]

The financial contribution from Australia didn't end there, according to this report. It stated that in April 2000 a courier from an Australian Islamic organisation was sent 'to deliver a huge amount of fund support from Australia'. The courier was identified as 'a certain Khalil Habidal aka Gerard'. The intelligence agency got his name slightly wrong, but the courier in question was well known in extremist circles in Sydney's Lakemba as 'Khalil the Filipino'. He worked as an x-ray technician at a Sydney hospital and was a regular at the Islamic Youth Movement's Haldon Street prayer room, the one kept under close watch by ASIO. After delivering the money to the Philippines, Khalil travelled on to Saudi Arabia and, at last report, had not returned.[22]

It was the dead of winter and the mercury was sliding towards zero as a posse of campers from Dee Why and Lakemba set off to trek through the Blue Mountains, west of Sydney. There were a dozen or so men, rugged up in parkas and thermals, and kitted out with rucksacks and hiking boots.

They stopped to take photos on the way, posing for a group snap at a public lookout over the rocky outcrops known as the Three Sisters. In one shot they appear lined up in rows like a footy team smiling for the camera, bedrolls and plastic water bottles on display. One wears a Nike beanie, another a *keffiyeh* headdress, Yasser Arafat style. Apart from that, they look like a group of friends out for a hike. But according to a witness statement later given to the Australian Federal Police (AFP): 'It was survival training — physical conditioning for the purpose of toughening a group of about 10 to 12 members of the jemaah for jihad.'[23]

In a second photo, some of the group are posing with their hands pointing skywards, in a gesture that signifies the first decree of Islam: 'There is but one God and Allah is his name.' At the edge of the group stands a tall, skinny man of about thirty in an oversized woollen jumper and knitted balaclava. This was the leader of the expedition, Asman Hashim, a Malaysian JI instructor dispatched to Mantiqi 4 to take charge of training in the Australian branch.

All of JI's territorial divisions were under instructions from Hambali to step up core activities such as recruitment and training. The arrival of Asman Hashim in Australia was the first step toward transforming Mantiqi 4 into an operational wing like the other three.

Asman arrived in Sydney in March 1998. He hailed from the Malaysian state of Sabah and was a graduate of Camp Abubakar, where he had completed the basic training course in weapons handling, explosives and guerilla warfare. Asman was both a close friend and brother-in-law of the Afghan veteran Abdul Rahman Ayub, who had arranged his assignment to Australia. Asman also knew Hambali from the chief's days in Sabah, which was a major transit point for JI recruits travelling from Malaysia and Indonesia for training in the Philippines.

Like his friend Abdul Rahman, Asman came to Australia full of tales of his exploits in the jihad. He boasted of his tours in the Philippines and Afghanistan 'fighting for Islam', and his expertise in martial arts. He seemed to have energy to burn and perhaps little wonder. According to Australian intelligence, Asman was a drug addict who had 'scrambled his brains' with amphetamines, before taking up the cause of jihad.[24]

Asman settled in Dee Why, where the original JI jemaah was still thriving, despite the Ayub twins having moved to Perth. He was put up at the JI safe house in Pittwater Road, the flat with the neatly stacked sleeping mats and the poster of Abu Bakar Bashir on the living-room wall. He later moved to another flat and got a job in a factory making roller doors in nearby Mona Vale. His tourist visa didn't allow him to work, so he used the name and tax file number of another member of the jemaah who had permanent residency in Australia.

Asman had dual roles — to organise the training camps for JI members and to keep an eye on the community at Dee Why for the Ayub brothers. 'He was the eyes and ears of the twins in Sydney,' one man in the jemaah told me. Asman would later return to Malaysia where he was arrested in February 2003 and detained indefinitely under the country's Internal Security Act for his involvement with JI.

Asman's bush training camps took place about once a month, according to the witness who called them survival training for jihad. The session in the NSW Blue Mountains when the photos were taken was in winter 1999. The group of about a dozen hiked for several hours through the forest to a camp site near Victoria Falls. For the less fit among them, it was a gruelling trek, the rocky path zigzagging for kilometres over boulders, in out of gullies and down a precipitous mountain to the spot where they made camp for the night. Directed by the jihad veteran Asman, the campers did physical exercises and military-style drills, then divided up into two sides to wage mock battles in the bush.

During some of these training sessions, the participants were equipped with regulation overalls and fake guns to make the exercises more lifelike. After the physical training, the group undertook intensive indoctrination sessions that went on far into the night. This religious and political drilling was done with the aid of manuals supplied earlier from Malaysia by Abdullah Sungkar and Abu Bakar Bashir.

One of the manuals used in this training was a dog-eared booklet with a green cover, entitled, in Indonesian, *A Course in Understanding Islam*. It outlined the JI leaders' theory of harnessing the three strengths of Islam — faith, community and military strength. The book was passed around among JI's Australian membership, along with the English translaton by Jack Roche.

'Allah ordered Muslims to develop armed strength by preparing arms and tanks, so as to strike fear into the hearts of Allah's enemies,' Bashir's manual declared. 'Human history shows that humans have known no time of greater justice, peace and prosperity than under Islamic rule. Once Islamic rule ended, human beings experienced oppression, chaos and tyranny. This situation will continue until power returns to the hands of Muslims.'[25]

The manual showed a diagram depicting Islam as a house, with faith as the foundations, Islamic law as the walls and jihad as the roof, protecting the house and its inhabitants. 'If there were no roof, the foundations and the walls would be destroyed, no matter how strongly they were built, and the house would be unfit to live in.'

After a weekend spent studying Bashir's dogma and doing jihad practice in the freezing forest, the expeditioners in the 1999 trip to the Blue Mountains hiked back to civilisation. 'It was very hard, some of them could barely make it back,' recalled one of the trekkers, Jack

Roche. The burly forklift driver relished the sessions himself, helping Asman organise the camping trips. Two years after swearing the oath of allegiance in Dee Why, Roche, known within the group as Khalid, was now an absolute devotee.

'In 1998–99 Jack Roche became more noticeably pro-jihad,' in the words of a close friend and fellow convert, Ibrahim Fraser. Like Roche, Fraser is a hulk of a man — more than six foot tall and weighing 180 kilograms, but also quietly spoken. A storeman and packer turned taxi driver, Ibrahim Fraser had converted to Islam in 1990 and met Roche at the Dee Why mosque. The pair became best friends. As Jack Roche became more 'pro-jihad', he confided regularly in Fraser.

'He told me that he wished he was involved in the conflict in Afghanistan,' Fraser said later in a statement to the Federal Police, after being cultivated as a witness against his friend. Roche couldn't afford to go to Afghanistan, where at this stage the ruling Taliban was fighting the Northern Alliance led by the warlord, Ahmad Shah Massoud. Roche had travelled to Malaysia, instead, to visit JI's leaders Sungkar and Bashir, before the latter's death. There he had been introduced to others in the JI hierarchy including Muklas.[26]

Roche had spent many hours listening to the JI leaders expound on their philosophy of jihad and translating their pronouncements into English for distribution in Mantiqi 4. In the process he had taken the motto in his mentors' 1998 manifesto to heart: 'Life in an Islamic state or death while striving to achieve it.'

Roche was now privy to the internal workings of Jemaah Islamiyah and its integral role in the international mujahideen network united under Osama bin Laden's umbrella group, al Qaeda.

Ibrahim Fraser revealed this to the Federal Police: 'Jack told me, and Abdul Rahim later confirmed it with me, that between 1996 and 1998 there had been a meeting in Afghanistan of all the emirs worldwide at which a worldwide strategy had been formulated for jihad. In that strategy, they had drawn up a plan so that one hand did not know what the other was doing. The purpose of compartmentalising in this way was to allow it to continue functioning should one group or cell be compromised.'

By late 1999, the main hub for JI activity on the eastern seaboard of Australia had shifted from Dee Why on the northern beaches to Lakemba in Sydney's southwest, the heart of the city's Muslim community. Before leaving for Perth, the Ayub twins had instructed their closest followers who remained in Sydney to boycott the new Dee Why mosque, which remained in the hands of their rivals, and to attend the more radical Haldon Street prayer room instead. The men from JI were welcomed there by its spiritual leader, Sheik Omran, and his star protégé, a fiery young preacher known as Sheik Feiz. The twins themselves had often attended the younger sheik's lectures, and had been invited for dinner at his home. 'They were very nice people,' Sheik Feiz said later. 'I never experienced any problems.'[27]

JI's most ardent supporters now based themselves around Lakemba. They included Jack Roche, who had moved from Dee Why, and the Mantiqi 4 deputy, Wandi, who ran a butcher shop in Haldon Street. The JI stalwarts prayed at the IYM prayer room and attended the weekly lectures by Sheik Feiz, whose blistering orations proved irresistible to the likes of Jack Roche.

'Oh you who believe, do not take as intimate friends, as advisers, those outside of your religion,' Sheik Feiz would intone in his sermons. 'Those who are non-Muslims — do not take them as intimate friends and advisers, for they will spare no efforts to corrupt you. They desire to harm you severely. Hatred has appeared from their mouths. However, what their hearts conceal is far greater, far worse ... These people are evil, they are cunning, they work in a subtle way!'

Sheik Feiz in full flight is a sight to behold. A brilliant demagogue and a striking man to look at — pale skin, jet-black beard, arched eyebrows and garbed all in black — his eyes flash and his hands gesticulate wildly as he delivers his spray. This sample is from a sermon entitled 'The Enemy's Plot', one of twenty Sheik Feiz lectures available on videotape at the Islamic bookshop in Lakemba and at Feiz's Global Islamic Youth Centre at Liverpool in Sydney's southwest.

The 'enemy' Feiz refers to is the Christians and Jews — or 'Zionist pigs' as he calls them — who rule Australia and the West, and their 'plot' is to destroy Islam by what Feiz calls an 'ideological invasion', a modern-day variation on the Christian Crusader invasions of mediaeval times.

'They have poisoned you, induced in you poison, and this war, this type of attack takes place by means of school curriculums, general education, TV, internet, vaccinations, fashion, publications, media, theories, philosophies . . . The attack is within your very home, your very lifestyle, the way you walk, the way you sit, the way you eat, the way you drink, the way you live. Look and reflect! The attack of the Christian Crusaders today is at its most intense.'

Sheik Feiz delivers his alarming invective in the unmistakeable Lebanese Australian accent of a young man born and raised on the streets of Sydney's southwest. In his former life, Feiz was a teenage boxer and body-building champion known as Frank the Beast.

'As a teenager I got a bit nasty, a lot of drugs, a lot of evil stuff,' he told a reporter from the *Australian*. 'I actually feared death or imprisonment because that was the next stage in my life.'[28] Searching for salvation, young Frank explored Christianity, Buddhism and even Judaism, and then finally, 'I found the truth.'

Like Jack Roche, 'the truth' for Frank the Beast was to be found in the stark simplicity of Islam in its most puritanical form. 'I don't believe in unclear concepts,' Feiz explained. 'Everything divine must be clear.' He became a follower of Sheik Omran's Ahlus Sunnah wal Jama'ah group and its fundamentalist Salafi brand of Islam. Sheik Omran then sent his young acolyte to Medina University in Saudi Arabia to learn Arabic and study the Koran.

The former Frank the Beast returned nine years later as Sheik Feiz and set up his Global Islamic Youth Centre at Liverpool. He fast became a role model for Muslim boys and young men. 'I understood the youth,' he explained. 'For the first time they were taught by someone who was one of them and who knew what they were experiencing — they understood me and I understood them.'[29]

The reformed pugilist certainly knows how to pull a crowd. Today hundreds of young men from Sydney's western and southern suburbs crowd into his twice-weekly lectures at Liverpool and snap up his sermons on videotape. In a community that has often felt marginalised and discriminated against, Feiz's stirring homilies are a powerful call to Muslim pride and solidarity. His appeal is strengthened by the unfolding dramas in the Middle East, as Feiz denounces the conflict in Iraq as 'nothing but a war on Islam and the Muslims, to ensure the Zionists — those pigs — the Zionist American domination in every corner of this earth.'

In 'The Enemy's Plot', Feiz rails that Australian Muslims have been seduced by the luxuries of their Western lifestyle and the 'cultivation' of material comforts, to the point where they are no longer willing to sacrifice their lives for Islam. Government assistance such as family allowances is seen as part of 'the enemy's plot', encouraging women to leave their husbands and let the government support them instead. Feiz feigns the scorn of a woman berating her husband for failing to match the government's largesse.

"'John Howard is paying for my bills, for my rent, for my electricity, my phone bill, he's giving me and giving me — and what are you giving me?'" Feiz then asks rhetorically, 'And how many homes have been destroyed because of governments as such? . . . This is a plot! It's a plot against us.'

Sheik Feiz harangues his flock for abandoning their faith, for cowering under their 'nice, warm doonas' and ignoring the call of jihad. His voice rises to a shout then falls to a whisper as he hectors and cajoles his congregation by turn, his tirade peppered with phrases in fluent Arabic from the Koran and *hadith*. 'When they succeed in this plot, what's gonna happen?' he demands. 'It's gonna be easy for them to assault us — to brutally shed our blood, to rape our children and women, to destroy our mosques! They are determined to wipe the name of Islam from the face of this earth.'

Sheik Feiz is almost shreiking as 'The Enemy's Plot' nears its finale. 'Brothers and sisters — what are you living for? What are we doing here? What's happening in the world? Go to Iraq today and see your brothers and sisters — see them, see what is happening there — it's gonna happen to you one day! Don't think because you're in Australia, you're comfortable . . . Look what's happening, brothers and sisters! Their heads are being blown off, their legs are being amputated, their arms, their bodies, their meat is being just thrown off their bodies. Look! And we are too comfortable with cultivation. We're too scared to go to jihad. What are you living for?!'

During one of Sheik Feiz's sermons in 1999, the Muslim convert and JI member Jack Roche was among those mesmerised in the crowd. This was at the time when Roche was becoming 'more noticeably pro-jihad', as his friend Ibrahim Fraser observed.

Sheik Feiz's apocalyptic message was an epiphany for Roche, according to Fraser, who was with him at the time. 'Jack said, "At long last we've met someone who has something to say about Islam. You get sick of all the rhetoric, of listening to all the bullshit,"' Fraser told me in 2003. Roche became a student of Sheik Feiz, attending his weekly lectures every Saturday night at the Haldon Street prayer room for the next two years. Roche later took his son Jens to Feiz to have him utter the declaration of faith to become a Muslim.[30]

Jack Roche was now willing to take his faith to its extreme. 'He told me that the greatest way to die was in jihad as you then become a martyr,' Ibrahim Fraser said in his statement to the police. 'He also told me in discussions that he had no problems in carrying out jihad against anyone, including Australians.'

❦

CHAPTER SIXTEEN

KHALID'S PLAN

JACK ROCHE WAS AT HOME in Lakemba when the call to jihad came in January 2000. It was the leader of Mantiqi 4, Abdul Rahim Ayub, on the phone from Perth. 'Abdul Rahim told me that there was something he needed to discuss with me and it regarded somebody going to Malaysia, and his decision was that that somebody was to be me,' Roche later testified at his trial.

The request for someone to be sent from the Australian branch to Malaysia had come right from the top, from JI's operations chief, Hambali, to the Ayubs. 'They wanted someone to go over to see him, preferably an Australian or Caucasian,' said Roche. Hambali and his al Qaeda masters were preparing to mount attacks on Western targets, in keeping with bin Laden's fatwa. The burly former Yorkshireman known as Khalid was just the kind of operative they needed.

'They were starting to think that if they were going to do something in a Western nation ... anybody of Middle Eastern appearance was suspected easily,' Roche told Colleen Egan of the *Australian*. 'I mean, it's not easy to get into Australia, it's not easy to get into the UK, it's not easy to get into the US, particularly if you're of Muslim appearance. So they started to think — I mean, this is all the way from Afghanistan — they started to think, and rightly so, that it would be better to get a local, because they're less suspicious. I mean, I shave my beard and I'm just Joe Blow, you know.'[1]

Roche was not Hambali's first choice. Hambali had requested Abu Ishmael, the Perth roof tiler the Ayubs had sent for training in Camp Abubakar. But according to Roche's testimony, Abu Ishmael was 'umming and ahing about whether to go' and Abdul Rahim said, 'Look, forget it. I'll get somebody else.' Roche leapt at the chance. 'Well I was full of all this fervour,' he explained later. 'You're sort of caught up in the fervour. You think, great — you're actually doing something useful.'

Roche immediately began planning for his trip. He quit his job as a forklift driver with BHP at Villawood and invited his son Jens to live in his flat in Lakemba while he was away. An excited Roche confided in his friend Ibrahim Fraser about his secondment. 'Jack told me that he was under a person in Malaysia. He was taking instructions from this person. This meant that he was no longer under the control of the Ayubs. At a later time Jack told me that this person was Hambali.'[2]

At first, Roche had little idea who Hambali was. He had heard the name from Mantiqi 4's deputy leader, Wandi, whom Roche testified 'knew Hambali well'. Wandi had recently returned from one of his frequent trips to Malaysia and was able to fill Roche in on Hambali's role in JI. There is no evidence beyond this that Wandi played any part in Roche's activities.

Roche discussed his trip further with the Ayubs, who explained that from Malaysia he would be sent for basic military training in Afghanistan, where, Abdul Rahim told him, 'possibly you will meet the sheik'. Abdul Rahim said this would be 'Sheik Sayyaf', the Afghan mujahideen leader responsible for JI's training in Afghanistan. Roche assumed he would finally get his chance to fight with the Taliban against the opposition Northern Alliance. 'He told me he was going for jihad,' Ibrahim Fraser testified. 'He did not expect to return and expected to die as a martyr.'

Before he left, Roche did the rounds of Islamic extremists in Sydney, raising funds 'for Osama bin Laden', he told his friend Fraser. As he made his final preparations, Roche penned a note to his son. 'My dearest Jens,' he wrote, 'hopefully you already know the situation regarding the flat. I will leave all relevant keys — doors, window, post box, etc, on the bed. The laundry keys are in the airing cupboard. Remember that I love you very much . . . It is the greatest sacrifice worthy of the highest reward from Allah that I am about to undertake . . . But as Muslims we are obliged to perform jihad to uphold the laws of Allah — the truth on this earth . . . As we see today the disbelievers are now out of control and believe that their ways — ways based on inequality, arrogance, etc — are right. I hate them for that and need to learn more about how to combat them. Please pray for me as I will pray for you . . . Your loving father, Khalid.'[3]

On 15 February 2000, Jack Roche flew out of Sydney for Jakarta. He kept a diary of his trip, the entry for day one stating: 'Tuesday 15/2/00 Jakarta arrive 1430. REST.' Also noted in Roche's diary was a mobile phone number and the name of a top JI leader in Indonesia he was to call on arrival, a man described to Roche as one of Abu Bakar Bashir's 'generals'. The name was Abu Hamzah, an alias of Thoriqudin (also known as Abu Rusdan), who would eventually replace Bashir as emir of JI. Roche made contact as instructed, then flew on to his next stop.

After the air-conditioned chill of Kuala Lumpur's sleek international airport, the tropical heat enfolded him like a blanket, as Roche made his way through the swarm of hotel touts and taxi drivers clamouring for custom on the roadway outside. Among the crowd was a driver waiting for the large, bearded foreigner, to take him on the 45-minute journey south to the secluded kampung of Sungai Manggis.

The taxi pulled up beside the cluster of bungalows in the banana grove. Roche was taken to a building he described as 'just a normal house . . . used as a mosque and an administrative centre.' A rotund, bespectacled man in robes and skullcap arrived on a motorbike shortly afterwards to greet the visitor from Mantiqi 4, and gave him a lift to his own home a few houses down.

I asked Roche much later what the infamous Hambali was like. He paused to think and then answered: 'I wouldn't say he's evil, that's not the word. He's very devoted to the cause . . . He believes very strongly in what he's doing and that he's found his cause in life.' Similarly intense, dedicated and quietly spoken, the two men got on well, Roche describing Hambali as 'serious but easy to get along with'. Thanks to Roche's fluent Indonesian, they could communicate with ease.

Roche stayed for two or three days at Hambali's home in Sungai Manggis. Hambali was relaxed, chatting about growing up in his lush but impoverished village in West Java. He told Roche that he still sent money home to his mother and that he had been back recently and nothing had changed. As Roche fended off the mosquitoes, Hambali's Chinese Malaysian wife prepared their meals, but stayed unseen by Roche in a curtained-off part of the house for the duration of his stay, in rigid accordance with the Prophet Muhammad's revelation, 'If you ask his wives for anything, speak to them from behind a curtain.' (Koran 33:53)

After what Roche called 'general chitchat', he and Hambali got down to business. 'Hambali's idea was to set up a cell in Australia that was a lot more committed than the group in general was in Australia,' Roche later recalled. Everyone knew there was little love lost between Hambali and the Ayubs, and the chief was plainly impatient with the slow progress in Australia, which came under the control of the more conservative Indonesian leadership of Mantiqi 2, his frustration recounted by Roche: 'Abdul Rahim has been in Australia for something like fifteen years ... fifteen years and nothing's really happened in Australia, and they're not bothered. I mean, not bomb-wise, but the development of the group as a whole has not really developed at all.'[4]

Now Hambali wanted to bring Mantiqi 4 under his own command, by establishing a cell that he would control. 'I was supposed to recruit a couple of people here and then send them over to Afghanistan for training,' said Roche. 'There just needs to be three, possibly four, people. I mean, this is an operational cell. Possibly four people who are committed, they work together, they have nothing to do with anybody else ... and their ultimate aim is to go for targets. To target something, to work on that, get that target and then to disappear. And then maybe in a few months' time, do it again.'[5]

Hambali had his eye on a major event that was looming in Australia. According to Roche's testimony, 'He inquired about the Olympic Games.' Roche kept a note of this brief discussion which referred to 'the possibility to do something in Sydney, during the Olympics Games there, this year.'

This was not the first time that disrupting the Olympics had been mooted. The possibility had been canvassed within Mantiqi 4 even before his trip to Afghanistan. 'The idea of doing something was floated around,' Roche told me much later. 'It was discussed in Sydney but they didn't do it because there was no point.' Australian investigators were told that 'it was seen to not further the interests of JI to attack the Olympics.'[6]

While the arrangements were made for Roche's travel to Afghanistan for 'basic training', Roche accompanied Hambali to Kuala Lumpur where the chief had other business to attend to. As Roche told it, Hambali 'was basically going around visiting business acquaintances' and Roche accompanied him. One of the offices they called in on was that of the JI

front company, the Mawashi Corporation.[7] Before the Australian flew
out, Hambali handed Roche 1800 Malaysian ringgit (A$800) and
instructed him not to discuss the details of his assignment with the Ayub
twins. Roche then returned to Sydney to prepare for his trip.

Two and a half weeks later, on 23 March 2000, Roche flew out of
Sydney again, bound once more for Kuala Lumpur. He travelled with
his friend Ibrahim Fraser who was en route to Singapore, where he was
living at the time. According to Fraser, Roche was in a buoyant mood
because he was finally 'going on jihad'. In KL the two friends took the
skytrain to Immigration then went their separate ways.

Roche checked into the Concordia Hotel then rang Hambali.
'Where are you?' the chief demanded. Hambali had sent his driver to
meet him at the airport but Roche had already taken off on the hotel
shuttle bus. Roche said later he had no wish for another stay in
Hambali's shack in Sungai Manggis — 'not with the amount of
mosquitoes that were in that house'. Hambali met Roche at his hotel,
where he gave him a phone number to call on his next stop, Karachi,
and a note to give to a man called Mukhtar.

On arrival in Pakistan, Roche was met by a rising star in the JI
hierarchy, an Indonesian named Abdul Rohim, the son of JI's leader,
Abu Bakar Bashir. His role in Karachi, according to Roche's testimony,
was as 'a go-between between JI and al Qaeda'.

The emir's son had long been groomed for a role as one of the next
generation of JI leaders. Brought up at the Ngruki school, he regularly
deputised for his father, swearing in new JI members in Solo.[8] The
concerns that Abu Bakar Bashir had voiced about Hambali being too
close to Khalid Sheik Mohammed were evidently fleeting. According to
Australian intelligence, Bashir's son was sent to serve his apprenticeship
with Hambali's friend 'the Brain', working in al Qaeda's information
division known as the Media Committee in the 1990s, when
Mohammed was running it.[9]

In Karachi, Bashir's son had founded a new JI cell known as al
Ghuraba, meaning the foreigners, which was set up as a training cell for
future JI leaders. Described by Australian intelligence as a 'junior varsity'
providing 'the equivalent of a Masters degree' in jihad for JI's next
generation, the cell sent members for training with both al Qaeda and
the Pakistan militant group Lashkar-e-Taiba. Hambali's younger brother
Rusman Gunawan, known as Gun Gun, later took over the running of
this group.[10]

After picking up Jack Roche at the airport, Bashir's son, Abdul Rohim, acted as intermediary to arrange Roche's rendezvous with his contact in Karachi, Mukhtar. Only much later would Roche realise that the suave Pakistani with the flawless English who came to greet him the day after his arrival was none other than 'the Brain' of al Qaeda, Khalid Sheik Mohammed.

Mohammed took Roche to stay overnight at his Karachi home, but their time together was fleeting; al Qaeda's operations chief was a busy man, deeply involved at this stage in preparations for the September 11 attacks on the United States. Mohammed allocated about one hour for his discussion with Roche. 'He was interested in Israeli interests in Australia,' Roche later testified. 'He was interested in airlines, especially American airlines.'

In his notebook, Roche recorded: 'I discussed with him about doing something in Australia — not at the Olympic Games in Sydney but looking for a target in Australia which if it happens will result in a heavy impact on the Jews in Australia . . . The main objective here is that this operation will not only be done once but issuing targets and disappear — in the future we will do something again.'

Khalid Sheik Mohammed instructed Roche to use the alias Abdullah on his travels and handed him a letter to pass on to 'the sheik'. Mohammed also introduced Roche to the man who would escort him across the border into Afghanistan.

Roche's guide was a German in his early thirties, who lived with his family in the al Qaeda camp that Roche was to visit.[11] Like all al Qaeda operatives, the German went by an assumed name, Abu Mohammed. His real name was Christian Ganczarski — a name now extremely well known to anti-terrorism authorities across Europe. 'This is a serious, dangerous jihadist,' one French official said later of Ganczarski, 'someone with several trips to Afghan camps behind him, who has met top al Qaeda leaders including bin Laden. He should have been behind bars long ago.'[12]

On the 600-kilometre bus trip to the Afghanistan border, Roche and Ganczarski found they had plenty in common. Ganczarski had grown up a Roman Catholic in Poland, moved with his family to Germany, then rebelled against his parents, dropping out of high school and getting an apprenticeship as a welder. Like Roche, Muslim workmates introduced him to the Koran, and he converted to Islam at age twenty, marrying another convert he met at a mosque. He went on to study at the University of Medina for two years, emerging committed to a life of jihad.

By the time he met Roche, Ganczarski had fought in Chechnya and Afghanistan, and become a specialist for al Qaeda in computers and telecommunications. He was so well trusted that he was used as a courier between bin Laden's camp in Afghanistan and Khalid Sheik Mohammed in Karachi. Ganczarski would later be charged over the suicide bombing of a Jewish synagogue in Tunisia in April 2002, which he allegedly orchestrated with Mohammed. According to German intelligence, the bomber phoned Ganczarski moments before the explosion; Ganczarski asked if there was anything more he needed, to which the bomber replied, 'I only need the command!' The command was given and the bomb was detonated, killing twenty-one people.[13]

Jack Roche was not the only Australian connection of Christian Ganczarski. When Ganczarski was eventually captured in Paris in June 2003 and French police began investigating all of his contacts, one of the names they turned up was Willie Brigitte, a Frenchman who had trained with Lashkar-e-Taiba in Pakistan. The French police learned that Brigitte was in Australia and tipped off ASIO, who had Brigitte arrested and deported to France. Brigitte would later confess to having been sent to Sydney to take part in 'a large-scale terrorist action in Australia'.[14]

In the company of Ganczarski, Jack Roche travelled north by bus across the bleak desert wastelands of Pakistan's Baluchistan province to the frontier town of Quetta. From there they took a taxi up the mountain highway and across the famed Khojak Pass, the same route on which the British Imperial Army had met its ruin after its effort to conquer the Pashtun warriors of Afghanistan. After crossing the border and passing through a series of Taliban checkpoints, they arrived at their final destination, an al Qaeda encampment about 10 kilometres from Kandahar.

The camp was a 1.5-kilometre walk from the main road. They entered it by foot through an archway, manned on either side by guards with Kalashnikovs. There were weapons everywhere, machine-guns, pistols, assault rifles, the lot. All eyes were on Roche. 'I was very conscious,' he remembered, 'of heavily armed people there and they're looking at me very — I mean, they're examining me.'

The guide, Ganczarski, led Roche to an administration building to be introduced, and then into a mess hall where about 200 men were just seating themselves on the floor for lunch. Ganczarski sat down to join them and a couple of men moved aside to make room for Roche.

'Between mouthfuls of food I happened to look around and I saw somebody looking at me,' Roche would later testify. 'I was quite shocked — it was Osama bin Laden — I was quite shocked . . . After a while I became conscious that I was actually staring at him and it really was shock, and I quickly, I thought, you know, staring is not a good thing in Islam. I don't think it's good in any society, so I immediately turned away.'

After the meal Roche went outside to wash his hands, but unwittingly exited the mess hall by a doorway leading to the living quarters reserved for married men in the camp, a faux pas he was later told could be punishable by death. Just as he did so, 'Osama bin Laden walked through with between eight and ten heavily armed — I assumed were guards, his personal guards.' Bin Laden gestured to Roche in a comradely fashion to go back inside, urging him with the words 'Please brother' in Arabic. Roche did as he was bid. Those were the only words they exchanged. As Roche put it, 'I nodded, he nodded and that was about it.'

But the al Qaeda chief knew who Roche was. Ganczarski had passed to bin Laden the note that Khalid Sheik Mohammed had given Roche in Karachi for 'the sheik'. Roche was told that bin Laden had read the note and would arrange for someone to speak to him 'about the purpose of his visit'.

Roche was introduced next to two of bin Laden's senior henchmen — his security chief, Saif el Adel, and his trusted military chief and long-time lieutenant, Abu Hafs. These two would be Roche's main contacts in the al Qaeda leadership for the duration of his stay. They asked first about the situation in the Philippines and Indonesia, and Abu Hafs inquired after his old comrade, 'Hussein', an alias of the Mantiqi 4 Afghan veteran Abdul Rahman Ayub. Then the discussion moved on to Roche's assignment.

'They asked me about airlines to and from — American airlines — to and from Australia. They asked me about Israeli interests in Australia . . . I think they had their eye on the Israeli embassy and they seemed to be interested in Joe Gutnick.' By Roche's account, the name of the Jewish Australian mining magnate, Joe Gutnick, was raised by Abu Hafs because of Gutnick's prominence as a supporter of Israel's recently resigned conservative former Likud Party leader, Benjamin Netanyahu.

Roche later told the Federal Police, 'They saw him as a link between the Israeli government and the Australian government . . . He seems to assist the Israeli government as much as possible, so they saw him as somebody who was a bit of a power broker and they thought his death would have had some sort of effect.'[15]

Saif el Adel arranged a ten-day course in explosives for Roche and gave him personal tuition in 'security methods' such as covert photography, instructing him to send his surveillance footage of potential targets back via Hambali. Abu Hafs briefed Roche further on Hambali's plan to recruit a cell. 'He basically said, "Look, if you can try and recruit other people with the idea to setting up some kind of cell in Australia . . ." He mentioned two or three. . . If it was possible for me to recruit them, to have them sent over to Afghanistan for training . . . One of them was to train in explosives, but a very intense — I mean, he was talking six months. And the other was to be trained in use of weapons and sniping.'

Roche agreed to carry out his allotted tasks, recording later in his notebook: 'Their decision is two important targets in Australia — Israel embassy and/or a Jews [sic] named Joe Gutnick. They decided to accept three white Australian Muslim to do training in Afghanistan. They will provide finance for these operations . . . In Australia my task is to look for a complete information on those targets and to find those three persons mentioned before. So I become the co-ordinator for the operations in Australia.'

After two and a half weeks in Afghanistan, Roche bade farewell to his new friends from al Qaeda. He stopped over again in Karachi for another brief meeting with Khalid Sheik Mohammed, who gave him US$3250 in cash and instructed him not to tell anyone in Australia what he was doing. He then flew on to Kuala Lumpur to see Hambali, who repeated Mohammed's instruction and gave him another US$4750, just delivered by courier from Pakistan. Finally, Roche headed for home.

Jack Roche flew back to Australia on 26 May 2000, to find the country in the grip of preparations for the most ambitious event it had ever staged — the Sydney Olympic Games. It was just over three months until the opening ceremony.

At the headquarters of the Sydney Organising Committee, SOCOG, things were getting hectic for Neil Fergus and his team at the Olympic Intelligence Centre. Fergus stepped out of the lift on the tenth floor, raised his right hand to the biometric scanner that activated the security door, then strode along the grey-carpeted corridor lined with 'Share the Spirit' posters to his corner office, waving good morning to the receptionist and staff in their open-plan cubicles on the way.

Fergus wore his usual amiable grin, but the veteran ASIO officer seconded to run intelligence for the Olympics had plenty to worry him. The Olympic torch was wending its way through the Pacific islands en route to Sydney, running the gauntlet of a bloody insurgency in the Solomon Islands, general lawlessness in Port Moresby and a coup in Fiji. The route was being changed daily for fear the torch would be hijacked by armed rebels as a PR stunt. At home, protestors were threatening to disrupt the open-air volleyball stadium on Bondi Beach and the anti-globalisation lobby was planning to rally at the Games. Those were the least of Neil Fergus's concerns.

There was a rising buzz of intelligence 'chatter' suggesting a terrorist strike at the Olympics was 'a very real possibility'. 'Al Qaeda and all of its sub-groups and aligned groups were regarded as the principal threat,' Fergus told me later. 'The consequence of them carrying out an attack would have been catastrophic, so that certainly was the focus of a great deal of energy.'[16]

Fergus and his team were working in two shifts over a sixteen-hour day, with personnel from the security intelligence organisation, ASIO, its foreign counterpart, ASIS, the NSW and Australian Federal Police, the army, Foreign Affairs Department, Customs Service, Defence Intelligence Organisation and Bureau of Criminal Intelligence. It was the biggest intelligence exercise in Australia's peacetime history. It would soon ratchet up to three shifts, operating around the clock.

The intelligence coming in from abroad was being processed at a separate Federal Olympic Security Intelligence Centre at ASIO headquarters in Canberra, then fed into the secure 'hub room' of Fergus's unit in Sydney. 'There were over 120 different intelligence investigations that had to be rigorously pursued,' said Fergus. 'A number of those related to people that were known to have links, and in many cases clear links, to al Qaeda or its surrogate groups.'

The main concern for Fergus and his associates was the extremists linked with the Islamic Youth Movement based in Lakemba, publishers of the radical magazine *Nida'ul Islam*, whose laudatory interviews with Osama bin Laden and others had brought it to the attention of ASIO. Their concerns would be heightened in the lead-up to the Games, with the discovery of a military-style camp, three hours' drive out of Sydney, on a property used by members of the IYM. A farmer had reported hearing automatic weapons fire in the bush and a local contractor had seen fifteen to twenty men setting up camp with rifles and shotguns for target practice. When they raided it, the police found automatic weapons cartridges and home-made explosives at the site, described by Neil Fergus as having 'all of the hallmarks of a full-blown terrorist training camp'. The men connected with the camp scattered after the raid, several of them heading overseas, and no arrests were made.

But despite the massive intelligence trawl preceding the Olympics, not one of the scores of leads flushed out related to al Qaeda's regional partner JI, or its Australian branch Mantiqi 4, or their newly activated operative Jack Roche. Seven years after its formation, JI remained completely unknown to the police and intelligence agencies of Australia, and, for that matter, their counterparts overseas. The authorities didn't even know who Jack Roche was, let alone that he was on his way to Sydney with instructions for a bombing.

In keeping with advice from his controllers, Roche had varied his route and changed his appearance before coming home. 'I went from Sydney and returned via Perth. I left with a beard and returned without a beard.'[17] His friend Ibrahim Fraser had never seen Roche clean-shaven. 'I didn't recognise him when I saw him. He told me it was to be low profile.'

Roche had been due to fly home via Sydney but had decided to move to Perth. He said later that he also wanted to brief Mantiqi 4 leader, Abdul Rahim Ayub and his brother, Abdul Rahman. In spite of Hambali and Khalid Sheik Mohammed's instructions not to discuss his mission with anyone, Roche said he felt that the Ayub brothers 'needed to be aware of what I'd just gone through.'

The Ayub twins came out to Perth airport to meet Roche on arrival, accompanied by the the bus driver from the Al Hidayah school, John Bennett, and the JI-trained Perth roof tiler, Abu Ishmael. They drove Roche to Abdul Rahim's house in Thornlie and had a cup of tea.

Roche stayed there for the next five days, the Ayub brothers quizzing him at length about his trip.

'I was basically debriefed as to what had taken place overseas,' Roche later testified. 'And they had no qualms whatsoever about me surveilling the Israeli embassy or gathering information about Joe Gutnick. I took it to mean that they were quite willing to go ahead with whatever was planned in Afghanistan.'

With the approval of the Ayub twins, Roche began preparing for his trip to the eastern states. He cruised the used-car yards along the Albany Highway with the Ayub twins and John Bennett, picking up a Toyota Tercel for $3000 in cash, using the money given to him by al Qaeda. The car was registered in Abdul Rahim's name, as Roche didn't have a valid driver's licence.

Next Roche set about recruiting a cell. His first choice was John Bennett, a committed convert and gun buff. 'He had a fascination with weapons . . . I saw him as a possible sniper as Abu Hafs had mentioned to me,' Roche later explained. Roche popped the question one day in the backyard of Bennett's home in Thornlie. 'I asked him, "Look, would you be interested in going to Afghanistan? Would you be prepared to do something against Israeli interests in Australia?" and I made a point of saying to him, "But whatever you do, don't tell the twins."'

Bennett was horrified. 'He wanted to do something against the Israelis here in Australia, maybe take out an Israeli embassy or something like that,' Bennett testified. 'I was probably in a state of shock, you know, coming out with something like that . . . I can't remember the exact words, but I made it clear that I wasn't happy with it, and that "You can't do that here." Islamically, it's against Islam.'[18]

Bennett's immediate reaction was to do what Roche had asked him not to — to tell the twins of Roche's attempt to recruit him into a separate al Qaeda cell. 'I immediately went around to their place,' Bennett recounted, 'and told them what this guy Hambali wanted to do here and they were pretty angry about it. They were quite furious and very upset that this guy, Hambali, who they knew . . .' Bennett's testimony was interrupted at this point in Roche's trial. But Roche went on to give his own version of why the twins suddenly switched from supporting his activities to being 'very upset'.

By Roche's account, the Afghan veteran Abdul Rahman was eager to go with him to Sydney: 'He wanted to partake in all of this, the planning from Afghanistan.' But Roche was in a hurry and Abdul

Rahman wasn't ready to go, so — to the twins' annoyance — Roche left without him. 'That was the cause of the falling out — I went alone and they were pissed off,' according to Roche.[19]

Roche elaborated in court: 'They wanted to control the situation. They were having problems with coming to grips with the fact that I appeared to be Hambali's man in Australia whereas they saw me as their man in Australia. They really did want to control the situation.' Roche's friend Ibrahim Fraser supported this view, explaining, in his words, 'The Ayubs were pissed off with Jack because he and Hambali were doing al Qaeda work in Australia.'[20]

The twins were also annoyed that Roche refused to hand over any of the US$8000 that he had got from al Qaeda. Ibrahim Fraser testified: 'The twins said that that money was for them, that that was their money, and supposedly he was given that money for them, but he always maintained that that money was for him to use. So it caused a falling out.'

Australian investigators accept these accounts of the Ayub brothers initially backing Roche's mission but then changing their minds due to their turf war with Hambali. A senior investigator briefed me: 'The Ayubs went cold because they felt left out. They weren't being consulted, they had no control of the money and we suspect Jack wasn't very smart and told them Hambali had said not to tell them. There was a sudden change to "We want this thing stopped and how dare Hambali get on our patch."'[21]

Roche made the long drive across the Nullarbor on his own. He was stopped by police at the South Australian border but, although he couldn't produce a licence, they let him go. He arrived in Sydney in early June, as the city counted down the days to the Games. The torch had made its way safely to Australia and was being carried through outback Queensland on its way to the Homebush Stadium. At the Olympic Intelligence Centre, Neil Fergus and his colleagues were on high alert, poring over every scrap of intelligence that might suggest a threat, oblivious to the movements of Roche.

Roche returned to his flat in Dennis Street, Lakemba. His friend Fraser, just back from Singapore, came and stayed with him. Roche talked freely of his plans. 'He stated to me that he had been instructed by Osama bin Laden to blow up the Israeli embassy in Canberra and that this should occur during the Olympic Games,' Fraser testified. Roche later told another contact that the plan was for suicide bombers to be brought in to carry out the attack.[22] He made inquiries about obtaining explosives from his friend Fraser, who used to be a shot firer in the mines of Western Australia. 'He said to me, "Where do I get 'tea' from?" And I said, "Well down the local coffee shop, mate." And he said, "No, TNT."'[23]

Roche used the internet to collect information on Joe Gutnick, claiming later to have got the businessman's home address through an online street directory. He didn't get as far as going to Melbourne, where Gutnick lived, to reconnoitre his home. The mining boss was shocked, two years later, to hear of how he was targeted. 'I learned about Roche's plans from the AFP, his plans to blow up the embassy in Canberra, his plans to blow up the consulate in Sydney and also he had targeted myself, to kill me,' said Gutnick. 'He knew where I lived and the synagogue I prayed in and he was planning to blow up a certain part of Caulfield.'[24]

In Sydney, Roche paid a visit to his old teacher Sheik Feiz, whose fiery sermons had been such an inspiration. The convert had a favour to ask of his sheik.

'He said, "Would you mind if a borrowed a video camera?"' Sheik Feiz recalled later. 'I said yes — but he didn't tell me what he wanted it for.' Feiz gave Roche the camera and showed him how to use it, but said he had no idea why Roche wanted it until ASIO knocked on his door two years later. 'They interviewed me and asked, "Did you give him the camera?" And I said, "Yes, I loaned it to him and that is all I know about it." They told me that he went to Canberra, they accused him of videoing embassies. I was shocked, I was absolutely stunned. If he had said to me "I want to film an embassy" — or a synagogue or something like that — I would have said "You're kidding!"'[25]

Armed with Sheik Feiz's camera, Roche took his son Jens on an outing to central Sydney, stopping near the Wynyard railway station. 'He had a video camera with him and he was filming up and down the street,' Jens later testified. Roche videotaped the office block housing the Israeli consulate in York Street, commenting to Jens as he filmed, 'Down on the corner from the building would be a good place to put a truck.'[26] But Roche later told Colleen Egan from the *Australian* that he quickly ruled out this target. 'There were far too many civilians around the place in York Street in Sydney when I looked at it, so I'd already basically decided that I wouldn't be doing anything there because there would be too many innocent people around.'

While Roche was in Sydney, relations with the Ayub twins continued to deteriorate. 'They were ringing me up all the time, telling me to come back,' he said later in court. 'I'm getting all these phone calls from the twins in Perth to "Stop whatever you're doing. Return to Perth. We need to talk to you." A lot of pressure from there, quite threatening.'

At the same time as the Ayubs were pressuring him to stop, Roche's controllers were chasing him to make sure he was going ahead. On 7 June, Roche had a conversation via an internet chat room with Abu Bakar Bashir's son, Abdul Rahim, the intermediary who had met him in Karachi and whom Roche described as 'a go-between' for al Qaeda and JI. On the internet, Bashir's son used the code name Sniper 21. 'He wanted to know what I was doing to further my surveillance in Australia,' said Roche. The translated transcript of their conversation was later tendered in evidence at Roche's trial.

Roche explained the conflict with the Ayub twins to Bashir's son. 'There are problems here between Abdul Rahim and Abdul Rahman and Hambali. Abdul Rahim and Abdul Rahman think that Hambali hasn't explained to your father about these duties in Australia. So those who are here do not want [to] help without approval from your father . . . They feel that Hambali has not had approval of these duties from your father . . . Abdul Rahim and Abdul Rahman are ill at ease because nobody has explained it to them.'

Bashir's son replied that it seemed to be a 'communication problem'. His comments suggest that there was no question in his mind that Roche's mission had the approval of Bashir, and that he too viewed the dispute as a question of who was in control. He told Roche, 'If I am not wrong, Hambali has already made agreement with Mukhtar's people here and feels that it has already been agreed to by the emir. So there is a possibility that the issue is [over] why Hambali takes members from Abdul Rahim and Abdul Rahman without their knowledge.'

Bashir's son believed it was up to Hambali to solve the problem with the Ayubs, advising Roche: 'You should contact Hambali again and tell him, so Hambali can clear up the problem . . . before it's too late.'[27]

It's unclear whether Roche took this advice and contacted Hambali. But Roche was obviously less concerned about pacifying the Ayub twins than about accomplishing his mission. A few days later, he set off for Canberra to complete his surveillance. He still didn't have a licence, so he asked a taxi-driver friend named Ahmed to drive him there in the Toyota Tercel. Once again Roche took his son Jens along for the ride. They arrived in Canberra mid-afternoon on 11 June, stayed overnight in a $70 cabin in a caravan park, and rose early the next day.

It was a cold, foggy Canberra morning. Security guard Geoffrey Harrison was on duty at his sentry box outside the Israeli embassy at 7.45 a.m., when he noticed a white Toyota, registration number 8BZ–352 stopped in a parking bay by the road. There were three men in the sedan. Harrison made a note in his occurrence book that the car's occupants were 'showing more interest than normal tourists', especially for that hour of the day.[28]

When one of the men got out and started filming, Harrison walked over. 'Morning. How you going?' asked Roche, in his broad Yorkshire accent.

'Good,' Harrison replied.

'It must be boring here by yourself,' Roche commented, making small talk, then added, by way of explaining why he was filming, 'Fascinated with the layout of Canberra.'

Harrison's rejoinder was caught on Roche's tape: 'Is that what it is? I didn't think you were going to go and bomb the joint or anything.'

After completing his filming, Roche made detailed notes of the layout of the embassy district, intending to send them with the footage to Hambali. While he had ruled out the consulate in Sydney because of the number of innocent civilians in the vicinity, he had no such qualms about the Canberra embassy, where he believed the casualties would be Israelis. 'Well, I could justify that. I mean, these Israelis I think I could destroy, because the whole idea of this, the state of the bombings, is to raise the awareness of the situation in Palestine. This is the whole idea of this, because what is going on in Palestine is evil.'[29]

By now, Roche's activities were becoming an open secret among the small but close community of Islamic radicals in Sydney and Perth — and a cause of growing disquiet. 'He wanted to tell everybody,' his friend Ibrahim Fraser remembered. 'You know, he told everybody, everybody in Sydney knew . . . I mean I heard about it and everybody else heard about it, and people would say, you know, this is madness . . . I remember speaking to someone in Sydney about it and saying, you know, "Have you heard what he's planning doing?" And that person said to me, "Oh we could never do that in Australia, because you know, our relationship with Australian society is pretty precarious anyway, so we wouldn't want to injure the good relationship that we're having, and look — we're here because we like this country. We don't want to destroy it, we don't want to see people get hurt.'"[30]

Among those Roche confided in after completing his surveillance was his former teacher who had lent him the video camera, Sheik Feiz. Ibrahim Fraser was with Roche when he spoke to Feiz, one Wednesday after the preacher's regular lecture at his Liverpool youth centre.

'After the discussion we went up and spoke to Feiz. Jack told him he had a plan, he said he wanted to take out the Israeli embassy . . . Sheik Feiz didn't want any part of it,' Fraser told me. Fraser said he later raised the subject with Feiz again, referring to Roche by his Muslim name, Khalid. 'I said to him, "This plan of Khalid's is the plan of a lunatic, it's very bad." Feiz agreed that it was very bad. He said, "I told him — no, no, no."'[31]

When Roche got back to Perth, the Ayub brothers didn't let up. 'They were every other day — if not every day — around, coming around to my place, putting pressure on me. It wasn't comfortable at all . . . Their main point of contention was what they saw as Hambali trying to control their situation in Australia,' Roche would later testify.

The Ayub twins sought backup to stop Roche and his plot. The brothers paid a visit to their old friend Sheik Omran, head of the Ahlus Sunnah wal Jama'ah organisation and regarded as the spiritual leader of radical Islamists in Australia. Sheik Omran was living in Perth at the time. The brothers sipped mint tea in his lounge room as they told the sheik what the convert known as Khalid was up to.

'They approached me and said this man wants to make some attacks on things . . . What do you want to do about it?' Sheik Omran later revealed.[32] The sheik said he told the Ayubs that Roche must be stopped. His view was that jihad should be waged in Islamic countries where Muslims were under attack — but not in Australia. 'I said, "Go back [to Roche] and if he doesn't stop thinking about it and talking about it, I am going to stop him."' What he meant was that he would tell the police, a threat the Australian authorities say was never carried out. The twins went home from their meeting with Sheik Omran and wrote a letter to Bashir, citing the Australian sheik's disapproval and urging Bashir to call Roche off.

By mid-July, according to his own account, Roche was getting cold feet. Al Qaeda's US$8000 had run out, his fervour had faded and his relationship with the Ayub twins was now beyond repair. Roche later claimed he wanted to extricate himself from the plot and decided the best way to do it was to go to the authorities before someone else got there first.

The phone rang at ASIO's branch office in Perth on 14 July 2000. The case officer on duty picked up the call as the automatically activated recording machine whirred into action. The ASIO man identified himself as 'Don' and asked the caller with the Yorkshire accent his name and place and date of birth. Roche then explained why he was calling.

'I said to them, "Look, I've just returned from Afghanistan, I've just met with Osama bin Laden, I'm extremely or very concerned about developments within — amongst — certain elements of the Islamic community here in Australia. I would like to have an interview with an ASIO officer and I would be —' I mean, this is my naivety, "I would be willing to work for ASIO should the need arise."' By Roche's account, the case officer agreed to arrange a meeting, but left the day and time to be confirmed.

A day or two after this, the Ayub twins showed up again at Roche's house in Perth. Abdul Rahim had his mobile phone with him and, in Roche's presence, he dialled a number in Indonesia. 'He phoned somebody and then after a little bit of hellos in Indonesian, he handed the phone to me. I took the phone and he said — it was Abu Bakar Bashir — and I was basically directed to go to meet him in Indonesia.' The Ayubs had been pestering Bashir for weeks and the emir had finally decided to resolve the dispute once and for all.

Roche bought himself a ticket for Jakarta for the following week. The day before he left, he rang the Perth ASIO office again. 'I said to them, "Look, I still want to have a meeting with an ASIO officer but I've got to go — tomorrow I've got to go to Indonesia to meet Abu Bakar Bashir . . . but I will return in approximately a couple of weeks' time and I'd like to have that interview then, please."'

Roche flew to Jakarta and rang his contact Abu Hamzah, a.k.a. Abu Rusdan, the deputy emir of JI. He was then escorted to Solo to see Bashir. He took with him a set of detailed notes he had made of the events of the past few months and an itemised account of the US$8000, in case Bashir asked how he had spent al Qaeda's money.

'Abu Bakar Bashir asked me what's going on over there,' Roche later testified. Roche explained to Bashir that he was only doing what he had been instructed to do by Hambali and the men from al Qaeda. 'He said to me, "Look, I don't know what it is that Hambali's asked you to do." He says, "I don't want to know."' Roche claimed that he and Bashir didn't discuss the details of his assignment, but at the end of their conversation, Bashir took Roche's side against the Ayubs: 'He said to me just to "Do what Hambali has told you to do."'

When Roche got back to Perth in early August, Abdul Rahim met him at the airport, eager to hear what the emir had decided. 'I told him, "Look, Abu Bakar Bashir had said to me that whatever Hambali told you to do, you do that,"' said Roche, 'and he just went — he was livid . . . to the point where I thought he was going to jump out of his van and try and attack me.' The Ayub twins demanded that Roche give back the computer they had given him for translating JI material, and swore this wouldn't be the last he would hear of it. 'They said, "We're going to send someone to Malaysia to fix Hambali."'[33]

Despite having Bashir's personal approval, Roche later claimed that he was still determined to abandon the plot. Two days after his confrontation with the Ayub twins, Roche placed a third call to ASIO. He asked again for the case officer he had spoken to before, but was told he wasn't in. 'I left a message for "Don", that, look, I'm back in Australia and I still want to have a talk, still want to have an interview.' Roche then waited for ASIO to return his call. 'I was expecting some kind of response but I got no response whatsoever.' Roche never did hear from ASIO again — until more than two years later, in the aftermath of the Bali bombings.

'The organisation stuffed up,' a senior intelligence source has since acknowledged. 'It wasn't the individual's fault. It should have been followed up. An organisation doing its job properly would have followed that through.'[34] If ASIO had followed through, it may have gained invaluable information from Roche — like the phone numbers and addresses of both Hambali and Khalid Sheik Mohammed, and an insider's account of the operations of al Qaeda and JI — more than a year before the September 11 attacks on the United States and the bombings in Bali.

This was not the only such opportunity that the Australian authorities missed. Roche's friend Ibrahim Fraser had returned to Singapore, by now deeply concerned. Fraser claimed that even after Roche's attempts to contact ASIO, he had continued discussing an attack on the Israeli embassy and making inquiries about obtaining explosives. Fraser rang the Australian high commission in Singapore and asked to speak to an Australian Federal Police officer attached to the mission. He was put through to an answering machine and left his name and number and a message asking someone to call him back. No one ever did. The AFP later claimed that Fraser had left the wrong number.[35]

Back in Perth, at Mantiqi 4 headquarters, the Ayub brothers kept up their barrage of complaints to anyone who would listen, including Abu Bakar Bashir. 'They were pestering him like a couple of mosquitoes,' according to Roche.[36] The dispute was causing deep discord within JI and rippling out through Islamist circles in Australia. It is not clear what caused Bashir to change his mind, but a week or so after Roche's return from Indonesia, the emir rang him to call the operation off. 'He rang me direct, directly, and basically just said, "Look, whatever it is you're doing, stop it."'

And that was the end of Khalid's plan. The scheme hatched by JI and al Qaeda to destroy the Israeli embassy in Canberra and assassinate the mining boss Joe Gutnick was aborted. The Sydney Olympic Games went off virtually without a hitch. Neil Fergus and his staff at the Olympic Intelligence Centre held their own celebration, quietly relieved that the terrorist attack they had feared had not materialised; they had no idea how close a call it had been.

But Australia was now squarely in al Qaeda's sights. In the wake of the Olympic Games and well after Jack Roche's job was scuttled, al Qaeda's top leadership continued to canvass attacks on Australian soil. Khalid Sheik Mohammed and Hambali considered bombing synagogues and other Jewish targets in discussions believed by Australian intelligence to have taken place in late 2000 and again in early 2001, and reportedly confirmed by both men under interrogation.[37] It would only be a matter of time before Australia found itself a target again.

CHAPTER SEVENTEEN

HAPPY CHRISTMAS

AMROZI WAS IN HIS WORKSHOP at home in Tenggulun when he got a call from Hambali in Malaysia. The chief had turned his attention back to JI's heartland, Indonesia; Hambali had a job for the grinning gofer and he needed it done now. '[He] told me to look for a car, around the 10 million rupiah price range. I didn't ask what for,' said Amrozi. 'The money would be taken care of by someone else, the person who handles finances. What was of utmost importance was to find a car.'[1]

The delinquent who had been such an embarrassment to his family had found a new role in life. As well as being the village repairman, fixing motorbikes and trading cars, Amrozi was now also the Mr Fixit for JI. Whatever the bosses needed, Amrozi could get — everything from vehicles to the chemical components for making bombs.

'Since 1999, I guess, I had been sourcing all the stuff from Surabaya — anything, from KCLO [potassium chlorate], sulphur, aluminium powder, all kinds of stuff . . . For those needing ammunition I would find and stock their supplies. As long as it's for jihad, if it's for jihad affairs, and as long as it's in the interest of Muslims I'll find it, no matter what the risks . . . whether it's weapons, ammunition or anything else, as long as it's for jihad I'll find it. My house was never ever lacking in all that stuff, I was prepared for anything that related to explosives, I had it readily available . . . It was ready for anyone — as long as they're not Christians, I'd give it to them.'

Most of Amrozi's stash of explosives had gone to feed the vicious civil war between Muslims and Christians in Ambon in the Maluku islands, which had begun in January 1999 and over the next few years would leave an estimated 9,000 people dead. Since the fall of Suharto and the JI exiles' return to their homeland, the local jihads in Ambon and Sulawesi had become the main focus of JI's efforts in Indonesia.

The provincial holy wars were also stoked by generous funding from overseas, according to the al Qaeda operative Omar al Faruq, who was working closely with JI and its affiliated militia groups in Ambon and Sulawesi. On one occasion, by Faruq's account, a Saudi sheik sent US$74,000 to Abu Bakar Bashir to buy weapons and explosives. A US intelligence report summarising Faruq's interrogation said that JI bought the explosives from the Indonesian armed forces, the TNI. 'Bashir sent his assistant Aris Munander to buy three tons of explosives from the TNI. They were loaded onto a cargo ship owned by the Bilny Shipping Company and headed for Ambon.'[2] The Indonesian version of this differs slightly, reporting that the explosives were bought 'from an ex-army soldier'.[3]

While Amrozi was doing his bit supplying explosives, his brother Ali Imron headed off to Ambon himself. 'I wanted to find out about the truth in Ambon. I wanted to get closer to the Muslims there ... I wanted to preach to them, preach to them about the real Islam. I also wanted to teach them about war itself. But they were already experts in bomb making, most of them were fishermen who used bombs on a daily basis.'

Ali Imron's classmate from Afghanistan and fellow teacher at Tenggulun's Al Islam school, Mubarok, was also busy sourcing provisions for JI. Mubarok had been assigned and financed by JI's military chief, Zulkarnaen, to make regular runs to the Philippines, returning with dozens of weapons including M16s and Colt 45s, plus caches of TNT, RDX powder, detonating cord and fuses.[4]

While the bloody provincial struggles in Indonesia were continuing, an event had taken place in the Philippines which infuriated JI and provided a fresh focus for its vengeance. In April 2000, the Philippine armed forces attacked and overran Camp Abubakar in Mindanao, the training site operated by the MILF and al Qaeda which was home to the Military Academy of JI. Although Camp Abubakar would later be re-established, the temporary loss of the training ground was a major blow to JI and its allies. For Hambali it was as good as a declaration of war.

Hambali and Bashir called a second meeting of their new pan-Asian alliance, the Mujahideen League. They met in Kuala Lumpur in mid-2000, with some fifteen delegates from JI's affiliate groups travelling from all over Southeast Asia to be there. One of those present, the JI treasurer, Abu Bakar Bafana, said the meeting was 'presided by Abu Bakar Bashir' and Hambali was appointed secretary-general. The group then passed a resolution, said Bafana, 'to attack Philippine interests.'[5]

It was not long after this meeting that Amrozi got the call from Hambali, in about July 2000, instructing him to get a car and bring it to Jakarta. The enterprising mechanic had to economise with the budget Hambali had allowed him. 'I thought, 10 million rupiah won't get us a Mitsubishi L300, so I bought a Suzuki carry van. In fact it just happened that I had already bought it because aside from everything else I trade in cars.'

After buying the vehicle, Amrozi got another call. His friend Dulmatin, the former explosives instructor from Afghanistan, had been in contact with Hambali too. Amrozi and Dulmatin both traded in cars — and explosives. 'He called and said that if the car is already available I should also provide "the stuff" — fertiliser — and if he said "fertiliser" it meant explosives. I was told to supply some 250 kilos,' Amrozi recalled. Amrozi got 'the stuff' from his regular supplier in Surabaya, Silvester Tendean, at the Tida Kimia chemical shop, then set off. 'After I had fixed the car up and it was ready, I took it to Jakarta . . . When I reached Jakarta, I delivered the goods to a mosque.'

Waiting for Amrozi in Jakarta was the group assigned by Hambali to assemble 'the stuff' he had brought. Among them were Dulmatin, Ali Imron, and Ali's classmate Mubarok. Also there was another old classmate from Afghanistan, Fathur Rahman al Ghozi, a graduate of Bashir's Ngruki school and one of the top bomb specialists in JI.

After making the delivery in Jakarta, Amrozi's job was done. 'That's where I gave them the car. I didn't ask and they didn't share any information with me about what it was for, where it would be used, I wasn't told a thing about it. So this car, I wasn't sure what they were going to do with it, I didn't know they were going to blow it up.'

Al Ghozi took over from there. 'I was taken by [two other JI members] on a tour of the Philippine ambassador's house and the Philippine embassy so we could determine where to stake out the ambassador,' al Ghozi later confessed.[6] This was to be a payback to the Philippine Government for its raid on Camp Abubakar.

The Philippine ambassador, Leonides Caday, pulled into his driveway in central Jakarta at lunchtime on 1 August 2000. The Suzuki carry van bought by Amrozi was parked outside, stuffed with explosives, which were detonated just as Caday's Mercedes Benz drove in. The ambassador had to be dragged out through the back window of his mangled car, with five leg fractures and serious burns. A security guard and a female street vendor were killed. It was JI's first car bombing and the event that signalled that Jemaah Islamiyah's jihad had begun.

The car bombing was just the opening salvo in JI's jihad. Hambali was now ready to launch a full-scale campaign. In early November 2000, he and Bashir called a third summit of their pan-Asian Mujahideen League.[7]

'It was during this meeting, where the bombings of Indonesian churches on Christmas Eve 2000 were planned,' Philippine intelligence later reported. 'It is also suspected that it was during this meeting that the JI attacks on the US and other Western installations were conceptualised.'[8]

Hambali knew that his plan to bomb Christian churches would be opposed by some within JI. So he had put his head together with two of his closest colleagues to agree on a justification for the attacks. Hambali's interrogators later described what transpired: 'They realised that the Islamic sharia law forbid them destroy [sic] a place of worship. In the attempt to solve the problem, the prisoner referred to Islamic verses and found parts that stated that if a place of worship was used for non-worship activities such as political ones, or to provoke other people, it was allowed to issue a fatwa to destroy the place. The three then agreed to use the verse to justify their plan.'[9]

After this, Hambali summoned his two key aides, Mantiqi 1 secretary Zulkifli Marzuki and JI treasurer Bafana, to meet him in Indonesia for a private session with Bashir. 'Hambali told me to go to the Ngruki Islamic boarding school in Solo,' Bafana later revealed. 'When I got to Solo, I had a meeting with Abu Bakar Bashir, Zulkifli and Hambali in the place I was staying near the Klewer Market.'

There were two items on the agenda — one was al Qaeda business, the other JI. First, said Bafana, 'The meeting discussed attacks on US interests in Singapore.' A year after giving its initial approval, al Qaeda was still keen to go ahead with an operation in

Singapore. According to an Indonesian police summary of Bafana's interrogation, 'This was the main objective of Sheik Osama bin Laden.'[10] When he later gave evidence in Bashir's court case, Bafana referred to the Singapore job as 'Program C' and testified, 'Program C was Osama's.'[11]

The second item discussed with Bashir at the meeting in Solo was 'plans for bombings targetting Christians on Indonesian soil during Christmas Eve celebrations in 2000.' In his interrogation, Bafana explained the rationale provided by Hambali: 'Muslims had been attacked by Christians in Ambon during celebrations marking the end of the fasting month in 1999, so it was better for Muslims to attack first.'

After two years of argument within Jemaah Islamiyah over how and when to wage jihad, Hambali and the militants had prevailed. The moderates had been sidelined and their push for a long-term strategy of building up JI while campaigning for an Islamic state had been spurned. And just to show the conservatives in the Indonesian branch, Mantiqi 2, who was in charge, the offensive would take place on their soil — JI's heartland, Indonesia.

The only question remaining was whether Abu Bakar Bashir would grant his approval to the campaign of terror that Hambali was planning. The operations chief clearly wanted the emir's imprimatur for such a major project. 'Bashir's approval was sought for Hambali's plan to bomb churches (in Indonesia) and US military interests in Sembawang, Singapore,' according to Bafana's account. The question was quickly resolved. By the end of the meeting, Hambali's proposals 'had the agreement and blessing of Abu Bakar Bashir.'[12]

A team of operatives hand-picked by Hambali assembled in Kuala Lumpur to map out the bombing blitz across Indonesia set down for Christmas Eve 2000. They gathered in the KL city office of one of the JI front companies set up by Mantiqi 1. Along with Hambali, Marzuki and Bafana, Muklas was there as well, in his role of providing spiritual guidance for the campaign.[13] Also on the 'advisory team', as Muklas called it, was Hambali's neighbour from Sungai Manggis, the young firebrand, Samudra, about to make his debut in the role of field commander for JI.

Back in his workshop in Tenggulun, Amrozi took another call from Hambali. The chief was coming to East Java and wanted a meeting. Amrozi went along with his brother Ali Imron, their friend Mubarok, and another Afghan veteran, Abdul Ghoni.

'We were summoned to Surabaya to the Egypt hotel,' said Ali Imron. 'We had a meeting there and he told us all about his jihad program.' Ali Imron, fired up by his role in the provincial struggle in Ambon, jumped at the invitation to take part in Hambali's plan. 'I happily welcomed his program because I wanted to do a real jihad just like he explained. It immediately hooked me, I readily, promptly, accepted. At that point the target we selected was a church in Mojokerto, because we were told to do it in East Java. Hambali told us there were others operating at different places.'

Hambali's plan was staggering in its scope — the simultaneous bombing of dozens of Christian churches and priests, in a wave of synchronised attacks across the archipelago. The project would need about forty men, working in eleven teams in eleven different cities. It would require meticulous planning, precision timing and extensive logistical support. Hambali took care of the planning himself, gave Dulmatin the job of making the timers, and seconded operatives from all over the JI network to do the dirty work.

The Malaysian biochemist Yazid Sufaat — host of the al Qaeda meeting in Kuala Lumpur in January 2000 — was brought in from KL. He was sent to Medan in Sumatra to head a team of five. His squad included a local businessman and Ngruki graduate whom the others nick-named 'Fatty' for his saggy face and paunch; his real name was Idris and his droopy eyes would later gaze out from police identikit photos of the Bali bombers.[14]

Samudra was assigned to the Indonesian island of Batam, just south of Singapore, and a contingent was sent from the Singapore branch to work with him. They included Muklas's brother-in-law Hashim bin Abas, the man whose surveillance tape of the MRT station had secured al Qaeda's approval for a bombing in Singapore.

One of the best brains in Jemaah Islamiyah was also seconded to Samudra's team — the former Adelaide Uni dropout and fondly described 'mad bugger' from UTM in Malaysia, Dr Azahari Husin. Dr Azahari had recently returned from his advanced explosives course in

Afghanistan, where he and four other JI members had been 'specially trained in urban warfare', in the words of a fellow trainee.[15] Azahari and his colleagues were about to try out the bomb manual he had written for JI.

Azahari's UTM colleague Wan Min Wan Mat was also involved in Hambali's intricate scheme. As leader of JI's Johor branch, Wan Min was to arrange the delivery of 'the goods' that Samudra would need in Batam, as later recounted by one of the Singaporeans on Samudra's team: 'I reported to Wan Min Wan Mat when I arrived in Johor . . . [He] ordered me to immediately transport the goods over to Batam . . . I was informed that it was firearms, small weapons to be used in the operations.'[16]

While Hambali's eleven squads of bombers fanned out across Indonesia, Hambali had another job for Fathur Rahman al Ghozi, the operative who had pulled off the attack on the Philippine ambassador. Al Ghozi was sent to the Philippines to purchase a large consignment of explosives from the MILF, using contacts from his days as an instructor in Camp Abubakar.

Al Ghozi headed to Mindanao to see his old friend Muklis Yunos, head of the MILF's Special Operations Group. Muklis Yunos was happy to help out with explosives but he wanted to do a deal. The MILF was eager to exact its own revenge for the raid on its base, Camp Abubakar; it wanted to do a bombing in Manila, but Yunos needed JI's help. 'He told me that they did not have the money to finance their program and he requested my assistance,' said al Ghozi. 'Their program needed money to buy 50 to 80 kilograms of explosives.'[17]

Al Ghozi relayed the request to JI's treasurer, Bafana, who 'agreed to give financial support' to the MILF. Bafana wired the money to al Ghozi, who then gave 250,000 pesos (A$6000) to Muklis Yunos to buy explosives for both JI and the MILF. The bombing in Manila would be a joint venture by the two groups, to be carried out by JI's al Ghozi with Yunos and a support team from the MILF, and timed to coincide with the church bombings in Indonesia.

Hambali and Bafana flew to the Philippines to discuss the Manila project with al Ghozi and the MILF. 'We met together in Manila on the first week of December 2000,' said al Ghozi. 'We fetched [Bafana] at the airport one afternoon and he was accompanied by Hambali.' Al Ghozi took them to the Norilyn Hotel, a dosshouse with dripping air-conditioners and a canvas awning, around the corner from the Quiapo mosque. There, said al Ghozi, they 'checked in and planned the bombings'.[18]

Even as they were formulating these synchronised attacks in Indonesia and the Philippines, Hambali and Bafana were thinking ahead to their next operation — the al Qaeda job in Singapore, referred to by Bafana as 'Program C'. The plans in Singapore were by now well advanced, with months of reconnaissance carried out. Only the target had changed — from the MRT station scouted in 1999, to Western embassies.

Al Ghozi was briefed on the Singapore job while Hambali and Bafana were in Manila. His instructions: 'to obtain five to seven tons of explosives intended for use in bombing the US and Israeli embassies in Singapore.'[19] But just in case Singapore proved too difficult, al Ghozi was asked to case the embassies in Manila as well.

Once preparations were under way in the Philippines, Hambali returned to Indonesia to supervise the countdown to Christmas Eve. He travelled to the island of Batam, where Samudra and his team were at work. Samudra had selected four Christian churches and taken delivery of 'the goods', including a batch of TNT and other chemicals. He was now holed up at the Happy Gardens guesthouse with his assistants from Singapore. Hambali checked into another guesthouse nearby, then went to give a pep talk to Samudra's team.

'Hambali came there to motivate us,' Samudra said in a police statement. 'To remind us to keep our intentions purely for Allah, to never neglect reading the Koran ... to be cautious and patient in determining our targets, meaning the church bombing targets, in which the main targets were the priests.'[20]

About ten days before Christmas, the last member of Samudra's squad arrived at the Happy Gardens guesthouse — Dr Azahari Husin, armed with the latest know-how from Afghanistan. 'He came with an instruction manual on how to assemble a bomb,' said Samudra. 'There was a printout from a computer and a picture of the assembly of the bomb [showing] how to connect the detonator to the explosive, which was written in by hand.' Using Azahari's manual, Samudra's team set to work.

Across the archipelago, Hambali's eleven teams of bombers were in place. In Tenggulun, Amrozi and Ali Imron were busily occupied with their friends. 'We decided that we wanted to make six bombs,' said Ali

Imron. 'We had three targets — three churches. Each church would be filled with two bombs, packaged up like parcels and then put in bags . . . The bombs were prepared at Amrozi's house. So Amrozi's house was indeed the terrorists' den!'

For many of JI's 'Afghans', the Christmas Eve operation marked their graduation from trained fighters to full-blown terrorists. It was a nerve-racking event. Samudra's team in Batam must have been in need of moral support because Samudra and Hambali both rang Muklas, the campaign's spiritual adviser, and asked him 'to drop by Batam' to provide some guidance.

Muklas travelled from Tenggulun to Batam and went to the guesthouse where the bombers were staying. 'The conversation went: "We are going to hold bombings in churches," and I was asked to give advice. The advice I gave concerned the need to strengthen one's faith, surrender to God's will, and the need for sincerity and brotherhood with fellow Muslims.'[21]

Reassured by Muklas that their task was the work of Allah, Samudra's group at the Happy Gardens guesthouse completed their preparations. Samudra later boasted: 'I made the bomb in Batam myself . . . I placed the bomb in a box and then placed the box inside a black or brown school bag. There were all kinds of them, according to everyone's creativity.' One of his team 'made a bomb in a gift parcel . . . decorated with a ribbon.'[22]

Early on Christmas Eve, Samudra set off with one of his operatives to make the drop. 'I left for the target, the church I was to blow up, at about 7 p.m. . . . I was riding on the back of a motorbike driven by Mahmud heading for the target, then after placing the bomb I returned to the guesthouse.'

Ali Imron and his mates in Tenggulun set out at about the same time, leaving the hapless Amrozi behind. 'Amrozi didn't come with us at the time because he was ill. Besides, Amrozi had never held a bomb before. We feared that he might get nervous and the bomb might explode in his hands . . . There were six bombs but only five people to deliver the bombs to these different places. So I volunteered and brought the [extra] bomb. I thought that the more bombs I delivered, the more I would be rewarded in the afterlife.'

Simultaneously across Indonesia, Hambali's bombing teams delivered their deadly packages to thirty-eight churches or priests, from Medan in northwestern Sumatra, to the island of Lombok, east of Bali. The bombs exploded between 8.30 and 10 p.m., except for the ones that misfired or were defused by police. Nineteen people were killed and 120 injured.[23]

Afterwards, Samudra's team reassembled at the Happy Gardens guesthouse to pray. 'I told them, those of you who succeeded in detonating a bomb . . . give thanks.'[24] If anyone had qualms about the bloody havoc they had wrought on the eve of one of Christianity's most sacred festivals, there would be no admitting it for now.

'We realised that there were other human beings that we were attacking and we didn't want to think much about it at that point,' said Ali Imron. 'We had decided that it was jihad so we didn't want to think about it. To be involved in jihad we need to have enemies, right? I dared not think about anything. And anyway we were bound by the jemaah . . . We were bound by that sacred *bai'at*, so that's it — not much questions asked.'

Six days after the church bombings in Indonesia, a series of explosions ripped through the Philippine capital, Manila, as the bombs made by JI's Fathur Rahman al Ghozi with his MILF cohorts were detonated. Another twenty-two people were killed and more than sixty wounded. The execution of two major attacks in two countries in the space of a week confirmed JI's emergence as a world-class affiliate in al Qaeda's deadly network. Jemaah Islamiyah had come of age.

Despite the heavy death toll, the Christmas Eve attacks had not gone entirely to plan. Many of the church bombs had failed to go off and one of Hambali's closest friends had been killed when a bomb exploded prematurely. The dead man was a comrade of Hambali's from Afghanistan, Jabir, the same man who had recruited Samudra into JI. Even as he celebrated their slaughter of scores of innocents, Hambali wept over the death of his friend.[25] Samudra, on the other hand — never one for sentiment — promptly nicknamed his late mentor 'Bang' Jabir.[26]

The brutal attacks had also deepened the schism within JI over how jihad should be waged. The murder and maiming of scores of church-goers shocked some members of JI, and revived the debate over the fatwas issued by Osama bin Laden and Hambali, sanctioning the killing of civilians. Among those now having serious reservations was one of the Singaporeans who had helped Samudra with the church bombings in Batam.

'After the operation I returned to Malaysia and heard about the deaths. It was after this that I began to wonder if Islam was about placing bombs, running away and watching women and children die. When I reflected on this, I was confused . . . confused with loyalty.'[27]

These regrets were echoed by Mohammed Nasir bin Abas, the leader of Mantiqi 3 and brother-in-law of Muklas, who had earlier refused to pass on Hambali's fatwa to his members. 'Those who followed the decree were people like Hambali and Muklas who carried out the bombings based on that decree. They bombed the churches and Bali . . . In the end, to me it was murder and I never understood the meaning of jihad in such acts, especially when civilians were the victims.'[28]

Hambali and his field commanders had no such qualms. They regrouped in Kuala Lumpur days after the church attacks, for an informal post mortem and to decide the next phase in JI's campaign. 'What we discussed during the meeting was whether we were to go on with the bombings or not,' said Samudra. 'It was decided then that we would.'[29]

But there was another hitch. One of Hambali's operatives had been arrested after the church bombings — and had given Hambali's name to the Indonesian police. The authorities still didn't know who had organised the attacks. The police suspected they were linked to the push for an Islamic state, while the media reported they were to avenge the deaths of Muslims in Maluku. Many people were blaming the military, the usual suspect in acts of extreme violence. In the case of one set of bombings, those in Medan, the perpetrators were found to be closely connected to Indonesian military intelligence.[30] It would be more than a year before the attacks would be connected with JI, whose existence remained unknown. But it was time for the chief of operations to make himself scarce.

'Hambali was known to be wanted by the Indonesian police force in relation to the bombings on Christmas Eve,' JI's treasurer, Bafana, later told the police. So in early 2001, the leadership met again at Bafana's home in KL, 'to discuss Hambali's escape to Pakistan'. Hambali surrendered his duties to Samudra, until a formal replacement could be made, according to Bafana.[31] At another meeting a month or so later, Muklas was appointed to replace Hambali as leader of Mantiqi 1 and 'chairman of the Mujahideen'. Muklas later told the Indonesian police, the appointment was made by Abu Bakar Bashir.[32]

Bashir himself was an enthusiastic supporter of the campaign of terror that JI had embarked on, according to Abu Bakar Bafana, and was eager to ensure it continued in Hambali's absence. In July 2001, Bashir called a meeting in Solo, described by Bafana to the Indonesian police. Bafana said the meeting was attended by five men — himself, Bashir and Amrozi, along with JI's military chief, Zulkarnaen, and another member called Arkam, a bomb maker and weapons instructor.

At this meeting, said Bafana, 'Abu Bakar Bashir told me to plan a bombing targeting Megawati, the President of the Republic of Indonesia and an attack on priests who were to hold a meeting in Manado.' A police summary of Bafana's statement said the plan to kill Megawati, who was then still vice president, was 'because she was seen to be supporting Christians'.[33]

Bashir's assassination plan didn't get far. By Bafana's account it was vetoed by the new head of Mantiqi 1: 'Muklas said that JI did not have the resources to do that, so the plan was cancelled.' Instead, JI proceeded with a string of smaller attacks, which Samudra arranged, including another five church bombings and the attempt on the Atrium shopping mall, which backfired when the bomb went off early and the bomber lost a leg.

While Bashir was no operational mastermind, he shared in equal measure Hambali's ruthless obsession. Bashir's lawyer later shed light on his one-eyed fixation. 'He is, first of all, a very simple man . . . but he is also a very determined man in his own way . . . His horizon is very primordial. Outside of Islam, he is very much ignorant in other matters.'[34]

Hambali, by this time, was ensconced in an al Qaeda hideout on the Pakistan–Afghanistan border. Osama bin Laden, evidently aware of the police investigation in Indonesia, was eager to extend his hospitality to Bashir as well. Bin laden relayed a message to Bashir, passed on by a Ngruki graduate and JI operative named Muhammad Rais, who was based in Afghanistan.

'Greetings from Osama bin Laden,' said the message, according to evidence later tendered at Muhammad Rais's trial. It continued: 'Osama bin Laden invites Ustad Abu Bakar Bashir to come to Afghanistan if the conditions for Ustad Abu Bakar Bashir have been made impossible in Indonesia.' Bashir did not take up the invitation and later flatly denied having received it.[35]

From bin Laden's mountain redoubt, Hambali would continue to pull the strings of JI. Buoyed by the bloody successes in Indonesia and the Philippines, Hambali was ready for another, even more ambitious attack. It was time to activate Program C.

❧

CHAPTER EIGHTEEN

THE SOURCE

A NEAT YOUNG MAN WITH a trimmed black moustache and crewcut made his way through the gleaming arrivals area of Hong Kong's new Chek Lap Kok Airport. With his boy-scout looks, fluent English and Canadian passport, twenty-year-old Mohammed Mansour Jabarah wouldn't have rated a second glance, as he followed the crowd off the overnight flight from Karachi and joined the queue in the cavernous customs hall.

It was the morning of September 11, 2001, and the world was about to change forever. The bleary-eyed travellers crowding around the luggage carousels in Hong Kong had no inkling of the horrors about to unfold in the United States. But young Jabarah knew that something was afoot.

In the al Qaeda camp that he had come from, Osama bin Laden had told them 'there were brothers awaiting the call to attack the United States' and had asked everyone to pray for them.[1] Before he had flown out of Karachi, his controller, Khalid Sheik Mohammed, had urged him 'make sure you leave before Tuesday'. These and other details were later revealed by Jabarah under interrogation, in one of the most extensive accounts provided by an al Qaeda operative, and summarised in a lengthy FBI report in which the young Canadian was identified as 'the Source'.

As he collected his luggage from the carousel in Hong Kong, Jabarah would have been too preoccupied with his own mission in Southeast

Asia to give much thought to what might happen the next day half way across the world. He headed straight for the tourist district of Kowloon City, where he checked into the hotel in which he would spend the next three days before flying on to his next stop, Malaysia.

It was early the following evening, Hong Kong time, when American Airlines flight 11 slammed into the north tower of the World Trade Center in New York, and sixteen minutes later when United Airlines flight 175 smashed into the south tower. Holed up in his Kowloon hotel room, Jabarah watched transfixed as CNN replayed over and over the collapse of the twin symbols of US supremacy in an avalanche of dust and rubble.

Suddenly the al Qaeda rookie was struck with awe and dread. He now knew what the 'big operation' was that bin Laden and Khalid Sheik Mohammed had hinted at. Now the potential impact of his own mission dawned on him and Jabarah became nervous. He 'began to question whether or not he could really handle the task at hand'. He even 'considered not carrying out the direction [and] ending the South East Asian Operation.'[2]

Alone in his poky hotel room, Jabarah probably sought solace in the Koran. He would have prayed for guidance. He certainly cast his mind back to the pledge of loyalty he had sworn to bin Laden and the repeated assurances that it was acceptable to kill innocents who were put in the way of the holy struggle. As the full horror of the attacks on America unfolded on his hotel TV set, Jabarah overcame his doubts. 'He felt . . . that as Osama Bin Laden had personally chosen him out of all the men in Afghanistan, he simply couldn't refuse.'[3]

Ever since he was a schoolboy growing up in a middle-class family in Canada, all Jabarah had wanted was 'to go and fight jihad'. He wasn't about to blow it now.

Jabarah had been born in Kuwait, one of four sons of a well-to-do Iraqi businessman, Mansour Jabarah, and his Kuwaiti wife. His father was a devout man and a member of the Muslim Brotherhood but wanted a Western education for his boys so, in 1994, the family left Kuwait and moved to the stately city of St Catharines, Ontario, twenty minutes' drive from Niagara Falls and just across the border from New York state.

Jabarah senior became president of the St Catharines Islamic Society and a respected figure at the local mosque, where he would pray several times a day, often with his twelve-year-old son in tow. In keeping with the family's middle-class aspirations, young Jabarah was enrolled at the Holy Cross Catholic Secondary School. He's remembered there as 'a very good boy', a diligent student who wanted to be a doctor, helped out at the mosque and volunteered to collect litter from the roads around Niagara. 'The boy was a gentleman,' recalled a family friend from the Islamic Society. 'He was working here in the mosque. Nice, polite boy.'[4]

For a boy from an Iraqi background, it was an awkward time to be growing up in North America. It was the aftermath of the first Gulf War when Canadian forces had joined the US-led coalition that drove Iraqi troops out of Kuwait. Jabarah's father had been eager for his family to escape the turmoil in the Arab world. But in the playground of the Holy Cross school there was no escaping Jabarah junior's Middle Eastern background and looks. 'People used to joke about it, to poke fun at him about bomb threats,' reported one former schoolmate.[5]

On school holidays, the family would fly home to their native Kuwait, where Jabarah and his older brother Abdul Rahman were caught up in the rising tide of resentment towards the United States. Their father had a friend called Suleiman Abu Gaith, who ran a youth group sponsored by the Muslim Brotherhood. Abu Gaith would take Jabarah, his brother and their friends out camping and playing soccer. Afterwards he lectured to them about Islam and showed them gruesome videotapes from conflicts like the one in Bosnia where Muslims were being slaughtered and, in the eyes of Islamic militants, the West was doing nothing to stop it.

His young acolytes may not yet have known it, but Suleiman Abu Gaith was a member of Osama bin Laden's inner circle, and would later become the spokesman for al Qaeda famous for his pronouncement after September 11: 'The Americans must know that the storm of airplanes will not stop, God willing — there are thousands of young people who are as keen about death as Americans are about life.'[6] Abu Gaith's sessions with Jabarah and his companions were part of the drive to tap into this vast pool of youthful recruits. By sixteen, Jabarah was ready to sign up. But al Qaeda needed educated young men, not schoolboys; Abu Gaith told him to go back to Canada and finish his studies first.

Back home in Canada, the eldest of Jabarah's brothers, Abdullah, had decided that a life of jihad was not for him. Abdullah was studying at university, living with his girlfriend and enjoying a typical student lifestyle that reportedly included drinking alcohol and smoking the odd marijuana joint. 'They made their choices and I made mine,' Abdullah said later, meaning he got to go out with women 'and they got to pray at the mosque'. As for his younger brother, Abdullah described Jabarah as 'a crazy bastard, fucking mad'.[7]

Jabarah graduated from the Holy Cross school in St Catharines in 1999 then headed straight for Afghanistan. His brother Abdul Rahman had already gone to sign up with al Qaeda. (Jabarah's brother was later named by the Saudi Government as one of a nineteen-man al Qaeda cell blamed for an attack in Riyadh in May 2003, when car bombs exploded inside three expatriate housing compounds, killing thirty people and injuring 200. When Saudi police stormed a house used by the group as a hideout, Abdul Rahman Jabarah was one of four men shot dead.)

Jabarah told his parents he was going to university in Kuwait but flew instead to Pakistan, his trip paid for and arranged by his mentor Abu Gaith. From Karachi he travelled with a guide and two other recruits to Peshawar, then drove to the border and walked for five hours through the mountains into Afghanistan.

Jabarah's destination was an al Qaeda camp north of Kabul, where he enrolled in the basic training course for new recruits, a fifty-day primer known as *Tahziri*, meaning beginning or preparation. A typical day in the al Qaeda boot camp started with dawn prayers, two hours of physical training, a shower from the well, breakfast, then two hours of classroom instruction, a nap, noon prayers, a lecture on the Koran and lunch. After chores were done and afternoon prayers completed, the rest of the day was taken up with training in weapons and explosives, then dinner, lectures on holy war, evening prayers and lights-out at 8.30 p.m.

Jabarah was taught to use an M16, an Uzi, an AK-47 and the later model Kalashnikov with the shortened barrel known as the Krinkov — Osama bin Laden's weapon of choice. He learned how to take out a low-flying plane from 5 kilometres away with a shoulder-fired Sam-7 or Stinger missile — possibly practising with some of the same ones inherited from the Americans at the end of the Soviet war. Jabarah and his classmates also learned how to destroy a tank with a disposable RPG, to booby-trap a field with landmines and make bombs using TNT and the plastic explosives C3 and C4.

As he went about his training, Jabarah would often see a rangy figure in flowing white robes and a straggly beard, his trademark Krinkov slung over his shoulder as he toured the camps. Osama bin Laden lived in a house nearby, from where he and al Qaeda's governing *shura* oversaw the training of the thousands of jihadists who passed through their camps. The freshmen like Jabarah hung on bin Laden's every word.

'Bin Laden would come to the camps and talk about the fatwas,' said Jabarah. 'The fatwas allowed them to kill any Americans . . . Bin Laden explained that the enemies of Islam were killing Muslims and hiding behind women and children. Bin Laden concluded that it was acceptable to kill those that are put in the way.'

After completing the basic training, Jabarah enrolled in an advanced course in urban guerilla warfare, which was open only to the top-rated graduates. They learned how to organise a terrorist cell and plan an assault on a building and did advanced weapons and physical-combat training. Jabarah did a brief tour with the Taliban on its front line against the Northern Alliance north of Kabul, but it was winter and there was no real fighting to be had. He heard there were skirmishes at Bamiyan and went to join in, only to find all was quiet there too. Instead, Jabarah and his friends took a side trip to see the ancient Bamiyan Buddha statues just before they were condemned as pagan relics and blown up by the Taliban.

Jabarah moved on to another camp to do a ten-week course in mountain warfare, covering ambush tactics, mountaineering and communications. The Canadian reported that there were 'hundreds of Arabs' at this camp, as well as some 'white guys' including 'two blonde Australians, approximately 30 and 25 years of age'.

At the end of the course, Osama bin Laden showed up to congratulate the graduates, accompanied by Jabarah's old mentor Suleiman Abu Gaith. Bin Laden told them that the reason they had been trained was so they could fight the Americans and the enemies of Islam.

'Osama bin Laden stated that America through their weapons and machinery were killing Muslim brothers in Palestine. He added that the US was responsible for killing innocent people in Iraq with their sanctions.' Bin Laden was referring to the UN sanctions imposed on Iraq for its refusal to comply with UN weapons inspections, a failure which would cause the United States and its allies to declare war on Iraq again in 2003. In his speech at Jabarah's graduation, 'OBL concluded that if America wanted to remove Saddam, it would have been done already. OBL was arguing that the US was not against

Saddam but was against Islam.' Before leaving, bin Laden urged his graduates to pray for 'the brothers' who were in America preparing to exact revenge.

Jabarah knew he had made it when his mentor, Abu Gaith, invited him to a gathering at al Qaeda's 'VIP guesthouse' in Kandahar. Bin Laden was there with his trusted adviser and deputy, Dr al Zawahiri. Also present were his military commander, Abu Hafs, and his security chief, Saif el Adel, the same two lieutenants who had briefed Jack Roche the year before. Jabarah knew that his mere presence among this company 'indicated to those in attendance that he was accepted'. Bin Laden gave another speech about the impending strikes against America, giving no details but making clear 'the attack would be severe'.

Jabarah was eager to formalise his membership of this exclusive clique, but he had to convince the man himself that he was worthy. 'He eventually made the decision to join al Qaeda some time in late May 2001 and asked . . . if he could see Osama bin Laden,' Jabarah told the FBI. A private audience was arranged, described, in a separate report by the Canadian Secret Intelligence Service, as 'an effort to convince bin Laden of his potential as an al Qaeda operative, by highlighting his excellent English skills, his clean Canadian passport and his high standing in his al Qaeda training courses.'[8]

Bin Laden told the young Canadian that if he wanted to join al Qaeda, 'he had to fight the enemy of Islam wherever it may be'. Bin Laden then took the young man's hand and asked him to repeat the *bai'at*. 'The oath was to fight against all those who hate Islam and stand by bin Laden until death.'

Not long after this, Jabarah met bin Laden again to be assigned his role. 'Bin Laden advised Jabarah that there was an outside mission. Bin Laden stated that it was because his English was so good and he had a good Canadian passport that he had been chosen for this mission,' reported the FBI. Jabarah was to travel to Pakistan to meet a man bin Laden called 'Mohammed the Pakistani', who 'would give Jabarah instructions and funds for an operation'. 'Mohammed the Pakistani' was yet another alias for Mukhtar, 'the Brain' of al Qaeda — Khalid Sheik Mohammed.

Jabarah flew from Peshawar to Karachi in August 2001 and made contact with Khalid Sheik Mohammed by phone. Mohammed picked Jabarah up at his hotel and took him back to his apartment, probably the same flat where he had hosted Jack Roche the previous year.

'The Brain' had been extremely busy since Jack Roche's visit. His masterplan for September 11 was well in place, his operatives in the United States counting down the days. Meanwhile, Mohammed had moved on to begin planning his next assault. Expecting massive retaliation after the attacks on New York and Washington, al Qaeda wanted to have another operation ready to go, to show it was still in business and could strike at will. After bin Laden abandoned the 'second wave' of plane hijackings originally planned to follow September 11, Mohammed had begun working on a different follow-up attack, to take place in Southeast Asia. This was the 'outside mission' for which Jabarah had been chosen.

In his apartment in Karachi, the al Qaeda mastermind briefed the young Canadian on his role. 'Jabarah's job would be to provide money for a suicide operation in the Philippines. Jabarah would be the go-between for the local South East Asian operatives and al Qaeda.' Jabarah was assured he was too valuable to be a suicide bomber himself — as Mohammed put it, there were 'hundreds of others in Afghanistan eagerly ready to fill that role'.

The 'local South East Asian operatives' that Jabarah was assigned to work with were al Qaeda's allies in Jemaah Islamiyah. The observation for the operation had already been done. Under instructions from Mohammed's old friend Hambali, the JI bomb maker and explosives supplier Fathur Rahman al Ghozi had surveyed the US and Israeli embassies in both Singapore and the Philippines. Al Ghozi had advised that the embassies in Manila would be easier to hit. All the JI team needed now was finance, which was where al Qaeda's man Jabarah came in.

Jabarah stayed with Khalid Sheik Mohammed, whom he knew as Muktar, in his Karachi home, taking what he called 'advice and lessons on how to prepare himself for al Qaeda missions'. Lesson one was Operating in a City Environment. Mohammed instructed Jabarah:

'Upon entering a city, he should obtain a guide book, like the type used by tourists . . . The guidebook would have the addresses of the United States and Israeli embassies, which Jabarah should note for target potential. Mukhtar also told Jabarah to take specific note of addresses for the offices of US and Israeli airlines . . . He should familiarise himself with the locations of cyber cafes and hotel business centres. These locations would be used for communications with group or cell members . . . He was told by Mukhtar to utilise silly names in obtaining email addresses [and] to try to use as many different cyber cafes as possible . . . Mukhtar advised Jabarah to create a fake business card for a cover story [and to] observe the dress and fashion of the local community and imitate it.'

In Karachi, Khalid Sheik Mohammed introduced Jabarah to the leader of the team he would be working with in Southeast Asia — Mohammed's old comrade, Hambali. Jabarah and Hambali had met before in Afghanistan, at the 'Islamic Institute' run by bin Laden's ally, the mujahideen warlord Abdul Rasul Sayyaf.

It was now four months since Hambali had fled Kuala Lumpur, after being identified by Indonesian police as a suspect in the Christmas Eve church bombings. JI's operations chief and al Qaeda's main operator in Southeast Asia had made Pakistan his new base. Hambali divided his time between bin Laden's mountain base in Afghanistan and his apartment in Karachi, where he drove around in a white Toyota Corolla. Hambali worked closely with Khalid Sheik Mohammed and bin Laden's military chief, Abu Hafs.

Hambali was by now operating principally under the auspices of bin Laden's group. He rose to such heights in al Qaeda that, by some reports, he became a member of its governing *shura*.[9] As far as Jabarah could tell, Hambali was al Qaeda: 'The Source stated that he believed Hambali to be a senior member of the group operating in Asia,' according to the FBI.

Hambali received Jabarah in his apartment in Karachi, where he briefed the Canadian further on his job. 'Hambali began giving Jabarah details regarding the planned operation in the Philippines, including targets such as the American and Israeli embassies. Hambali told Jabarah he would be working with a Malaysian named Mahmoud.'[10] This was an alias of Abu Bakar Bafana, the treasurer of JI. Bafana would be Jabarah's first point of contact for the job. His second contact would be Azzam, an alias for the secretary of Mantiqi 1, Zulkifli Marzuki.

Hambali told Jabarah that the person with whom he would work most closely on the operation was an Indonesian called Saad. This was one of the many names used by Fathur Rahman al Ghozi, the bomber who had earned his stripes with the attack on the Philippines ambassador in Jakarta and the bombings in Manila in December 2000. Al Ghozi had already cased the embassies and was now sourcing explosives for the job ahead.

During his sessions in Khalid Sheik Mohammed's apartment in Karachi, Jabarah had a fellow trainee — a Saudi, about twenty-five years old and married with three children. His name was Ahmed Sahagi and he had been a bodyguard for bin Laden. Sahagi didn't speak much English, but he wouldn't need it for his role — as a suicide bomber. Nor was he considered irreplaceable. Jabarah was told: 'If the suicide driver, Ahmed Sahagi, was arrested, Jabarah would call Mukhtar and get a replacement ... Hambali had indicated to Jabarah that he had numerous people willing to act in suicide roles.'

Jabarah and Sahagi were drilled by Khalid Sheik Mohammed for weeks. They were taught the encoding system used by al Qaeda to disguise phone numbers. The system known as the '0–5 method' is based on the principle that the original number and the replacement number should add up to 10. So nine becomes one, seven becomes three, five is five and so on. If the original number is 309 223 850, for example, then the coded number would be 701 887 250.

They were also given code words to be used when communicating by email or SMS. 'Wedding' referred to the coming event; 'market' meant Malaysia; 'soup' Singapore; 'terminal' Indonesia; and 'hotel' the Philippines. The code word for Americans was 'white meat'.

Jabarah observed that Mohammed 'was very busy with Al Qaeda business and there was not time for much else'. One day Mohammed joked that 'after he is through with operations, he will go and be with Ramzi Yousef'. Mohammed's nephew Yousef was in a US prison doing 240 years for his bombing of the World Trade Center in 1993.

By the second week in September, Jabarah's tuition was complete and it was time to go. The young Canadian was given a ticket for Malaysia via Hong Kong. Hambali gave him a phone number to call in Kuala Lumpur and an email address set up by the group in Malaysia for the operation: bob_marley@yahoo.com with the password LLCoolJ6.

Before he left, Khalid Sheik Mohammed gave Jabarah US$10,000 in cash and instructions to let him know if he needed more. After reminding Jabarah to 'make sure you leave before Tuesday', Hambali and Khalid Sheik Mohammed sent him on his way.

Two days after September 11, Jabarah flew out of Hong Kong for Kuala Lumpur. After overcoming his initial shock at the carnage, Jabarah felt 'happy with the success of the operation' in America, which he said 'inspired him as to his own mission'.

Jabarah booked a room at the Garden City Hotel in Kuala Lumpur and went to find an internet cafe to check for his next instructions. In his inbox was an email from Muktar — Khalid Sheik Mohammed — telling him that the suicide bomber, Ahmed Sahagi, had also arrived in KL, and that the two of them should meet. Jabarah found Sahagi in his hotel room, where the Saudi filled him in on the latest news from Karachi.

'Sahagi told Jabarah that he was in Karachi with Mukhtar on 9/11 and that all of the video equipment in Mukhtar's apartment was set to record the news that day. Sahagi said that Mukhtar was disappointed at first because the plane hit the top of the towers [but] became very happy when the buildings came down. Sahagi said the fourth plane was intended for the White House . . . Sahagi told Jabarah that OBL had been preparing for the 9/11 attacks for two years.'

A week after his arrival, Jabarah met up with Hambali's men in Kuala Lumpur — JI's treasurer, Abu Bakar Bafana, and Mantiqi 1 secretary Zulkifli Marzuki. The location in which they chose to plot their offensive against America and its allies was a McDonald's store in KL.

Bafana told Jabarah that Khalid Sheik Mohammed had already supplied US$10,000 for the project. Bafana explained that the money had been allocated by al Qaeda after his earlier trip to Afghanistan, when he had shown the surveillance footage shot in Singapore to bin Laden's military chief, Abu Hafs. As Bafana explained to Jabarah: 'Any group who has the ability and the people will send a representative to Afghanistan to meet Osama bin Laden and pitch a plan to OBL for support. This is what was done in Asia.'

Bafana and Marzuki briefed Jabarah on progress so far. Bafana said 'there was a brother working on buying explosives but that they had only amassed 300 kilograms of TNT so far'.[11] This was al Ghozi, who had been off stocking up in the Philippines. They also had four tonnes of ammonium nitrate, supplied by the Malaysian biochemist Yazid Sufaat, the man with the condo in KL. Bafana instructed Jabarah to go to the Philippines to find out from al Ghozi what else was needed.

Jabarah took off for Manila with the suicide bomber Ahmed Sahagi and checked into the Horizon Hotel in Makati, where they met up with al Ghozi. Al Ghozi told Jabarah he needed more time and more money and that he was concerned about the targets. He took the pair on a tour to see the embassies for themselves, then the three of them flew back to Kuala Lumpur to brief Bafana and Marzuki. 'Al Ghozi told the group that the targets in the Philippines were too hard to hit. He said that the US embassy was too far from the street and there were only a couple of Israeli citizens actually working at the Israeli embassy.'[12]

Al Ghozi's gloomy assessment brought the plan for a bombing in the Philippines to an end, for the moment at least. But it was only a hiccup in the overall operation. With the flexibility and opportunism that are the hallmarks of both JI and al Qaeda, the group planning the operation simply switched targets — right there and then.

They already had another plan to turn to — the plan known as 'Program C', referred to by Bafana as 'Osama's' — a plan for a bombing in Singapore. The sparkling city-state was Asia's own symbol of Western affluence and corporate success, the regional equivalent of New York's twin towers. A bombing in Singapore would devastate Southeast Asia as surely as September 11 had shattered the United States. Jabarah and al Ghozi were sent on their way.

❧

CHAPTER NINETEEN

PROGRAM C

Jabarah jumped off the bus from Kuala Lumpur outside the Hotel Royal in Newton Road, the hectic heart of downtown Singapore. Al Ghozi was waiting there to meet him. They made their way through the crowds heading for Newton Circus, where the open-air food stalls were doing a raucous trade, the air thick with chilli fumes from blazing woks and the shrill cries of hawkers: 'Chilli Mud Crab!' 'Laksa!' 'Salt and Pepper Prawn!' 'Best in Singapore!'

Al Ghozi had with him three Singaporeans whom he introduced to Jabarah as Simpson, Alex and Max. The local JI members had yet to be briefed on their role. All they knew was that Bafana had phoned ahead to his brother, Fathi, a prominent member of the Singapore branch, with the instruction to 'assist a foreign friend code-named Mike'. The 'foreign friend' was al Ghozi, using yet another of his aliases — 'Mike the bomb maker'. Jabarah was introduced to the Singaporeans as Sammy.

After picking up Jabarah at the bus stop, the five men drove to Marina South, an expanse of parks, golf ranges, bowling alleys and restaurants on the southern side of Singapore island. They stopped there in a public carpark and sat in the Singaporean Alex's car while Jabarah briefed them on 'Sammy's plan', as it was referred to by the local men. Their interrogations would later form the basis of a White Paper published by Singapore's Ministry for Home Affairs, detailing the plot:

'The terrorist plan was to rig up six truck bombs, each with three tonnes of ammonium nitrate and to simultaneously attack six locations in Singapore . . . The local cell would conduct the reconnaissance, set up the logistics and, when all was ready, 'Sammy' would bring his own people down to Singapore to rig the bombs.'[1]

Six separate trucks, packed with a total of 17 tonnes of ammonium nitrate — as the Singaporean authorities later put it, 'the consequences would have been catastrophic'.[2] Each of the truck bombs would be as powerful as the ammonium nitrate bomb used by Timothy McVeigh in Oklahoma City in 1995, which demolished a nine-storey building, killed 168 people and injured hundreds more.

Jabarah explained that the role of the local operatives would end when the truck bombs were ready to go. 'The trucks would then be driven and parked at designated points near the targets . . . The local cell members would then leave the country as unknown suicide bombers arrive. These suicide bombers (believed to be Arabs) would be brought down to Singapore just a day before the planned attack.' One of the suicide bombers would be the former bin Laden bodyguard, Ahmed Sahagi, tutored in Karachi with Jabarah by Khalid Sheik Mohammed.

Nothing about the three Singaporeans sitting in the car with Jabarah and al Ghozi would have alerted the city-state's vigilant authorities to the fact that they were planning a bombing. They certainly passed for law-abiding citizens. Alex was a tubby-faced civil engineer, Max a motor mechanic turned ship traffic assistant, and Simpson a manager who held the rank of lieutenant-corporal in the Singapore armed forces. All three had done their compulsory national service and were still serving in the army reserve.

With its squeaky-clean affluence and obsession with civic order, Singapore was the last place you would expect to find a cell of would-be bombers working to al Qaeda. Nicknamed the 'nanny state' of Southeast Asia, Singapore was ranked number one in the world for 'social cohesion as a priority for the government'. In the wake of September 11, it was declared the second safest city (after Luxembourg) as a result of its attention to security.[3]

The government and its citizens would later struggle to understand how terrorists had emerged in their midst. Home Affairs Minister Wong Kan Seng spoke for many when he remarked, 'They were people with education, they have proper jobs, they have families, they have HDB [government] flats and they are like any ordinary Singaporeans . . . so why would they want to allow themselves to be engaged in activities like that?'⁴

The trio in the car with Jabarah and al Ghozi had all begun by attending religious classes held by a man called Ibrahim Maidin. He was a 52-year-old Indian Singaporean who managed a powder-blue block of luxury apartments called The Belmont in leafy Holland Road. Outside the condominium an iron gate glides open to admit the residents in their black BMW and gold Mercedes Benz sedans, while a security man on a walkie-talkie shoos away intruders. The well-heeled tenants felt so secure there that one later remembered joking with the solemn, bespectacled condo manager, Maidin. 'I remember telling Ibrahim right after September 11, "You better shave off your beard or you'll be mistaken for one of Osama's men!"'⁵

After work, Maidin returned to his modest government flat where he held Islamic study sessions, which attracted men from all walks of life. The Islamic resurgence spurred on by the Iranian revolution and the resistance in Afghanistan had caught on in tiny Singapore as well. For its minority Muslim population, who sometimes felt like second-class citizens, it brought a new sense of identity and pride. People were returning to the mosques and to traditional dress and taking a fresh interest in the Koran.

Maidin's pupils included a chauffeur, a butcher and a foot reflexologist, along with businessmen, managers and engineers. When psychologically profiled later by the Singapore authorities, they listed religion followed by material wealth as their most important values. Some were after religious knowledge, others 'needed a sense of belonging'.⁶

An adherent of the puritanical Wahhabi stream of Islam, Maidin had become a follower of the firebrand Malaysian preacher, Abu Jibril, one of the original JI loyalists who had first fled into exile with Abu Bakar Bashir and later featured in a JI recruitment video holding a gun and a Koran. Singapore was part of Abu Jibril's patch and on one of his regular visits in the late 1980s, he had inducted Ibrahim Maidin into the group. Maidin later swore the *bai'at* to Bashir and was appointed leader of JI's Singapore branch.

Abu Jibril would sometimes come along as a guest speaker to Maidin's class. At other times, Bashir or Hambali would travel from Malaysia to give lectures to the Singapore group. The visitors preached a stridently anti-American line, which was echoed by Maidin. Their call to drive out the infidels struck a chord with those who resented the presence in Singapore of more than 17,000 Americans and the extensive US military and commercial interests. Those who felt strongly enough to stay on after class for further discussion were singled out by Maidin for more intense personal tuition and finally, about eighteen months later, recruitment into JI. The psychological profiling characterised the men who were recruited by their 'high compliance, low assertiveness and high levels of guilt and loneliness', and noted that inclusion in such an inner circle provided 'a strong sense of exclusivity and self-esteem'.

One of Maidin's pupils was Mohamed Nazir bin Mohamed Uthman, a gaunt 28-year-old of Indian origin with bushy eyebrows and an intense gaze. Nazir was the motor mechanic who worked as a ship traffic assistant and the JI cell-member who went by the code name Max.

When Maidin began sending his recruits off to Afghanistan for training in the early 1990s, Max had been one of the first to volunteer. Everything was arranged by Hambali, starting with a false letter from a religious school in Pakistan to say the recruit had been accepted there for Islamic studies. This gave them an alibi for their employers and families, explaining why they would be away from Singapore for three and six months. The recruits were sent to Hambali in Malaysia for preparatory religious and physical training before going on to Afghanistan.

By the time Max went off to Afghanistan, he was ready to sacrifice everything. His JI branch sent Hambali a letter advising that its eager volunteer was 'ready for *istimata*' (martyr's death), 'should the party over there need him'. If this was not required, the letter continued, the branch would like him to undergo 'specialist training' as follows: 'a) sniper, b) field engineering, c) assassin.' The letter to Hambali pointed out, however, that Max might be missed at home. '[He] is a bachelor who is good at practical [more] than theory. He can continue with the training as he has time. We do not have members who are trained commandos here. However he needs to write to his mother from a distant country so that she would not look for him.'[7]

Max returned from his five months in Afghanistan eager for action and was assigned to a JI cell, along with a civil engineer named Adnan bin Musa, who used the code name Alex, and a manager and army reservist called Mohammed Ellias, known as Simpson. It was this cell that was seconded to work with the al Qaeda operative Jabarah.

By the time Jabarah hopped off the bus at the Hotel Royal, the local JI branch had been preparing for an attack for years. They had been surveying potential targets since 1999, when their footage of the MRT station had been taken to Afghanistan by Bafana to get Abu Hafs' approval for a bombing.

The Singapore branch had also surveyed Changi Airport, a radar station and airbase, the pipelines carrying the city's water supplies from Malaysia and the shipping channels off the island, marking a 'kill zone' on a Defence Ministry map. Hambali had directly supervised the various plans, meeting regularly with Maidin and his deputies across the causeway in Johor. A few months before Jabarah's arrival, the Singapore branch's several dozen members had been summoned for a compulsory 'recall and operational exercise' to test their readiness and update their skills.

For Max and his colleagues it was time to put their training into practice. Maidin had told them: 'They had to attack Americans wherever they were so long as they were doing things against Islam. [Maidin] said there was no right or wrong in this. In selecting US targets in Singapore, he conceded that innocent Singaporeans would be killed, just as innocent Muslims were killed when the US bombed Afghanistan and al Qaeda members.'[8]

In a final test of their commitment, the Singaporeans had been asked to take part in a survey stating how far they were willing to go. The form handed to each operative stated: 'I understand my responsibilities and capabilities and I am prepared for . . .' and then listed the various ways in which they could do their part. The options ranged from offering ideas and money to 'conducting sabotage inside Singapore against US interests'. The ultimate task that members could volunteer for was the act of *istim* — death for the cause. Five of the group, including Max, signed up for death.

On Jabarah's first night in Singapore, Max and his cell members took the Canadian from al Qaeda on a tour. They cruised the flashy boulevard of Orchard Road, with its chrome-and-glass shopping plazas and swank hotels, passed the grand old colonial mansions alongside the Botanic Gardens, and finally came to the embassy strip along Napier Road.

The US embassy would have looked formidable by night, a fortress-like grey edifice with slits for windows behind wrought iron, and set back from the road. Next door was the more humble cream-brick facade of the Australian high commission, with its prominent coat of arms, the metallic kangaroo and emu, gleaming in the moonlight.

Jabarah had nominated three top-priority targets for the bombings — the US and Israeli embassies and the US naval base at Sembawang Wharf. When he asked the three locals for other possible targets, one of them suggested the Australian high commission and the British mission further along Napier Road, 'because of their proximity to the US embassy'.[9]

The day after their moonlit reconnaissance, Max came by with a new video camera for al Ghozi, who would make the final decision on targets. While one of the locals did the driving, al Ghozi videotaped the exterior of the US embassy and the security post at its entrance from a bus stop and from the carpark of a block of flats across the road. They then tracked past the Australian high commission, where al Ghozi zoomed in on the checkpoint at the gate, and continued filming as the car cruised by the British high commission. The footage of the embassies was downloaded onto a videodisc and labelled 'Visiting Singapore Sightseeing'. The team reconnoitred a host of other targets as well, among them the Israeli embassy, the Caltex oil company, the US Naval Shipyard, the American Club and the city office tower housing the Bank of America.

After six days in Singapore, Jabarah and al Ghozi held a meeting to discuss what was needed to pull off the job. The bomb maker was in his element. Al Ghozi 'was the most eager for the operation to succeed', according to Jabarah.[10] Al Ghozi had even expanded the already ambitious plan and now proposed to set off seven truck bombs, which would require a massive 21 tonnes of ammonium nitrate.

The group already had 4 tonnes of ammonium nitrate in storage, obtained by the biochemist Yazid Sufaat through his company, Green Laboratory, in Kuala Lumpur. Yazid Sufaat's chemistry skills were, by this stage, in great demand. In 2001, when bin Laden's military chief, Abu Hafs, was looking for a scientist to take over al Qaeda's biological weapons program, Hambali volunteered the US-educated Sufaat. According to the interrogation of Khalid Sheik Mohammed, Hambali introduced Sufaat to bin Laden's deputy, Ayman al Zawahiri, in Kandahar, Afghanistan. Sufaat then set up a laboratory near Kandahar airport where he spent several months working on cultivating anthrax for al Qaeda.[11]

With four tonnes of ammonium nitrate already purchased, the Singaporean Simpson was told to find another 17 tonnes. Meanwhile Max was to locate a secure warehouse where the truck bombs could be assembled. They would then be driven to locations near the targets where the suicide drivers would take over.

According to the Singapore White Paper, 'The suicide bombers . . . would be shown the route and their vehicle. They would then proceed to operate individually and mount the attack on their assigned target between 8.00 am and 10.00 am the following morning.'

After completing the video surveillance, Jabarah and al Ghozi flew back to Kuala Lumpur with the footage to give Hambali's deputies, Bafana and Marzuki, a progress report on the operation. But there was major consternation in the JI office when they arrived.

'The news was bad,' said Jabarah. 'Malaysian intelligence had shown an interest in Bafana so it was necessary to cut contact with Bafana.'[12] JI's long-serving treasurer, Faiz bin Abu Bakar Bafana, had been identified to the Malaysian authorities after the arrest of several members of an Islamic extremist group in Malaysia linked to JI.[13] Any further contact with Bafana was now too dangerous; he was immediately cut off and the operation proceeded without him.

Mantiqi 1 secretary Marzuki was now in control of the project in Singapore. Marzuki was shown the surveillance footage and, according to Jabarah, 'It was decided that the US embassy, Israeli embassy, British embassy, Bank of America AIA Tower and US naval ships would be the targets, with the American embassy and Israeli embassy as the most important.'[14] The Australian high commission was not on the final list. Al Ghozi said he would need more money for explosives and more surveillance to be done by the local cell. 'Al Ghozi asked that Max, Simpson and Alex video the US naval docks and asked Marzuki about the possibility of using boats for the operation and how much explosives they would carry.'[15]

Al Ghozi took off again to the Philippines to buy TNT, while Jabarah stayed on in KL, moving into a rented apartment with the Saudi suicide bomber, Ahmed Sahagi. Needing more money from al Qaeda, Jabarah rang Khalid Sheik Mohammed in Karachi, only to be told that Mohammed 'had fled to Afghanistan to hide after 9/11'. Jabarah told Mohammed's secretary he needed US$50,000. The secretary assured Jabarah that he would take care of it, and told him to await an email with further instructions.

A week later the promised email arrived, instructing Jabarah to phone a man called 'Youssef' in KL. According to Jabarah, they met in the City One Plaza shopping mall, where 'Youssef' handed Jabarah US$10,000 in $100 bills tied by an elastic band in an envelope. It was the first of three such meetings over five days, during which Jabarah was given a total of US$30,000 in cash. Jabarah described his benefactor as 'the money man in Malaysia for al Qaeda'.[16]

Back in Singapore, Max and his fellow cell-members had been busy carrying out their allotted jobs. The trio did the reconnaissance requested by al Ghozi of Sembawang Wharf and the US warships berthed at the Changi naval base, filming from a seafood restaurant across the water and a passenger ferry that passed the base. The footage was downloaded onto another disc and labelled 'MP3 — Rock 'n Roll'. While al Ghozi was off sourcing TNT in the Philippines, the local cell was still tracking down the huge load of ammonium nitrate needed for the job. Simpson made contact with a friend who knew someone working at a chemical import company and made inquiries about placing a large order.

But as the plot moved toward its climax, Max and his associates were being watched — unknown to them. Singapore's Internal Security Department (ISD) had been tipped off after September 11 that a local man was boasting of having fought in Afghanistan with bin Laden. The man, who was placed under watch, was a close friend of the JI operative, Simpson, and the ISD's surveillance led them to the JI cell planning the truck bombings.[17]

The ISD watched with growing suspicion as the cell members converted US$3500 into local currency, continued their inquiries about buying ammonium nitrate and were 'observed to be in close contact with several foreigners' — later identified as Jabarah and al Ghozi. Oblivious to the surveillance, the cell carried on with its preparations.

Things were hotting up overseas as well. Jabarah was still in Kuala Lumpur waiting for news on the explosives when he got an email: Hambali was back in town and he wanted to meet.

Hambali had been in Kandahar in Afghanistan when the United States began its bombardment of al Qaeda's bases in retaliation for the attacks of September 11. Bin Laden had lost his longtime military chief, Abu Hafs, a close associate of Hambali and the man who had authorised the Singapore operation. Abu Hafs had been killed when a US missile flattened his Kandahar home.

As al Qaeda's leadership scattered, Hambali had fled across the border to Pakistan and then flown back to Kuala Lumpur. Exhausted and obviously rattled by the death of his associate, he had almost blown his cover. Hambali was travelling, as usual, on a false passport, but made a nearly fatal mistake, as he told Jabarah: 'Because Hambali was tired he accidentally listed his real name and information on his arrival papers. When he was questioned about his real name by immigration officials he told them that he made a mistake, and for unexplained reasons they let him pass.'[18]

Hambali summoned Jabarah, Marzuki and the would-be suicide bomber, Sahagi, to a meeting at a Kuala Lumpur shopping mall. Hambali was clearly unnerved by events in Afghanistan and concerned at how long the operation in Singapore was taking.

'Hambali advised that he met with Abu Hafs two days before he was killed and Hafs wanted the operation done quickly,' Jabarah later told the FBI. But the local cell was having trouble sourcing ammonium nitrate at home and al Ghozi, who was still in the Philippines, had advised that it could take more than a year to smuggle the explosives into security-conscious Singapore. Meanwhile, one of JI's local members had been picked up for questioning, and the ISD would soon be on their trail.

So Hambali decided to call the whole thing off — and revert back to the earlier plan. According to Jabarah, 'Hambali stated that they should cancel the Singapore operation and move the target back to the US and Israeli embassies in the Philippines. Hambali said this operation could be accomplished sooner since the explosives would already be in the Philippines. Hambali said that if the targets were not considered good, they should find better targets in the Philippines.'[19]

But Hambali moved too late. Even as he was aborting the operation, Singapore's Internal Security Department was moving in. The ISD swooped on 9 December 2001, arresting six men including Max, his fellow operatives Simpson and Alex, and their cell leader, Fathi bin Abu Bakar Bafana, brother of the JI treasurer. The arrests continued for days with fifteen men captured in December and more to follow.

Those who escaped the crackdown went into hiding in Singapore or fled across the causeway to Johor, but there was scant refuge to be had there, as the Malaysian Government had launched its own wave of arrests. It would not be long before Max and his friends would succumb to the ISD's expert interrogation techniques and reveal the existence, leadership and activities of JI, which had remained secret until now. It seemed that the game might be up for Jemaah Islamiyah.

CHAPTER TWENTY

HAMBALI'S REVENGE

Hambali was fuming. As the arrests continued in Singapore, he mobilised those of his men who had escaped the ISD's dragnet and convened a meeting across the causeway in Johor. Those who attended reported later that the operations chief was bent on revenge: 'He urged them to persist with the bombing plans to demonstrate that they could still mount the attacks, albeit on a smaller scale, as well as to retaliate for the ISD arrests.'[1]

There was more bad news to come for JI. The al Qaeda operative Jabarah was still in Kuala Lumpur when he got an email headed 'Problem'. As the Canadian later recounted: 'Bafana had been arrested. He knew everything about the planned operations and everyone was being rounded up.'[2]

Hambali's loyal aide and treasurer, Abu Bakar Bafana, had been picked up in Singapore on 17 December 2001, after returning to his home town to celebrate the Muslim festival Eid with his mother. His arrest was a devastating blow. Bafana knew all there was to know about JI and it was only a matter of time before the Internal Security Department would prise loose his secrets.

Mantiqi 1 was in disarray, its leadership on the run. Marzuki told Jabarah, 'Get out of Malaysia.' The Canadian left the next day, taking a bus to Hat Yai in southern Thailand then a train to Bangkok where he checked into the Plaza Hotel to keep his head down and wait for instructions.

In Singapore, the ISD's interrogations quickly yielded results. Thirteen of the fifteen men arrested in December confessed to being members of 'a clandestine organisation which calls itself Jemaah Islamiyah',[3] uncloaking JI as a terrorist group for the first time. Several of them, including the Singapore branch leader Ibrahim Maidin, identified Abu Bakar Bashir as the group's emir and Hambali as its chief of operations. They also revealed some facts of intense interest to Australia.

On 15 December, a cable arrived at ASIO headquarters in Canberra. It was a Saturday, so only a skeleton staff was on duty. But they soon snapped to attention when they saw what was in the dispatch from ASIO's operative at the Australian high commission in Singapore. It contained the first sketchy details of the planned truck bombings, including the fact that the Australian mission had been scouted as a potential target.

'Shit! We'd better get busy!' was how one staffer later recalled the reaction at ASIO HQ. That was on the Monday, when everyone got back to work after the weekend. ASIO issued a new Threat Assessment for the high commission in Singapore, upgrading the threat level to HIGH, and a team of agents cancelled their plans for Christmas holidays and set to work.

The cable from Singapore was the first that any Australian authority knew of the existence of JI. 'It was not on our radar screen as a terrorist organisation before December 2001,' ASIO chief Dennis Richardson later confirmed.[4] Intelligence had failed — not only in Australia but across Southeast Asia. A terrorist group with thousands of members in half a dozen countries had thrived for almost a decade, while every police force and intelligence agency in the region remained oblivious to it. 'There was the failure of ASIO, the failure of the Australian intelligence community, the failure of regional intelligence communities and others to identify the transition of JI into a terrorist organisation,' Richardson acknowledged. 'I think that should have happened. That is not hindsight. We are paid to identify things like that and we did not.'[5]

The news of the group's existence and its elaborate plot in Singapore confirmed longstanding fears within the Australian intelligence community that Australia itself was now in the cross hairs of al Qaeda and the fanatics it sponsored. Bin Laden himself had announced as much only a month before in a tirade aired on the Arab TV network Al Jazeera. Bin Laden had singled out Australia for the first time, likening its role in helping secure independence for East Timor to the brutal Christian Crusades: 'The crusader Australian forces were on Indonesian shores, and in fact they landed to separate East Timor, which is part of the Islamic world.'[6]

Bin Laden's statement had prompted a classified assessment from ASIO in November 2001, that Australia should now consider itself a target: 'The statement must be seen within the context of [Osama bin Laden's] statements since 1996, which consistently have laid down general markers for subsequent terrorist action,' ASIO warned. 'Previous statements have referred to the US and its allies. [Bin Laden's] specific reference to "crusader Australian forces" thus represents a significant upgrading of Australia's profile. Looked at against OBL's track record, ASIO considers this statement will have force and significance for at least the next 18 months.'[7]

ASIO's assessment pointed to Indonesia as the most likely place for an attack on Australians. 'Certainly [bin Laden's] statement will be seen as particular encouragement for individuals or groups in Indonesia who are followers of OBL and who may have the capability to commit violent acts . . . OBL's al Qaeda network does have the capability to commit violent acts of terrorism in Indonesia.' In ASIO's view, any Australian could become a target. '[Bin Laden] has been explicit in stating there is no distinction between military personnel and civilians; both Australian official representation in Jakarta and other identifiable Australian interests would certainly be seen as extensions of the Australian "crusader" forces.'

As the flow of intelligence continued from Singapore, ASIO learned that there was even greater cause for alarm. Under ISD interrogation, the Singaporean detainees revealed the existence of a JI branch in Australia, with a presence in three cities, Sydney, Melbourne and Perth. Most of this information came from JI treasurer Abu Bakar Bafana, who would have tracked the steady flow of money sent from Australia to head office and allocated the funds for Bashir and Sungkar's frequent trips to Mantiqi 4. Bafana had also travelled to Australia himself, visiting Perth in September 2001 on a private business trip.[8]

Other Singaporean JI members had travelled to Australia as well. One of them was Muklas's brother-in-law, Hashim bin Abas, who had cased the Singapore MRT station for a bombing in 1999. Hashim travelled to Australia three times in 2001, visiting Perth and Brisbane. He later revealed that while in Australia he met with members of

Mantiqi 4, though it is not known what they discussed. Another of the Singaporeans travelled frequently to Melbourne where his daughter attended an Islamic school.

The first skerricks of information from Singapore didn't give Australian authorities a great deal to go on, but it was enough. 'The initial advice was very generalised, but it was valuable, because it was the only information we had,' a well-placed intelligence source told me. The early details did include two specific clues, the names of two men described as being key members of the Australian branch. They weren't even full names, just a first name — Abdul Rahim — and a nickname — Wandi. But it was sufficient for ASIO to launch a major covert investigation.

The danger posed by JI was now starkly apparent. A month after the tip-off from Singapore, ASIO and the Office of National Assessments (ONA) issued a classified report to advise the Australian Government: 'Southeast Asian Islamic extremists have established cells in the region and, with al Qaeda involvement, planned terrorist attacks against Western targets in Singapore.' The report noted that JI's contact with 'outside terrorists', some time before 1999, had marked its transition 'from militant organisation into terrorist group'.[9]

By January 2002, ASIO had identified the Australian leadership of JI. They knew that JI had a fully fledged Australian branch with followers in three states. They also knew that JI and al Qaeda were in league, that they were planning bombings and that Australians had been identified as targets.

In Singapore and Malaysia, the revelations from JI prisoners were enough to prompt a massive crackdown, dozens of arrests and the break-up of JI branches. But in Australia there were no such drastic results. There was no evidence yet of criminal offences having been committed or planned on Australia soil. And unlike Malaysia and Singapore — to the regret of some in the intelligence community — Australia has no draconian Internal Security Act allowing arrest on mere suspicion and long-term detention without trial.

So while their counterparts in Malaysia and Singapore were scooping up and incarcerating JI suspects by the dozen, ASIO ploughed on with its undercover surveillance and secret investigation. For the next ten months there would be no arrests, no raids and no information released about the terrorist branch operating in Australia; in fact, nothing at all to show for the investigation publicly until after the Bali bombings in October 2002.

Getting out of Malaysia as instructed, Jabarah sat tight at the Plaza Hotel in Bangkok waiting for someone to make contact. Christmas and New Year came and went. Finally in early January 2002, the Canadian got an email with a number to call in the Thai capital. Hambali answered the phone and told Jabarah to come and meet him the next day.

Hambali was holed up with his secretary, Marzuki, at the Chaleena Hotel, an incongruous setting for a couple of fanatical Islamists. The 278-room 'three star' Chaleena is conspicuous for its Parthenon-style white-tiled facade with mock Corinthian columns and an outdoor bar featuring a flashing neon palm tree and cocktails called Mad Dog and Sex on the Beach. Inside is a dim-lit karaoke bar with sunken vinyl lounges and enticements to 'Thai traditional massage — service at hotel room'. Crowded with Asian budget travellers and businessmen, it was unlikely that anyone would recognise Hambali and his fellow fugitives there.

It was a tense little gathering when Jabarah arrived. Hambali and Marzuki were clearly nervous. According to Jabarah's interrogation, 'They told him about [Bafana's] arrest and told Jabarah that his picture might be in the news. Jabarah was told to leave and that [Marzuki] and [Hambali] would take care of the rest.' 'It will be a very big hit for us if you're arrested,' Hambali told him during the meeting.'[10]

The three men met again a few days later. By Jabarah's account, 'Hambali said that the name Sammy [Jabarah's alias in Singapore] was circulating so they knew people who were arrested were talking to the authorities. Hambali told [Jabarah] to go through Myanmar and return to Pakistan.'[11]

JI had just suffered another major setback with the capture of 'Mike the bomb-maker', the Indonesian Fathur Rahman al Ghozi in Manila. After the cell was busted in Singapore, al Ghozi had carried on, placing an order for six tonnes of TNT in the Philippines. He had then bought himself a ticket to Bangkok to meet up with Hambali and the others to get more funds. Al Ghozi was almost due to leave for the airport when police acting on a tip-off smashed open the door of his room at the City State Hotel. The veteran bomber led police to his cache — fifty boxes of TNT, 300 detonators and seventeen M16 rifles, buried in the backyard of a house in General Santos City, Mindanao.

JI's operations in Singapore and Malaysia had been thoroughly disrupted, its plans and modus operandi exposed, key operatives arrested and its leadership named. A less committed band might have decided to give it away. But Hambali had a new plan, which he revealed to Jabarah before they parted ways in Thailand in mid-January 2002.

From now on, said Hambali, his group would avoid highly secured objectives like Western embassies and military bases, and focus instead on softer targets which were easier to hit. 'His plan was to conduct small bombings in bars, cafes or nightclubs frequented by Westerners in Thailand, Malaysia, Singapore, Philippines and Indonesia.'[12] Hambali did not reveal which country he would target first, but told Jabarah he had 1 tonne of high-powered PETN explosive ready to go in Indonesia.

After his final meeting with Hambali, Jabarah made good his escape, flying out to the United Arab Emirates and then Oman. By this stage, the Canadian's name and photograph had hit the newspapers, after he was exposed as a key suspect in Singapore. He was picked up two months later in Oman and handed over to the FBI, under whose relentless interrogation he provided his incredibly detailed confession in May 2002.

Jabarah was a major catch and Australian investigators were eager to talk to him. 'We sought access to him then,' an Australian intelligence contact told me, 'but for a variety of reasons that access was denied.' The FBI was keeping its valuable new witness to itself, taking the attitude — in the words of this contact — 'Stand aside, we're looking after this.' Australia would never get access to the man the FBI code-named 'the Source'.

Jabarah's revelations, including the crucial tip-off that Hambali was planning to bomb nightclubs, were contained in an FBI report running to several dozen pages entitled 'Information Derived from Mohammed Mansour Jabarah', and dated 7 May 2002. The voluminous confession was the most solid account to date of the relationship between al Qaeda and JI and their plans to conduct joint attacks. And it was the critical first and only clue pointing to Hambali's new strategy of attacking nightclubs frequented by foreigners.

This information would have been of enormous interest to Australian investigators, if only they had known. But not only was Australia refused access to Jabarah personally, it was also denied the benefit of the treasure trove of facts he had provided. Jabarah's information was distributed widely throughout Southeast Asia in mid-2002 — but not to Australia.

The FBI explained later, 'This information did not indicate specific
threats against Australia, but was provided to those countries deemed to
be at risk of terrorist attack.'[13] The FBI did not explain why it deemed
Australia not to be at risk, despite the Australian high commission in
Singapore having been cased as a potential target; nor did it explain why
it refused Australia's repeated requests for access to Jabarah. 'The Source's'
account was never handed over to Australia until after the Bali
bombings, by which time it was too late.

Publicly, Australian authorities have downplayed the significance of
the Jabarah report and the FBI's failure to pass it on, insisting it would
not have helped to prevent the Bali bombings. But in private, some
Australian officials were extremely angry over the United States' failure
to share with its trusted ally Australia the best intelligence it had at the
time on the threat posed by al Qaeda and JI. 'Of course we should have
had it,' one official told me. 'The FBI is the most hopeless organisation
in the world when it comes to information management . . . They
probably didn't even know where Australia was.'

❧

Bangkok now became the new command centre for Hambali and his
team. With its seven million people, vast urban sprawl and erratic
policing, the Thai capital proved a perfect place to hide and plan JI's
comeback.

After Hambali's secretary, Marzuki, arranged new false passports, JI's
Malaysian leadership quickly regrouped. The next to arrive was Muklas,
who had been in Johor when the Malaysian Government shut down
the Luqmanul Hakiem school as part of its crackdown on Islamic
militants linked to JI. 'In January 2002 I escaped to Thailand because I
was assumed to be involved with the Malaysian Mujahideen Group,'
Muklas recounted. 'In Thailand I met with Zulkifli [Marzuki] . . . Then
about 15 days later Wan Min arrived as well, and about one week later
came Dr Azahari and Noor Din.'[14]

The three academics from UTM in Malaysia had made it across the
border barely a step ahead of the Malaysian police. As their colleagues
were being rounded up by the authorities, the popular 'mad bugger', Dr
Azahari, had got the phone call at home warning him he was on the

list. Azahari had grabbed his overnight bag, kissed his wife and children and left. His fellow academics, Wan Min Wan Mat and Noor Din Mohammed Top, fled at about the same time.

Azahari and his colleagues reconvened with Hambali, Marzuki and Muklas in Bangkok. The six men saw themselves as neither criminals nor escapees from justice. They called themselves the *muhajarin*, the term used by the Prophet Muhammad for the faithful companions who had accompanied him on his historic *hijrah* from Mecca to Medina. Muklas explained: 'What I mean by the Muhajirin is people who flee from one place to another seeking safety, because Azahari, Wan Min, Noor Din, Hamb'ali, Marzuki and myself at the time were fugitives . . . who were being sought by the Malaysian police.'[15]

Hambali presided over a meeting of the six men in Bangkok, a crucial gathering held in February 2002. According to Australian police, JI's emir, Abu Bakar Bashir, travelled from Indonesia to be there as well.[16] At this session JI's leaders resolved to carry on their campaign. 'Azahari and Noor Din had received orders from Hambali to prepare a proposal for an operation,' Wan Min Wan Mat later disclosed.[17]

Now a wanted man in Indonesia, Malaysia, Singapore and the Philippines, it was time for Hambali to once again make himself scarce. 'It was suggested that Hambali keep his distance from our group because he was the one most wanted by the authorities,' reported Wan Min. 'The meeting decided that Muklas would become the head of our group.' Muklas had already replaced Hambali as head of Mantiqi 1 the previous year, when the operations chief had gone into hiding in Pakistan and Afghanistan. Now Muklas was elected to a new position, 'Chair of the Muhajarin'. But as long as Hambali remained present, the chief was still calling the shots.

The 'proposal' that Hambali had asked Azahari and Noor Din to prepare was the standard written submission to al Qaeda to seek approval and funding for an operation. It had been done previously for the aborted project in Singapore and was now being done again. 'From my discussions with Azahari and Noor Din in Bangkok, I learned that the proposals they were preparing were for operations in Singapore and Indonesia,' said Wan Min. That they would even contemplate another attempt in Singapore was testament to the extraordinary resilience of JI. However, with the ISD's crackdown continuing, Singapore was not a realistic proposition. That left Indonesia.

While Azahari and Noor Din wrote up the proposal, Wan Min was told to arrange for the transfer of funds through an account held in southern Thailand. The next decision was who would take operational command. Hambali was gone and Mantiqi 1 in Malaysia had been crippled, its headquarters evacuated and its leaders now in hiding in Bangkok. So Muklas decided to hand control of operations over to Mantiqi 2 in Indonesia. There was just one hitch: senior Mantiqi 2 leaders were still opposed to bombings. So Muklas decided to bypass the main mantiqi leadership and pass the baton instead to JI's hawkish military chief, his old comrade from Afghanistan, Zulkarnaen.

'There was an order from Muklas that all proposals concerning operations needed to be referred to Zulkarnaen and discussed with him in his capacity as the Military Head of JI headquarters in Indonesia,' Wan Min told the police. 'Muklas had decided that all the proposals should be taken to Indonesia first, so that decisions about them could be made by a team headed by Zulkarnaen.'[18]

The location for JI's next joint venture with al Qaeda had been decided; it would take place in JI's heartland, Indonesia. The target had yet to be chosen, but it would be in keeping with Hambali's directive — for bombings in bars and nightclubs frequented by Westerners.

By early 2002, as Hambali and his offsiders were starting to plan their next atrocity, pressure was building on the Indonesian Government to move against JI. The detainees in Singapore had by now exposed the organisation and fingered Abu Bakar Bashir as its leader. The Singapore Government would soon name Bashir as 'the controlling figure in the plot' to truck-bomb Western embassies.

As the pressure for action mounted, the Indonesian police took Bashir in for questioning at the National Police Headquarters in Jakarta in January. A phalanx of TV cameras trailed him in, the emir having become an instant media celebrity on the strength of being branded a terrorist. For six hours, Bashir denied any knowledge of JI to the police, who then released him, saying they had no evidence against him. The defiant Bashir issued a statement, announcing 'I am not a member of al Qaeda. However, I really praise the fight of Osama bin Laden, who has dared to represent the Islamic world to combat the arrogance of the US and its allies.' Bin Laden, he declared, was 'a true Muslim fighter', while 'the real terrorist' was the United States.[19]

The US and Singapore governments lobbied hard for more decisive action, with Singapore accusing Indonesia of endangering the city-state's safety by failing to act. 'It is a fact that we were saved from a disaster that nearly happened, but it is also true that this could happen again later, since the leaders are still at large and free in Indonesia,' Singapore's Foreign Minister complained.[20]

But in Indonesia Bashir seemed untouchable. Already well known in Islamic circles for his role as president of the Indonesian Mujahideen Council, his standing was only enhanced by his celebrated detention and release, his steely defiance and his televised contempt for the United States.

It was not only Islamic extremists who rallied to support Bashir. Politicians with an eye on the Islamic vote rushed to defend him, led by President Megawati's wily deputy, Hamzah Haz, leader of the United Development Party. 'It is not true that extremist terrorists are in connection with Indonesia,' announced the Vice President, insisting that he would lodge a formal complaint with Singapore over its claims. The Singaporean ambassador was summoned to the Foreign Ministry in Jakarta for a rebuke.[21]

Encouraged by the top-level backing, Bashir fired off a writ for slander to the Singapore embassy demanding a trillion rupiah in damages and calling the accusations against him an insult to Muslims, 'when in truth the so-called terrorists are Muslim warriors'.[22]

While publicly denying it, Jakarta knew very well by this time that al Qaeda was active in Indonesia. In February 2002, Indonesian intelligence reported the presence of an extensive training camp in Sulawesi, manned and funded by al Qaeda. The setup described by Indonesian intelligence 'consisted of 8–10 small villages located side by side on the beach, equipped with light weapons, explosives and firing range. Participants in the training are not only local people but also from overseas. The instructor of the physical training in the camp is Parlindungan Siregar, a member of al Qaeda's network in Spain.'[23]

The existence of this camp in Indonesia was uncovered during investigations into an al Qaeda cell in Spain led by the notorious Abu Dahdah, based in Madrid. The Spanish al Qaeda chief reportedly visited Sulawesi in 2001 and arranged funding for the camp as a training site for jihadists from Europe, North Africa, the Middle East and Southeast Asia.[24] The camp was later linked to the devastating train bombings that took place in Madrid in 2004, with media reports that some of the terrorists responsible had been trained in Indonesia.[25]

Like the Singaporeans, the Spanish authorities had been pressuring Jakarta for months to move against the suspected terrorists operating in Indonesia. As early as December 2001, the Spanish authorities had requested the arrest of the al Qaeda instructor Parlindungan Siregar. *Time* magazine reported the nonchalant response from an Indonesian official: 'You can go and talk to him if you want, we'll give you his address.'[26]

As the evidence mounted, the Indonesian authorities remained in dogged denial. In an extraordinary show of sympathy, Vice President Hamzah Haz hosted Abu Bakar Bashir to a dinner at his home. He also invited the head of the infamous Laskar Jihad, Jafar Umar Thalib, and another fanatical Islamist, Habib Riziq, whose Islamic Defenders Front was also in the news for trashing bars and nightclubs in Jakarta.

'None of them have an extreme character,' said Hamzah Haz of his guests. 'They only want to see that Indonesia has a religious society.' A four-hour chat over dinner with Bashir and his fellow extremists was enough for the Vice President to announce he was 'certain that there are no terrorists in Indonesia'.[27]

∗

In March 2002, Muklas farewelled his five colleagues in Bangkok and headed back to Indonesia. He travelled south by bus to the crossroads town of Yala near the Thai border with Malaysia. At the terminal there he met up again with Wan Min, the designated bagman for the coming operation. Wan Min handed Muklas $US15,500 in cash, the first of three instalments totalling US$30,500 provided by Hambali. Muklas stated later that 'Since Hambali is not known to have any other big funding sources' he assumed that the money 'came from Afghanistan, namely Sheik Osama bin Laden'.[28]

Muklas took a bus via Kuala Lumpur to Johor, then crossed the Malacca Strait to Sumatra with a boatload of illegal Indonesian workers.

'I waited for my wife and children to arrive,' he recounted. 'Then together with my family I returned on a ship heading for Jakarta.'[29]

Muklas was back in Java in time for the biannual meeting of JI's Central Leadership Council, the Qiyadah Markaziyah, held in the city of Bogor, south of Jakarta, in April 2002. It proceeded much as normal except that, by one account: 'The meeting should have been chaired by Abu Bakar Bashir, but he was unable to attend.'[30]

Bashir was too busy in Solo fending off the escalating calls for his arrest. The gathering was chaired instead by his deputy, Abu Rusdan, who had already been slated as the next emir. They discussed the detention of JI's treasurer, Bafana, before moving on to the progress reports from the mantiqis and other routine affairs. Despite the purge in Singapore and Malaysia and the clamour for a crackdown in Indonesia, it was pretty much business as usual for JI.

At the close of the two-day meeting, Muklas returned once more to his family home in Tenggulun and turned his attention to the operation at hand. 'After I arrived in my village I thought about how I could carry out the plan.'[31]

While Muklas was in Tenggulun, a team from the elite Criminal Investigation Corps of the Indonesian National Police was winging its way to Singapore. While publicly continuing to deny any evidence of terrorism in Indonesia, the authorities in Jakarta were taking up Singapore's invitation to interview the JI detainees and learn the truth for themselves.

On 18 April, JI's captured treasurer, Faiz bin Abu Bakar Bafana, was taken from his cell in Singapore for yet another round of interrogation. After four months of relentless grilling, Bafana was gaunt and defeated. He had already made an extensive confession to Singapore's ISD. Now, in the course of a two-day interview, he repeated his story for the Indonesian police.

'It is true that I am the Jemaah Islamiah treasurer in Malaysia and Singapore,' admitted Bafana. 'Hambali is its chairperson. And Abu Bakar Bashir is the emir of JI.' With Bashir himself denying any knowledge of JI, this revelation was dramatic in itself. But Bafana went on to give away even more explosive details.

He told of the formation of the militant alliance the Mujahideen League by Hambali and Bashir, and its resolution to 'attack Philippine interests', and how this had led to the bombing of the Philippine ambassador in Jakarta. He described the gathering in Solo just before

Christmas 2000 when the plans to bomb Indonesian churches and US targets in Singapore had won 'the agreement and blessing of Abu Bakar Bashir'. And he detailed the later meeting called by the emir in 2001 where, he said, Bashir 'told me to plan a bombing targeting Megawati'.[32]

Bafana's interrogation was a bombshell — first-hand testimony from a key lieutenant, confirming Bashir's leadership of JI and his personal role in planning terrorist attacks. The Indonesian authorities now had the evidence they had been denying for months.

But still Jakarta refused to act. And senior politicians continued their public endorsement of Abu Bakar Bashir. In late May, Hamzah Haz dropped in on Bashir at his home in Solo to pay his respects. Photographers were invited along to record the event. The Vice President and the terrorist leader posed for the cameras, shaking hands and beaming like old friends. Hamzah Haz declared later: 'If you arrest Abu Bakar Bashir, you'll have to arrest me first.'[33]

On a wintry Canberra evening, a delegation of top intelligence analysts strode briskly through the twilight chill descending on Australia's Parliament House. The temperature was just seven degrees and a strong southerly whipped across the forecourt. There was a sense of urgency about the four men heading for the office of Australia's Minister for Foreign Affairs, Alexander Downer. 'We went up there to say, "We have increasing information about a regional terrorist network and we want to brief you on it,"' one of them later recalled.[34]

It was June 2002 and there was growing disquiet within ONA, the body that analyses incoming intelligence for the Australian Government. The agency had requested a special meeting with Downer to explain its unease. 'The purpose of that briefing was to provide him with our views, as they were then, on the threat of terrorism in Southeast Asia and particularly on the information we then had about Jemaah Islamiah and its operations,' said ONA's then Director-General, Kim Jones.[35]

As he headed for Downer's office, Jones had with him three of his best experts — the head of his Pacific branch, Dr Richard Gordon;

Southeast Asia specialist Dr Bill O'Malley; and senior analyst David Farmer, who specialised in Indonesian security issues and terrorism.

David Farmer was worried. Formerly with the Army Intelligence Corps, Farmer had spent most of his working life for the past six months poring over the steady flow of intelligence pointing to a likely terrorist attack in Indonesia. Back in September 2001, in the immediate wake of September 11, Farmer had authored a report for ONA predicting how Islamic groups in Indonesia would react to the US-led 'war on terror'. His report said: 'The threats by Muslim extremists of violence against the citizens and assets of the US and its close allies must be taken seriously. At the very least, increasingly hostile anti-Western protests and harassment of Westerners are likely . . . they have a history of resorting to terrorist methods.' Farmer had also warned, 'Militants may target Australian citizens and interests.'[36]

David Farmer's sense of foreboding had been borne out three months later with the discovery of Jemaah Islamiyah and its plot in Singapore. The flow of intelligence since then had begun to show how closely connected JI and al Qaeda were. Their alliance was now well known to Indonesian intelligence too; even as Jakarta politicians were feigning ignorance, their intelligence agency, Badan Inteligen Nasional (BIN) was briefing its Australian counterparts in March 2002 on 'the way in which Jemaah Islamiyah was organised . . . and establishing connections with al Qaeda'.[37]

As David Farmer arrived for the meeting with Foreign Minister Downer, his gut feeling that an attack could be looming had been strengthened again by a major al Qaeda catch in Indonesia. The big fish was the al Qaeda operative Omar al Faruq. The CIA had homed in on Faruq near his home in Bogor in June, after his captured controller, Abu Zubaydah, named him as 'the senior al Qaeda rep in Southeast Asia'. Faruq was nabbed at the behest of the Americans at a mosque, handed over to the CIA and then spirited away to the top-security Bagram air force base in Afghanistan for interrogation.

By mid-June, Faruq was just beginning to talk. 'Some of the debriefing material was coming out,' David Farmer later recalled. 'So we were at that stage a little firmer in our view of interconnections between Southeast Asia and terrorism elsewhere in the world.'[38] ONA reported to the government in the month that Faruq was arrested: 'Al Qaida has a longstanding presence in Indonesia . . . al Qaida is actively supporting extremists who are prepared to conduct terrorist acts in support of global jihad while advancing their own agendas; in particular Al Qaida has been active in fostering a relationship with Jemaah Islamiyah.'[39]

On that crisp Canberra evening on 18 June 2002, David Farmer and the ONA team laid out their concerns in disturbing detail for Foreign Minister Downer. Exactly what transpired at this meeting has since been the subject of exhaustive scrutiny by a Senate committee set up to examine whether Australians should have been more clearly warned about the dangers of travelling to Indonesia prior to the Bali bombings.

The ONA's Bill O'Malley testified about the meeting with Downer: 'We were trying to make the impact on the minister of our knowledge up until then and explain the danger . . . Much, but not all, of the briefing was confined to Indonesia. We were talking about the problems elsewhere in Southeast Asia as well at the time — our concerns, particularly in the Philippines but also in Thailand or Malaysia or Singapore . . . We knew that there was no shortage of explosives and no shortage of weapons. We made these points clear. We said that basically they had the intention, they had the capability, and getting access to the kinds of equipment they needed would be no problem.'

The Foreign Minister certainly took them seriously. When Downer had to leave for a dinner appointment, he asked the ONA team to come back to continue the briefing the following day. By the end of it, he was left in no doubt about the gravity of the threat from al Qaeda and JI. He then posed the question: what would be the most likely targets in the region?

David Farmer had an answer ready. 'When the question was asked I responded by saying Bali and describing why I thought Bali would be a target and what possible targets there would be. I then went on and said that Singapore and Riau had similar circumstances that might lead them to be targeted as well.' Singapore had already been picked out as a target by JI, while Riau in Sumatra was considered risky because it was the centre of Indonesia's oil industry. But it was Bali, with its saturation of Western tourists and virtually no security, that was uppermost in Farmer's mind.

Farmer had thought for months that the popular resort island was an obvious target. In his report the previous September, Farmer had canvassed the possibility of 'tourist hotels on Lombok or Bali' being hit by Islamic extremists. This was before the existence of JI was even known; at that time Farmer's concerns were focused on the brutal militia group Laskar Jihad. Farmer had reported that there was no sign of any such attack being planned, but pointed out that extremists saw tourist hotels as 'havens of Western decadence'. He warned 'a tourist hotel in Bali would be an important symbolic target'.

Farmer had raised the spectre of an attack on Bali again when he attended a US-sponsored seminar on the future of al Qaeda in April 2002. By this time, JI had been clearly identified as the main terrorist risk in Indonesia. 'We had a scenario-planning exercise to try and identify where al Qaeda would be in the future,' Farmer testified. 'We broke up into a range of groups to investigate certain aspects . . . To build a case for our argument we actually used the scenario of al Qaeda elements linking up with terrorists in Southeast Asia and attacking Bali.'

In the session with Foreign Minister Downer, Farmer and his colleagues ran through the specific locations in Bali where terrorists might strike. 'We covered a range of possible targets,' said Farmer. 'Hotels, nightclubs, airlines and the airport in Denpasar were all covered. We did not do those specifically because there were Australians there; it was because they were seen to be very viable targets for Jemaah Islamiyah.'

The mere thought of a terrorist attack on Bali must have put the Foreign Minister on edge. Bali was the most popular destination for Australians holidaying overseas, with up to 25,000 Australians heading there each month at peak times of the year. And Downer's department was responsible for issuing travel advisories informing Australians of any safety risks in travelling abroad.

Ever since September 11, ASIO had kept its Threat Assessment for Indonesia at HIGH. But the travel advisory issued by the Department of Foreign Affairs and Trade (DFAT) for Indonesia was more low key. It advised Australians to 'keep themselves aware of developments that may affect their safety' and 'maintain a high level of personal security awareness'. It warned against travel to trouble spots like Ambon, Aceh and West Timor, but noted: 'Elsewhere, tourist services in Indonesia are operating normally, including in Bali.'

But now, in the view of one of Australia's top intelligence analysts, Bali was no longer necessarily safe. The main question facing Foreign Minister Downer was whether the travelling public should be told. According to a DFAT staffer, Bill Paterson, who was with him at the briefing, 'Mr Downer, in a general way to those present, in effect, said,

"Well, I wonder whether that means we should be changing our consular advice."' Hours of evidence has been heard over what was said next. According to the only notes that were taken of the meeting, the ONA analysts replied that 'there was no specific intelligence' to warrant any change. The men from ONA were later at pains to emphasise that giving travel advice was not part of their brief, but ONA chief Kim Jones, confirmed: 'We did not see a basis for changing it on the information that we had.'

Witness after witness would later repeat that there was 'no specific intelligence' to justify a warning about Bali. Amid the scramble to avoid and apportion blame in the wake of the Bali bombings, Foreign Minister Downer would dismiss the warnings of David Farmer and his colleagues as mere 'hypothesising and theorising'.⁴⁰ However, staff in Downer's department were so concerned about the intelligence warnings that they wanted more information from ONA. Exactly what information was sought and what was provided was later the subject of intense conjecture during the Senate committee hearings.

According to the ONA accounts, DFAT staffer Bill Paterson requested a follow-up briefing after the initial sessions with Downer. David Farmer testified, 'He came out of our brief — after listening to the brief to the foreign minister — and said that a lot of this was new to him and he was concerned that we were so agitated about the issue, and he asked if we could come and brief members of his division.' Nine days later, DFAT sent an email to ONA under the heading 'Terrorism Questions', posing a series of queries including, 'What evidence or theory is behind the idea that terrorists might target Western interests in Bali?'⁴¹

DFAT and ONA subsequently provided startlingly conflicting accounts of how ONA responded to this request. DFAT claimed it never received any response at all, while ONA claimed that its response was to provide another detailed briefing for DFAT's Bill Paterson and three of his colleagues. The ONA men, David Farmer and Richard Gordon, testified that this follow-up briefing was held in Paterson's office in late June or early July and went for about two hours. They said they provided the DFAT team with much the same information they had given to Downer, using the same briefing notes. 'I basically revisited the same points we had made to the Foreign Minister,' recounted Farmer. 'I addressed why I thought Bali would fit the profile as a target for terrorists.' Gordon remembered discussing the amount of explosives that terrorists would need to use and citing the Oklahoma bombing as an example. DFAT categorically denied that this meeting took place. The department's First Assistant Secretary, Ian Kemish, testified: 'As far as DFAT is concerned this meeting did not happen.'

In the absence of any notes or diary entries to verify the meeting, the Senate committee, which reported in August 2004, concluded that the meeting almost certainly did not take place. It reported 'ONA warrants criticism for failing to respond adequately to the DFAT's direct and unambiguous questions about a highly significant issue for Australians and Australian interests abroad — namely terrorism.'

As the concerns about Indonesia were mounting in 2002, the issue of threat advice was hotly debated within intelligence circles. ASIO, which had maintained its HIGH Threat Assessment, was accused of 'scare-mongering' by the Defence Intelligence Organisation (DIO), which never shifted its risk advice for Indonesia above 'low to medium'. The advisories were also a sore point among operators in the travel industry, for whom Bali meant big business, chief among them the national airline Qantas.

ASIO's Threat Assessment for Indonesia so rankled with Qantas that in mid-2002 the airline requested a separate assessment be done for its interests in Jakarta and Denpasar, Bali, in the hope of being given a lower rating. This hope was dashed by ASIO's curt reply on 3 July: 'The general threat to Qantas interests in Jakarta and Denpasar cannot sensibly be differentiated from the general threat to Australian interests in Indonesia; currently assessed as HIGH.'

ASIO advised that Australia's profile as a potential target for a terrorist attack by Islamic extremists had been raised by its involvement in the war on terrorism, and that there were very good reasons to assume that airline interests *would* be an obvious target. It reminded Qantas of Operation Bojinka in 1995, in which JI and al Qaeda had plotted to hijack and blow up passenger planes in Southeast Asia. ASIO also noted that the authorities had not yet caught up with a Singaporean JI leader who had discussed with Hambali crashing a hijacked jet into Singapore's Changi Airport in revenge for the ISD's arrests.[44] It mentioned that JI and al Qaeda figures had transited both Jakarta and Denpasar airports in the past. 'Given the JI presence in Indonesia, neither Jakarta nor Bali could be considered exempt from attack,' ASIO concluded.[45]

Despite ASIO's rebuff, Qantas tried again, this time approaching ASIO chief Dennis Richardson directly to request another separate assessment for Bali. Once again the response from ASIO was blunt: 'The Director General advised that it was not possible to separate the threat to Qantas in Bali from the threat to Qantas in Jakarta or in Indonesia generally.'

As 2002 wore on, the intelligence grew steadily more ominous. A new ONA report in late July stated: 'Reports of planned terrorist violence in Southeast Asia are coming more frequently.' It warned, 'Al Qaida's strength in Southeast Asia . . . is likely to grow as Al Qaida members flee pressure elsewhere,' adding 'Suicide attacks have not been part of militants' modus operandi in Southeast Asia. But that may be changing.' In another report issued on the same day, ONA pointed to 'reports that Indonesian Islamic extremists intend to launch attacks in Indonesia in August and in Southeast Asia in September'. It said that these could include 'attacks on Christians, raids on brothels and nightclubs, bomb attacks or terrorist attacks on US or other Western targets'.[46]

The tone of the warnings grew urgent in early August, when ASIO issued a new threat assessment for Indonesia. 'Islamic extremists may be planning a series of co-ordinated "actions" across Indonesia, and subsequently Southeast Asia in the August September period,' it warned. The actions 'appeared likely to range from demonstrations to terrorist attacks' and Western interests including those of Australia 'were among the intended targets'.[47]

A terrorist attack in Indonesia now seemed almost inevitable — at least to those in the know. But ordinary Australians, including those excitedly planning their holidays in Indonesia, were not privy to any of these classified assessments by ASIO or ONA, which were for government eyes only, not for public release. And the travel advisories issued by DFAT reflected none of the growing sense with intelligence circles that a disaster was imminent.

As for Bali, there was still 'no specific intelligence' of a possible attack. In the twenty reports it issued between June and October, ONA did not mention Bali again, despite David Farmer's rising unease. And Bali was never included in the travel warnings issued by DFAT, except for the bland reassurances that the situation there was 'calm' and 'normal'.

'I think we did the right thing all along,' Foreign Minister Alexander

Downer commented later to the *Australian*. 'We can't keep changing travel advice on the basis of speculation.' Downer said he had been told of 'hundreds' of possible terror targets in the past eighteen months; if he changed the travel advice every time, 'our travel advisory system would be a shambles'.[48]

The Senate committee took a different view. In its report, it found that the travel advisories 'did not adequately reflect the content of the threat assessments that were available by that time, that specifically warned that Australians in their own right were now seen as terrorist targets in Indonesia'. The report stated that travellers should have been warned that Australians in Indonesia 'were of potential interest to al-Qa'ida/JI'. It noted that the advice about Bali being 'calm' and 'normal', while strictly correct, reinforced 'a benign (and erroneous) view' of the island as a safe haven. The report concluded that 'DFAT, with is heightened focus on terrorism, should have been in little doubt that an explicitly anti-Western terrorist attack of some kind would eventuate and that Australian interests, including soft targets such as tourists, could not be considered immune.'

❦

CHAPTER TWENTY-ONE

FOR ALL YOU CHRISTIAN INFIDELS

The mobile phone on Amrozi's workbench in Tenggulun beeped to signal an incoming text message. If he hadn't been such a pious man now, Amrozi might have cursed; he had enough to do already and didn't need any more work. 'I was extremely busy, I never had any breaks,' he said later. 'There were always people coming to ask me to fix things — their kitchen was a mess or their washing machine was out of order or their electric fan was broken. I never got a break.'[1]

But as he hit the READ command on his cell phone, Amrozi knew immediately that everything else would have to wait. The sender was Samudra. 'The message said that they will have an operation and they should meet in Solo.'[2]

After returning to Tenggulun in April, Amrozi's older brother Muklas had made contact with Samudra to tell him he had funding and approval for a bombing. Muklas had asked Samudra to come up with a proposal. Samudra was now assembling his team and devising a plan.

Amrozi jumped in his white Toyota sedan and drove to Solo where he picked up Samudra and his friend, the explosives specialist Dulmatin. They were accompanied by a third man, the Ngruki graduate known as 'Fatty', who had taken part in the church bombings in 2000, and whose real name was Idris. The four men drove around in Amrozi's car then stopped near a petrol station. Samudra had an announcement: 'Today we have begun a big project. Today we have declared war on America.'[3]

The former honours student and computer geek from West Java was now thirty-two. Under Hambali's tutelage, Samudra had become one of JI's top field operatives, driven by a burning hatred, but cool and professional in his work. He was also a skilled recruiter, whose forceful personality and tales of jihad in Afghanistan proved irresistible to the young men he cultivated from the Islamic high schools and religious study groups of provincial West Java. Even though he had no formal training, he was known by the honorific, Imam Samudra.

General I Made Mangku Pastika, the urbane police chief tasked with solving the Bali bombings, would later describe Samudra with a measure of respect: 'From all these members of the group . . . the most intellectual is Samudra . . . He is very calm. He is an engineer and a tertiary graduate, although we have not traced which university he attended.'[4] In fact Samudra had never been to university at all; it was just the impression he gave. Nor was he always calm. Samudra's arrogance and quick temper were the cause of constant friction with his colleagues in JI.

By early 2002, Samudra's notoriety was spreading. He was now on a wanted list drawn up by the Indonesian police. Samudra had been named in relation to the bungled attempt to bomb the Atrium shopping mall in Jakarta in August 2001. Two men, including the courier who lost a leg when the device exploded, had identified Samudra as the organiser. He had also been named by some of the Singaporean detainees. As a result, in September 2001, police had raided a jungle training camp run by Samudra in Pandeglang, south of his home town, Serang, arresting thirteen recruits and seizing a cache of firearms and ammunition.[5]

In February 2002, Samudra had been identified by an Indonesian police spokesman as an orchestrator of the Christmas Eve church bombings in 2000. His name and mug shot appeared beside Hambali's on a police flow chart headed 'Uncovering the Bomb Cases', and which listed them as the top suspects in the Christmas Eve bombings, the blast at the Atrium shopping mall and another five smaller attacks on Christian churches in 2001. A separate flow chart listed Hambali, Samudra and seven others under the heading 'Network of Bombing Perpetrators in Jakarta'.[6]

Even Australian intelligence was aware of Samudra. 'By the middle of the year 2002 we knew enough about Imam Samudra to know that he was experienced and he was dangerous,' ONA's Southeast Asia specialist Dr Bill O'Malley told the Senate committee inquiry in 2003. 'But we had absolutely no capability to trail him, to know where he was or to know in specific terms what he was doing.'

If anyone had that capability it was the Indonesian police. The police flow charts show that the Indonesian authorities had Samudra's name, occupation, photograph and date of birth; they also had his address and his home and mobile phone numbers. They had the same details for Hambali as well, along with records of the phone contacts between the two of them and other suspects. The police had even set themselves an action plan: 'Intensify search and investigation for the wanted people — Hambali and associates — in West Java and other places they use as hiding places.'[7]

But the action plan barely got off the ground. 'There was no real political will to push it. There's no getting around it — there was no political will,' commented one Australian investigator close to the Indonesian police. While the police commander in charge of the bomb cases was 'going hell for leather', he was given scant resources and luke-warm backing from higher up. In a country with a long history of political violence, much of it fomented by the police and armed forces themselves, investigating a string of bombings simply wasn't a priority. 'If it was a Western police force, they'd be dropping everything, there would be hundreds of people working on it,' the Australian investigator told me. 'But they just went, "Yeah, yeah, we're investigating it."'[8]

The reluctance became political when evidence started to emerge that Islamic extremists were behind the attacks, according to this source. In the prevailing political climate in Jakarta, 'No one wanted to overtly point the finger at Muslims.' The lack of interest turned to downright obstinacy when pressure was applied by foreign governments, such as the United States and Singapore, claiming Indonesia was harbouring terrorists. 'What Singapore was saying was a real affront to the Indonesians,' said the Australian investigator. 'When it became personalised like they thought it was — they just went "Stuff you!"'

Free to carry on with his activities, Samudra was determined to take his fight to a wider stage. Previously his hatred had been directed largely at Christians in Indonesia; now he was ready to execute the fatwas from bin Laden and Hambali authorising the killing of civilians from the United States and its allied countries.

On a website he set up later 'to answer Muslims' questions about the Bali blast', Samudra would cite the US bombing of al Qaeda bases in

Afghanistan and the UN sanctions against Iraq as justification for his acts. He called his website istimata.com, which translates in English as martyrdom.com, and issued his tirade under the banner of his self-proclaimed International Suicide Battalion.

'For all you Christian infidels! If you say that this killing was barbarous and cruel and happened to "innocent civilians" from your countries, then you should know that you do crueller things than that. Do you think that 600,000 babies in Iraq and half a million Afghan children and their mothers are soldiers and sinful people who should have to endure thousands of tonnes of your bombs???!! Where are your brains and your consciences??!!! The cries of babies and the screams of Muslim women . . . There is no way they will ever be able to stop your barbarity! . . . So here we are, Muslims!! So here we are, the brothers of those who have died from your barbarous actions!! . . . Our hearts have been wounded and are filled with pain at the deaths of our brothers and sisters. We cannot allow unjust and barbarous actions against our Muslim brothers and sisters in any corner of the world.'[9]

Samudra called the enemy the 'Coalition army of the Cross', whose member countries he named as 'America, England, Australia, Germany, Belgium, Japan and almost all members of NATO and so on'. He singled out Australia over its role in securing independence for East Timor, declaring: 'Australia had taken part in efforts to separate East Timor from Indonesia, which was all an international conspiracy by followers of the Cross.' For all his verbose rhetoric, Samudra's motivation was simple enough. As a police officer who witnessed one of his tirades later put it: 'He has a deep hatred for Westerners.'

Samudra and Amrozi scouted for targets for weeks. Their first choice was the US embassy in Jakarta, according to Amrozi: 'We went to look at the embassy and we thought — Wow! If we were able to, this would be it! . . . But everyone was thinking about how expensive that operation would be and how much preparation it would take.'[10]

In keeping with Hambali's directive to avoid heavily secured installations, they considered softer targets away from Java in places like Sumatra or Batam island, but found there were few Westerners there to be killed. It was Samudra who came up with the resort island of Bali. None of the group had actually been there, said Amrozi, but 'someone — I forget who — had said there were lots of Caucasians there'. Amrozi returned to Tenggulun to report back to Muklas, who later told the Indonesian police: 'I found out from my younger brother Amrozi that Samudra had a plan to execute bombings in Bali. I approved and supported the idea and provided the funds.'[11]

Muklas and Amrozi went by the Al Islam school to invite their brother Ali Imron to join in. 'I didn't hesitate for a second. I immediately said yes,' Ali Imron recalled.[12] Their friend Mubarok, who worked at the school and lived next door to Amrozi was enthusiastic as well. The four men then set out for Solo in Amrozi's Toyota, stopping on the way to pick up Dulmatin.

Their destination was a village on the outskirts of Solo and the home of a man called Hernianto, a follower of Abu Bakar Bashir. They drove through the fading dusk to a mossy timber bungalow surrounded by banana palms on a dusty road. It was after nightfall when Amrozi's white Toyota pulled up and the five men trooped inside, entering through a doorway leading to a private room, separate from the rest of the house, where they would not be disturbed. It was 14 August 2002.

Empty except for a shelf stacked with Islamic texts, the tiny room was now filling with people. The new arrivals were greeted by JI's military chief, Zulkarnaen, who had called the meeting. Zulkarnaen would have operational carriage of the project without playing a direct role. Also in the room were Samudra, Idris and Abdul Ghoni, who had worked with Ali Imron's team on the church bombings in 2000.[13]

As the night deepened, the nine men sat in a tight circle on the floor of the dingy room. The host, Hernianto, whose wife was on night duty as a nurse at the local hospital, brought refreshments as the meeting got under way.

'It was I who opened the meeting and gave advice,' Muklas revealed to the police, 'because I was considered to be in charge, in view of my age, knowledge and experience'. Muklas would be the controller of the operation, his main role to keep the group focused and motivated. The key to this was their conviction that what they were doing was sanctioned by God. As Samudra put it: 'All that we did, we did for Allah.'

'The advice I gave them was that they needed to remain sincere and constant in carrying out acts of devotion including jihad or holy struggle,' said Muklas. He told them the objective was 'to avenge the despotic behaviour of the United States and its allies towards Muslims everywhere so they cease such behaviour.' He explained that Bali had been chosen 'because there are many places in Bali that are visited by tourists from the targeted countries such as the US, England, France, Australia, Israel and other countries who behave despotically towards Muslims.'

At the end of his pep-talk Muklas handed over to Samudra, whom he had assigned as field commander. Samudra explained that the precise targets would be chosen once they arrived in Bali, then asked if everyone was in favour of the plan. 'We all agreed including myself,' Ali Imron later confessed. 'After the agreement Imam Samudra distributed the jobs and the date and time of the bombing in Bali. It was to be around September 2002.'[14]

While everyone was enthusiastic about the proposal, there was concern about the date chosen by Samudra, who wanted the attack to mark the first anniversary of September 11. 'There was a quarrel about the timing,' said Ali Imron. 'Samudra was the field leader. He wanted to do it in Bali as soon as possible. Most of us disagreed with him. We believed that if it was done in a hurry we wouldn't get perfect results.'[15]

After a vigorous discussion, the date was left unresolved. 'The meeting finally decided that we must first prepare the materials including the car, chemicals, the timing of the explosions, etc. When they were all ready, then we would leave for Bali. The timing would be determined by when everything was ready.'

Before they parted, each team member was allotted his tasks: Amrozi would buy the car and chemicals; Ali Imron would assist Samudra; while Mubarok would help with the driving. Idris would be the logistics man, handling money and accommodation. Abdul Ghoni would mix the chemicals, leaving Dulmatin to construct the bomb. The meeting finished at 10 p.m. Hernianto served rice and refreshments and the nine men who would bomb Bali went their separate ways.

It was the first and only time the core group would assemble in one room; there was no need for them to meet again. 'All those present understood the mission,' Muklas later explained. Samudra elaborated: 'I gave them full freedom, because they had all done this before. This was merely a repeat of previous work. It's not like they were children who had to be told everything they had to do.'[16]

cℳo

While the core team set about its preparations, Samudra was assembling a second cell — a clique of young disciples enlisted from the Islamic high schools of West Java and groomed to die for the cause. The group Samudra called Team Lima was made up of five impressionable youths from a religious study circle he had formed in Banten, near his birthplace, Serang.

One of Samudra's initiates was a recent graduate of Bashir's Ngruki school called Abdul Rauf, who had gone on to study journalism before being inspired by Samudra to choose a career in jihad instead. Twenty-year-old Abdul Rauf had introduced Samudra to four of his friends — Yudi, Agus, Amin and Arnasan — all from a tiny town called Malimping in the backblocks south of Serang.

Imam Samudra was quite a guru to these young men, brought up on the folklore of the old Darul Islam movement. He preached to them about the persecution of Muslims, showed them videos of atrocities committed by Christians in Ambon and Sulawesi, and explained 'the victory' of September 11. Then he took them to his jungle training camp at Pandeglang and taught them to fire rifles and fight with machetes.[17]

The poorest of the boys, Arnasan, lived with his parents in a shack with no electricity on the outskirts of town, where they shared a single rice paddy with a neighbour. Arnasan was a plump boy with 'a dark, pimply, wrinkled and sad face', a description from Ali Imron, who met him later.[18] 'He was a little bit naughty when he was young,' Arnasan's mother told a journalist. 'He liked to play more than study. But he was a good boy. He was quite devoted, prayed five times a day and always observed Ramadan.'[19]

Arnasan's family couldn't afford his school fees so he had dropped out after the second year of junior high school. Finding a mentor like Imam Samudra opened up a whole new world. Samudra introduced Arnasan and his friends to computers and the internet, entranced them with his war stories from Afghanistan and indoctrinated them with his mantra that 'jihad has to be executed first'. The young gang was in his thrall, especially Arnasan whom Samudra described as 'the most prominent in spirit and motivation'.

Samudra had been coaching his five young followers for more than a year. Now he was ready to send them into action. Their first job would be to stage a bank robbery to raise funds for the bombing in Bali. The money wasn't really the point — JI already had funding from al Qaeda; it was more a test of how far his young novices would go.

The target of the heist was the Chinese-owned Elita goldsmith's shop in Samudra's home town, Serang. He told his recruits the robbery could be justified under Islamic law. 'The term is to carry out *fa'i* — which means taking back what is rightfully owned by the Islamic community but has been stolen by the infidels, particularly by the Chinese infidels,' Samudra explained.[20]

Two of the team stood guard outside the shop while Abdul Rauf let off a firecracker down the road, the signal for Arnasan and the other youth to storm the shop armed with guns provided by Samudra. They made their getaway on motorbikes with five million rupiah and 2.5 kilograms of gold handed over by the jeweller. The gold was later sold and the total takings of 400 million rupiah deposited in a bank account set up by Idris for the bombing. Team Lima had passed its first test.

Samudra moved to Solo, shifting into a house rented for him by Idris which became his new base. The neighbours thought it odd when he showed up there with his wife and four children but hardly anything else, not even kitchen utensils. There was no furniture in the house, not even chairs, and when guests came they would always sit outside. Samudra's wife, Zakia, wore the head-to-toe burkah and dark glasses to cover her eyes.

An inquisitive neighbour named Anisah watched with interest as Samudra came and went, keeping very odd hours. 'Sometimes he would go out in the afternoon and not come home until the following morning. He would get home at five-thirty in the morning and go straight inside and then he wouldn't come out. I would ask the kids where he had been and why he had stayed out all night. "I don't know, Aunty," they would say.'[21]

Back in Tenggulun, Amrozi set off with Ali Imron and Idris to buy a car. In a village 50 kilometres' drive away they found just the thing — a white 1984 model Mitsubishi L300 wagon, with Bali plates as Samudra had instructed. Ali Imron would later blame Samudra's haste for providing the Indonesian police with one of their first clues after the bombing.

'Amrozi was pressured by Imam Samudra to get the car as quickly as possible,' said Ali Imron. 'Amrozi should have bought that L300 van from some far away place. But he bought it from a place nearby — the owner who sold it even knew Amrozi quite well.'[22]

Amrozi drove the car home to his workshop where he replaced its racing wheels with standard ones and stripped out what they didn't need. 'I also removed the air-conditioning and the back seats as ordered by Samudra, so the car could carry one tonne of chemicals. The reason I removed the wheels, tyres, AC and seats was because the L300 would be exploded in Bali.'[23] Amrozi later went to work with his toolkit, filing and re-etching the chassis number engraved on the L300 so the vehicle couldn't be traced.

Next, Amrozi visited his regular supplier, the Tidar Kimia shop in Surabaya, where he had previously bought chemicals to send to Ambon. This time Amrozi wanted more than the shop had in stock; he had to go to the warehouse and rent a pickup truck to get his forty sacks of potassium chlorate, each weighinbg 25 kilograms, back to Tenggulun. A few days later he returned to the shop for 50 kilograms of aluminium powder and two sacks of sulphur.

Waiting in Solo, Samudra received a text message from Amrozi: 'He told me everything was ready.'

A sense of menace surrounded the US embassy in Jakarta on 11 September 2002. Security guards with walkie-talkies and assault rifles prowled the perimeter, while newly erected barricades diverted traffic in a wide arc around the compound. The embassy was closed after 'credible and specific threat information', jargon for new intelligence that al Qaeda and JI were intending to blow it up.

Inside his heavily secured residence, Ambassador Ralph 'Skip' Boyce had been worrying for weeks. 'I was calling on a wide range of senior people in the Indonesian Government to convey our concerns about what we felt was a deteriorating security situation here,' Boyce told me in an interview in 2003. 'This was coupled with the enhanced visibility of al Qaeda . . . and concerns that they might be in touch with, or in league with, some of these Indonesian groups.'[24]

Like any good ambassador, Boyce was being diplomatic. By September 2002, he knew for a fact that al Qaeda and JI had joined forces and were preparing to attack. But his repeated warnings to the Indonesian Government had gone unheeded.

Boyce's fears were finally corroborated by the captured al Qaeda operative Omar al Faruq. Arrested in June and whisked away to the Bagram air force base in Afghanistan, Faruq had provided only tidbits at first. But eventually, after three months of interrogation, al Qaeda's rep in Indonesia had broken down. It's not known exactly how the Americans got him to talk, but the 'stress and duress' techniques used on terror suspects at bases like Bagram, such as keeping detainees blindfolded, sleep deprived and standing or kneeling in painful positions for hours on end, are now well known.

Two days before the anniversary of September 11, his US interrogators had finally extracted an elaborate confession out of al Faruq. It led the United States to issue a worldwide 'orange alert', indicating a 'high risk' of terrorist attack. The reasons for the alert were highlighted in a CIA report circulated on September 10. It stated that Faruq had confessed to having prepared 'a plan to conduct simultaneous car/truck bomb attacks against US embassies in the region to take place on or about 11 September 2002'.

Faruq also nominated Australia as a target of al Qaeda and JI, informing his interrogators that Australian interests in East Timor had been canvassed for possible attacks.[25] ASIO raised its Threat Assessment for East Timor to HIGH, while the Australian diplomatic mission in Dili was temporarily closed and most of its staff evacuated. The DFAT travel advisory for Indonesia had been upgraded in July to warn: 'Bombs have been exploded periodically in Jakarta and elsewhere in the past, including areas frequented by tourists. Further explosions may be attempted.' It was now strengthened again to advise that 'in view of the ongoing risk of terrorist activity, Australians should maintain a high level of personal security awareness at all times'. The advice that tourist services in Bali were 'operating normally' didn't change.

But the real bombshell in Faruq's confession was his account of the direct involvement of Abu Bakar Bashir, summarised in the CIA's report. 'Faruq admitted that Abu Bakar was a co-ordinator of this plan to bomb regional embassies, including Jakarta. Bashir authorised Faruq to use JI operatives and resources to conduct this large scale operation.'[26]

The CIA reported that Faruq claimed this was not the first time that Bashir had played such a role: 'Faruq admitted to being the mastermind behind all the Christmas 2000 bombings in Indonesia. These bombings were planned with the complete knowledge, approval, logistical and financial support of Bashir . . . Faruq also revealed that Bashir ordered the April 1999 bombing of the Istiqlal mosque in Jakarta and blamed Christians for the act to foment sectarian strife.'

Faruq's sensational allegations supported the testimony provided five months earlier by the detained JI treasurer Abu Bakar Bafana, providing another first-hand account of Bashir's direct involvement in planning terrorist attacks. But a political furore erupted when details of Faruq's confession were published in *Time* magazine, in a leak apparently designed to pressure the Indonesians into arresting Bashir. Islamic groups condemned the CIA report as 'the black propaganda of the US'. Their cynicism stemmed in part from memories of the CIA's role in destabilising Sukarno decades before, the CIA's involvement only serving to exacerbate anger over what many saw as US interference in Indonesia's affairs.

Taking their cue from the extremists, government ministers rushed to support Bashir. 'Who accuses him of being a terrorist?' demanded the Justice Minister Yusril Ihza Mahendra. 'It's a new accusation from the US . . . The Department of Justice will defend him.'[27] Vice President Hamzah Haz scoffed at the new evidence against his former dinner guest, dismissively stating: 'If a terrorist network is discovered to be operating in Indonesia the government will take action.'[28]

The new accusations further enhanced Bashir's cachet. In Solo, 5000 of his followers rallied to support 'the preacher wanted by America', as he was promoted on fliers for the rally. 'Bashir is a great man, a great preacher,' said one protestor. 'He is no terrorist. Bush is the terrorist. America is the terrorist.' The Islamic Defenders Front announced, 'Everyone who attended the rally is waiting for instructions from their leaders to stage a jihad against America.'[29]

Publicly Bashir was buoyed by the new wave of support. 'Bring me Omar al Faruq and those arrested in Singapore and Malaysia!' he insisted. 'The Americans and the CIA must not talk if they cannot show me the evidence. They are talking nonsense.'[30]

But privately Bashir was alarmed at being incriminated by Faruq. After the front-cover splash in *Time* magazine, JI members were reportedly called to a series of meetings across Java where the emir advocated a change of course.

'[Bashir] argued strenuously that bombings and the armed struggle for an Islamic state should be put on hold for the time being because they would have negative repercussions for the movement,' wrote Sidney Jones of the International Crisis Group. According to JI members she interviewed, Bashir argued: 'The moment was not ripe to go forward because the US and Indonesia acting in concert could crack down on Muslim activists. It was not that [Bashir] disagreed with violence as a tactic. He was concerned that the timing was wrong.'[31]

But the emir's about-face was anathema to the militants whose views now prevailed in JI. According to Sidney Jones, '[Bashir's] advice went down poorly among JI members and while they continued to show respect and acknowledge him as the de jure head of JI, the radicals began searching for new leaders closer to their way of thinking.'

Bashir's push for a backdown was given short shrift by the JI bombing team, whose members were now at work separately in Solo and Tenggulun. However, Ali Imron, for one, was unnerved by the chorus of demands for Bashir's arrest. 'I recall asking Amrozi and Mubarok whether or not the plan could go ahead considering the news from Malaysia and Singapore that Ustad Abu Bakar Bashir was going to be arrested,' Ali Imron said later. 'Amrozi and Mubarok said it was OK, meaning that we could proceed with the Bali plan.'[32]

As the political storm raged in Jakarta and Solo, preparations for the bombing moved quickly. In the third week of September, JI's bomb master, Dr Azahari Husin, travelled to Tenggulun, which was now the command centre for the operation. Azahari was accompanied by his colleague from UTM in Malaysia, Noor Din Mohammed Top.

The two visitors stayed overnight with Muklas in his modest family home in the village, catching up on events since their last meeting in Bangkok. 'Dr Azahari told stories about his hideouts . . . in Malaysia and explained about the plan to bomb America's interests in Singapore as well, but said that it was not feasible and so he came to join the bombing team in Indonesia,' Muklas revealed.

The man assigned to assemble the bomb, Dulmatin, arrived in Tenggulun the next day. Dulmatin picked up Azahari and Noor Din and took them to stay at his home in Solo, eager to brainstorm with the author of the JI bomb manual. 'At Dulmatin's house, Dr Azahari and Dulmatin discussed exploding systems in massive amounts,' said Muklas. 'They talked until around five o'clock in the morning about the technical side of bombing.' They stopped to pray at dawn then continued their discussion for another full day, before Azahari and Noor Din returned to Jakarta.

In Tenggulun, Amrozi and Idris began breaking up the chunks of potassium chlorate into powder and packing the chemicals into twenty large cartons emptied of their former contents, clove cigarettes. 'I packaged them up in those Gudang Garam boxes, those cigarette boxes,' said Amrozi. 'Then I wrapped them in a sack and sewed it up. Then I just put them on the bus.' Idris and Ali Imron helped Amrozi cart the boxes of potassium chlorate, sulphur and aluminium powder to the terminal at Surabaya from where they were sent off by bus to Denpasar. 'I just said to the bus crew to please take this package and drop it at the terminal at the other end. They asked, "Who will pick it up?" I said, "Someone will, someone will."' After this, Amrozi and the others in Tenggulun simply had to bide their time. 'The departure to Bali was not yet determined,' said Amrozi. 'We had to wait for an SMS message from Samudra.'

The field commander had been busy. After an initial trip to Bali in early September to arrange accommodation and begin reconnaisance, Samudra had returned to his base in Solo. From there he emailed his five young acolytes who had staged the gold-shop robbery, to tell them the time for jihad had come.

The boys from Team Lima came by bus: the ex-journalism student, Abdul Rauf; the pimply sad-faced boy named Arnasan; and their friends from Malimping, Yudi, Agus and Amin. Idris picked them up at the station and took them to Samudra's rented house in Solo. Samudra's inquisitive neighbour remembered them well.

'There were five people staying here,' Anisah said. 'They were here for about a week, but I couldn't tell you their names. They said they were uni students but I don't know. I asked them, "You five men living here together, are you all working?" They said, "No I'm not working, I'm still at uni." That's all they said. They were only here for a week.'[33]

The five youths were undergoing some final intensive priming by Samudra. 'We discussed jihad and the plans for *syahid* bombings in Bali,' Samudra later explained. 'I conveyed to them the condition of oppressed Muslims . . . especially the slaughter committed by American terrorists and their allies towards other Muslim countries.' After a week of preaching, prayer and indoctrination, Samudra posed the question.

'I asked them, "Brothers, are you or are you not capable of going on jihad on behalf of Muslims with a martyr's bombing?" I told them they shouldn't do it if they felt pressured, or to be seen as courageous, or to gain popularity, or for any other bad reasons. They should only do it for Allah.'

At first no one volunteered. 'He invited us to carry a martyr's bomb . . . but we all remained silent,' one of the five youths, Agus, later testified. Samudra then quizzed them one by one. 'I answered "I am not ready,"' said Agus. Neither were three of his friends. 'At the time, the only one of us who was ready was my friend . . . Arnasan.'[34] Samudra knew the sad-faced high school dropout, also known as Iqbal, was the most likely candidate. 'Bal, is the martyr bomber ready?' Samudra asked him. 'Yes,' Arnasan replied. Arnasan and his friends in Team Lima were then sent off to Bali by bus to await their next instructions. The others were 'still deliberating on the courage that was needed,' in Samudra's words.

By early October, everything was set. But as they moved toward the final stages, the group received some sobering news. Dr Azahari's fellow lecturer from UTM and the bagman for the bombing, Wan Min Wan Mat, had been arrested in Malaysia. One of the six men who had been at the key planning session in Bangkok, Wan Min was a senior member of the JI team and his capture was a significant blow. But JI was set up precisely to accommodate such losses. Its organisation and operations structure was so compartmentalised that if any one member was arrested the group could still carry on as planned — which is exactly what it did.

Finally, Amrozi and the others waiting in Tenggulun got the signal to move. 'I received an SMS message from Samudra which said that the chemicals had arrived in Bali,' Amrozi recounted. 'I was asked to send "the white one" — meaning the L300 van — as quickly as possible to "the place" — meaning Bali.'

Amrozi contacted his brother Ali Imron with the message, 'We leave for Bali in the L300 at 1 p.m.' The next day the team assembled hastily at Amrozi's house: Amrozi and Ali Imron, their friends Dulmatin and Mubarok, and the bomb master, Dr Azahari, who arrived in Tenggulun again on the day of their depature, 5 October 2002. Muklas came by to give the team his blessing before they set off for Bali.

CHAPTER TWENTY-TWO

COCKY AUSTRALIA, BEWARE!

It was close to midnight on Friday 6 October when the bombers' convoy arrived in Bali. The capital, Denpasar, was still steaming from the heat of the day, as they wound their way through its dimly lit streets. 'It was very late at night, by the time we got there I had fallen asleep,' Amrozi recalled.

The Mitsubishi L300 driven by Mubarok and a green Suzuki with Ali Imron at the wheel pulled into a petrol station near the bus terminal on the city's outskirts. Mubarok shook Amrozi awake. 'You were invited to come to Denpasar, why did you fall asleep?' he scolded his neighbour.[1]

Ali Imron jumped into the driver's seat of the L300, which was stacked with filing cabinets they had purchased during a stop on the way. Ali Imron took off alone in the van to stow it in the garage of a house rented by Samudra. Amrozi and Mubarok got into the Suzuki with Azahari and Dulmatin and drove on.

They pulled over when they spotted a cracked timber sign with square black letters announcing 'Hotel Harum'. Under the sign was a cluttered shopfront with sacks of rice stacked to the ceiling beside a pair of scrawny cocks in a wicker cage. The pet monkey which usually screeches a raucous welcome from its perch in the frangipani tree would have been fast asleep.

When the four men stepped out of the Suzuki, there was a small welcoming party there to greet them. 'On arrival at the Hotel Harum we met up with Samudra,' said Amrozi. With him were three other men — Idris and Abdul Ghoni, who had both been at the planning session in Solo, and a newcomer to the plot named Umar Patek, an instructor at the JI Military Academy. 'We met at the side of the road in front of the hotel,' Amrozi recounted. 'Then Samudra and Idris went into the hotel to order a room.'

At 50,000 rupiah a night, barely A$10, the dingy rooms of the Hotel Harum were a world away — though only fifteen minutes' drive — from the flash resorts and neon-lit discos of Kuta Beach. After renting two rooms, the group crowded into room 101, a windowless rectangle with mouldering yellow walls and two narrow wooden beds. The field commander quickly recapped everyone's tasks. It didn't take long. As Amrozi said, 'We knew what to do . . . we've done it five times before, we know our jobs.'[2]

The next day the bombing team reassembled at the house Samudra had rented in Jalan Pulau Menjangan, a quiet, leafy street in a well-to-do suburb of Denpasar, with little passing traffic except for the occasional food hawker pushing a cart. The house Samudra had leased was a salmon-pink two-storey villa behind a high green wrought-iron fence. It had everything the bombers needed — security, five bedrooms, two bathrooms and, most importantly, a lock-up garage in which the L300 was already hidden away. Samudra had paid a full year's rent up front, wiring the 10 million rupiah (A$2000) through a local bank.

Inside the house, Abdul Ghoni was already at work mixing the chemicals sent in the cigarette boxes by Amrozi. He had two assistants, the JI instructor Umar Patek and another veteran named Sarjio, who had helped with the attack on the Philippine ambassador in Jakarta. The three men spent days mixing the sacks of potassium chlorate with the sulphur and aluminium powder in batches of twenty-five kilograms each, then pouring the mixture into plastic bags and storing them in one of the spare rooms. It was a tedious and dirty job; there were chemicals spilt all over the tiled floor and so much dust that Sarjio got sick from it and had to stop working.

When the experts Azahari and Dulmatin arrived they took over. There was almost a rebellion when Azahari announced that he needed several dozen small plywood boxes, which he wanted the assistants to make, to pack the explosives in. It was the first of numerous arguments and mishaps among the irritable team of conspirators over the coming week. 'The people here got very upset,' related Ali Imron. 'How was it possible for us to make such a large number of boxes? It had already been decided that we would use filing cabinets and they had been bought.'[3] Azahari finally agreed to settle for the plastic filing cabinets and work resumed.

'We worked and worked, lining up the filing cabinets and filling them with explosive detonating cord. We worked all through the night,' said Ali Imron. 'During the night time we started to fill the drawers of the filing cabinet with the black powder that had already been mixed.'

There were twelve plastic filing cabinets, each four drawers high — so forty-eight drawers in all — loaded with the deadly mixture, with holes drilled through the cabinets so the detonator cord could be looped through. 'We put the formula into the filing cabinets and put the detonating cord through the holes on both ends. When the cabinets were nearly full we sealed them with paper cartons. All 48 drawers were prepared in this way . . . Each drawer was connected by detonating cord and placed in the back of the car. So then the car was full of ready-to-blow explosives, which couldn't be seen from the outside because the car windows were black. Another box containing TNT was put right next to the driver.'

As the laborious preparatory work ground on, secrecy was paramount. For the six days and nights that the core group spent there, the bomb makers didn't leave the house, sleeping and eating where they worked and taking turns to stand guard outside. Each team member had a Balinese alias. They communicated in code, referring to the bomb as *dodol kudus*, the name of an Indonesian sweet fruit cake. They stayed in contact mainly by SMS and changed their mobile phone numbers constantly. If anyone received a call from a number they didn't recognise, the numbers would be changed again. Each man was told only as much as he needed to know. Some of the younger ones didn't even know who Dr Azahari was; they knew him only as 'Alan' or 'Lan'.

There were about a dozen men all told in Bali; the core group of nine who had met in August in Solo, plus the assistants mixing the chemicals and a local fixer named Masykur, who helped to find the accommodation and rental cars. While the bomb makers stayed at the house in Menjangan Street, Idris and Samudra were holed up in separate quarters, and Amrozi and Mubarok were billeted elsewhere in the five different hotels and boarding houses around Denpasar where Idris had rented rooms. Only Idris knew where everyone was and he moved constantly himself. 'I never asked why Idris had three places to live in one city, because the more I asked the greater the risk to me,' said Samudra.

Stuck on his own in a suburban guesthouse, Amrozi was bored; his job as gofer was basically done. 'It's fair to say that I had nothing to do. There were so many people there, all given tasks according to their skills. I don't have the skills that the others have.'[4] Amrozi was mostly kept away from the crucial preparations and told to stay put in his room. 'I was left there alone while Samudra, Idris and Dulmatin stayed somewhere else that I didn't know . . . Idris and Samudra often visited me and brought me food and I didn't do anything except eat and sleep,' Amrozi complained. 'It was like being kept in detention.'

Samudra came and went as he pleased between the bomb house in Menjangan Street and his garden room in a boarding house behind the Banyuwangi cafe in Denpasar's Muslim quarter. Samudra stayed there on and off for a month; the owners and other tenants got to know him quite well, later recalling the look he adopted for his stay in Bali — red hat, thin moustache, laptop and black Crypton motorbike. He told them he was a tour guide, which explained his odd hours.

While his colleagues were mixing chemicals, Samudra whiled away his time at the local internet cafe or on the veranda of the boarding house, chatting to his neighbours and giving sweets to their kids, who called him 'Uncle Andre'.[5] 'He was friendly, he was nice,' recalled the landlady, Nilos Wandari. 'He behaved quite normally, quite well — not suspiciously.'[6]

A voracious reader as always, Samudra spent hours poring over the local papers for the latest news. He may well have seen an interview with Abu Bakar Bashir published in an Indonesian tabloid, in which the emir lashed out at Australia's Foreign Minister, Alexander Downer, who had stated that Bashir should be investigated. Bashir called Australia a 'cocky trouble-maker' whose real agenda was to destroy Islam. The article was headlined: 'Cocky Australia, beware!'[7]

Samudra's swanning around and imperious manner annoyed some of the crew doing the dirty work at the bomb house, where nerves were beginning to fray. 'Most of his time in Bali he just went to internet cafes, that's about all he ever did, he hardly ever checked out the activities at Menjangan Street,' complained Ali Imron. 'Samudra hadn't even decided how many bombs would be exploded. He just wanted to blow up as much as possible, but we didn't have the capacity to do that . . . Samudra demanded that even his superiors obey him . . . Those were the kinds of clashes that were happening.'[8]

It was at night-time that Samudra did his share of the work, heading out to case the tourist strip along Legian Street in Kuta Beach. Samudra kept the nightclubs favoured by foreigners under surveillance on and off for weeks, starting with his first trip to Bali in early September.

There was one particular spot that caught Samudra's eye — the popular drinking barn the Sari Club, a legend among regular Australians visitors to Bali. Samudra later described to police one surveillance outing in early October, when he played tour guide for Idris and Ali Imron.

'When we got to Legian Street in Kuta, we sat in the car in front of the Sari Club. I saw lots of whiteys dancing, and lots of whiteys drinking,' Samudra recalled. It was 9 p.m. and the Sari Club was just starting to jump. The streetside hawkers would have been doing a lively trade in wooden carvings and pirated DVDs, while the traffic along the strip slowed to its usual late night crawl, exhaust fumes mingling with the sweet scent of clove cigarettes. A cacophony of music blared from the open-air bars while, further up the road, Jimmy Barnes was belting out his Aussie working-class anthems at the Hard Rock Hotel.

The Sari Club's huge covered dance floor, with its thatch-roofed bars on either side protected from the weather by corrugated iron sheeting, would have been packed. The Sari could jam in 800 people on a good night. Outside, flags with the words 'welcome' fluttered under its coloured lights. Its clientele were all foreigners, in keeping with the club's policy of barring entry to Indonesians.

Inside would have been the usual Sari Club scene, colourfully described in the 'Bali by Night map 'n guide': 'Another heaving Australian hangout with rousing chorus singsongs, courtesy of the army of sizzled, sweaty, bare-chested lads and tipsy female tourists. Video screens back the rammed dance floor with local ladies of the professional ilk screening the game. Chucking up and out time is around 3 a.m.'

To the revellers inside, it was all just good fun. To Samudra, watching from the outside with Idris and Ali Imron, the 'whiteys' in the Sari Club were evil incarnate. 'I saw a lot of foreigners there engaged in immoral acts. That place is the biggest centre of immoral activities in Bali . . . It is a gathering place for all the nations of imperialists, terrorists, oppressors and destroyers of the virtue of Indonesian women . . . Bali is one of the world's largest and most popular places for sex outside marriage . . . This is an irony which shames us in the presence of Allah.'

Diagonally opposite the Sari Club was Paddy's Bar, another favourite haunt of visiting Australians, similarly described in 'Bali by Night': 'The raucous boozed-up crowd of predominantly young Aussies bounce around to the likes of Men at Work while downing beakers of potent Jungle Juice (made from local Arak). Fun and friendly, and if you're prowling for a little holiday romance, this could be the place to find it.'

Samudra had found his target. 'That place, Kuta, and especially Paddy's Bar and the Sari Club, was a meeting place for US terrorists and their allies, who the whole world knows to be monsters,' he later told the Indonesian police.

The five young suicide bombers Samudra was grooming would soon know their fate. The separate cell he called Team Lima had arrived in Bali a few days before. Arnasan and his friends were split into two groups and kept in separate lodgings, away from the main team making the bombs. 'They were told to stay where they were and read the Koran as much as they could to guard their heart and conscience and to firm their intentions in the name of Allah,' said Samudra.

Meanwhile at the bomb house in Menjangan Street, an accident with the chemicals almost gave the whole game away. It happened while the team was moving the filing cabinets packed with explosives. 'There were remnants of black powder stuck on the ceramic floor that hadn't been properly cleaned off,' said Ali Imron. 'Instead of lifting the filing cabinet we dragged it around, which caused an explosion. All the neighbours came out. Idris and I were on guard outside.'[9]

The pair assured the anxious neighbours that nothing was wrong. 'Idris said that it was probably the sound of a flat tyre or an exploding balloon.' But inside the place was a mess, as Ali Imron found. 'When I got inside the house was full of smoke . . . After that we all left . . . We cleared out of the house. We were worried that the neighbours might get more suspicious if they thought there was something to worry about. But nothing more happened that night so we resumed working the next morning.'

After this accident, the team discovered a serious flaw in their work. The filing cabinets had been overpacked; the chemicals had expanded and the drawers were bulging. Abdul Ghoni, who had returned to Java, received an urgent SMS message ordering him back to Bali, where he had to start the arduous job of packing the chemicals all over again, refilling the drawers with smaller quantities then wrapping them with elastic bands.

By this time the youngest of the team, Ali Imron, was starting to panic. The doubts that he had stifled during the church bombings of Christmas 2000 now came flooding back, or so he claimed. 'I kept praying to Allah: Please stop me . . . please stop me,' Ali Imron would later testify in his defence.[10] He told Samudra he wanted to go home, using the excuse that he had exam papers to mark at the Al Islam school in Tenggulun. But according to Ali, Samudra 'acted like a tough man' and made him stay.[11]

After several days, the controller and spiritual guide of the operation, Muklas, paid a visit to Bali, in his words 'to check on the plan for the bombing'. By Ali Imron's account, he was brought in to smooth over the tensions in the team. This would have been a sensitive task. According to Ali Imron, the always prickly Samudra was protective of his turf and was immediately offended if he felt Muklas, as the overall controller of the operation, was usurping his role as field commander.

Muklas travelled by bus under cover of night from Tenggulun to eastern Java and then by ferry and bus to Denpasar. 'On the way to Denpasar I contacted Idris by SMS on my mobile phone to say that I was coming to Bali and would arrive around dawn and to please pick me up,' Muklas later told the police. The sun was just rising when he stepped off the bus. 'I immediately looked for the prayer room at the Denpasar terminal to perform the dawn prayer ritual. Before praying I rang Idris to tell him I had arrived . . . After praying I headed for the waiting room at the terminal and met Idris there.'

Tight security surrounded Muklas's visit. The controller changed his mobile phone number ten times in the course of the operation and only Idris knew where he was staying and the details of his movements. Like the others, Muklas used a Balinese pseudonym for his stay. He chose the alias 'Rama', from the mythological Hindu hero whose name epitomises chivalry, courage and obedience to sacred law.[12]

After picking Muklas up at the bus stop, Idris took him to one of the rented rooms, white-tiled and bare except for a mattress, a floor mat and a broom. Muklas locked himself in and 'slept alone while Idris left, without informing me where he was going. I did not ask where he lived for reasons of security.' Idris came back in the evening with Amrozi, bringing rice and water for dinner. 'Over the 3 days I was at

Idris's rented house I met once with Amrozi and a man I did not know who was brought by Idris. We shook hands but did not say our names for reasons of security,' Muklas explained.

The following night, Muklas was taken to Legian Street to see the targets for himself. 'As I walked from the car I was shown the Sari Club and Paddy's Bar across the street . . . I saw their signs as we passed and I also saw that most of the people inside were whiteys.'

Muklas had been keen to bomb the US consulate, located in a suburb of Denpasar. 'The American embassy in Renon was actually our original target . . . But after we saw it we saw it was just a quiet building with almost no-one around, so we decided not to make it the main target. So the main targets were the Sari Club and Paddy's. The Sari Club was surveyed for nearly a month and we concluded that there were none of our people there, I mean Indonesians, because Indonesians aren't allowed in . . . But at Paddy's some are still allowed in, therefore we decided to make the bomb at Paddy's smaller.'

Muklas paid a visit to the house at Menjangan Street to give the bomb makers his blessing before returning to Java. On the way back to the bus station, he stopped off to farewell Samudra and the anxious Ali Imron. 'The two of them were standing waiting for me by the side of the road . . . I was in the car at the time and was only able to say "How are you?" and they answered "Fine." I do not know for sure who answered because we were still moving even as I shook hands and I said I was going home to Java.' Muklas parted from Idris at the bus stop with the words 'Let us pray that we succeed.'

On the morning of 10 October, the bombers loaded up the L300 van. A sheet of plywood was cut to fit its base. Then the twelve filing cabinets were placed in the back, three across and four deep, each bolted to the floor. 'All twelve filing cabinets were filled with four racks or drawers and they were all filled with the black powder . . . plus one extra drawer filled with TNT,' said Ali Imron, who was still happy to brag about their work after the event, despite his misgivings. The forty-ninth drawer packed with TNT was placed behind the driver's seat, hard up against the other drawers.

While the van was being loaded, Samudra summoned his young recruits from Team Lima. It was obvious which one would be chosen. Sad-faced Arnasan was ready to trade a life of drudgery in his family's rice paddy for Samudra's promise of eternity in paradise. The other four were sent home, some perhaps disappointed, others no doubt relieved, all assured that they would get another chance. 'Everyone was instructed to remain patient and await their turn to commit *syahid* bombings if another jihad assignment arises,' said Samudra.

Samudra instructed Arnasan to write a will. As always, he did as he was told, handing it to Ali Imron. He also wrote letters to his family and friends. 'I want to say sorry to you. But all I want to do is commit myself to jihad . . . I ask for all your prayers [because] there is so much work that must be completed for the sake of the struggle. I pray that my martyrdom will be the trigger for the growth of the mujahideen . . . If you all truly want to create a return to glory . . . you must spill your blood, in order that you are not all ashamed before Allah.'[13]

Samudra had by now found another volunteer who was equally willing to spill his blood. He was a tall, thin, blue-eyed young man named Feri from Central Java. Ali Imron knew him from a visit Feri had made to the Al Islam school in Tenggulun earlier in the year. It's not known exactly how Feri was recruited or when he arrived in Bali, but he was brought into the plot in its final stages and briefed by Samudra: 'I told him to carry a backpack or rucksack filled with one kilogram of TNT and put a switch into the TNT. Only after he had entered the target area was he to press the button.'

The device that Feri would carry into Paddy's Bar was being constructed by Dr Azahari at the house in Menjangan Street. It wasn't a rucksack but a vest, modified for the purpose, as Ali Imron described: 'First we sewed pieces of cloth onto the front part of the vest. The cloth functioned as long pockets. There were three pockets in all; we did the same at the back. In the pockets we put pieces of PVC pipe, each 1.5 centimetres wide, already loaded with TNT and detonating cord. Then we bundled the six ends of the detonating cord and connected them to the detonator which was attached by cables to a small battery-powered switch box; that was in the right pocket of the vest.'

The work of the bomb makers was almost done. It had taken half a dozen men almost a week to build the car bomb. Dr Azahari and Dulmatin had also rigged up a small device made of TNT to be planted outside the US consulate in Renon, Denpasar; this would be JI's calling card, a message to the United States that it was the primary target.

Amrozi's last errand was to help Idris and Ali Imron buy a new motorbike to be used for their getaway. 'I rode the motorcycle to the house in Menjangan Street,' said Ali Imron. 'When I got there the bomb makers were still loading the bomb into the car. That night, Thursday 10

October, they finished loading. At around nine o'clock the vest bomb and the bomb to be placed at Renon were finished. On the same night Dulmatin and 'Lan' (Azahari) left the house in Menjangan Street. Before leaving, they told me how to activate the switch on the vests, on the car and on the bomb at Renon.'

Azahari and Dulmatin had left nothing to chance, preparing four separate systems for detonating the car bomb. There was a switch to activate the bomb manually and a separate device to set it off by mobile phone. There was also a timer set on a 45-minute countdown just in case, and, as a final backup, a pressure-release mechanism that would go off if the filing cabinets were disturbed. Azahari and Dulmatin left Bali that night, driving back to Java with Amrozi in the green Suzuki.

By the afternoon of Friday 11 October, only three key operatives remained on the island — Samudra, Idris and Ali Imron, along with the suicide bombers, Arnasan and Feri. There were just over twenty-four hours to go.

◈

By early October, Western intelligence knew that a massive terrorist act was in the making — somewhere in the world. On 6 October, Osama bin Laden had issued a chilling new warning to the West: 'As Allah is my witness, the youth of Islam are preparing things that will fill your hearts with tears.' It was followed two days later by another ultimatum from his deputy, Ayman al Zawahiri. 'Our message to our enemies is this: America and its allies should know that their crimes will not go unpunished.'

Prompted by these missives, the US State Department issued a formal Worldwide Caution, reminding its citizens of 'the continuing threat of terrorist actions that may target civilians' and warning them away from soft targets like clubs and restaurants. The US advice was echoed by Australia's DFAT in its own worldwide bulletin, advising that the US authorities believed new attacks were being planned but could not provide further information on 'specific targets, timing or method of attack'.

Those closest to the steady buzz of intelligence felt that all the signs were pointing in one direction. 'We knew something was going to happen in Indonesia,' an intelligence source told me in 2004. The premonition was strengthened by a new CIA report, passed on to Australia, which identified a series of locations across Indonesia as high-risk targets — among them Bali. 'This intelligence was assessed by agencies,' Prime Minister John Howard told parliament on 16 October 2002, 'and the view was formed by them that no alteration in the Threat Assessment level — then at a high — applying to Indonesia was warranted'.[14] It was the same as before; there was 'no specific intelligence', so the reassuring travel advice that everything in Bali was 'normal' went unchanged.

On 8 October, ASIO issued a new Threat Assessment about JI, warning that it may be planning attacks throughout Southeast Asia, possibly within days; a date of 9 October was mentioned. It issued another assessment on 10 October, advising that bin Laden's and al Zawahiri's statements suggested 'another large scale attack or attacks by al-Qa'ida are being prepared'.[15] A catastrophe was imminent, but everyone was helpless to stop it.

⚬✺⚬

It was Friday evening and Samudra was in a playful mood, killing time at the boarding house behind the Banyuwangi cafe. He chatted to the neighbours and sweet-talked a young single mother who lived nearby, asking if she had a boyfriend and what her plans were for Saturday night.[16]

Over at Menjangan Street, Idris and Ali Imron eased the laden L300 out of the garage to take Arnasan on a test drive in rehearsal for the following night. But they were confronted with a major problem that Samudra had failed to pick up on. 'When he got here, he couldn't drive!' exclaimed Ali Imron. Neither could the second suicide bomber, Feri. Ali Imron was furious at Samudra for overlooking this crucial point: 'The ones who had been prepared by Samudra — who told us, "These people are prepared to drive as part of their holy bombing" — apparently couldn't even drive!'[17] Arnasan could only steer the car in a straight line but couldn't turn corners or change gears; someone else would have to drive. Terse words were exchanged according to Ali Imron: 'It was a real misunderstanding — in fact an argument.'

The next day was Saturday, 12 October. It dawned as brightly as any other perfect Bali day. The bombers rose at dawn to pray and seek Allah's blessing. Arnasan and Feri probably hadn't slept at all. At 9 a.m. Samudra left his boarding house and rode to Menjangan Street, where Idris and Ali Imron assured him everything was ready.

If Ali Imron was still doubt-stricken he certainly wasn't letting on, as he went about his final crucial duties. First he rigged up a series of switches on the getaway motorbike bike so the lights illuminating its number plates could be turned off. Then it was time to bring in the suicide bombers. 'At around noon, Idris brought Arnasan and Feri to the house in Menjangan Street,' Ali Imron related to the police. Next came his most critical task — relaying Dr Azahari's instructions on how to detonate the bombs.

'I showed Feri how to put on the bomb-loaded vest and how to ignite the switch to detonate it. I also told Arnasan how to use the switches on the box connecting the batteries with the detonator in the car.' Ali Imron went through these instructions over and over again throughout the afternoon. 'Then I told both Arnasan and Feri to repeat what I had taught them. When I was sure they understood the system I ended the lesson.'

Early in the evening, Ali Imron took off on the Yamaha motorbike to deliver the small TNT package to the US consulate. He had tried to persuade Idris to do it but the logistics man wasn't willing to transport a bomb, so Ali Imron did it himself. The device had a cell phone attached as a detonator and was wrapped in plastic bags. Ali Imron evidently enjoyed this particular task because he added a personal touch. Before leaving the package by the road, he later confessed, 'I put human faeces in a plastic bag and placed it on top of the bomb.'[18]

Back at the house in Menjangan Street, Arnasan and Feri were waiting to set off on their final journey. The argument over who would drive had not been resolved and tempers were on edge.

'I wasn't speaking to Idris because I was still very upset,' said Ali Imron. 'I know it's terrible but I must be honest, I was very upset, because he didn't want to take the bomb to Renon on the motorcycle when I asked him — and I was also the one asked to deliver the car bomb. I asked him to drive the car, but he wouldn't do that either. He said he was afraid because it was an even bigger bomb.' So Ali Imron drove himself.

'We headed out around 10.25 p.m.,' Ali Imron related. 'I got the L300 ready and drove it out of the garage. Arnasan sat in the middle. I was behind the wheel and Feri sat next to the left door with his vest bomb.'

The cargo in the back weighed more than a tonne and the van was sluggish and hard to handle, as Ali Imron turned out of Menjangan Street and headed south towards Kuta Beach. 'The van was quite heavy so I drove very slowly, only about 40 kilometres an hour.' He was afraid it would blow up before they even got to the targets.

The traffic along Legian Street was bumper to bumper as the L300 turned into the strip. Every night was party night in Kuta Beach but Saturday was the biggest night of all. The dance floor at the Sari Club was packed and throbbing to the strains of Eminem. Late-night diners and nightclubbers spilled out of the crowded bars and restaurants, while taxi drivers hustled for fares. A local cabbie named Aris pulled into the queue of taxis; his wife would dream that night of Aris telling her, 'I am not going to be able to join you tonight darling . . . I will be sleeping.'[19]

As the L300 crawled towards the Sari Club, Ali Imron gave Arnasan and Feri their last instructions. 'I told Feri to put the vest on and told Arnasan to connect the cables from the detonator to the switches in the box.' The switches were flicked to standby and Ali Imron stopped the car. 'I told Arnasan to take over in the driver's seat. That was it. Then I got out of the car and went to meet Idris who was waiting for me on the motorcycle.'

Arnasan steered the groaning L300 the last few hundred metres down Legian Street. No one knows what words may have passed between the two young men inside. Ali Imron's version is the closest there is to a first-hand account of what happened next. 'Near the Sari Club, Feri — the one with the vest — got out of the van. He then walked towards Paddy's Bar. While he was walking to Paddy's Bar, Arnasan drove the van — slowly, he drove the van.'

Idris and Ali Imron sped off on the Yamaha motorcycle and stopped a few blocks away to detonate the bomb. Still seated on the motorbike, Idris pulled out his mobile phone to dial the number of the cell phone supposedly wired up to the van. As he was about to punch in the numbers, Idris asked Ali Imron about the phone with wires attached that had been back at the house.

'I was stunned,' said Ali Imron. 'The mobile phone with wires attached was supposed to be used as the remote device for the van. The remote that should have been in the car had been forgotten — it was on the table, at the house at Menjangan Street. Idris was the last one to leave the house. He didn't mention it — the phone had been forgotten.'[20]

So much for the fail-safe plan. As they cursed their stupidity, Idris called the number of the phone attached to the TNT package outside the US consulate. Several kilometres away in Renon the device went off, causing minor damage. But the bombers had no way of setting off the massive car bomb — it was now up to Arnasan.

Outside the Sari Club, Arnasan pulled up in the L300 and parked the van on the wrong side of the road, next to the entrance. Horns began blaring as the traffic quickly banked up behind him, while inside the van Arnasan locked the ignition and removed the keys, as he had been told to do by Ali Imron: 'When he got to the front of the Sari Club, Arnasan was supposed to turn off the engine and lock all the doors. He wasn't allowed to park there because it's on the right hand side. Even if people knocked on the window, even if they beat on the car, he had to wait for the vest bomb in Paddy's Bar to explode.'

It was 11.07 p.m. as Feri pushed his way through the crowd on the dance floor at Paddy's Bar, his hand in the pocket of his vest. Two metres from the DJ's booth, Feri flicked the switch. There was a split second, a flash and a roar, then the crashing of brick and wood and glass, flames and people screaming.

From the bars nearby people poured into the street to see what had happened — just as the bombers knew they would. 'That was the intention of the bomb,' said Ali Imron. 'When the explosion happened the people inside the Sari Club would also come out — then the van would be blown up. We expected there would be lots of victims on the street. That was the scenario we had planned.'

At 11.08 and 23 seconds, Arnasan hit the switch on the car bomb. It was as though the whole world had exploded. 'There was a fizzing, a glow of orange light flying through the air. I turned my back and I was knocked to the ground,' an Australian survivor later testified. From the inferno, a woman's voice was heard screaming 'Oh my God, it's hot, please help me, quick, quick, quick . . .'[21]

A local man who rushed to help when he heard the explosion, later sobbed in court as he described the scene. 'Everywhere I looked in the Sari Club, there were bodies. Some had been blown against the north wall and most were in a horrible condition . . . I carried some away, a person's head in one arm and an arm in the other . . . I will always remember this white lady. She had been cut by a piece of glass . . . I could see her heart beating through her chest . . . Then I saw her heart stop beating and she died in my arms. I closed her eyes with my hands and cried.'[22]

Sitting on the back of the Yamaha a few blocks away, Ali Imron was shaken by the blast, which had the force of a small earthquake and was heard 25 kilometres away. He watched the sky glow orange from the massive fireball. 'The bomb exploded, lives were taken, so we hit the US and its allies in the face. I was happy and very tense.'

But as the pandemonium started, Ali Imron said his elation evaporated. 'That was when I heard the ambulance sirens. The memory of carrying my own child in the ambulance all those years ago came back to me. I only held that child once. It made me terribly sad. I thought there must have been more than 100 victims. The ambulance sirens never ceased, they went on and on, over and over.'[23]

Ali Imron and Idris circled around on the motorbike for an hour, stunned, not knowing where to go. Finally, at 3 a.m., they found Samudra at the internet cafe, tapping away as though nothing had happened. 'He seemed to be tuned into whatever Internet activities he was doing,' remarked Ali Imron. Idris and Ali Imron took off again and dumped the motorbike at a mosque.

Later in the morning Samudra would take his usual seat at the Banyuwangi cafe and order chicken soup, as he watched the blackened bodies of his victims being pulled from the rubble on the TV screen in the corner.[24] After his capture, the Indonesian police later asked him how he had felt. 'I felt that I feared only Allah,' Samudra responded. 'My efforts, which had been so small, had caused the deaths of so many people. But if those killed were not Muslims, but Americans, Christians, then I was grateful.'

In Java, Muklas was listening to the radio for news when the first reports came through at 11.45 on the night. 'Firstly I was shocked because the explosion was extremely intense, beyond our expectations. I had figured that only the Sari Club and Paddy's would be destroyed. Secondly I felt grateful. The mission and its objectives had been achieved because there were many casualties from amongst American allies including Australian citizens. Thirdly I sought Allah's forgiveness because apparently there were also some victims who were Muslims.'

A forensic examination done by the Bomb Data Centre of the Australian Federal Police showed that the devastation could have been far worse. The analysis found that the ratio of chemicals had been inconsistent and they had been poorly mixed by hand. The plastic bags that the mixture was stored in were not airtight, allowing the chemicals to deteriorate due to humidity, and there were air gaps in the filing cabinet drawers, which 'greatly reduced the explosive force produced by this bomb.' As a result, only the few drawers in direct contact with the drawer full of TNT actually exploded; the rest of them simply burned. The analysis concluded: 'It could have been far greater if the whole 1150 kilograms of explosives had exploded as anticipated.'[25]

For Amrozi, it was good enough. Back home in Tenggulun, he heard the news when he switched on the radio the next day. His first thought was for his friends who had stayed behind in Bali to execute the attack. 'I prayed for their safety and prayed that they would be spared from any danger.'

When he learned of the damage and casualties, Amrozi laughed out loud. 'I was very happy . . . How can I describe it — it was like when I was still a bachelor, trying for a girl and you finally get to meet her, it was that sort of excitement. But this was even better.'[26] Amrozi shrugged off the news that Indonesian Muslims had been among those killed. 'I figured even if they didn't die there, they would die somewhere else, right?'

⚜

CHAPTER TWENTY-THREE

A MILLION AMROZIS

Abdul Rahim Ayub was in a hurry. The leader of Jemaah Islamiyah in Australia had a plane to catch; his ticket was paid for and his bags were packed. It was three days after the Bali bombings. In Indonesia a massive manhunt was swinging into action, and in Sydney, Perth and Melbourne, investigators from ASIO and the Federal Police were getting ready to move in on the Australian branch of JI. But Abdul Rahim was a step ahead of them. Summoned to return to Indonesia, he would soon be on his way, unless someone stopped him.

Abdul Rahim had made no secret of his plans. Two weeks earlier, in late September, he had taken leave from the Al Hidayah school in Perth at the end of the school term, saying he was going home to Indonesia for the school holidays to see his sick mother. 'He was due back in late October,' said the school's administrator, Umar Abdullah. 'He left his family here; he was expected back after the holidays.'[1]

Abdul Rahim hitched a ride with a friend across the Nullarbor, travelling via Melbourne to Sydney, to brief members of the jemaah before he left. He got to Sydney in early October and was dropped off in one of his old stamping grounds, Lakemba, where he stayed at the home of a JI member who ran a clothing store in Haldon Street near the office of the Islamic Youth Movement.

Abdul Rahim did the rounds of JI in Sydney, meeting up with members of the local jemaah and dealing with the ongoing disputes over money. The Sydney group was still complaining that Jack Roche had 'stolen' the money he had been given in 2000 by Hambali and Khalid Sheik Mohammed, which the locals believed belonged rightfully to the Australian branch.

In Lakemba Abdul Rahim caught up with an old uni friend from Melbourne, Ahmed the taxi driver, who had driven Jack Roche around the Israeli embassy in Canberra while Roche cased it for a bombing. Abdul Rahim and Ahmed had dinner together at the Island Dreams cafe in Haldon Street, a favourite hangout of Sydney's radical Islamic set, where they bumped into Roche's friend and fellow convert Ibrahim Fraser.

Fraser remembered later that Abdul Rahim was his usual cheery self, as he spoke of his forthcoming trip to Indonesia. 'He was smiling as always. He was bragging that someone had paid his fare.' He also mentioned that he had 'very important business' to attend to in his homeland.[2]

Abdul Rahim had no idea that he had been under investigation now for almost a year, since being identified as the Australian leader of JI after the tip-off from Singapore in December 2001. Abdul Rahim and other key JI figures had been bugged, watched and investigated by ASIO for ten months. 'From the day they were told that JI was in Australia they worked 100 per cent flat out from then,' an investigator close to the case told me. 'They worked their butts off.'[3]

Publicly, there will still nothing to show for the inquiry. The case had been cloaked in total secrecy; neither the investigation nor the known presence of a JI branch in Australia was announced. 'Our aim was to identify an operational cell. We wanted to identify all of the JI members but the main aim was to find any operational cell.' There was some debate within ASIO about when to start knocking on doors and getting warrants for searches. But the investigators knew that as soon as they did so everyone would go to ground, so they kept it undercover.

By October 2002, no evidence of criminal activity in Australia had been picked up. What the surveillance had revealed was a JI network of some thirty members and 100 supporters across three states, whose main activities seemed to be recruiting, fundraising and physical training; paintball sessions were still being held in the bush, the latest one at Blackwood outside Melbourne in April 2002. The investigators were confident they had JI in Australia pegged: 'We learned pretty much all there was to know.'

ASIO never did find the operational cell it was looking for. Incredibly, even after ten months of investigation, they knew nothing of Jack Roche, his recruitment by al Qaeda or his plot to blow up the Israeli embassy during the 2000 Sydney Olympic Games. The cell they were after had been disbanded in its infancy two years before. Roche's plan had been an open secret in the radical Islamic community — but Australia's premier ietlligence agency never even got a whiff of it. The investigators working on the case believed the Australian branch acted only as a support group for JI headquarters and that Indonesia was the place where JI was likely to strike. 'We knew the Australian group was part of the Indonesian group. We were really worried about something happening in Indonesia.' Their fears were realised on 12 October in Bali.

Ibrahim Fraser watched horrified in his lounge room in Lakemba as the aftermath of the bombings unfolded on the Sunday night TV news. 'I was dumbfounded,' Fraser recalled. 'I couldn't believe why anyone would do that.' First thing the next morning, said Fraser, 'There was a knock on the door. It was a guy from AFP counter-intelligence.' ASIO and the Federal Police had gone into overdrive. As one veteran investigator told me, 'After Bali it was chaos.' Suddenly desperate to find out what JI might be up to in Australia, the two agencies were scrambling to follow up on the leads they had previously missed or ignored.

Ibrahim Fraser had plenty to tell the agent from the AFP. Fraser had been waiting for someone to look him up for two years — since he had phoned the Federal Police office in Singapore in September 2000 to try to tell them about Jack Roche and his plans. After the AFP failed to get back to him, Fraser had begun telling journalists he picked up in his taxi about JI's activities in Australia. One of the reporters Fraser talked to was Martin Chulov of the *Australian* newspaper. Fraser told him about Abu Bakar Bashir's numerous visits, the paintball sessions used as 'jihad training' and the fundraising by JI in Australia, and mentioned the names of key JI members, including Jack Roche and Abdul Rahim Ayub. Chulov had been so worried about what Fraser told him that instead of just writing the story, he had rung the AFP's counter-terrorism hotline in April 2002 and passed on what he had been told, without disclosing who had told him.

Like Ibrahim Fraser, Chulov waited for a call back. And waited. It wasn't until five months later that he heard back from the Federal

Police; the agent who rang him wanted to talk to his source. 'He said they were prioritising and assessing calls made to the hotline,' said Chulov. 'They felt that this one warranted further investigation.'[4] This was in late September, just before Bali. Chulov had tried contacting Ibrahim Fraser to pass on the AFP agent's message, but Fraser's phone had been switched off.

Now, in the shocking wake of the bombings, the AFP was intent on talking to anyone with information on JI, and Fraser was top of the list. The agent to whom Chulov had spoken tracked the taxi driver down on the Monday morning after the bombings. 'He asked me, "Are you Ibrahim Fraser? Are you a Muslim? Do you speak fluent Indonesian?" I said, "Yes." Then he started asking questions.' Fraser was more than ready to talk — but not right away; his wife and kids were at home and he didn't want to talk in front of them. So he arranged to meet the AFP agent in the city two days later to tell what he knew.

While the AFP and ASIO were playing catch-up, Abdul Rahim Ayub was heading for the airport to catch his plane. It was 15 October, three days after the bombings. After his final round of meetings in Melbourne and Sydney, the Australian JI leader had returned to Perth to farewell his family, who would follow him three months later.

Abdul Rahim was dropped off at Perth airport and made his way to the Qantas desk to check in for QF139 to Jakarta. The terminal was crowded with tearful friends and relatives, there to greet members of the local Kingsley Football Club flying home from the horror in Bali, grief-stricken over the death of one of their team-mates in the bombings.

As Abdul Rahim wended his way through the crowd towards the flight gate, the ASIO agents who had been monitoring his movements for the past ten months were nowhere to be seen. In contrast to the huge manhunt in Indonesia, there was apparently no great urgency about keeping tabs on the Australian head of JI. 'He wasn't even under surveillance,' one well-placed source told me, a fact confidentially confirmed by a senior intelligence officer in 2004.

As he parted with his passport at the immigration desk, Abdul Rahim must have been sweating, wondering if he would be stopped. Although he wasn't under surveillance, ASIO knew enough about his movements to know he was about to leave the country. But Abdul Rahim had nothing to fear. 'We did not have a lawful reason to prevent him leaving Australia,' an intelligence source told me. 'There was firm advice that we had no basis to prevent him leaving.'[5] His passport was stamped and Abdul Rahim was sent on his way.

While Abdul Rahim was winging his way out of the country, Ibrahim Fraser was making his rendezvous with the AFP where he laid out the whole JI story in the first of a series of interviews. 'I said to them, "You know about Jack Roche, of course? You know about the bombing they wanted to do?"' Fraser was stunned at the response. 'They didn't know anything — like, nothing. They didn't know of Jack Roche, hadn't even heard of him.'[6] In the course of a few hours with Ibrahim Fraser, Australian investigators discovered more about JI's activities in Australia than they had learned from ten months of investigations.

On the night of 27 October, a squad of Federal Police and ASIO agents with guns drawn and a sledgehammer burst into a house in Lakemba in the first of a series of raids in Sydney, Melbourne and Perth. 'We heard this loud bang and we all woke up. All of a sudden our door broke down and all these policemen with big handguns screamed at us to get down.' After months of taking the softly-softly approach, ASIO would now be publicly lambasted for going in too hard.

The families of the JI men who were targeted complained vigorously to journalists about their treatment. 'They pushed my dad onto the floor, they handcuffed him and one of the police officers stepped on his ear and told him not to move,' said Yulyani Suparta, whose father, David, had been JI's treasurer in Sydney and had later hosted Abdul Rahman Ayub in Perth and testified for him at the Refugee Review Tribunal. 'They grabbed my mum, they told us to get on the floor and pointed guns at us. I was really scared. One of them pushed me and told me to put my hands on the floor and lay on my stomach.'[7]

The men whose homes were raided were key members, supporters and office-holders of Jemaah Islamiyah. All of them protested their innocence, some claiming they had never heard of JI, others insisting they had only gone along to hear Abu Bakar Bashir speak at the mosque. 'How can they accuse us of being terrorists? We haven't done anything,' said the JI veteran in Sydney known as Wandi. In the raids, a handwritten note was found listing JI's leadership, which confirmed Wandi's position as deputy leader of Mantiqi 4.[8]

On 30 October, ASIO and the AFP raided Jack Roche's home in Perth. Among other things they found documents about jihad, directions to and from the US and Israeli embassies and his surveillance photographs of the Israeli consulate in Sydney. They then obtained warrants to bug Roche's flat and his phone. Over the next few days the agents monitoring the intercepts listened in astonishment as Roche divulged the extraordinary saga to journalist Colleen Egan of the *Australian*, who had contacted him after the raids. Roche told Egan of his meetings with Hambali, his encounter with bin Laden in Afghanistan and his instructions to form an al Qaeda cell. 'This is an operational cell,' Roche told Egan. 'To target something, to work on that, get that target, and then to disappear.'

ASIO had finally found the operational cell it had been searching for for almost a year. Previously ignorant of Jack Roche's existence, they now had him on a plate. Roche was taken in for questioning by the AFP and, in the course of a nine-hour taped interview, happily repeated his whole story, as the two AFP agents interviewing him struggled to keep up with the mass of dates, names and details that he volunteered.[9] He 'essentially put the noose around his own neck,' one of the AFP officers observed. Roche would eventually plead guilty and be sentenced to nine years' jail.

During his elaborate admission, Roche told the AFP about his repeated attempts to tip off ASIO more than two years before, when he had phoned ASIO's Perth office and asked for a meeting but the agent he had spoken to had not followed up on his calls. 'The last time I called ASIO no one seemed to be particularly interested in what was going on,' he told them. 'I have been sitting in Thornlie and in South Perth waiting for somebody to come knocking on my door. And eventually it happened.'

❧

Abdul Rahim Ayub was home free. After his flight from Perth to Jakarta, the Mantiqi 4 chief travelled to Solo in Central Java, the home town of JI's leader, Abu Bakar Bashir. But Abdul Rahim didn't drop in to visit his old friend and mentor. With JI being named as the number one suspect in the Bali bombings, Bashir had his hands full already; and in any case, Abdul Rahim had a meeting to attend.

His destination was the mountain retreat of Tawangmangu, east of Solo, a picturesque resort town popular for its natural springs, forest walks and frisky monkeys. High above the heat and hustle of Java's cities, Tawangmangu had been chosen as the location for the bi-annual meeting of JI's Central Leadership Council, the Qiyadah Markaziyah. The conference was held, not at some secret safe house, but at a villa on the mountainside owned by an Islamic NGO, the Al Irsyad Foundation. Just days after the Bali bombings, it was almost business as usual for JI. According to one of those who attended, Mantiqi 3 leader Mohammed Nasir bin Abas: 'The meeting should have been chaired by Abu Bakar Bashir but he had been arrested by the government.'[10]

Finally jolted into action, the Indonesian police had gone to the US military base where the al Qaeda operative Omar al Faruq was being detained, to corroborate his account of Bashir having authorised previous bombings. 'The *Time* magazine reports were confirmed by Faruq,' announced the national police spokesman. 'We have named Bashir as a suspect following the results.'[11]

A police summons was issued for Bashir to face questioning in Jakarta. Meanwhile, journalists and TV crews had descended on Solo — myself and a team from *4 Corners* among them. We witnessed Bashir's tirade on the 'ravine of hate' at the silver-domed mosque and then his press conference at the Ngruki school, where he denied any knowledge of al Faruq and blamed the CIA: 'The United States intelligence agency is behind the Bali bombings in an attempt to justify their accusation that Indonesia is a terrorist base.' Straight after this, Bashir was rushed off to hospital, his supporters claiming he had collapsed from stress. He failed to show up for the interrogation scheduled by the police.

In Bashir's absence, the meeting of the Central Leadership Council in Tawangmangu was chaired by his deputy, Abu Rusdan, a JI veteran and former instructor in Afghanistan. Bashir had sent a message of support, recounted later by Nasir bin Abas to the police. 'Bashir in his capacity as emir of JI said, "Continue the jemaah and I will continue to defend it." This message was received by Abu Rusdan who then conveyed it to those present at the meeting . . . so that JI members would know and would continue to maintain the JI struggle, even though the emir was under threat.'[12]

The meeting dealt with the usual JI housekeeping, hearing reports from each of the Mantiqi leaders including Abdul Rahim Ayub, who brought his colleagues up to date on recent events in Australia.[13] They discussed a request from Muklas, who was also present in his capacity as leader of Mantiqi 1, asking for donations to support the families of JI detainees in Malaysia and Singapore. Then they moved on to discuss the looming arrest of Abu Bakar Bashir. Without further ado, according to Nasir, 'We decided to look for a new JI emir.' Bashir's deputy, Abu Rusdan, was appointed to replace him.

Aside from the main business of the meeting, all the buzz among JI's leadership was about the recent bombings in Bali. Not all of the men on the Central Leadership Council had been privy to planning the attacks, and nor did all of them approve.

'I kept saying to Muklas, 'Who did this thing in Bali? Are you responsible for this?' Nasir bin Abas later revealed. '[Muklas] looked at me and smiled and said, "Are you suspicious of me?"' Two days later, Muklas confessed to Nasir that his suspicions were well founded. 'He said to me that he and the brothers were responsible.'[14] The massacre would further inflame the friction within JI over slaughtering civilians to achieve its ends, Muklas's own brother-in-law Nasir emerging as the most vocal critic of the terror campaign: 'I knew right then that this was not the way. Jihad is not like that. It is about protecting Islam if it is under attack.'

⁂

Smashed glass and twisted metal still littered Legian Street in Kuta Beach, as Graham Ashton picked his way through the debris to the blackened ruins of the Sari Club and Paddy's Bar. Surrounded by mangled car wrecks and mounds of rubble, the AFP's General Manager for Southern Operations swore that the men behind this carnage would be hunted down.

'It's a massive inquiry that lies ahead of us,' said Ashton. 'The public sentiment in Australia is enormous to see these perpetrators brought to justice . . . No stone will be left unturned in doing that.'[15] Appointed to co-lead a joint Indonesian–Australian investigation, Ashton was as good as his word. Two hundred Australian police would soon be on the ground to help the Indonesians track down the bombers.

From the devastation at the crime scene, thousands of scraps of wreckage were collected, sorted, examined and tested by the scores of investigators at work in the joint forensics laboratory. The piles of rubble quickly yielded clues — and eventually a trail of evidence the bombers had left behind, thanks to Samudra's haste, Amrozi's sloppiness and Ali Imron's panicking in the aftermath of the bombings.

The first clue was a scorched bit of metal imprinted with a chassis number, GB 011280. Some of the numerals had been filed away and re-etched to disguise them. But the person who had done the filing — Amrozi — hadn't noticed a second number engraved on the van, a compulsory registration code for vehicles big enough to be used for public transport. This number was found intact, enabling the police to trace the Mitsubishi L300's previous owner, 50 kilometres from Tenggulun, who remembered having sold it to Amrozi. The next clue was the Yamaha motorbike dumped by Idris and Ali Imron at the Denpasar mosque. It was tracked back to the showroom where staff provided descriptions which led to identikit pictures of three of the bombers.

When the police searched Amrozi's house in Tenggulun, they found empty sacks with the name of the Tidar Kimia store, whose owner promptly confessed to having sold the chemicals to Amrozi. 'That was an excellent moment,' Graham Ashton later recalled.[16] The hapless mechanic was asleep in bed when the police arrived. 'I didn't suspect anything. I didn't have any idea that I would be arrested,' mused Amrozi. 'But I was always prepared because I knew the risks involved.'[17]

Amrozi's arrest led quickly to the others. After a set of phone numbers was found in the house in Tenggulun, Samudra's mobile phone was tracked to Serang in West Java, where the field commander was about to board a ferry at the same port where he used to hang out and watch the ships as a boy. 'Ironically that was the place I was captured,' Samudra mused with a chuckle. 'That was such a coincidence, that was fate indeed.'

Arrested in January, Ali Imron claimed he was relieved to be caught, his conscience having finally got the better of him during his three months on the run. 'After I became a fugitive that's when I snapped. My thoughts and beliefs changed. I knew I was wrong. It wasn't supposed to be the way it turned out. I looked back at the history of the Prophet Muhammad and our Muslim predecessors and I realised there was no such kind of jihad . . . So when I was caught by the authorities I gave in. I didn't resist, because I felt guilty, I knew that what I did was wrong.'

His big brother Muklas had no such regrets when he was picked up near Solo and paraded for the press cameras in Denpasar shackled in leg-irons and wearing a bright orange t-shirt bearing the slogan 'Misfits'. Muklas would later sack his lawyer for suggesting he express remorse in the hope of getting a lighter sentence. 'This is jihad, not drugs,' said Muklas. 'We are not sorry at all.'[18]

Within three months of the bombing, the cell responsible for it had been smashed and the Indonesian Government had rushed through new anti-terrorism laws, introducing the death penalty for the bombers soon to face trial. The investigation led eventually to more than 100 arrests across the archipelago. However, key JI operatives remained at large, among them the bomb master, Dr Azahari, his assistants, Dulmatin and Noor Din Mohammed Top, and JI's military chief, Zulkarnaen.

And even as Australians applauded the success of the investigation, the bombers' idol, Osama bin Laden, delivered a grim postscript to the attacks. 'The killing of the British and Australians in the explosions in Bali . . . is but a reaction and a retaliation undertaken by the zealous sons of Islam . . . We have warned Australia before against taking part in the war in Afghanistan, and about its despicable effort to separate East Timor. It ignored the warnings until it woke up to the sounds of the explosions in Bali. Then it falsely claimed that its people were not targeted.'[19]

Bin Laden's communique, broadcast on the Al Jazeera network, was a sobering reminder that Bali was just one ambush in an ongoing campaign against the United States and the countries aligned with it. 'What do your governments want from their alliance with America?' bin Laden demanded. 'And I specifically mention Britain, France, Italy, Canada, Germany and Australia . . . If you have been aggrieved and appalled by the sight of your dead and the dead from among your allies . . . remember our dead children in Palestine and Iraq who perish every day . . . Why should fear, killing, destruction, displacement, orphaning and widowing continue to be our lot, while peace, security and happiness are yours? This is unfair. It is time to get even. You will be killed just as you kill, and bombed just as you bomb. And wait for more calamity.'

The carnage in Bali galvanised fresh international support for an all-out campaign against al Qaeda and the terrorist groups under its wing.

Prime Minister John Howard, who won support for his steadfast response to the tragedy, told Parliament that bin Laden's latest message was 'a chilling reminder of the evil and perverted character of the apparent leader of the deadliest terrorist threat the world has had.'[20]

Despite the successes in Indonesia, the region-wide crackdown on JI and the damage inflicted on al Qaeda in Afghanistan since September 11, it was obvious to everyone that the so-called 'war on terror' was far from won. The terrorists' infrastructure might be damaged, but their hatred had been sharpened by the retaliation. CIA chief George Tenet told the US Congress: 'They have reconstituted, they are coming after us.'

But even as bin Laden's network was being proclaimed 'the deadliest terrorist threat' ever, the war on terror was being diverted to fight another enemy. With bin Laden still eluding capture, the United States had resolved to turn its wrath against its other arch-enemy, the Iraqi dictator Saddam Hussein. The US had been gearing up for this for months, citing Iraq's refusal to surrender its reputed stockpiles of chemical and biological weapons. 'Fuck Saddam, we're taking him out,' President Bush had reportedly told colleagues.[21] As for Saddam's supposed stockpiles: 'I don't think they existed,' the UN's chief weapons inspector would eventually admit.[22]

To ensure public backing for his redirected offensive, President Bush sought to link the Iraqi dictator with the terrorists of al Qaeda, although no clear connections between them had ever been established. 'You can't distinguish between al Qaeda and Saddam when you talk about the war on terrorism,' Bush insisted. 'They're both equally as bad, and equally as evil, and equally destructive. The danger is that al Qaeda becomes an extension of Saddam's madness and his hatred and his capacity to extend weapons of mass destruction around the world.'[23]

The United Nations was unwilling to sanction military action and few countries ready to take the gamble, so Bush needed all the support he could get. Australia came to the party, Prime Minister Howard echoing President Bush's dubious justification for war. 'The ultimate terrorist nightmare would be if weapons of mass destruction were to fall into the hands of Osama bin Laden and his cohorts . . . It follows from that that efforts must be sustained by the nations of the world to remove from the hands of people who might capriciously use them, weapons of mass destruction.'[24]

With many Australians profoundly wary of joining a US-led invasion, the Prime Minister moved to harness the public outrage over

Bali to secure support for a war on Iraq. 'We now understand, after the
events in Bali and those of 11 September 2001, that we are living in a
world where unexpected terrorist attacks on free and open societies can
occur in ways that we never before imagined possible,' the Prime
Minister told Parliament in February 2003. 'The atrocity in Bali
demonstrated something Australia had never fully understood until then
— that we are truly vulnerable. In light of this we have reappraised the
way we view and deal with the threat of terrorism. We understand the
danger of leaving threats unaddressed.'

Six weeks later, on 20 March 2003, US cruise missiles bombarded
Baghdad as the first of 20,000 troops from the US Army's Third
Infantry Division streamed across the Kuwaiti border into Iraq.
Australian SAS commandos were already on the ground; a White House
staffer briefed President Bush: 'The Aussies are in.'[25] As columns of
armoured vehicles rumbled north across the desert, for those with an
eye to history there were eerie reminders half-buried in the desert sand;
the rusted hulks of bombed-out tanks and trucks, left from the previous
Gulf War twelve years before — the one that provided the catalyst for
bin Laden's jihad.

Within weeks it seemed, briefly, that the war was won. Victorious
coalition forces took Baghdad, the expected fierce resistance from the
Iraqi army evaporating into hardly even a fight. The giant statue of
Saddam Hussein was dragged crashing to the ground. The dictator
himself would soon be pulled, bearded and dishevelled, from a dirt hole
beneath a farm house near his home town, Tikrit. In Washington,
President Bush announced: 'For all who love freedom and peace, the
world without Saddam Hussein's regime is a better and safer place.'

But, while few mourned the demise of the Iraqi tyrant, there was
scant evidence that the world was a safer place, or that the real threat —
that posed by terrorism — had been reduced. There were plenty of
experts who believed the opposite was true. The International Institute
for Strategic Studies in London reported that al Qaeda was 'more
insidious and just as dangerous' as ever, with 18,000 operatives in ninety
countries and a network that would take 'a generation to dismantle'.[26] It
pointed out the source of bin Laden's appeal — his ability to 'sell the
cultural humiliation of Islam'. This potent selling point had only been
enhanced by the West's latest offensive against a Muslim nation, Iraq.

As the months passed after the invasion, we knew for sure that the
world was not a safer place. The newspaper headlines said it all: 'Suicide

bomber kills 10 in Jerusalem.' 'Wave of bombings in Shiite shrines across Iraq — 150 dead.' And later: 'Carnage in train attacks in Madrid, 191 killed.'

The folly of claiming that the war on Saddam would strike a blow against the forces of terror was scathingly exposed in a report by the Strategic Studies Institute of the US Army War College, penned by a veteran military analyst and historian, Professor Jeffrey Record. 'Strategically, Operation Iraqi Freedom was not part of the global war on terrorism; rather it was a war-of-choice distraction from the war of necessity against al-Qaeda . . . This was a strategic error of the first order . . . [It] has created a new front in the Middle East for Islamic terrorism and diverted attention and resources away from . . . an undeterrable al Qaeda.'[27]

Professor Record also exposed President Bush's much vaunted 'war on terror' as a false premise that set the scene for strategic failure. For one thing, there is no clearly identifiable enemy. As another expert noted: 'al Qaeda is not a single terrorist group but a global insurgency'.[28] For another, there is nothing conventional about this conflict. 'Terrorist organisations do not field military forces as such and . . . are not subject to conventional military destruction,' wrote Professor Record. 'It is difficult to obtain conclusive military victories against irregular enemies who refuse to quit precisely because they cannot be decisively defeated.'

Professor Record echoed the view of a growing body of commentators that the description 'war on terror' was and remains a serious misnomer. 'Talk of a war itself encourages people to believe in a clear and not-too-distant victory, whereas the apocalyptic spirit of al Qaeda may be around for decades,' editorialised the *Economist*. 'The public would be able to cope better with such trials if it understood that the al Qaeda peril is one with which it will have to learn to live for the foreseeable future.'[29]

After the initial jubilation following the fall of Saddam, Iraq slid steadily into anarchy. The toll of US soldiers killed in the aftermath soon exceeded the number who died during the war itself. Bombings became an almost daily occurrence, followed later by the kidnapping and beheading of foreign hostages, their footage of their deaths broadcast on the internet. The terrorism expert Jessica Stern noted: 'America has taken a country that was not a terrorist threat and turned it into one.'[30]

The truth of this was tragically demonstrated in August 2003 when a truck bomb demolished the UN office in Baghdad, leaving scores of people injured and seventeen dead, among them the UN High Commissioner for Human Rights, Sergio Vieira de Mello. The hopes for a quick and peaceful transition to democracy were dead as well.

The day after the destruction of the UN office, Australia's deputy Prime Minister John Anderson rose in Parliament, grasping to find some meaning to it all. 'It is not enough to talk of senseless hatred, senseless violence or senseless evil, no matter how abhorrent or hard it may be for us to understand,' Anderson argued. 'We need to understand that there must be very powerful — dark and evil, but very powerful nonetheless — and identifiable ideas behind the terrorism of the sort we now see all too frequently.'[31]

His speech enunciated a widely shared grief and shock — and the steadily dawning reality that no amount of military supremacy would be enough to win this fight. 'Surely, we need to recognise that only the most powerful of beliefs, not mere ill-defined prejudices or unfocused irrational hatred, could produce such carefully premeditated, planned, callous, wanton evil . . . It is going to be very important for us in the battle against terrorism — a battle we cannot lose — to seek to understand those dark and powerful ideas.'

Balinese ceremonial guards in sarongs and armed with daggers milled around the entrance to the hot and stuffy courtroom, where a sign warned: 'Explosives prohibited.' Vendors had set up food carts to sell snacks and soft drinks to the crowd. Australian survivors in burns suits and on crutches fought back tears and rage as they prepared to face the men who had left them scarred for life. 'Go to hell you bastard!' someone yelled as Amrozi was led handcuffed and grinning into court, on day one of the trials of the Bali bombers.

Amrozi's brother Muklas was in a celebratory mood after the birth of his sixth child, a son he named Osama. From his jail cell, Muklas sent a letter to his wife urging her to raise their newborn to 'inherit the attitude of Osama bin Laden', whom he called 'a divine gift from Allah' sent to enrich 'the whole Muslim world'.[32] Undaunted by the prospect of execution, Muklas announced: 'Until bombs stop dropping on Muslims around the world, we will keep going — we will never stop.'

As if by way of demonstration, on 12 May 2003 a series of deadly truck bombs ripped through three housing compounds in the Saudi capital, Riyadh, killing more than twenty people and wounding 200. Samudra gloated for the TV cameras as he was led to a police van: 'After Riyadh there will be another one. Allahu Akhbar! — God is Great! — America will be destroyed!' Meanwhile, the chiefs of al Qaeda urged their followers on to new attacks, bin Laden's deputy, al Zawahiri pronouncing, 'Oh Muslims, muster your resolve and hit the embassies of America, England, Australia and Norway, their interests, their companies and their employees. Set the ground ablaze under their feet.'

As he awaited sentencing, Amrozi held an impromptu press conference in his cell, posing for photographers and bragging about his efforts on behalf of oppressed Muslims. 'We will continue to fight for them. Even though I am dead, our children and grandchildren will continue . . . There will be a million Amrozis to come. They might not be called Amrozi but they will behave just like me. And their smile, that too will be different from mine.' Amrozi even warbled a song he had composed for the occasion:

This is us — the young warriors,
This is us — the army of Allah,
We don't fear the death sentence.
Continue to do jihad, whatever happens. . .
Kick out the mean zionists,
Kick out the filthy people of the crucifix,
God is great![33]

As the trials continued, the bombers were transported one by one to Jakarta to testify in the case against their leader, Abu Bakar Bashir, who was on trial facing charges of treason over the Christmas 2000 church bombings and the alleged plot to assassinate Megawati Sukarnoputri.

The bombers gave confusing and contradictory accounts of Bashir's role. The remorseful Ali Imron testified that Bashir had taken over as leader of JI in 1999. Muklas denied Bashir was the leader but admitted knowing him in Malaysia, to which Bashir responded: 'I don't know him. His story about Malaysia is also not true.' Samudra scoffed at suggestions that Bashir had sanctioned the attacks in Bali: 'Why would I ask for his blessing? His sermons bored me.'[34] The star witness, former JI treasurer Abu Bakar Bafana, testified tearfully from Singapore that Bashir had approved the Christmas church bombings and the plan to kill Megawati.

In the lead-up to his trial, Bashir's colleagues on the Central Leadership Council held another of their regular six-monthly meetings. Despite the enormous crackdown and the arrest of the emir and dozens of its members, JI's organisation and leadership hierarchy remained largely in place and able to function. Its leaders were so confident and defiant that they discussed attempting a jail break to free Bashir. 'It was suggested by Rusdan that we should try to save Abu Bakar Bashir,' Mantiqi 3 chief Nasir bin Abas told the police. The idea was abandoned, said Nasir, 'because Bashir had once said, "Let me be tried and jailed." Bashir had also refused to leave town before he was arrested, saying, "Just let me stay here." So we decided not to try and save him.'[35]

As was previously done for those arrested in Singapore and Malaysia, the new emir authorised payments to support the families of members arrested over the Bali bombings. At the end of the meeting they parted, with instructions to take even greater care than normal to ensure the struggle continued, according to Nasir: 'Each leader was to go home to their respective places and warn the jemaah to be careful about where they travelled and to limit the use of their cell phones.'

While JI's support base and fundraising capacity had been disrupted, the flow of funds from al Qaeda could still be depended on. JI had earned itself a bonus with the operation in Bali. According to the later interrogation of Hambali, 'Al Qaeda was highly satisfied with the Bali bombing and as a result they provided additional money . . . again without condition.'[36]

Since the bombings, al Qaeda had sent two payments to JI of US$50,000 each, the first in December 2002, the second in February 2003, by Hambali's account. The money was sent by courier from Hambali's old friend 'the Brain', Khalid Sheik Mohammed, not long before his capture in Pakistan. From his hideout in Thailand, Hambali distributed US$45,000 to JI in Indonesia, keeping the rest to support his own activities. Al Qaeda was keen for JI to keep up the good work, according to Hambali. Of the money sent to Indonesia: '$15,000 was supposed to be used to support the families of those involved in the Bali bombings . . . The rest of the money was to be used for a JI terrorist operation.'

Even as the clampdown continued, JI was readying itself to strike again. The Indonesian police began to suspect another operation was in the offing in mid-2003, when they intercepted an email from a former student at Bashir's Ngruki school. It said, 'I have graduated from a masters program and I want to marry soon,' which was known to be JI code for carrying out a bombing.[37]

The alarm bells rang louder when a huge cache of arms and explosives was seized in a raid on a house being used as a bomb factory in Semarang, Central Java. The stash included thirty sacks of potassium chlorate and four boxes of TNT; one of the men arrested said a separate load of explosives had already been sent to Jakarta. The police also found a list of targets, including five-star hotels and shopping malls, and a 25-year plan for recruitment and training drawn up by JI. The co-leader of the joint police taskforce, General Pastika, warned that since the crackdown started there had been 'a change in the mind of the terrorists'; they had become 'more radical, more committed'. Once again, all the intelligence was pointing to another attack. And once again, the authorities were powerless to stop it.

On 5 August 2003, a young man named Asmar Latin Sani drove an overloaded blue Toyota van into the circular driveway leading to the entrance of the Marriott Hotel in Jakarta. Twenty-six-year-old Asmar had been a pupil at Bashir's Ngruki school for eight years. 'He was just an ordinary student,' said the principal; he had wanted to become a teacher there but his grades weren't good enough.[38] It was Asmar's email the police had picked up a few weeks before.

Asmar had been recruited by the fugitive bomb master Dr Azahari and his assistant, Noor Din Mohammed Top. The two men had been on the run for nearly a year since Bali. As they criss-crossed Indonesia ahead of the authorities, they had holed up in the remote fishing port of Bengkulu in Sumatra, where for a few weeks they found refuge in Asmar's home town.

Not content to simply evade capture, Azahari and Noor Din had taken delivery of the US$30,000 dispatched by Hambali from al Qaeda and were planning another bombing. The pair of now hardened desperadoes handpicked and coached young Asmar for his role in it.

'They talked a lot about the need for sacrifice to achieve glory for Islam and Muslims,' said a school friend of Asmar's whose house was used to store explosives. '[Noor Din] once told me that we are surrounded by enemies. We must work hard to destroy the enemies around us. He told me, "You have never suffered yourself, but I know how it feels to be chased down. Just imagine — when I was relaxing at home and suddenly someone knocked at my door there was a good chance that I was going to be arrested or killed . . . We have to destroy our enemies before they destroy us."[39] The two JI veterans sent a team to case a number of prospective targets including the Australian International School in Jakarta, but finally settled on the Marriott because it was American-owned.

As Asmar eased the van stuffed with explosives around the hotel driveway, he was approached by two security guards. He apparently panicked and detonated the bomb too soon, before the van got to the main doorway of the hotel; if he had got any closer, the devastation would have been even greater. As it was, the explosion killed twelve people. Asmar's head was recovered from the fifth floor of the shattered hotel.

The Bali bombers were elated. 'Thanks be to God!' yelled Samudra to the assembled media outside the court where his trial was continuing. 'If it's Muslims who have done this, then I am happy,' adding 'Go to hell, Australia!' Amrozi, being escorted to a prison van on the eve of his sentencing, simply yelled 'Bomb!' Al Qaeda was quick to claim credit, bin Laden's man, al Zawahiri, hailing the attack as 'a fatal slap on the face of America and its allies in Muslim Jakarta, where the faith has been denigrated by the dirty American presence and the discriminatory Australian presence'.

The next day was judgment day for 'the smiling assassin', Amrozi, the first of the Bali bombers to learn his fate. The Denpasar court was packed with journalists, survivors and relatives of some of his 202 victims. It took all day to read the 328-page judgement to the court, after which Chief Judge I Made Karna announced his verdict at 4.10 p.m., with three raps of his gavel on the bench.

'The accused Amrozi has been proven legally to be guilty in committing a terrorist act. The judges give the accused the penalty of death.' The court erupted in cheers and applause. The survivors and bereaved family members embraced and wept with relief. They must have longed for some signal of repentance, or at least fear of death, even a moment of introspection from the condemned killer. But Amrozi's reaction was to raise his right fist in triumph then turn around grinning broadly to give a jubilant thumbs-up to the court.

In the eyes of the world, justice had been done. But in the minds of the bombers, their families and supporters, the court's judgement was of little consequence. The only judge whose verdict they awaited was Allah, and they remained completely confident that He was on their side. Amrozi's mother could finally cease despairing over her wayward son. 'Yesterday I was really shocked and I couldn't believe my cutest son could be sentenced to death,' said Tariyem. 'But today I feel better because all of these problems I have left in Allah's hands and I have asked Allah to find a solution for Amrozi.'[40]

Just as the survivors and the bereaved took comfort from the grim pronouncement of justice, the bombers and their families drew solace from their unshakable belief that their struggle and their actions were sanctioned by God. Their conviction that they were right was as profound and solid as the certainty of their victims and accusers that they were wrong. Alive or dead, the grinning face of Amrozi as he was sent to death row would become a lasting symbol of that unshakable faith, and an inspiration to the 'one million Amrozis' he believed would follow him.

Of all the main bombers, only Ali Imron expressed remorse, in a lengthy apology delivered at his trial. It appeared to be genuine, though it was no doubt aimed in part at winning him a reprieve from execution. 'Firstly, I apologise to all the victims, their families and those who have suffered loss, especially the Balinese,' Ali Imron told the court. 'I apologise to the Government and people of Indonesia. I am sorry that what I have done has smeared the name of Islam . . . I apologise to my family and my wife as I frequently lied to them. What I have done is wrong and I regret it. Please don't follow my actions. Especially to my friends, family and students, don't ever do what I have done.'

'Secondly, to my friends in the struggle, what benefit has there been from this violent struggle? The Bali bombing has brought no benefit to humanity and religion. Let this be a lesson. Take me as a clear example that these actions are wrong. Jihad conducted under human desire and revenge is a grievous mistake.'

❦

CHAPTER TWENTY-FOUR

THE FORTRESS OF FAITH

Hundreds of the emir's faithful turned out to hear the verdict against Abu Bakar Bashir. Riot police with shields, dogs and water cannon surrounded the Central Jakarta District Court. Bashir flashed his trademark buck-toothed grin and waved to the throng, saintly as always in his white ensemble as he was jostled into court by a scrum of loyalists, media and police. 'Believe me, it doesn't matter how many years the judges decide on, we will win,' he assured his followers.[1]

The judgement ran to 220 pages, but the key finding was contained in a single sentence: 'The panel of judges found it has not been legally proven that the defendant Abu Bakar Bashir is the leader of Jemaah Islamiyah.'[2]

The court erupted with shouts of 'Allahu Akhbar!' — 'God is great!' Bashir beamed in triumph and strode to the bench to pump the hands of his prosecutors. His conviction and four-year jail sentence on the charge of treason was a fraction of the fifteen years the prosecution had sought and, to his followers, only reinforced his image as a fearless dissident being persecuted for his religious and political beliefs. His acquittal of being a terrorist leader was a resounding win.

The September 2003 verdict was the first in a confused and contradictory series of judgements in the case against Bashir. The court found it was 'true and correct that JI does exist' and that Bashir had formed the group in collaboration with Abdullah Sungkar and helped to draw up its rule book, the JI *Guidelines for Struggle*. But it found there was no evidence he had formally been appointed as leader after Sungkar died.

A separate appeal court later found that Bashir had given 'a blessing' for a series of bombings, including church attacks at Christmas 2000 and the bungled attempt on the Atrium shopping mall. In an example of the sometimes bizarre rulings of the Indonesian judiciary, this court accepted that Bashir had also approved the attacks on the Sari Club and Paddy's Bar in Bali, even though, at this stage, he had not been charged over these bombings and the prosecution had tendered no evidence to indicate his involvement in them. The court went on to find that although all the bombings constituted acts of terrorism, they did *not* constitute an attempt to overthrow the government, as the targets were not symbols of the state.[3]

On the strength of this strange ruling, Bashir's treason conviction was overturned and his jail term was reduced to three years. By the end of the case, all that Bashir was found guilty of was falsifying residency documents and illegally leaving and re-entering Indonesia. Another, subsequent appeal court reduced his sentence yet again, to eighteen months.

In the eyes of his backers, who had all along called the accusations 'black propaganda', Bashir had been vindicated. The emir's former dinner host, Vice President Hamzah Haz, went on the attack. 'They have accused us of aiding terrorists. We are being cornered and Islam is being scrutinised,' he insisted. 'Who is the real terrorist? It is the United States for they have attacked Iraq. In fact they are the king of terrorists.'[4]

In the wake of Bashir's absolution, Indonesia lurched back into denial. The government was still refusing to outlaw JI and argument was once again raging over whether the organisation existed at all. 'I've never heard of JI and the people I meet have never heard of JI either,' said Hasyim Musadi, leader of Indonesia's biggest Islamic group, NU, and later a candidate for vice president. 'JI is a strange name to us. The government has never officially informed us whether JI exists . . . They must prove it.'[5]

Emboldened by Bashir's exoneration, JI itself was keen to set the record straight. An announcement headed 'Official Statement from Jemaah Islamiyah' was prepared by JI's Indonesian leadership on 6 October 2003. 'We would like to take this opportunity to openly and officially state that: Jemaah Islamiyah indeed exists and has consistently carried the mandate of Allah as . . . the bringer of hope, victory and glory for all Muslims,' the JI statement proudly declared. 'It continues to position itself as the opponent of oppression and arrogance of anyone who prevents mankind from following the path of Allah.'[6]

The statement was drafted amid the continuing debate within JI over its aims and methods, which had intensified in the wake of the bloodshed in Bali. Many JI members, especially in Indonesia, were horrified by the atrocity and by JI's evolution from an organisation working for an Islamic state into a terrorist group. The formal statement was apparently aimed at smoothing over the rifts and reaffirming the original raison d'être of JI. In the end the document was never formally released, apparently because there was also dissension over going public. The draft document was obtained and authenticated by Sidney Jones of the ICG.

Despite the ongoing division, the bold rhetoric of the JI declaration spoke for itself. It showed that, a year after the Bali bombings, Jemaah Islamiyah was far from defeated. Despite the disruption and damage it had suffered and the ongoing disagreements over modus operandi, the shared conviction of its leaders and disciples was clearly far greater than any differences between them.

'Jemaah Islamiyah will always position itself as the enemy of infidels, as the obstructor of tyranny and torture of one group of human beings by another and as a barrier to evil and vice . . . [We] will always confront with all our spirit and to the last drop of blood anyone who stands in the way of proselytisation of jihad in the path of God.'

Thai Airways flight 992 from Sydney thumped onto the tarmac and lumbered to a standstill at the Don Muang International Airport on a steamy night in Bangkok. Inside the terminal, police with sniffer dogs prowled the arrivals lounge. Outside, a black armoured personnel carrier from the Royal Thai Police stood sentinel, a marksman with an M16 keeping watch from the turret while police in commando gear with submachine guns patrolled the roadway.

It was October 2003. I had flown in with a *4 Corners* crew following the trail of JI in the year after Bali. Bangkok was in a state of tense anticipation, with US President George Bush and twenty other world leaders due to arrive within days for the Asia-Pacific Economic Cooperation (APEC) summit. The Thai authorities had learned while preparing for the convention that the airport, Western embassies and other key targets had been cased for bombing by an al Qaeda suicide squad working to Hambali.

The normally traffic-clogged streets of the Thai capital were eerily empty as we drove from the airport into downtown Bangkok; the government had ordered a five-day public holiday to clear the city before APEC. As we checked into the Conrad Hotel, security guards were using mirrors on sticks to check under cars for bombs. The Conrad had also been on Hambali's hit list.

Nearby at the Australian embassy, Chubb security guards with blue Akubras and walkie-talkies manned metal detectors at the gate, guarded by Thai paramilitary police with assault rifles. The Australian mission had been picked out as a target as well, circled in blue ink — along with the US and other Western embassies — on a tourist map found in the home of one of Hambali's accomplices, according to Thai police.

Hambali's chief scout in Bangkok was a young Malaysian known as Lillie, who had swapped architecture studies in Kuala Lumpur for jihad training in Afghanistan. While there, he had sworn allegiance to bin Laden, who told him 'his duty was to suffer'. Lillie later confessed to being a member of a three-man suicide squad chosen after September 11 for a similar mission in Thailand. According to a classified report of his interrogation, 'Lillie claimed that he did not know the kind of suicide operation that was assigned to him but he stated that he [believed] the operation would involve a plane in a way that was more or less the same as the September 11 attack.'[7]

Lillie's squad had also cased nightspots along the popular neon-lit tourist strip, Khao San Road. He told his interrogators that the operations chief was planning another Bali-style attack. 'Hambali wanted to choose targets like bars and discos where Westerners and Japanese gathered and where the businesses were owned, operated or used by Israelis.'

From Bangkok, we followed Hambali's trail a thousand kilometres south to the Thai frontier town of Narathiwat near the Malaysian border. A bedraggled fishing port at the bottom of the skinny Thai peninsula, Narathiwat is the capital of one of the restive Muslim-majority provinces strung out along Thailand's southern boundary.

Under the gaze of a giant golden Buddha, which smiles serenely from its hilltop over the jungle, Muslim rebels have been fighting sporadically for a separate state since the 1970s. More recently, their on-again off-again insurgency has provided fertile ground for the spread of JI's jihad.

As our propeller-driven Fokker 50 rattled in to land and bumped across the potholed tarmac at Narathiwat airport, the provincial military police were readying themselves for trouble. The violence had escalated in recent months. 'There is a feeling of fear across the whole region,' the local commander Major General Thani Tavitsri told me at his sandbagged jungle base outside Narathiwat. A policeman had just been shot dead, the eighth of Major General Thani's men to be killed in a spate of attacks, gunned down while riding his motorbike, in revenge for the deaths of several militants in a shootout.

The renewed clashes had come amid reports that JI had infiltrated the local insurgency. 'The fastest way for JI to increase their membership is to make contact with the old [militant] groups who still have a following in these areas,' the Major General explained. The Thai authorities believe that up to 1000 local fighters have undergone training in Indonesia and the Middle East, prompting Major General Thani's sombre prediction: 'The worst may be yet to come.'

Just south of Narathiwat, an old iron bridge spans the lazy brown Kolok River at the border checkpoint of Sungai Kolok, the busiest crossing point between Malaysia and Thailand, and home to 'a huge number of brothels to accommodate visiting Malay gentlemen', according to the proud boast on a Thai Government website. Outside the chaotic passport office on the Thai side, a faded sign offers a polite but cautionary greeting: 'Welcome to Sungai Kolok. WARNING. You are involved with drug, you are illegal using drug in entertainment club, you will be charged. Best regards, Narathiwat province police.'

A hundred metres upstream — in full view of the bridge and the official checkpoint — we watched a thriving smuggling trade go on. Timber longboats shuttled back and forth across the river carrying groaning cargoes of contraband and travellers who prefer to dispense with the formalities at the official crossing. It was across this porous border that Hambali and his fellow fugitives fled on their escape north after the crackdown in Singapore and Malaysia, finding sanctuary in the jungles of southern Thailand before continuing on to Bangkok.

Hambali later revealed that his al Qaeda bosses had been canvassing a hit in Thailand for years. Khalid Sheik Mohammed and Abu Hafs had asked him back in 2000 to report to them on potential targets. At that time, well before Lillie's arrival in Thailand, Hambali had sent a JI team to conduct surveillance in conjunction with the local Thai rebel groups. They had cased the Bangkok tourist strip and also surveyed the popular island resorts of Pattaya and Phuket, sending surveillance footage back to al Qaeda headquarters in Afghanistan. But according to Hambali 'the local mujahideen groups in Thailand had rejected the idea of targeting tourist spots', apparently believing — like the dissidents in JI's own ranks — that foreign holidaymakers were not legitimate targets. By Hambali's account, the plan to hit Thai tourist resorts was abandoned as a result.[8]

Hambali had settled on Western embassies instead. One of his deputies based himself in Narathiwat to cultivate new foot soldiers for the operation — a local doctor, a religious teacher, a driver and a labourer, who were all eventually arrested and charged. According to the police reports of their interrogations, the doctor asked his colleagues: 'Are you brave enough to put a bomb on your body and walk into the US embassy?' to which one of the group replied, 'Yes, I think I can do that.'[9]

In the months after our trip to southern Thailand, the fears of it becoming a new battleground for jihad were grimly borne out. In January 2004, Muslim rebels stormed an army battalion base in Narathiwat, shooting dead four soldiers who were guarding the armoury and seizing more than 300 guns. The Thai Government responded by declaring martial law across the south. Spurred on by their success and armed with their new military-issue weapons, the rebels went on a rampage.

At dawn on 28 April 2004, Islamic militants staged simultaneous attacks on police stations and security checkpoints across three southern Thai provinces. In the ensuing gunbattles, dozens of Muslim fighters, many of them teenagers, were killed. In Pattani province, one band of desperates retreated to an old mosque where, under siege and vastly outnumbered, they yelled through loudhailers that they were ready to die as martyrs. The security forces opened fire with teargas and bullets; when they finally stormed the mosque, thirty-two bodies were found piled on the stone floor. In all, 108 rebels were killed in what *Time* magazine called 'an unprecedented outbreak of carnage that has stunned this predominantly Buddhist nation'[10] Their families reportedly buried the bodies unwashed, believing they had already been purified by jihad.

In raids afterwards, police discovered a seven-point plan to achieve an Islamic state in southern Thailand. The blueprint called for the recruitment and training of 30,000 holy warriors, followed by an armed rebellion to impose Islamic law.[11] The government's bloody crackdown did little to dampen the militants' deadly fervour. 'I am so angry now I will kill to defend my family and my faith . . . I want revenge,' said one young man whose father was shot dead in the mosque.[12]

The day after the bloodbath, the longstanding separatist group the Pattani United Liberation Organisation posted a warning on its website: 'Dear People of the World, persons who plan to visit Thailand NOW are warned not to travel to Pattani.' The warning included the popular holiday resorts of Phuket and Krabi — which had been seen by many travellers as safe alternatives to Bali. Once declared off-limits for attack by Thailand's Islamic militants, the tourist spots frequented by foreigners were now seen as fair game. The website ultimatum concluded: 'Pattani people are not responsible for what happens to you after this warning.'

Hambali's schemes were finally thwarted when the JI mastermind was captured in August 2003, in the most significant blow struck so far against JI. The breakthrough came with the arrest of the Malaysian, Lillie, and another member of the suicide squad that bin Laden had sent to Thailand. Their admissions led the CIA and Thai intelligence to an apricot-coloured apartment block in the temple city of Ayutthaya, north of Bangkok, with a 7–Eleven store on the corner and a Dunkin' Donuts across the road. Hambali was at home with his wife when Thai special forces smashed down the door of his rented flat.

His apprehension was hailed by the United States as the biggest win for the war on terror since the arrest of his friend 'the Brain' a few months before. 'In the last few days we captured a major terrorist named Hambali,' announced President Bush. 'He's a known killer who is a close associate of September 11 mastermind Khalid Sheikh Mohammed. Hambali is one of the world's most lethal terrorists.'

But Australia's Defence Minister cautioned against celebrating too soon. 'We have no indications that the ongoing arrests of JI members across the region have seriously damaged JI's command and control,' Robert Hill told a defence conference in Canberra. 'JI has been able to continue planning and executing terrorist attacks despite the arrest of over 200 members, including some of its most senior operatives since 2001 . . . Hambali's arrest may have disrupted operational planning in Bangkok and southern Thailand. Planned operations in Jakarta have probably not been disrupted, with bombs and terrorist cells still in circulation.'[13]

The capture of Hambali and hundreds of his cohorts was certainly a relief. But the more arrests that take place, the more we understand about JI, and the depth and extent of this sophisticated, resilient, and fearless organisation. Before December 2001, its existence was completely unknown other than to its own initiates. Now we know that its history spans generations, dating back to the birth of the Darul Islam movement in Indonesia in the 1940s, and that its fury dates back further still, to the centuries of the Christian crusades. A network built up over decades with a philosophy rooted in ancient history is not about to be dismantled in a few months — or even years.

Estimates of the size of JI's continuing membership and support base vary widely. The Australian Government has calculated 'somewhere between three and five thousand adherents' in Indonesia alone.[14] This may be a conservative estimate, given that in its own 1998 Seminar Report, JI claimed then to have 2000 members and 5000 trainees. As Australian Federal Police Commissioner Mick Keelty has commented, there seems to be 'an almost endless supply of people willing to take up the radical and fundamentalist cause'.[15]

The Indonesian authorities have struggled to confront the eruption of Islamist terror, a politically fraught issue in the world's most populous Muslim nation. While resolute in hunting down the Bali bombers, the government of Megawati Sukarnoputri, was eager to blame the West for their murderous acts. 'The motives and justifying arguments of their movement apparently arise from the prolonged unjust attitude exhibited by big powers towards countries whose inhabitants profess Islam,' the then president told the United Nations General Assembly, in a speech applauded in the Islamic world. 'Many eminent Muslims in Indonesia believe that once the major powers behave in a more just manner and make clear their impartiality in the Middle East, then most

of the root causes of terrorism, perpetrated in the name of Islam —
which in any circumstances cannot be justified — would have been
resolved.'[16]

There was some truth in her assertion. There was also some truth
in the advice from the head of the Islamic group Muhammadiyah that
poverty and injustice were helping to fan the flames of terror. 'When
the deprived see that the state and the government have not come to
their defence they feel abandoned . . . When the state becomes an
accomplice in maintaining the gap between the privileged and the
deprived, they get angry. Confusion, frustration, despair and anger
soon find expression in many forms, some through violent means
aimed at what they see as injustice, moral decadence and religious
bankruptcy.'[17]

But amid the contention over causes and solutions, there lies
another, bleaker truth. Those who wage terror in the name of Islam are
motivated not only by politics, religion, injustice or revenge; some of
them are impelled by a sheer and implacable hatred as well, which no
amount of foreign policy change or social and economic reform will
ever mollify. For these die-hards, there is no room for compromise or
conciliation, no point to negotiation, and no place for the compassion
and tolerance invoked in the Koran. It is the same pitiless resolve
encapsulated in the words of Abu Bakar Bashir in the silver-domed
mosque in Solo: 'Between you and us there will forever be a ravine of
hate.'

Throughout the Indonesian archipelago, dozens of militant religious
schools continue to preach the philosophy championed by Bashir. His
own pesantren at Ngruki is currently educating some 2000 youngsters
in keeping with Bashir's credo: 'We must nurture both comprehension
of and zeal for jihad, so that love for it and for martyrdom grows in the
soul of the mujahideen.'

In these many small cradles of militancy, Muklas, Amrozi and
Samudra are revered. 'I think there are lots of Indonesians who
sympathise with them,' said a teacher in one school. 'They see them as
fighters, as heroes.'[18] In 2003, Indonesian academics and Islamic teachers
began a long-term project to counter these views, inviting students
from pesantrens known for their JI sympathies to attend workshops
aimed at promoting tolerance and building bridges of communication.
The optimistic view is that given a decade — though others say a
generation — it may be possible to moderate the culture of violent

extremism that provides the seemingly endless source of new jihadists for JI.

From his prison cell in Jakarta, Bashir remained a powerful force in Islamic politics and continued to steer the course of JI's struggle. In April 2004, after renewed sectarian clashes in Ambon, Bashir convened a meeting in his cell with leaders of his Indonesian Mujahideen Council, the Islamic Defenders Front and other Islamist groups, where they resolved to send reinforcements to join the fighting.[19] The violence in Sulawesi had also flared afresh. The ICG's Sidney Jones blamed the emergence of a rash of new militant groups, spawned by the same ideology but 'leaner, meaner and quicker' and even 'more dangerous' than JI.[20]

By this time, however, the Indonesian authorities were tired of Sidney Jones and her negative reports on JI and the country's provincial trouble spots. In the lead-up to the 2004 presidential elections, Jones was accused by the Indonesian intelligence agency, BIN, of spreading slander about the country, threatening its security and damaging its reputation abroad. Her working visa was cancelled and Jones was expelled from Indonesia.

❖

A riotous reception awaited Abu Bakar Bashir on 30 April 2004, the day he was due to walk free from Jakarta's Salemba prison. Hundreds of his followers had massed in the pre-dawn darkness outside the jail, where Bashir had completed his eighteen-month sentence for immigration offences. A force of 1000 riot police was ready with batons, shields and water cannon mounted on armoured trucks.

At first light Bashir emerged, only to be bustled into a police van and transferred to the national police headquarters to face a new round of terrorism charges. The mob erupted in rage. Supporters hurled stones, bricks and home-made fire bombs at the police, who pelted back blasts of water and teargas.

A furious Bashir blamed the United States and Australia for lobbying to stop his release. 'America has demonstrated its arrogance towards other nations by forcing its will on the Indonesian Government,' he railed. 'America has attempted to slander me and tried to implicate me in terrorist activities . . . The police are to question me again about a case for which I have previously been charged but which could not be proved in court.'[21]

For Australia, Bashir had only contempt. 'The Australian Government is the lackey,' he remonstrated. 'The Australian Government plans to help America crush Islam. It is one of the enemies of Islam. It is clear it has already opened a front against Islam and Muslims.'[22]

The angry scenes in Jakarta came as the first pictures of Iraqi detainees being abused and tortured by US forces in Baghdad's Abu Ghraib prison were being broadcast to the world. One image showed a hooded prisoner apparently connected to electrical wires standing on a box; others depicted US guards jeering at naked and hooded Iraqis forced into contorted poses for the camera. More pictures would follow; a cowering prisoner being terrorised by a snarling dog straining at its leash, another, naked and smeared in what looked like shit.

The universal outrage was at its most intense in the Muslim world. 'The American forces have now committed the kind of brutalities and human rights violations that will live on in Middle Eastern memories for decades,' commented the Australian Islamic scholar, Amin Saikal. An Arab language website said it all in a simple caption, run beside the now famous photograph of US Private Lynddie England holding a prostrate Iraqi prisoner on a leash. The caption read: 'And they ask: "Why do they hate us?"'

Iraq was supposed to have been a defining victory in the so-called war on terror, a triumph for democracy over tyranny, freedom over oppression. 'Ultimately, it is a contest of conviction,' Australian Prime Minister John Howard told us, 'whether the free world is prepared to protect and encourage democratic values . . . whether the powerful call for freedom can overcome the destructive force of terror.'[23]

Instead, Iraq had become a new cause célèbre for the forces of militant Islam — a fresh symbol of the Arab world's 'humiliation and disgrace' cited by bin Laden to justify his holy war. For Bashir and his ilk, it was a powerful new symbol in the propaganda campaign. The ravine of hate — or was it misunderstanding? — seemed to inch even wider as we watched.

Bashir thundered from his jail cell that the United States had become 'a barbarous nation which continuously desires to colonise and terrorise other nations. Their wealth and technological advances have been made the means by which to pressure, terrorise and make war on small, weak nations. We are now seeing how arrogant the American Government is, using the power it possesses to act like a policeman who rearranges the world just as it wishes . . . Such arrogant actions by America will clearly lead to resistance by those who have been oppressed and such a situation will lead the world into a clash of civilisations between nations and religions and will trigger all-out war.'[24]

Bashir's tirades were by now predictable. But the views he expressed were not confined to a fanatical fringe. For many moderate Muslims as well, the abuses in Iraq — supposedly a new beacon of democracy and freedom — reinforced what they saw as the hypocrisy of the West. 'An increasing majority of Muslims are beginning to see the world as a clash between Muslim civilisation and western civilisation,' said Husain Haqqani of the Carnegie Endowment for International Peace in Washington. 'Every incident of the use of force against Muslims, justified or unjustified, is interpreted as a manifestation of that clash.'[25]

The Australian scholar Amin Saikal put it another way, defining the confrontation as 'a clash of extremisms'. On each side the conflict was being defined by extremes: Good versus evil. Democracy against tyranny. Freedom or terror. The Party of God versus the Party of Satan. Us and them. Each side was fortified by an equally unshakable belief — an absolute certainty that it commanded the moral high ground, that good — and God — were on its side, that its beliefs would eventually prevail.

A contest of conviction, the Prime Minister called it. A test of 'determination and resolve'. A battle to uphold 'those values Australians cherish — tolerance, opportunity, security and respect for one's neighbours'. If only it were that simple. Once, being Australian had made us feel secure, cocooned by our distance, our easygoing spirit and our nation's medium size, comfortable bit players in world affairs. Not any more. An al Qaeda targeting memo publicised in April 2004 rammed home the point: 'We have to turn the land of the infidels into hell as they have done to the land of the Muslims . . . Their importance is as follows: Americans; British; Spanish; Australians.' In Indonesia, Australians were placed at the top of the list.[26]

A contest of conviction. As a label, it was supposed to hold out some hope, and it was certainly more heartening than the prospect of an unrelenting, undeclared war. But while it may be more encouraging than an unwinnable 'war on terror', there is something deeply discomfiting about a contest of this kind. Any other contest — of military might, weaponry, knowledge, technology — we could surely at least hope to win. But a contest of conviction?

Because it is clear now that the 'enemy' is not simply Osama bin Laden or Abu Bakar Bashir, or their grinning foot soldier, Amrozi, waiting happily on death row. The enemy is the implacable conviction that drives them, the 'dark and powerful ideas' nurtured through the centuries; the idea, in essence, that the Abode of Islam has been, and continues to be, brutalised and oppressed, and that fighting back with whatever means and whatever force can be mustered is a struggle sanctified by God.

This is a conviction so profound that it brooks no fear of death and no contemplation of defeat. It was summed up by one of Bashir's followers, waiting in the crowd outside the Jakarta jail. 'In Islam, there is no failure. Dying is winning. Success means victory in this world. Death means victory in the world beyond.'[27]

After his transfer from prison, Bashir was shifted to a newly refurbished and air-conditioned suite of cells in the Jakarta police headquarters, with five rooms, an en suite and a small garden. 'He is old, so in the name of humanity we have given him a place to pray,' a police spokesman explained. 'As religious people, we have to respect each other.'[28]

As he awaited the new charges against him, the political tide appeared to be rising further in favour of Bashir. In June 2004, the frontrunner in Indonesia's presidential elections, Susilo Bambang Yudhoyono, announced that JI would not be outlawed by his government, because it had only been proven to exist in neighbouring Malaysia. 'Actually there is no formal organisation called JI in Indonesia,' he pronounced while campaigning in West Java. 'By our law, by our rules of the game, we cannot dismiss the organisation that does not exist formally.'[29]

A month later there was even greater cause for celebration for JI, when Indonesia's Constitutional Court struck down the hastily drafted terrorism regulations rushed into law in the wake of the Bali bombings. Hearing an appeal against the conviction of Maskyur, the assistant who helped Samudra arrange cars and accommodation in Bali, the Court found that the retroactive laws were invalid under the Constitution, which states that the right not to be prosecuted retrospectively is a 'basic human right that cannot be diminished under any circumstances at all'.[30] The convictions of dozens of jailed JI members, including the death-row prisoners Muklas, Amrozi and Samudra, were suddenly thrown into doubt, with the country's Justice Minister conceding that the bombers could apply for judicial reviews.

The effect of the ruling was brought home in August 2004, when the last of the captured Bali bombers, Idris, appeared before the South Jakarta District Court to hear the verdict against him. One of the core bombing team, Idris had confessed freely to his role. He had attended virtually all of the planning meetings, assisted Amrozi to buy the L300 and pack the chemicals, helped prepare the suicide driver, Arnasan, and detonated one of the bombs himself, the small TNT device outside the US consulate. 'Yes, I'm responsible,' he admitted on the day he appeared for sentencing. 'That's why I'm here.'[31]

The charge against Idris over his role in Bali was dismissed, the chief judge in the case explaining apologetically that, as a result of the Constititional Court's earlier decision, the judges had no choice but to set aside the charge. Idris was convicted on a separate count of having transported explosives used in the bombing of the Marriott Hotel and was sentenced to ten years in jail. 'This is fine,' he said cheerily after the hearing. 'God willing, this is my destiny for today. But who knows what will happen tomorrow.'

The following day, Abu Bakar Bashir was transferred from his suite of cells at police headquarters to Jakarta's Cipinang prison, to await his new trial. Arriving at the prison, Bashir waved and grinned confidently for the crowd. Four months after his re-arrest, the anti-terrorism laws were in disarray and the Indonesian authorities were grappling to find a way to prosecute him. With the laws passed after Bali in limbo, they announced he would be tried instead over the Marriott attack, even though he had been in prison when it occurred. His lawyer scoffed at the charges. 'I want to remind everyone again that at the time of the Marriott bombing, Ustad had already been detained for eight months.'[32]

As Bashir prepared afresh to face his accusers, the terrorists were mobilising to wreak yet more havoc. This time their retribution would be aimed squarely at Australia.

At 10.30 a.m. on Thursday, 9 September 2004, one month out from a federal election, a Daihatsu van cruised past the Australian embassy in Jakarta, did a quick U-turn and pulled in front of an Indonesian police truck stationed outside the mission. Seconds later, the van and its deadly cargo were detonated, apparently by a suicide bomber inside. 'It was just a massive explosion — it was like someone had punched you in the stomach,' said a diplomat who was sitting at her desk in the embassy when the bomb went off. Outside, the impact was far greater. In the words of an Indonesian man queuing for a visa, 'It was like an earthquake.'

A massive ball of white smoke billowed into the sky above central Jakarta. The glass facades of nearby buildings were shattered for a block around, windows smashing as high as fifteen storeys above the street. Bloodied security guards writhed in agony outside the wrecked embassy guardpost. A severed head and leg were strewn on the road, and the body of a passing motorcyclist lay crumpled across his bike.

A man ran from the wreckage carrying the seemingly lifeless body of a five-year-old girl, naked except for a pair of tiny pink plastic sandals; the force of the blast had torn the clothes from her body. Elizabeth Manuela Musu had been visiting the embassy with her mother to pick up her brand-new Australian passport, having received her Australian citizenship the week before. The critically wounded child, who was rushed to Singapore for emergency surgery, was among more than 100 casualties; her mother, 27-year-old Maria Kumalawati, was one of nine people killed in the bombing.

Indonesia's police chief immediately named the fugitive JI bomb master, Dr Azahari, and his associate, Noor Din Mohammed Top, as the prime suspects. The police claimed that two months earlier they had foiled a plot to assassinate President Megawati and visiting Australian dignitaries at the opening of a new Australian-funded anti-terrorism centre in Semarang, Central Java. The thwarted plotters had then shifted to Jakarta instead. The police said they had tracked Azahari and three others to a boarding house in the city's west, but the group had fled just before their hideout was raided, reportedly the third time Azahari had narrowly eluded capture. The gang was thought to include at least two suicide volunteers, whose task was to stay with the van and detonate it as close as they could get to the embassy gates, as parking there was prohibited.

Within hours of the bombing, a statement was issued in Arabic on a public web forum, purportedly claiming responsibility for the attack on behalf of JI. 'We, the Jemaah Islamiyah in East Asia, have sent messages to the Christian government in Australia but it did not respond to us or to our call, yet still the Australian Government took part in the war against our brethren in Iraq and supported the invading forces. We have decided to bring Australia, which is considered one of the most vehement enemies of God and the religion of Islam, to account . . . this is only the first of many replies that are coming, God willing, which is why we advise all Australians in Indonesia to leave or else we will make it their graveyard. We also advise the Australian Government to withdraw its forces from Iraq, and if our demands are not met, we will direct many painful strikes against them, God willing. The columns of booby-trapped cars will not end and the lists of martyrs are still full and will not end . . . Our raids will not stop and our jihad will go on until the liberation of the lands of Muslims.'[33]

Prime Minister John Howard responded: 'The day any country surrenders decisions on those things to the dictates of barbarism and terrorism is the day a country loses control over its future.'[34] As the Australian and Indonesian governments swore not to bow to the terrorists, a team of Australian Federal Police flew out to Jakarta to join a new investigation.

And so the grim task of tracking down the perpetrators and bringing them to justice began all over again. No doubt there will be more arrests and more trials. Another round of JI operatives will be captured and jailed. Abu Bakar Bashir himself will be tried — perhaps convicted and jailed for life, perhaps acquitted and set free. The Bali bombers may be dispatched to their deaths; their icon bin Laden might even be hunted down.

But more blood will be spilled. And none of these separate defeats will quench the deadly conviction of those who wage terror in the name of Islam, or extinguish the dark and powerful ideas that nourish that conviction. For every holy warrior caught or killed, there will almost certainly be another willing to take his place, to answer the ancient and irresistible call to jihad, echoed in the defiant rhetoric of the 2003 'Official Statement from Jemaah Islamiyah'.[35]

'Let us face the enemies of Islam with all the courage we possess. Let us build confidence and unity among ourselves so that we cannot be divided by the enemy. Let us stand shoulder to shoulder with JI upholding Islam. Know that however great their power, it is nothing more than a spider's web in the face of the fortress of faith.'

Chapter 2 Jihad is Our Way

1 As reported in 'A Quiet Voice Echoes Among Islamic Radicals', *Washington Post*, 3 January 2003.

2 Abu Bakar Bashir, statement to Indonesian police, January 2003. For details of Bashir's early life, I have also drawn on Sidney Jones's reports for the International Crisis Group; and 'Meeting Ustadz Abu', by Tim Behrend, University of Auckland, December 2002. The common Indonesian spelling of Bashir's name is Abu Bakar Ba'asyir. I have chosen to use the anglicised form more familiar to Australian readers.

3 Abu Bakar Bashir, statement to Indonesian police, *op. cit.*

4 'The Latest Indonesian Crisis: Causes & solutions', by Abdullah Sungkar & Abu Bakar Bashir, published by *Nida'ul Islam* magazine, July–August 1998. I have amended the original translation slightly to clarify its meaning.

5 The Political Consequences of Military Operations in Indonesia 1945–99, PhD thesis by David J. Kilcullen, UNSW, 2000. For the history of Kartosuwiryo and the Darul Islam movement I have also drawn on *A Nation in Waiting*, Adam Schwarz, Allen & Unwin, 1999; and Sidney Jones's reports for the ICG.

6 The Political Consequences of Military Operations in Indonesia, *op. cit., ibid.*

7 'Darul Islam and Jemaah Islamiyah: An historical and ideological comparison', Greg Fealy, ANU, 2004.

8 'Indonesian Society in Transition: A Study of social change', W.F. Wertheim, Greenwood, 1956, cited in The Political Consequences, *op. cit.*

9 'Darul Islam and Jemaah Islamiyah', *op. cit.*

10 *A Nation in Waiting, op. cit.*

11 *Ibid.*

12 'Waiting in the Wings', David Jenkins, *Sydney Morning Herald*, 26 June 2003.

13 'Suharto's "Detect, Defect and Destroy" Policy Towards the Islamic Movement', interview with Abdullah Sunkgar published in *Nida'ul Islam*, February–March 1997. For Sungkar's background I have also drawn on 'Al-Qaeda in Southeast Asia: The case of the Ngruki network in Indonesia', Sidney Jones, ICG, 8 August 2002.

14 *A Nation in Waiting, op. cit.*
15 'The Latest Indonesian Crisis', *op. cit.* The following quote also comes from this article.
16 'The Southeast Asian Terrorist Network (as of 20 September 2002) Overview', classified report by regional intelligence agency.
17 'Indonesia, Democracy, Priests, Parliament and Self-made Gods', Abu Bakar Bashir, *Nida'ul Islam* October–November 1996.
18 'Al-Qaeda in Southeast Asia', *op. cit.*
19 System for the Caderisation of Mujahidin in Creating an Islamic Society', Abu Bakar Bashir, address delivered at the first Indonesian Mujahideen Congress, 5–7 August 2000, Yogyakarta, translated by Tim Behrend.
20 'Al-Qaeda in Southeast Asia', *op. cit.*
21 'The Latest Indonesian Crisis', *op. cit.*
22 'Al-Qaeda in Southeast Asia', *op. cit.*
23 'Indonesia — the Imprisonment of Irfan Suryahardy', Amnesty International, July 1986. See also 'The Imprisonment of Usroh Activists in Central Java', Amnesty International, October 1988.

Chapter 3 Brothers

1 'I Just Want to See My Son Before He Dies', Martin Chulov & Afrizal Samad, the *Australian*, 8 August 2003. I have also drawn on 'Brothers in Arms', Matthew Moore, *Sydney Morning Herald*, 16–17 November 2002; and 'The Bombers' Kin', Sian Powell, the *Australian*, 1 September 2003.
2 Ali Imron, interview with BBC TV, provided by Sarah McDonald. For the early history of the brothers I have relied principally on the reports of their interrogations by the Indonesian police. However, all direct quotes from Ali Imron, Muklas and Amrozi in this chapter, unless otherwise indicated, are from interviews recorded by the BBC in 2003 for the documentary series, *The Third World War*.
3 'The Family Behind the Bombings', Simon Elegant, *Time* magazine, 25 November 2002.
4 Interview with *4 Corners*, recorded January 2003.
5 'Allah's Assassins', Eric Ellis, the *Bulletin*, 5 March 2003.
6 'Islamic Leader Warns Indonesia', Indira A.R. Lakshmanan, *Boston Globe*, 17 October 2002.
7 'Happy-faced Mukhlas in Plea for Life', Sian Powell, the *Australian*, 5 September 2003.
8 Results of the Interrogation of the suspect, Amrozi, 6 November 2002.
9 'Inside the Bali Plot', Simon Elegant, *Time* magazine, 9 December 2002.
10 'A Quiet Voice Echoes Among Islamic Radicals', Alan Sipress & Ellen Nakashima, the *Washington Post*, 3 January 2003.
11 'Politics and Religious Renewal in Muslim South East Asia', Robert W. Hefner, from *Islam in an Era of Nation-States*, eds Robert W. Hefner & Patricia Horvatich, University of Hawaii Press, 1997.
12 'Al-Qaeda in Southeast Asia: The case of the Ngruki network', Sidney Jones, ICG, 8 August 2002.
13 'Indonesia — The Imprisonment of Usroh Activists in Central Java', Amnesty International, October 1988.
14 *Ibid.*
15 *Ibid.*
16 'Indonesia: Arrests of Muslim activists relating to the Tanjung Priok incident of 12 Sept 1984', Amnesty International, July 1985.
17 'Al-Qaeda in Southeast Asia', *op. cit.*
18 'Indonesia — the Imprisonment of Usroh Activists', *op. cit.*

19 'Indonesia — The Imprisonment of Irfan Suryahardy', Amnesty International, July 1986.
20 Abu Bakar Bashir, statement to Indonesian police, January 2003.
21 'The Malaysian Connection', *Tempo* magazine, 9 November 2002.

Chapter 4 Exile

1 Abu Bakar Bashir, statement to Indonesian police, January 2003.
2 'Al-Qaeda in Southeast Asia: The case of the Ngruki network', Sidney Jones, ICG, 8 August 2003.
3 *Het Parool*, Netherlands newspaper, 2 January 2003.
4 *Suara Hidayatullah*, magazine October 2002.
5 'Al-Qaeda in Southeast Asia', *op. cit.*
6 Abu Bakar Bashir, statement to Indonesian police, *op. cit.*
7 *Ibid.*
8 'The Malaysian Connection', *Tempo* magazine, 9 September 2002.
9 Interview with BBC TV. Unless otherwise indicated, all direct quotes that follow in this chapter from Muklas, Amrozi and Ali Imron are from interviews with the BBC recorded in 2003 for the documentary series *The Third World War.*
10 The National Police of the Republic of Indonesia. The Investigation Team for the Bali Bombing Case. Report on interrogation of Muklas, 2003.
11 'Australians Inspired Amrozi's Hatred', Martin Chulov, the *Australian*, 13 June 2003.
12 Official Report of Further Interrogation of Amrozi, 14 December 2002.
13 Examination Report by the Indonesian Police on the interrogation of Samudra, dated 21 October 2002.
14 'Jemaah Islamiyah in South East Asia: Damaged but still dangerous', Sidney Jones, ICG, 26 August 2003.
15 Abu Bakar Bashir, statement to Indonesian police, *op. cit.*
16 'The Osama bin Laden and al-Qaeda of South East Asia', Marc Erikson, *Asia Times*, 6 February 2002.
17 Central Jakarta Office of the Counsel for Prosecution, Indictment of Abu Bakar Bashir, Jakarta, April 2003.
18 Abu Bakar Bafana, statement to Indonesian police, Singapore, 18 April and 30 April 2002.
19 Briefing with Singapore Ministry of Home Affairs, Singapore, January 2003.
20 Examination Report of Samudra, *op. cit.*
21 Abu Bakar Bashir, statement to Indonesian police, *op. cit.*
22 'Muslim Militants Led Double-Life in Malaysia', *Washington Post*, 16 December 2002.
23 This account was given to me by Australian JI member Jack Roche, who met Hambali in Malaysia in 2000.
24 *Seeds of Terror*, Maria Ressa, Free Press, 2003. For Hambali's early life, I have also drawn on 'Hambali Plotted Terror Campaign', the *Star*, 1 January 2003; 'Dead End for Hambali', *Tempo* magazine, 25 September 2003; and *Militant Islam in Southeast Asia: Crucible of terror*, Zachary Abuza, Lynne Rienner Publishers, 2003.
25 *Seeds of Terror*, ibid.
26 'Asia's Own Osama', Simon Elegant, *Time* magazine, 1 April 2002.
27 'Moderate Indonesia is Put to the Test', *Financial Times*, 14 October 2003; and 'Indonesia Needs One Universal Legal System', Ulil Abshar-Abdala, Institute of Information Flow Studies, 20 June 2001.
28 *Seeds of Terror*, *op. cit.*
29 'Hambali Plotted Terror Campaign', *op. cit.*
30 'Muslim Militants Led Double-Life', *op. cit.*

31 'Fugitive's Fall Was Inevitable: Landlord', *Sydney Morning Herald*, 26 August 2003. I have also drawn on 'Inside Hambali's School for Terror', Kimina Lyall, the *Australian*, 1 November 2002.
32 'Clerics Groomed Students for Terrorism', *Washington Post*, 2 February 2002.

Chapter 5 The Battle of Lion's Den

1 For names of JI recruits trained in Afghanistan, see 'Jemaah Islamiyah in South East Asia: Damaged but still dangerous', Sidney Jones, ICG, 26 August 2003.
2 Muklas, statement to Indonesian police, 13 December 2002.
3 Interview with BBC TV recorded in 2003 for *The Third World War* documentary series.
4 Ahmed Rashid, *Taliban: Militant Islam, oil, and fundamentalism in Central Asia*, Yale Nota Bene, 2001.
5 *The Fragmentation of Afghanistan*, Barnett R. Rubin, Yale University Press, 2002.
6 *Soldiers of God: With the Mujahidin in Afghanistan*, Robert D. Kaplan, Houghton Mifflin, 1990. p. 49, cited in: *Holy War Inc.: Inside the secret world of Osama bin Laden*, Peter L. Bergen, Phoenix, 2001.
7 *Taliban, op. cit.*
8 *To Heart and Cabul: A story of the first Afghan war*, G.A. Henty, republished by Saeed Jan Quereshi, Saeed Book Bank, 1983, cited in *Holy War Inc., op. cit.*
9 *The Traveler's Dictionary of Quotation*, ed. Peter Yopp, Routledge, 1988, cited in *Unholy Wars*, John Cooley, Pluto Press, 1999.
10 Cited in *Unholy Wars, ibid.*
11 *Holy War Inc., op. cit.*
12 'Afghanistan, Graveyard of Empires', *Foreign Affairs*, Vol. 80, Issue 6, 1 November 2001.
13 *Unholy Wars, op. cit.*
14 *Ibid.*
15 *Holy War Inc., op. cit.*
16 *Ibid.*
17 *Taliban, op. cit.*
18 Police interrogation reports of Samudra and Ali Imron refer to their training in Sayyaf's camp. See also 'Jemaah Islamiyah in Southeast Asia', *op. cit.*
19 'Jemaah Islamiyah in South East Asia', *op. cit.*
20 Muklas, statement to Indonesian police, *op. cit.*
21 Interview with Robert Fisk, the *Independent*, 1993, cited in *Unholy Wars, op cit.*
22 *Holy War Inc., op. cit.*
23 *I Met Osama bin Laden*, BBC TV documentary.
24 Interview with Paksitani journalist Hamid Mir, September 1998.
25 *Bin Laden: the man who declared war on America*, Yosef Bodansky, Prima Lifestyles, 2001.
26 *Taliban, op. cit.*
27 'Osama my Best Friend', Catherine Taylor, the *Australian*, 16 January 2003.
28 *I Met Osama bin Laden*, BBC TV documentary.
29 *Taliban, op. cit.*
30 *Unholy Wars, op. cit.*
31 Information provided to author by Professor William Maley, ANU, Canberra.
32 *Holy War Inc., op. cit.*
33 Muklas, statement to Indonesian police, *op. cit.*
34 Interview with JI veteran cited in *Militant Islam in Southeast Asia: Crucible of terror*, Zachary Abuza, Lynne Rienner Publishers, 2003.
35 Interview with BBC TV, *op. cit.*
36 'Jemaah Islamiyah in South East Asia', *op. cit.*
37 Interview with BBC TV, *op. cit.*

38 'Al Qaeda Figure Seized in Thailand', *Washington Post*, 15 August 2003.
39 'Jemaah Islamiyah in Southeast Asia', *op. cit.*
40 'Indonesia Finds New Terror Links', Timothy Mapes, *Asian Wall St Journal*, 13 December 2002. Sidney Jones of the ICG believes the number of Indonesians from Sungkar and Bashir's network who trained in Afghanistan fell somewhere short of 300.
41 Muklas, statement to Indonesian police, *op. cit.*
42 *Holy War Inc.*, *op. cit.* See also *Inside Al Qaeda: Global network of terror*, Rohan Gunaratna, Columbia University Press, 2002.
43 *The Jihad Fixation: Agenda, strategy, portents*, Wordsmiths, 2001.
44 *Holy War Inc.*, *op. cit.*
45 'Anti-Soviet Warrior Puts His Army on the Road to Peace', Robert Fisk, the *Independent*, 6 December 1993. The anecdote about bin Laden's weapon is from *Bin Laden*, *op. cit.*
46 Egyptian journalist Essam Deraz, cited in *Holy War Inc.*, *op. cit.*
46 Interview with BBC TV, *op. cit.*
47 *Unholy Wars*, *op. cit.*
48 *Inside Al Qaeda*, *op. cit.*
49 Interview with Peter Arnett and Peter Bergen, CNN, May 1997.

Chapter 6 Be Brave if You're Right

1 Interview with BBC TV. All direct quotes from Muklas in this chapter are from BBC interviews recorded in 2003 for *The Third World War* documentary series, unless otherwise indicated.
2 'Jemaah Islamiyah in South East Asia: Damaged but still dangerous', Sidney Jones, ICG, 26 August 2003.
3 'The Family Behind the Bombings', Simon Elegant, *Time* magazine, 25 November 2002.
4 Muklas, statement to Indonesian police, 13 December 2002
5 Jaafar Anwarul, JI detainee, interview with TV3 Malaysia, April 2004.
6 'Malaysian Muslim School had a Militant Secret', Reuters, 25 November 2002. I have also drawn on 'The School that Taught JI Network', Kimina Lyall, the *Australian*, 22 November 2002; and 'Trail of Blood Leads from Remote School', Mark Baker, *Sydney Morning Herald*, 22 November 2002.
7 Abu Bakar Bashir, statement to Indonesian police, January 2003.
8 'Villagers Say Bali Bombing Suspect a Radical', AP, 10 November 2002.
9 Interview with BBC TV. The quotes from Amrozi and Ali Imron in the following pages of this chapter are likewise from BBC TV interviews.
10 'Jemaah Islamiyah in South East Asia', *op. cit.*
11 *Bin Laden: The man who declared war on America*, Yosef Bodansky, Prima Lifestyles, 2001.
12 'The Declaration of Jihad on the Americans Occupying the Country of the Two Sacred Places', released by Osama bin Laden, 23 August 1996.
13 From Osama bin Laden's 1998 announcement of the World Islamic Front for Jihad.

Chapter 7 Striving in the Path of God

1 *Muhammad, Prophet and Statesman*, W. Montgomery Watt, Oxford University Press, 1961. For the life of Muhammad, I have also drawn on *Muhammad*, Maxime Rodinson, Tauris Parke Paperbacks, 2002; N.J. Dawood's introduction to the *Penguin Koran*, 1989;

'Islam and the Muslim Community', Frederick M. Denny, in *Religious Traditions of the World*, ed. H. Byron Earhart, HarperCollins, 1984; *A History of the Arab Peoples*, Albert Hourani, Faber & Faber, 1991; and *A History of Islamic Societies*, Ira M. Lapidus, 2002.

2 *Muhammad, ibid.*

3 *Islam: A guide for Jews and Christians*, F.E. Peters, Princeton University Press, 2003.

4 *Islam: A guide, op. cit.*

5 *Ibid.*

6 *Ibid.*

7 *What Went Wrong? The clash between Islam and modernity in the Middle East*, Bernard Lewis, Phoenix, 2002.

8 *Ibid.*

9 *Islam: A thousand years of faith and power*, Jonathan Bloom & Sheila Blair, Yale University Press, 2002.

10 *Milestones*, Sayyid Qutb, International Islamic Federation of Student Organizations, [1964] 1978.

11 *The Crisis of Islam*, Bernard Lewis, Weidenfeld & Nicolson, 2003.

12 *The Jihad Fixation: Agenda, strategy, portents*, Wordsmiths, 2001.

13 *Ibid.*

14 *Ibid.*

15 Ala al-Din Ali ibn Husam al-Din al-Muttaqi, *Kanz al'Ummal*, Vol. 2, pp. 252–286.

16 *Islam and the West*, Amin Saikal, Palgrave Macmillan, 2003.

17 *The Jihad Fixation, op. cit.*

18 *Islam: A short history*, Karen Armstrong, Modern Library, 2000.

19 *Islam and the West, op. cit.*

20 *What Went Wrong?, op. cit.*

21 See *Islam and the West, op. cit.*; *Islam: A guide, op. cit.*, and others.

22 *What Went Wrong?, op. cit.*

23 *Islam and the West, op. cit.*

24 Bin Laden, videotaped speech, 7 October 2001.

25 As cited in *Islam and the West, op. cit.*

26 Safar al-Hawali, 1991, cited in *Holy War Inc.: Inside the Secret World of Osama bin Laden*, Peter L. Bergen, Phoenix, 2001.

27 *Bin Laden: The man who declared war on America*, Yosef Bodansky, Prima Lifestyles, 2001

28 *43 Days: The Gulf War*, Ian Bickerton & Michael Pearson, Text Publishing & ABC Books, 1991.

29 *Ibid.*

30 *I Met Osama bin Laden*, BBC documentary.

31 Muklas, additional statement to Indonesian police, 3 December 2002.

Chapter 8 The Field Commander

1 Samudra, statement to Indonesian police, 29 November 2002. This chapter is based primarily on the series of statements made by Samudra to the Indonesian police.

2 'Allah's Assassins', Eric Ellis, the *Bulletin*, 5 March 2003.

3 *Ibid.* I have also drawn on 'Bombers' Faces Revealed Amid Warnings to Public', Darren Goodsir, *Sydney Morning Herald*, 18 November 2002.

4 Interview with BBC TV, recorded in 2003 for *The Third World War* documentary series. The direct quotes from Samudra about his early life are from this interview unless otherwise indicated.

5 'Indonesia Backgrounder: How the Jemaah Islamiyah terrorist network operates', Sidney Jones, ICG, 11 December 2002.

6 'Indonesia Backgrounder', *op. cit.*

7 *Ibid.*

8 'Genealogies of Islamic Radicalism in Post-Suharto Indonesia', Martin van Bruinessen, 2002.

9 Examination Report by the Indonesian Police on the Interrogation of Samudra, dated 21 October 2002.

10 'How the Jemaah Islamiyah Terrorist Network Operates', *op. cit.*

11 Interview with BBC TV, *op. cit.*

12 Examination report of Samudra, *op. cit.* The direct quotes that follow from here in this chapter are all from Samudra's police interrogations unless otherwise indicated.

13 *Bin Laden: The man who declared war on America*, Yosef Bodansky, Prima Lifestyles, 2001.

14 Ali Imron, statement to Indonesian police, 26 January 2003; and 'Jemaah Islamiyah in South East Asia: Damaged but still dangerous', Sidney Jones, ICG, 26 August 2003.

15 'Jemaah Islamiyah in South East Asia', *ibid.*

16 Testimony of Singapore JI member Jafar Mistooki at trial of Abu Bakar Bashir, *Straits Times*, 27 June 2003.

17 'Shy Boy Became a "Mass Killer"', Don Greenlees, the *Australian*, 20 November 2002.

18 'Allah's Alumni', Sian Powell & Sandra Nahdar, *Weekend Australian*, 20 September 2003.

19 *The Jihad Fixation: Agenda, strategy, portents*, Wordsmiths, 2001.

20 'Jemaah Islamiyah in South East Asia', *op. cit.*

21 'Allah's Assassins', *op. cit.*

22 Interview with BBC TV, *op. cit.*

23 'The Malaysian Connection', *Tempo* magazine, 9 November 2002.

24 'Hambali Plotted Terror Campaign', the *Star*, 1 January 2003.

Chapter 9 The Jemaah

1 Interview with *4 Corners*, recorded May 2003.

2 Confidential author interview. This chapter is based primarily on accounts obtained from former JI members and followers, most of whom spoke on condition of anonymity.

3 *Ibid.*

4 Briefing with Australian investigator, 2004.

5 Confidential author interview.

6 Refugee Review Tribunal: Decision and reasons for decision, 5 February 1999, ruling in case of Abdul Rahman Ayub.

7 Briefing with Australian investigator, 2004.

8 This story is based on confidential author interviews with two separate sources.

9 Confidential author interview.

10 Briefing with Australian investigator and accounts from former JI followers.

11 Confidential author interview.

12 RRT: Decision, *op. cit.*

13 The first joint visit by Sungkar and Bashir to Australia recorded by Australian immigration authorities was in January 1991. Sungkar arrived in Sydney on 13 January, while Bashir arrived on 20 January. Bashir made an earlier visit to Australia on 12 April 1990, flying into Melbourne, and is also believed to have made an even earlier one in 1998 or '99, of which there is no official record.

14 'An Offer of Help – but ASIO Preferred to Raid', Linda Morris, *Sydney Morning Herald*, 4 November 2002.

15 Briefing with Australian investigator, 2004.

16 Transcript of speech delivered by Abu Bakar Bashir, supplied to *4 Corners* by Linda Morris of the *Sydney Morning Herald*.
17 Confidential author interview.
18 Jack Roche, interview with ABC TV, November 2002.

Chapter 10 The Islamic Military Academy of JI

1 Testimony of Achmad Roihan in the Indonesian trial of Abu Rusdan, August 2003, cited in 'Indonesia Backgrounder: Jihad in Central Sulawesi', Sidney Jones, ICG, 3 February 2004.
2 Confidential author interview.
3 'Official Statement from al-Jamaah al-Islamiyah', 6 October 2003.
4 'Suharto's "Detect, Defect and Destroy" Policy Towards the Islamic Movement', interview with Abdullah Sungkar, *Nida'ul Islam*, February–March 1997.
5 The National Police of the Republic of Indonesia, The Investigation Team for the Bali Bombing Case. Report on interrogation of Muklas, 2003.
6 'Terror Connections of Abubakar Basyir; and Further Details on Terrorist Connection and Activities of Umar Faruq', CIA, September 2002.
7 US intelligence report on activities of al Faruq, undated.
8 Interview with Hashim Salamat, *Nida'ul Islam*, May 1998.
9 'Southern Philippines Backgrounder: Terrorism and the peace process', Sidney Jones, ICG, 13 July 2004.
10 *Seeds of Terror*, Maria Ressa, Free Press, 2003.
11 'The Southeast Asian Terrorist Network (as of 20 September 2002) Overview', classified report by regional intelligence agency.
12 Badan Inteligen Nasional (BIN) report on activities of Umar Faruq, September 2002.
13 *Seeds of Terror, op. cit.*
14 Philippine intelligence report, September 2002.
15 US intelligence report.
16 'Jemaah Islamiyah in South East Asia: Damaged but still dangerous', Sidney Jones, ICG, 26 August 2003.
17 'In Terror Pact – City Airport, Seaport Bombings Part of Plot', *Mindanao Times*, 16 April 2003, cited in 'Jemaah Islamiyah in South East Asia', *ibid*.
18 Interrogation report of Mohammad Nasir bin Abas, head of Mantiqi 3, 18 April 2003.
19 Central Jakarta Office of the Counsel for Prosecution, Indictment of Abu Bakar Bashir, Jakarta, April 2003.
20 Report on interrogation of Muklas, *op. cit.*
21 'Jemaah Islamiyah in South East Asia', *op. cit.*
22 Jemaah Islamiyah Seminar Report, (undated) obtained by the author.
23 Record of Interview, Mohammad Nasir bin Abas, Jakarta, 9 May 2003.
24 *Inside Al Qaeda: Global network of terror*, Rohan Guneratna, Columbia University Press, 2002.
25 'Osama, My Best Friend', Catherine Taylor, the *Australian*, 16 January 2003.
26 Philippine police intelligence report on Mohammed Jamal Khalifa.
27 *The New Jackals*, Simon Reeve, Andre Deutsch, 1999.
28 *Seeds of Terror, op. cit.*
29 *Ibid.*
30 Cited in *Seeds of Terror, op. cit.*
31 *The New Jackals, op. cit.*
32 *Holy War Inc.: Inside the secret world of Osama bin Laden*, Peter L. Bergen, Phoenix, 2001.
33 'Bojinka' has been widely reported to be a Serbo-Croatian word meaning 'big bang'. The *9/11 Commission Report* noted that Khalid Sheik Mohammed revealed in his April

2003 interrogation that, in fact, 'bojinka' was 'a nonsense word he adopted after hearing it on the front lines in Afghanistan'.

34 *9/11 Commission Report*.

35 Republic of the Philippines, National Headquarters, Philippine National Police Intelligence Command. 'After Intelligence Operation Report: Neutralisation of international terrorists', 27 February 1995.

36 *Seeds of Terror, op. cit.*

37 'Chronological Activities of Rose Mosquera', Philippine police intelligence report (undated).

38 *Inside al Qaeda, op. cit.*

39 Interview with John Miller, ABC News, broadcast 28 May 1998.

40 Tactical Interrogation Report of Abdul Hakim Murad, Philippine National Police, 9 January 1995.

41 Interview with Colonel Rodolfo Mendoza, former head of Special Operations Group, Philippine National Police. I have also drawn on 'Indonesian Cleric Tied to '95 Anti-US Plot', *LA Times*, 7 February 2002.

42 Philippine police intelligence report.

43 Briefing with Australian investigators, April 2004.

44 *Ibid*.

45 *Seeds of Terror, op. cit.*

46 Philippine police intelligence report.

47 'Osama My Best Friend', *op. cit.*

48 'Planner Reveals How 9/11 Might Have Been Worse', Christina Lamb, *Sunday Times*.

Chapter 11 A Bit of a Mad Bugger

1 Author interview, December 2003 and January 2004.

2 Confidential author interview. The source, a former close colleague of Azaharis in Malaysia, spoke on condition of anonymity. 'Dani' is not his real name.

3 *Islamic Revivalism in Malaysia*, Zainah Anwar, Pelanduk Publications, 1987.

4 *Ibid*. I have also drawn on *Malaysia — Mahathirism, hegemony and the new opposition*, John Hilley, Zed Books, 2001.

5 This account of campus life at UTM is based on the recollections of John Cooper.

6 'Bali Bomb: Cops quiz ex uni man', Reading University magazine, October 2002.

7 John Cooper, author interview.

8 'Whisper to a Scream: Bomber's wife tells her side of the story', Megaswary Ramakrishnan, the *Australian*, 13 September 2004.

9 *The Jihad Fixation: Agenda, strategy, portents*, Wordsmiths, 2001.

10 Muklas, additional statement to Indonesian police, 30 December 2002.

11 Wan Min said in his interrogation (11 March 2003) that they met earlier, in 1993.

12 'Top Jemaah Islamiyah Bomb-maker is Born-again Muslim', Simon Cameron-Moore, Retuers, 18 August 2003.

13 Shamsul Bahri Hussein, Malaysian JI detainee, interview with TV3 Malaysia, April 2004.

14 Muklas, additional police statement, *op. cit.*

15 Interrogation deposition of Wan Min Wan Mat, 11 March 2003, cited in 'Jemaah Islamiyah in South East Asia: Damaged but still dangerous', Sidney Jones, ICG, 26 August 2003.

16 English translation of Dr Azahari's bomb manual, obtained by author.

17 Ahmed Rashid, *Taliban: Militant Islam, oil, and fundamentalism in Central Asia*, Yale Nota Bene, 2001.

18 'Interpreting the Taliban', William Maley, in *Fundamentalism Reborn? Afghanistan and the Taliban*, ed. William Maley, Hurst & Co., 1998.

19 *Taliban, op. cit.*

20 Cited in *Taliban, op. cit.*

21 Cited in 'The Jemaah Islamiyah Arrests and the Threat of Terrorism', White Paper to the Singapore Parliament, 7 January 2003.

22 *Ibid.*

23 *Holy War Inc.: Inside the secret world of Osama bin Laden*, Peter L. Bergen, Phoenix, 2001.

24 'The Declaration of Jihad on the Americans Occupying the Country of the Two Sacred Places', released by Osama bin Laden, 23 August 1996.

Chapter 12 Mantiqi 4

1 The National Police of the Republic of Indonesia. The Investigation Team for the Bali Bombing Case, report on interrogation of Muklas, 2003. This report refers to the date in 1996 when the Guidelines (known by their Indonesian acronym PUPJI) were approved. PUPJI itself contains a reference to the 1995 date when it was originally endorsed. Wan Min's account of the books being destroyed is from his Record of interview, 6 January 2003.

2 The Malaysian JI member Asman Hashim told authorities that Mantiqi 4 included the Maldives. Some Australian investigators discount this claim. The information that the Australian branch came under the Indonesian JI leadership was provided to the Singaporean authorities by JI detainees. It is referred to in the Singapore Government White Paper and was confirmed to the author in a briefing with the Singapore Ministry of Home Affairs, January 2003.

3 Report on interrogation of Muklas, *op. cit.*

4 Abdul Rahim was identified as the leader of Mantiqi 4 by numerous JI detainees, including Muklas and Mohammad Nasir bin Abas.

5 Confidential information supplied to author.

6 Testimony to Australian Refugee Review Tribunal, 1998 and 1999.

7 Mantiqi 3 leader Mohammad Nasir bin Abas reported Abdul Rahim Ayub's presence at a Qiyadah Markaziyah meeting in October 2002, just after the Bali bombings. Reports that Abdul Rahim attended earlier Markaziyah meetings are believed to be incorrect, a result of confusion between the Mantiqi 4 chief and another JI leader with a similar name, Abdul Rohim, the son of Abu Bakar Bashir, who is known to have attended the earlier Markaziyah meetings.

8 Testimony from Jack Roche during his trial in Western Australia in 2004.

9 Information obtained in briefings from Australian investigators and author interviews with former JI members and followers. Other information on Wandi in this section is also from briefings with Australian investigators.

10 Confidential author interview.

11 'Bombing Suspect Humble, Passionate', Kara Lawrence, *Herald-Sun*, 23 October 2002.

12 Interview with *4 Corners*, recorded May 2003.

13 Comments about the flat in Dee Why leased by Ahmad, and about its residents, are from confidential author interviews, conducted February 2004.

14 Jack Roche's given name was Paul Holland. He changed his name to Jack Roche in Perth in 2001 in order to obtain a WA driver's licence. I have used the name Jack Roche for him throughout to avoid confusion.

15 Conversation with author. The information and quotes in this chapter were obtained directly from Jack Roche unless otherwise indicated.

16 Interview with ABC TV News, November 2002.

17 *Nida'ul Islam* website.

18 The term 'Salafism' comes from the Islamic phrase *minhaj as-salaf*, or method of the early Muslims. Salafis believe that the Koran and *sunna* should be interpreted as the

early generations of Muslims interpreted them and not subject to any innovation. In modern Islam, Salafi has come to describe a Saudi-based group of fundamentalist Muslims who seek to 'purify' modern Islam and subscribe to the rigid interpretations of early jurists such as Ibn Taymiyya.

19 CIA report, mid-June 2002, obtained by author.

20 Central Court of Instruction, Madrid. Reported by Sarah Ferguson, *Insight*, SBS, 30 October 2003. I have also drawn on 'Muslim vs Muslim', John Lyons, *Sunday* program, 1 April 2003.

21 'A Word from the Wise', Cameron Stewart & Colleen Egan, *Weekend Australian*, 18–19 October 2003.

22 *Ibid.*

23 *Ibid.*

24 Confidential author interview.

25 Jack Roche testified that when he visited Afghanistan in 2000, Abu Hafs inquired of him 'How's Hussein?', using the name by which he knew Abdul Rahman Ayub.

26 Briefing with Australian investigator.

27 Confidential author interview.

28 Interview with *4 Corners*, recorded 2004.

Chapter 13 — Tear Them to Shreds

1 Abu Bakar Bashir, statement to Indonesian police, January 2003.

2 'The Latest Indonesian Crisis: Causes & solutions', by Abdullah Sungkar & Abu Bakar Bashir, published by *Nida'ul Islam* magazine, July–August 1998.

3 'Al Qaeda infrastructure in Indonesia', Indonesian intelligence report, February 2002, cited in *Inside Al Qaeda: Global network of terror*, Rohan Gunaratna, Columbia University Press, 2002. The letters are also described in *Seeds of Terror*, Maria Ressa, Free Press, 2003; and in 'The Plot Thickens, But Mostly Outside Singapore', *Straits Times*, 26 January 2002.

4 *Holy War Inc.: Inside the secret world of Osama bin Laden*, Peter L. Bergen, Phoenix, 2001.

5 *Ibid.*

6 Recounted by Pakistani journalist Rahimullah Yusufzai in *I Met Osama bin Laden*, BBC TV, *op. cit.*

7 *Bin Laden: The man who declared war on America*, Yosef Bodansky, Prima Lifestyles, 2001

8 *Ibid.*

9 Abu Bakar Bashir, statement to Indonesian police, *op. cit.*

10 Central Jakarta Office of the Counsel for Prosecution. Indictment of Abu Bakar Bashir, Jakarta, April 2003.

11 Interrogation report of Mohammad Nasir bin Abas, head of Mantiqi 3, 18 April 2003, and 'Jemaah Islamiyah in South East Asia: Damaged but still dangerous', Sidney Jones, ICG, 26 August 2003.

12 Record of Interview, Wan Min Wan Mat, 6 January 2003.

13 Interview with BBC TV, recorded in 2003 for *The Third World War* documentary.

14 'Suspect Confesses to Bali Bombings', the *Guardian*, 8 November 2002.

15 'Brothers in Arms', Matthew Moore, *Sydney Morning Herald*, 16–17 November 2002.

16 Interview with BBC TV, *op. cit.*

17 The National Police of the Republic of Indonesia. The Investigation Team for the Bali Bombing Case. Report on interrogation of Muklas, 2003.

18 'Jemaah Islamiyah in South East Asia', *op. cit.*

19 Interview with BBC TV, *op. cit.*

20 'Indonesia Backgrounder: Jihad in Central Sulawesi', Sidney Jones, ICG, 3 February 2004.

21 Document obtained by author.

22 US intelligence report, 2002.

23 'Jemaah Islamiyah in South East Asia', *op. cit.*

24 US intelligence report, 2002.

25 Badan Inteligen Nasional (BIN) report on activities of Umar Faruq, September 2002.

26 Regional police intelligence report, 30 June 2002. See also 'Indonesia Backgrounder: How the Jemaah Islamiyah terrorist network operates', Sidney Jones, ICG, 11 December 2002

27 'Terrorist connections of Abubakar Basyir; and further details on terrorist connection and activities of Umar Faruq', CIA, September 2002.

28 *Deliverance: The Inside Story of East Timor's Fight for Freedom*, Don Greenlees & Robert Garran, Allen & Unwin, 2002.

29 *Ibid.*

30 Confidential author interview.

31 *Deliverance, op. cit.*

32 *Ibid.*

33 'Suharto's "Detect, Defect and Destroy" Policy Towards the Islamic Movement', interview with Abdullah Sunkgar published in *Nida'ul Islam*, February–March 1997.

34 *Seeds of Terror, op. cit.*

35 BIN report, *op. cit.*

36 The other two co-conspirators were named in the BIN report as Abdul Azis al Qahar from Makassar, and al Bukhari, a Chinese Muslim from Singapore. Abu Bakar Bashir was not named as a conspirator in this plot.

37 *Seeds of Terror, op. cit.*

38 CIA report, *op. cit.*

39 Examination Report by the Indonesian Police on the Interrogation of Samudra, dated 21 October 2002.

40 How the Jemaah Islamiyah terrorist network operates', *op. cit.*

41 'The Jemaah Islamiyah Arrests and the Threat of Terrorism', White Paper to the Singapore Parliament, 7 January 2003.

42 Faiz bin Abu Bakar Bafana, statement to Indonesian police, Singapore, 18 April and 30 April 2002.

43 *Ibid.* See also 'How the Jemaah Islamiyah terrorist network operates', *op. cit.*

44 'The Southeast Asian Terrorist Network (as of 20 September 2002) Overview', classified report by regional intelligence agency.

Chapter 14 The Springboard

1 Report of the US Senate Select Committee on Intelligence & the US House Permanent Select Committee on Intelligence. Joint Inquiry into Intelligence Community Activities Before and After the Terrorist Attacks of September 11, 2001. December 02.

2 *Ibid.*

3 CIA Director, George Tenet, testimony to US Senate Select Committee, *ibid.*

4 'Post-September 11, 2001, Southeast Asia', *American Diplomacy*, 9 July 2002.

5 Tenet testimony, Report of US Senate Select Committee, *op. cit.*

6 'The Southeast Asian Terrorist Network (as of 20 September 2002) Overview', classified report by regional intelligence agency.

7 Report of US Senate Select Committee

8 9/11 Commission Report: Final report of National Commission on Terrorist Attacks upon the United States, 22 July 2004.

9 *Ibid.*

10 *Ibid.*
11 *Ibid.*
12 *Ibid.*
13 Report of US Senate Select Committee, *op. cit.*
14 *USA v Zacarias Moussaoui*, Grand Jury Indictment, June 2002.
15 *USA v Zacarias Moussaoui*, Appellee Brief.
16 US Senate Select Committee Report and 9/11 Commission Report, *op. cit.*
17 9/11 Commission Report, *op. cit.*
18 'The Southeast Asian Terrorist Network (as of 20 September 2002) Overview', classified report by regional intelligence agency.
19 Muklas, statement to Indonesian police, 20 December 2002.
20 *Seeds of Terror*, Maria Ressa, Free Press, 2003.
21 The material here from Hambali and Khalid Sheik Mohammed's interrogations is cited in the 9/11 Commission Report, *op. cit.*
22 Mohammed Nasir bin Abas, interview with TV3 Malaysia, April 2004.
23 Malaysian JI detainee Shamsul Bahri Husein, interview with TV3 Malaysia, April 2004.
24 'Indonesia Backgrounder: Jihad in Central Sulawesi', Sidney Jones, ICG, 3 February 2004
25 'Did Anyone Really Know Them?', *Straits Times*, 19 January 2002. The account of the Singapore cell is based on information in 'The Jemaah Islamiyah Arrests and the Threat of Terrorism', White Paper to the Singapore Parliament, 7 January 2003, and attached documentation.
26 Transcript of videotape recovered from Afghanistan, voice of Hashim bin Abas, released by Singapore Government.
27 Singapore Parliament White Paper, *op. cit.*
28 Regional police intelligence report.
29 US intelligence report on activities of Omar al Faruq, undated.
30 'Summary of Information: Subject — Umar Faruq'. Intelligence report on activities of Faruq.
31 Regional police intelligence report.

Chapter 15 The Enemy's Plot

1 Interview with *4 Corners*, recorded May 2003.
2 *Ibid.*
3 The Al Hidayah Islamic School of Bentley, WA, press release, 8 May 2003.
4 Refugee Review Tribunal (RRT): Decision and Reasons for Decision, 5 February 1999.
5 Letter on file of RRT.
6 Testimony to RRT.
7 Confidential information supplied to author.
8 RRT, letter to 'Mr Abdullah', 10 February 1999.
9 Confidential author interview.
10 Copy obtained by author.
11 Jack Roche's account to author.
12 Interview with *4 Corners*, recorded May 2003.
13 John Bernett, testimony in Jack Roche trial, WA, 2004.
14 'The Man Roche Couldn't Recruit', Jan Mayman & Vanda Carson, the *Australian*, 20 November 2002.
15 Interview with *4 Corners*, recorded May 2003.
16 Confidential author interview.
17 Briefing with Australian investigators.

18 The information on the role of Abu Ishmael is drawn from confidential author interviews with former JI members and followers, and from briefings with Australian investigators.
19 Information from former intelligence analyst.
20 Classified report to regional police chief, undated.
21 Regional intelligence report, undated.
22 Confidential author interview and briefing with Australian investigator.
23 Statement of Ibrahim Fraser to Australian Federal Police, 18 November 2002.
24 The information on Asman Hashim is drawn from confidential author interviews with former JI members and followers, and from briefings with Australian investigators.
25 Copy of manual obtained by author.
26 Information supplied to author by Jack Roche.
27 'Heroes and Lost Souls', Cameron Stewart & Colleen Egan, *Weekend Australian*, 20–21 December 2003.
28 *Ibid*.
29 *Ibid*.
30 Sheik Feiz, testimony in Jack Roche trial.

Chapter 16 Khalid's Plan

1 Interview with Colleen Egan, the *Australian*, November 2002.
2 Statement by Ibrahim Fraser to Australian Federal Police, 20 November 2002.
3 Letter tendered as evidence at Roche's trial in WA, 2004. Information in this chapter, including direct quotes from Jack Roche, is based on trial evidence, unless otherwise indicated.
4 Interview with Colleen Egan, the *Australian*.
5 *Ibid*.
6 Briefing with Australian investigators.
7 Information supplied by Australian investigators.
8 Some of the JI members sworn in by Bashir's son, Abdul Rohim, were erroneously reported in the media to have been sworn in by Mantiqi 4 leader Abdul Rahim Ayub, a mistake due to the similarity of their names.
9 Confidential intelligence briefing, 2004.
10 For information on the al Ghuraba cell, I have drawn on 'Transnational Terrorism: The threat to Australia', report by Les Luck, Department of Foreign Affairs and Trade, 2004, and confidential intelligence briefing, 2004.
11 Trial documents in case against Christian Ganczarski.
12 'The Alliance Lives!', *Time Europe*, 23 June 2003.
13 'Sydney Terror Suspect Linked to al Qaeda Bombers', Ellen Connolly & Darren Goodsir, *Sydney Morning Herald*, 18 November 2003.
14 'Presentation of the Facts', by Deputy Presiding Judge Jean-Louis Bruguiere & Chief Examining Magistrate Jean-Francois Ricard.
15 Jack Roche, record of interview with Australian Federal Police, November 2002.
16 Interview with *4 Corners*, recorded May 2003. All Neil Fergus quotes in this chapter come from this interview. I have also drawn on 'Intelligence After Action Report, Sydney 2000 Games', produced by the Olympic Intelligence Centre.
17 Interview with Colleen Egan, the *Australian*.
18 John Bennett, testimony in Jack Roche trial.
19 Conversation with author.
20 Author interview.
21 Briefing with Australian investigator.
22 Information supplied confidentially to author.
23 Author interview.

24 Interview with *4 Corners*, recorded May 2003.
25 'Heroes and Lost Souls', Cameron Stewart & Colleen Egan, *Weekend Australian*, 20-21 December 2003.
26 Trial testimony of Jack Roche's son, Jens Holland, in Jack Roche trial.
27 Transcript of conversation, tendered at Roche's trial. In the transcript, the term 'your father' was incorrectly translated as 'Mister Antum'. Roche explained in his evidence that this should have read 'your father'.
28 Testimony in Jack Roche trial.
29 Interview with Colleen Egan, the *Australian*.
30 Author interview.
31 *Ibid*.
32 'A Word From the Wise', Cameron Stewart & Colleen Egan, the *Australian*, 18–19 October 2003.
33 Conversation with author.
34 Confidential author interview.
35 'Number Left in Terrorist Call "Wrong,"' Martin Chulov, the *Australian*, 1 June 2004.
36 Conversation with author.
37 Briefing with Australian investigators.

Chapter 17 Happy Christmas

1 Amrozi, interview with BBC TV. All quotes from Amrozi and Ali Imron that follow in this chapter are from the BBC interviews recorded in 2003 for *The Third World War* documentary, unless otherwise indicated.
2 US intelligence report on activities of Omar al Faruq.
3 Badan Inteligen Nasional (BIN) report on activities of Umar Faruq, September 2002.
4 Mubarok, statement to Indonesian police.
5 Faiz bin Abu Bakar Bafana, statement to Indonesian police, Singapore, 18 April and 30 April 2002.
6 Interrogation of Fathur Rahman al Ghozi, as reported by newsflash.org
7 Bafana, statement to Indonesian police, *op. cit.*
8 'The Southeast Asian Terrorist Network (as of 20 September 2002) Overview', classified report by regional intelligence agency.
9 Classified report of Hambali's interrogation, 26 August 2003. The two colleagues were Suhaip and Jabir, who was killed in the Christmas Eve bombings.
10 Bafana, statement to Indonesian police, Singapore, 22 October 2002.
11 'Terror Turncoat Tells of Australian Branch', Matthew Moore, *Sydney Morning Herald*, 27 June 2003.
12 Bafana, statement to Indonesian police, Singapore, 18 & 30 April 2002.
13 The National Police of the Republic of Indonesia. The Investigation Team for the Bali Bombing Case. Report on interrogation of Muklas, 2003.
14 For a detailed investigation of the Christmas Eve 2000 bombings, see 'Indonesia Backgrounder: How the Jemaah Islamiyah terrorist network operates', Sidney Jones, ICG, 11 December 2002.
15 Malaysian JI detainee Amran Mansor, interview with TV3 Malaysia, April 2004.
16 *Ibid*.
17 Fathur Rahman al Ghozi, sworn statement, 31 January 2002, Camp Crame, Manila.
18 Fathur Rahman al Ghozi, statement, Camp Crame, Manila, 16 February 2002.
19 *PNP Intelligence Group v Faiz bin Abu Bakar Bafana*, Manila, Philippines, 11 October 2002.
20 Examination Report by the Indonesian Police on the interrogation of Samudra, dated 21 October 2002.

21 Muklas, statement to Indonesian police, 29 December 2002.
22 Examination Report of Samudra, *op. cit.*
23 'How the Jemaah Islamiyah terrorist network operates', *op. cit.*
24 Examination Report of Samudra, *op. cit.*
25 'How the JI terrorist network operates', *op. cit.*
26 Examination Report of Samudra, *op. cit.*
27 Amran Mansor, interview, *op. cit.*
28 Mohammed Nasir bin Abas, interview with TV3 Malaysia, April 2004.
29 Examination report of Samudra, *op. cit.*
30 'How the Jemaah Islamiyah terrorist network operates', *op. cit.*
31 Bafana, statements to Indonesian police, Singapore, 18 and 30 April 2002.
32 The National Police of the Republic of Indonesia. The Investigation Team for the Bali Bombing Case. Report on interrogation of Muklas, 2003.
33 Bafana, statements to Indonesian police, Singapore, 18 and 30 April 2002, and 22 October 2002.
34 'Cleric Stays Calm Despite Terror Accusations', Agence France-Presse, 16 October 2002.
35 'Bin Laden "Invited Bashir to Afghanistan" Just Before Attacks on US', Sian Powell, the *Australian*, 2 February 2004.

Chapter 18 The Source

1 'Information Derived from Mohammed Monsour Jabarah', US Department of Justice, Federal Bureau of Investigation, 7 May 2002. Information in this chapter about Jabarah is from this report, unless otherwise indicated. The FBI report refers to Jabarah as 'the Source'. To avoid confusion, when quoting from this report, I have replaced some references to 'the Source' with 'Jabarah'.
2 Canadian Secret Intelligence Service (CSIS), Interrogation Report of Mohammed Mansour Jabarah, 2002.
3 *Ibid.*
4 'Canadian al Qaeda Suspect Handed Over to US by CSIS', *Globe and Mail*, 29 July 2002.
5 *Ibid.*
6 Broadcast on Al Jazeera, 13 October 2001.
7 Institute for Defence and Strategic Studies, NTU, Singapore, interview conducted in Canada, May 2003, cited in *Seeds of Terror*, Maria Ressa, Free Press, 2003.
8 CSIS report, *op. cit.*
9 Numerous commentators, including Rohan Gunaratna, Maria Ressa and Zachary Abuza, have written that Hambali became a member of al Qaeda's governing *shura* (reportedly some time after September 11). The author has not seen any investigative or intelligence material that supports this and Australian investigators remain sceptical of this claim.
10 CSIS report, *op.cit.*
11 *Ibid.*
12 *Ibid.*

Chapter 19 Program C

1 'The Jemaah Islamiyah Arrests and the Threat of Terrorism', White Paper to the Singapore Parliament, 7 January 2003.

2 ISA Advisory Board's recommendation, 30 May 2002, Singapore.
3 *World Competitiveness Yearbook 2002*, and Mercer Human Resource Consultancy, March 2003, cited in Singapore Tourism Board Advisory, 'Singapore Committed to Safety of Visitors, Residents and Citizens', 28 March 2003.
4 Interview with MediaCorp Radio, 11 September 2002.
5 'Manager's ISD Arrest Shocks Residents', *Straits Times*, 13 January 2002.
6 White Paper, *op. cit.*
7 Annex B, White Paper, *op. cit.*
8 ISA Advisory Board's recommendation, *op. cit.*
9 Summary of Case against Jemaah Islamiyah (Singapore), Annex A, White Paper, *op. cit.*
10 Canadian Secret Intelligence Service (CSIS), Interrogation Report of Mohammed Mansour Jabarah, 2002.
11 The 9/11 Commission Report: final report of the National Commission on Terrorist Attacks upon the United States: 22 July, 2004.
12 'Information Derived from Mohammed Monsour Jabarah', US Department of Justice, Federal Bureau of Investigation (FBI), 7 May 2002.
13 The Kumpulan Mujahideen Malaysia (KMM), formed in the mid-1990s, was closely linked with the Malaysian opposition party, PAS, and with JI. Many of its members trained in Afghanistan or in the MILF camps in the Philippines. KMM's existence was discovered by the Malaysian authorities in August 2001, when they arrested several of its members over a bank robbery, carried out to raise funds for its jihad activities.
14 FBI report, *op. cit.*
15 CSIS report, *op. cit.*
16 *Ibid.*
17 The man named in the tip-off was a Singaporean of Pakistani extraction, Mohammad Aslam bin Yar Ali Khan, who flew out of Singapore for Pakistan on 4 October 2001 and was later arrested by the Northern Alliance while fighting with the Taliban in Afghanistan.
18 FBI report, *op. cit.*
19 *Ibid.*

Chapter 20 Hambali's Revenge

1 'The Jemaah Islamiyah Arrests and the Threat of Terrorism', White Paper to the Singapore Parliament, 7 January 2003.
2 Canadian Secret Intelligence Service (CSIS), Interrogation Report of Mohammed Mansour Jabarah, 2002.
3 Singapore Government Press Statement on ISA Arrests, 11 January 2002.
4 Testimony to Senate Foreign Affairs, Defence and Trade References Committee, 18 June 2003 (see note 5).
5 'Bali 2002. Security threats to Australians in South East Asia', report of Foreign Affairs, Defence and Trade References Committee, August 2004.
6 Statement broadcast on al Jazeera, 3 November 2001.
7 ASIO submission to Senate FADTR Committee, *op. cit.*
8 The information about JI members' travel to Australia was provided in confidential briefings by Australian investigators.
9 ONA submission to Senate FADTR Committee, *op. cit.*
10 CSIS report, *op. cit.*
11 'Information Derived from Mohammed Monsour Jabarah', US Department of Justice, Federal Bureau of Investigation (FBI), 7 May 2002.
12 *Ibid.*
13 FBI statement, 10 July 2004, provided to Margot O'Neill, *Lateline*, ABC TV.
14 Muklas, statement to Indonesian police, 20 December 2002.

15 *Ibid.*
16 Confidential briefing with Australian investigator.
17 Record of interview, Wan Min Wan Mat, 6 January 2003.
18 *Ibid.*
19 'The Osama bin Laden and al-Qaeda of Southeast Asia', *Asia Times*, 6 February 2002.
20 'Reaction Over Terrorism Takes Singapore by Surprise', *Kompas Online*, 23 February 2002.
21 'Pressure Builds on Jakarta to Toe the Line on Bush's "War on Terrorism"', www.wsws.org/articles/2002
22 'Muslim Cleric to Sue Singapore Government', CNN, 8 March 2002.
23 'Al Qaeda infrastructure in Indonesia', Indonesian intelligence report, February 2002, cited in *Inside Al Qaeda: Global network of terror*, Rohan Gunaratna, Columbia University Press, 2002.
24 Ken Conboy, Intel (Jakarta 2003), cited in 'Indonesia Backgrounder: Jihad in Central Sulawesi', Sidney Jones, ICG, 3 February 2004.
25 'Britain Links JI to Spain Bombs', Cameron Stewart, the *Australian*, 13 May 2004.
26 'Taking the Hard Road', Simon Elegant, *Time*, 30 September, 2002.
27 'Indonesian Vice President's Dinner Sorts Out Terrorists From Nice Guys', *Washington Post*, 16 May 2002.
28 The National Police of the Republic of Indonesia. The Investigation Team for the Bali Bombing Case. Report on interrogation of Muklas, 2003.
29 Muklas, statement to Indonesian police, 20 December 2002.
30 Mohammed Nasir bin Abas, statement to Indonesian police, 9 May 2003.
31 Muklas, statement to Indonesian police, 20 December 2002.
32 Abu Bakar Bafana, statement to Indonesian Police, Singapore, 18 April and 30 April 2002.
33 Hamzah Haz, as quoted on *Lateline*, 14 October 2002.
34 Kim Jones, (then) Director-General, ONA, testimony to Senate FADTR Committee, *op. cit.*, 20 June 2003.
35 *Ibid.*
36 ONA submission to Senate Committee FADTR, *op. cit.*
37 ONA testimony to Senate FADTR committee, *op. cit.*, 24 September 2003.
38 David Farmer, ONA, testimony to Senate FADTR Committee, *op. cit.*, 20 June 2003. The quotes that follow from the ONA officers are from their testimony to this committee, unless otherwise indicated.
39 ONA submission to Senate FADTR Committee, *op. cit.*
40 'Bali Warning a "Theory"', the *Australian*, 18 June 2003.
41 Report of Senate FADTR Committee, *op. cit.*
42 Confidential briefing.
43 ASIO submission to Senate FADTR Committee, *op. cit.*
44 According to the Singaporean authorities, the local JI member Mas Selamat Kastari discussed this proposal on at least two occasions with other JI members. Kastari escaped from Singapore to Malaysia and Thailand but was subsequently captured.
45 ASIO submission to Senate FADTR Committee, *op. cit.*
46 ONA submission to Senate FADTR Committee, *op. cit.*
47 ASIO submission to Senate FADTR Committee, *op. cit.*
48 'Bali Warning a "Theory"', *op. cit.*

Chapter 21 For All You Christian Infidels

1 Interview with BBC TV, recorded in 2003 for *The Third World War* documentary.
2 General I Made Mangku Pastika, Indonesian leader of Bali bombings investigation, comment to journalists.

3 Police statement of Amrozi. This chapter is based principally on the police statements of the bombers and evidence presented at their trials.

4 '"Hat Man" Kept Cool on Police Watch', Robert Martin & Martin Chulov, the *Australian*, 18 November 2002.

5 'Indonesia Backgrounder: How the JI Terrorist Network Operates', Sidney Jones, ICG, 11 December 2002.

6 Indonesian police documents obtained by author.

7 *Ibid.*

8 Confidential author interview.

9 Printout of www.istimata.com, cited in Imam Samudra police interview, 12 January 2003.

10 Interview with BBC TV, *op. cit.*

11 Muklas, statement to Indonesian police.

12 Interview with BBC TV, *op. cit.*

13 This description of the meeting at Hernianto's house is taken from the police statements of Muklas, Samudra, Amrozi, Ali Imron and Mubarok. The participants provided contradictory accounts of who was present and what took place at this meeting. Where their accounts conflict, I have relied principally on Ali Imron, whose testimony appears to be the most truthful.

14 Ali Imron, statement to Indonesian police, 26 January 2003.

15 Interview with BBC TV, *op. cit.*

16 Interview with BBC TV, *op. cit.*

17 'How the JI Terrorist Network Operates', *op. cit.*

18 Ali Imron, statement to Indonesian police.

19 'Allah's Assassins', Eric Ellis, the *Bulletin*, 5 March 2003.

20 Samudra, statement to Indonesian police.

21 Interview with *4 Corners*, recorded January 2003.

22 Interview with BBC TV, *op. cit.*

23 Amrozi, statement to Indonesian police.

24 Interview for *4 Corners*, recorded October 2002.

25 Briefing with Australian investigators.

26 'Terrorist connections of Abubakar Basyir; and further details on terrorist connection and activities of Umar Faruq', CIA, September 2002.

27 'No Proof, So No Abu Bakar: Indonesia', *Straits Times*, 24 September 2002.

28 'Politics: Authorities divided on Megawati plot', Laksamana.net, 23 September 2002.

29 'Thousands of Militant Muslims Declare Holy War in Mass Anti-US Rally in Surakarta', *Jakarta Post*, 25 September 2002.

30 'Accused Terrorist Challenges US', Michael Casey, AP, 24 September 2002.

31 'How the JI Terrorist Network Operates', *op. cit.*

32 Ali Imron, statement to Indonesian police. The quotes that follow in the remainder of this chapter from Muklas, Amrozi and Samudra are all from their police statements.

33 Interview with *4 Corners*, recorded January 2003.

34 'Ruthless Enforcer Pulled the Strings', Darren Goodsir, *Sydney Morning Herald*, 11 September 2003. The quote that follows is from 'Investigations Stir Terror's Nest', Sian Powell, the *Australian*, 3 July 2003.

Chapter 22 Cocky Australia, Beware!

1 Amrozi, statement to Indonesian police. This chapter is based principally on the police statements of the bombers and evidence presented at their trials. All quotes used from the bombers are from their police statements, unless otherwise indicated. Their accounts are contradictory in many respects, e.g. in the dates and details of the trip to

Bali and who travelled with whom. In these cases, I have relied principally on Amrozi, whose version is most consistent with the known facts. (Amrozi, in his police statements, refers to Samudra by the alias Fatih. To avoid confusion, I have changed these references to read Samudra.)

2 'JI Targeted Bangkok Tourism, Say Thais', Mark Baker & Wayne Miller, *Sydney Morning Herald*, 13 June 2003.

3 Interview with BBC TV, recorded in 2003 for *The Third World War* documentary.

4 *Ibid.*

5 'Andre, a Bold and Charming Bomber', Wayne Miller & Stephen Gibbs, *Sydney Morning Herald*, 4 December 2002.

6 Interview with *4 Corners*, January 2003.

7 'Bashir Threat to Australia Before Bomb', Kimina Lyall, Don Greenlees & Martin Chulov, the *Australian*, 7 November 2002.

8 Interview with BBC TV, *op. cit.*

9 Interview with BBC TV, *op. cit.*

10 'Man With an Iron Mask', Darren Goodsir, *Sydney Morning Herald*, 26 August 2003.

11 'Ruthless Enforcer Pulled the Strings', Darren Goodsir, *Sydney Morning Herald*, 11 September 2003.

12 'Man With an iron mask', *op. cit.*

13 'Deadly Puzzle's Final Face', Cindy Wockner & Komang Suriadi, *Daily Telegraph*, 31 July 2003.

14 Australian Parliament Hansard, 16 October 2002.

15 ASIO submission to Senate Foreign Affairs, Defence and Trade References Committee. Report 'Bali 2002. Security threats to Australians in South East Asia', released August 2004.

16 'Andre, a Bold and Charming Bomber', *op. cit.*

17 Interview with BBC TV, *op. cit.*

18 'Bali Attack Originally Planned to Mark 9/11', Sian Powell, the *Australian*, 22 August 2003.

19 Testimony of Aris's wife during Bali bombing trials.

20 Interview with BBC TV, *op. cit.*

21 'Bomb Victim's Fury Boils Over', Wayne Miller, *Sydney Morning Herald*, 24 June 2003.

22 'I Saw the Heart of a Bali Victim Stop as She Lay in my Arms', Martin Chulov, the *Australian*, 29 May 2003.

23 Interview with BBC TV, *op. cit.*

24 'Ruthless Enforcer Pulled the Strings', *op. cit.*

25 Report by Kevin Cuthbertson, bomb technician, Australian Bomb Data Centre.

26 Interview with BBC TV, *op. cit.*

Chapter 23 A Million Amrozis

1 Interview with *4 Corners*, recorded May 2003.

2 Author interview.

3 Confidential comments to author.

4 Author interview.

5 Confidential comments to author.

6 ASIO had been on Roche's trail without even knowing it. Investigators knew that someone named Paul Holland (Roche's real name) was involved with JI, but didn't know who he was. They thought that 'Paul Holland' was probably an alias used by one of the Ayubs, the confusion apparently caused by the fact that Roche had bought a car using Abdul Rahim's name.

7 'Muslims Condemn "Heavy-handed" Tactics', *Sydney Morning Herald*, 1 November 2002; and 'Guns Put to Children's Faces in ASIO Raid', AAP, 1 November 2002.

8 Copy of document obtained by author.
9 Jack Roche's record of interview, tendered at his trial in WA in 2004.
10 Mohammad Nasir bin Abas, statement to Indonesian police, 9 May 2003.
11 'Bashir Named as Suspect, But Calls in Sick', *Jakarta Post*, 19 October 2002; and 'Al Faruq Admits RI Ties', *Jakarta Post*, 18 October 2002.
12 Record of interview, Mohammed Nasir bin Abas, 10 July 2003.
13 Mohammed Nasir bin Abas told police that Abdul Rahim Ayub attended this Markaziyah meeting and provided a report as Mantiqi 4 leader.
14 'Secrets of a Terror Turncoat', Martin Chulov, *Weekend Australian*, 17 July 2004.
15 Interview with *4 Corners*, recorded October 2002.
16 'The Hunt', Martin Chulov, *Weekend Australian*, 11 October 2003.
17 Interview with BBC TV, recorded in 2003 for *The Third World War* documentary. The quotes that follow from Ali Imron and Samudra are also from BBC TV interviews.
18 'Raise Our Son as Osama', Martin Chulov, the *Australian*, 21 May 2003.
19 Audiotape broadcast on Al Jazeera, 12 November 2002.
20 Australian Parliament Hansard, 14 November 2002.
21 'Tales of the New Arabian Knights', Paul McGeough, *Sydney Morning Herald*, 29 May 2004.
22 'Maybe Iraq Had No Banned Weapons: Powell', the *Australian*, 26 January 2004.
23 'Bush: Hussein, al Qaeda Linked', *Washington Post*, 26 September 2002.
24 Australian Parliament, Hansard, 14 November 2002.
25 *Plan of Attack*, Bob Woodward, Simon & Schuster, 2004. I have also drawn on 'Troops Find Little Resistance at Border Crossing', *New York Times*, 22 March 2003; and 'Race to Baghdad', Craig Nelson & Marian Wilkinson, *Sydney Morning Herald*, 22 March 2003.
26 'Al Qa'ida Back to Full Strength', the *Australian*, 15 May 2003.
27 'Bounding the Global War on Terrorism', Jeffrey Record, Strategic Studies Institute, US Army War College, December 2003.
28 'Scoring the War on Terrorism', Daniel Byman, the *National Interest*, 2003.
29 The *Economist*, 10 January 2004.
30 Comment made in August 2003, cited in 'Bounding the Global War on Terrorism', *op. cit.*
31 Australian Parliament Hansard, 20 August 2003.
32 'Raise Our Son as Osama', Martin Chulov, the *Australian*, 21 May 2003. For the trials, I have also drawn on 'Bali Survivor Sees Beyond an Eye for an Eye', Martin Chulov, the *Australian*, 13 May 2003; and 'Smile, It's Judgement Day in Denpasar', Matthew Moore & Wayne Miller, *Sydney Morning Herald*, 13 May 2003.
33 'In the Name of Jihad, Amrozi Sings for his Crime', Sian Powell, the *Australian*, 1 August 2003.
34 'Bashir is Boss of JI, Bomb Suspects Tell Court', Matthew Moore, *Sydney Morning Herald*, 29 May 2003.
35 Mohammed Nasir bin Abas, statement to Indonesian police, 18 April 2003.
36 Classified report of Hambali's interrogation, 22 August 2003.
37 ABC TV News, August 2003; and *Tempo* magazine, 17 August 2003.
38 The *Australian*, 12 August 2003.
39 Indonesian Police Official Report, interrogation of Sardona Siliwangi, 28 August 2003.
40 'Poetic Justice of Death Sentence', Martin Chulov, *Weekend Australian*, 9–10 August 2003.

Chapter 24 The Fortress of Faith

1 'Bashir Jailed for Four Years', Sian Powell, the *Australian*, 3 September 2003. I have also drawn on 'Bashir Guilty but Cleared of Leading JI', Matthew Moore, *Sydney Morning*

Herald, 3 September 2003; and 'Acquitted, but the Suspicion Still Lingers', Matthew Moore & Catharine Munro of AAP, *Sydney Morning Herald*, 4 September 2003.

2 Judgement number: 547/PID.B2003/PN.JKT.PST, Central Jakarta Court, 2 September 2003.

3 The series of judgements is summarised in Judgement number: 29/K/Pid/2004, Indonesian Supreme Court, 3 March 2004.

4 'Indonesian Deputy's "King of Terrorists" Attack on US Raises Fears of Split', Matthew Moore, *Sydney Morning Herald*, 5 September 2003.

5 'Top Muslim's Challenge: Prove JI exists', Matthew Moore, *Sydney Morning Herald*, 9 September 2003.

6 'Official Statement from Al Jamaah Al Islamiyyah', 6 October 2003, draft document supplied to author by Sidney Jones, International Crisis Group. Sidney Jones's translation uses the more typical Indonesian spelling of JI's name. I have amended this when quoting from the statement, in keeping with the spelling used throughout this book.

7 Classified report of Lillie's debriefing, mid-August 2003.

8 Classified report of Hambali's interrogation, 22 August 2003. The account states that Hambali 'discussed targets in southern Thailand with the mujahidin chief in Thailand, Abdul Fatah, alias Muhamad Haji Jaeming'. Hambali then assigned Yazid Sufaat to work with a Thai operative, Abu Hisham, to choose targets. The report goes on: 'Fatah told [Hambali] that Dr Ismael Lutfi Japagiya, head of the Wahhabi movement in Thailand, did not agree with the targets and that Fatah should not be involved … [Hambali] told Muktar that the local Thai mujahidin were not supportive and that ended the feasibility.'

9 Thai police interrogation of Muyahid.

10 'The Road to Jihad', *Time Asia*, 10 May 2004; and 'Islamic Fervour and Modern Grievances a Toxic Brew in Thailand's South', Louise Williams, *Sydney Morning Herald*, 8 May 2004.

11 'Thai Violence Leaves Country in Crisis', Peter Lloyd, *7.30 Report*, ABC TV, 26 May 2004.

12 'The Road to Jihad', *op. cit.*

13 Australian Defence Minister Robert Hill, Speech to Regional Terrorism, Global Security and the Defence of Australia, RUSI Triennial International Seminar, Canberra, 9 October 2003.

14 Estimate by Australian Foreign Affairs Minister Alexander Downer, 'Terror Army on the Rise, says Downer', Tom Allard, *Sydney Morning Herald*, 18 March 2004.

15 Comment reported in the *Australian*, 7 August 2003.

16 Speech to UN General Assembly, New York, 23 September 2003.

17 'Muslim Leader Blames Corruption for Radical Surge', Matthew Moore, *Sydney Morning Herald*, 10 December 2003.

18 'Lessons in Jihad', Matthew Moore, *Sydney Morning Herald*, 30 August 2003.

19 'War Fears Resurface in Ambon', Sian Powell, the *Australian*, 27 April 2004.

20 'Indonesia Backgrounder: Jihad in Central Sulawesi', Sidney Jones, ICG, 3 February 2004.

21 'Opposing American Intervention', by Abu Bakar Bashir, *Republika* newspaper, 20 April 2004.

22 'Bashir Defiant Before Release', Sian Powell, *Weekend Australian*, 13–14 March 2004.

23 Address to the Institute of Public Affairs, Melbourne, 29 May 2004.

24 'Opposing American Intervention', *op. cit.*

25 'Attacks by Israel, US Will Likely Fuel Perception of War on Islam', Knight Ridder, 20 May 2004.

26 'Al Qaeda Targeting Guidance', 2 April 2004, reported by Margot O'Neill, *Lateline*, ABC TV.

27 'Bashir to be Arrested After Release', Sian Powell, the *Australian*, 30 April 2004.

28 'Bashir's Suite Deal with Police', Sian Powell, the *Australian*, 15 May 2004.
29 Reported by Rob Taylor, AAP, 16 June 2004.
30 'Review is Not a Release', Tim Lindsey, Simon Butt & Ross Clarke, the *Australian*, 27 July 2004.
31 'Idris Escapes Bali Bombing Conviction', Tim Palmer, *7.30 Report*, ABC TV, 24 August 2004.
32 'Bashir to be Charged Over Bali Blasts', Sian Powell, the *Australian*, 26 August 2004.
33 Statement posted on www.islamic-minbar.com 9 September 2004.
34 'Terror at our Door', the *Australian*, 10 September 2004. For details of the bombing I have drawn on coverage by ABC TV News, the *Australian*, the *Courier Mail* and the *Sunday Mail*.
35 'Official Statement from Al Jamaah Al Islamiyyah', *op. cit.*

bai'at	path of allegiance
dakwah	proselytisation (religious conversion through preaching)
Darul Islam	Abode of Islam
emir	leader
fa'i	raising money through attacking enemies of Islam
fatwa	Islamic decree issued by religious scholar
hadith	reports of the sayings and deeds of the Prophet
hajj	pilgrimage to Mecca
hijrah	migration of the Prophet
halaqah	study group
Hizbullah	God's warriors
imam	religious leader
jihad	striving or struggle
jemaah	community
kafir	infidel
mati syahid	martyr's death
mujahideen	holy warrior
Negara Islam Indonesia	Islamic State of Indonesia
pesantren	Islamic boarding school
Qiyadah Markaziyah	Central Leadership Council
sharia	Islamic law
shura	council
sunna	ways of the Prophet
ulama	learned experts
usroh	family groups
ustad	teacher
Wahhabism	the doctrine pioneered by Muhammed ibn Abd al-Wahhab to renew and purify the Islamic faith by returning to the fundamentals of the Koran and the Prophet Muhammad's teachings; adopted by Saudi Arabia as its state creed.

Note on spelling: There are many transliterations of Arabic and Indonesian names. We have used those forms least foreign looking to Australian readers.

∾∿∾